Acknowledgements

The authors and publishers would like to thank the teachers and students who trialled and commented on the material: Argentina: Alicia Balsells, Liliana Luna; Brazil: Angela Cristina Antelo Dupont; France: Anne Cosker, Harry Crawford; Germany: Vanessa Coughlan, Nicole Gaudet; Greece: Christine Barton, Gaynor Williams; Poland: Anita Trawinska, Tadeusz Z. Wolanski; Spain: Henry Burke, Brendan Smith; Switzerland: Helena Lustenberger; UK: Jenny Cooper, Simon Gooch, Bernie Hayden, Sarah Hunter, Roger Scott, Clare West. The authors would also like to thank the staff at EF International Language School, in particular, Mick Davies, Simone Khairi, Amy Langmead, Andrea Southgate and Alan Wilson. Special thanks to our editors, Charlotte Adams, Meredith Levy, Sue Ashcroft, Judith Greet and Claire Thacker who all gave invaluable help and support. The publishers are grateful to Annette Capel and Wendy Sharp for permission to reproduce their original course book concept in *Objective CAE* and in all other *Objective* examination course books.

The author and publishers are grateful to the authors, publishers and others who have given permission for the use of copyright material identified in the text. It has not been possible to identify the sources of all the material used and in such cases the publishers would welcome information from copyright owners. p. 12: 'Close encounters of the British kind', reproduced from *British Shibboleths, One language, different cultures*, edited by Eddie Ronowicz and Colin Yallop, with permission of the publishers, The Continuum International Publishing Group Ltd; p. 15: extract from *The Magic Toyshop* by Angela Carter. Copyright © Angela Carter 1967. Reproduced by permission of the Estate of Angela Carter c/o Rogers, Coleridge & White Ltd, 20 Powis Mews, London W11 1JN; p. 18: extract from *My Family and Other Animals* by Gerald Durrell, reproduced with permission of Curtis Brown Ltd, London, on behalf of the Estate of Gerald Durrell, 1956. Copyright Gerald Durrell; p. 22: interview reproduced with permission of GMTV; p. 27: adapted extract from *The Cambridge Encyclopaedia of the English Language*, 1995, by David Crystal, reproduced with permission of Cambridge University Press; p. 29: extract from 'How to improve your memory' © Mind Tools Ltd, 1995–2007. Reprinted with kind permission of MindTools.com; p. 35: extract from *The Writing Center Online Handouts – Ten secrets of writing business letters*, reproduced with permission of Arizona State University; p. 36: *Dian Fossey*, extract adapted from the Encyclopaedia Britannica © 2007 Britannica.com Inc; p. 38: extract from 'Kiwi Surprise', *Living etc*, May 1999, reproduced with permission of IPC Media; p. 39: *Michael Flatley* by John H. Mathews, extract from Encyclopaedia Britannica 1994-1999, reprinted with permission from the Encyclopaedia Britannica © 1998 Britannica.com Inc; p. 43: extract from 'In my opinion: hello...', from Online Connected Dotcom Telegraph 29.07.99, © Telegraph Group Limited (1999); p. 45: extract from 'Bums on seats is not the answer' by Susannah Kirkman © NI Syndication 24.03.2000; p. 46: adapted extract from 'The Psychology of Success', by Jo Gardiner, reproduced with permission of the author; p. 52: extracts from *Patently Absurd!* (http://www.patent. freeserve.co.uk), reproduced with permission; p. 59 (2): extract from *Russia: A Concise History, Revised and Updated edition* by Ronald Hingley, pages 74–75, Thames & Hudson, 1991, reproduced with permission of the publishers; p. 59 (3): extract reproduced from *The Midas Touch* by Anthony Sampson (Copyright © Anthony Sampson 1990) by permission of PFD on behalf of Anthony Sampson; p. 59 (4): extract from *Every Man's Own Lawyer* by A.Barrister (Judge Brian Galpin), Macmillan Reference Books, 1981, reproduced with permission of Macmillan, London, UK; p. 59 (5): extract from *Sense and Nonsense in Psychology*, by H. J. Eysenck, published by Penguin 1958, reprinted with permission from The HJ Eysenck Memorial Fund; p. 70: headline 'What the public really thinks of the Royal Family', © Daily Mail 26.03.2001; p. 70: headline 'Human Cloning is closer than you think', © 2001 Time Inc, reprinted by permission; p. 70: headline 'Boost Your Metabolism' from Zest Magazine, April 2001; pp. 70–71: adapted article 'Talking clothes get our measure', by Paul Nuki © NI Syndication 21.03.1999; pp. 76–77: extract from *The Dream* from *Collected Short Stories Volume 2* by W. Somerset Maugham published by Heinemann. Used by permission of The Random House Group Limited; p. 80: adapted extract from *Mission: implausible*, Guardian Unlimited, © Jo Queenan; p. 83: extracts from *Titanic Trail Guided Tours*, reprinted with permission, www.titanic-trail.com; p. 86 extract from *Bel Canto* by Ann Patchett. Reprinted by permission of HarperCollins Publishers Ltd, © Ann patchett, 2002; p. 87 adapted text from Darcey Bussell and Igor Zelensky 'Kiss' review, Ian Palmer, Ballet.co at www.ballet.co.uk, 21 December 2006; p. 87: extract from 'The KISS principle' by Leif Solberg, *Family Practice Management* Vol. 10, no. 7, 2003; p. 89: extract from 'Evolutionary factors of language' (http://www.ling.lancs.ac.uk/monkey/the/ linguistics/LECTURE4/ 4evo.htm), reprinted with permission; p. 91: extract from 'Why was this tutorial created'? (http://www.kumc.edu/SAH/OtED/jrade/ preparing_talks/101.html), reprinted with permission of the University of Kansas Medical Centre; p. 92 (a): extract from *Magic Carpet Theatre*, Cambridge Drama Centre leaflet, January-April, www.magiccarpet. demon.co.uk, reprinted with permission; p. 95: 'What these kids need is discipline', by Ann McFerran © Ann McFerran/NI Syndication 22.08.1999; p. 98: extract from *The Way Up To Heaven*, from *Kiss Kiss* by Roald Dahl, publisher Michael Joseph, published by Penguin Books, 1962. Reproduced with permission of David Higham Associates; p. 99: adapted extract from 'The $25,000 Levi's', *Daily Mail* 16.05.2001 © Daily Mail 2001; p. 101 (a): extract 'I stumbled on the George ...' from an article by Ingrid Kennedy first published in *The Independent on Sunday* 25th June 2000; p. 104: extracts from film review page, *Hannah and Her Sisters* and *It All Starts Today, Radio Times* 3–9 February 2001. Reprinted with permission of *Radio Times*; p. 107: text from 'Tips for preparing a successful proposal' from http://www.wested.org/ tie/grantips.html, © 1995–2007 WestEd. All rights reserved; p. 112: extract from *On The Outskirts* Copyright © Michael Frayn, 1964 (Collins, London: 1964), reproduced by permission of Greene & Heaton Ltd; pp. 116–117 extracted from an article by Philip Hensher 'Don't be fooled: the Queen is not speaking our language', first published in *Independent* 22nd December 2000; p. 119 (1): extract from *Eating Out: Social Differentiation, Consumption and Pleasure*, by Alan Warde and Lydia Martens, published by Cambridge University Press 2000; p. 119 (2): extract from *Frozen Food* by Robert Uhlig & Constable Robinson Publishers, © Telegraph Group Limited; p. 119 (3): extract from *The Painter's Daughters*, The Sunday Telegraph Magazine, 18.06.2000 © Telegraph Group Limited 2000; pp. 126–7: adapted extracts from *Mini Sagas*, editor Brian Aldiss, 1997. Reproduced with permission of Sutton Publishing Ltd; p. 128: 'Art's old masters draw the queues' by Maev Kennedy, 10.02.2001, reproduced by permission of *The Guardian*; p. 132: extract from *Full Circle* by Michael Palin reproduced with the permission of Random House Group Ltd. Copyright © Michael Palin 1997; p. 137: extract from 'What's the Weather?' in *New Scientist* 16.09.2000, reproduced with permission from New Scientist magazine, the global authority on science and technology news © RBI 2000 www.NewScientist. com; p. 150: article 'If bingeing on chocolate ...' by Paul Kendall, *Daily Mail* 23.04.2000, © Daily Mail; p. 151: adapted extract from 'Beaten by a tomato...' by David Munk, *The Guardian* 24.04.2001 © Guardian 2001/David Munk; pp. 158-159: extracts from *Team Development Manual* by Mike Woodcock, reproduced with permission of Gower Publishing Company; p. 160: adapted extract from 'Treasure Island', *Flightbookers, Travelling Freestyle Magazine*, Autumn 2000, by permission of River Publishing; p. 161: extracts from *Running a hotel on the roof of the world* by Alec Le Sueur, published by Summersdale, reproduced with permission; p. 163 (4): extract from 'Jacques Brel hostel', *The Rough Guide to Belgium & Luxembourg*, April 1999, written by Martin Dunford et al, published by Rough Guides Ltd, reproduced with permission; pp. 167–8: extract from 'The Open Window' by Saki (H.H. Munro) from www.classicshorts.com; p. 173: extract from 'Oh, what a carry on!' © The Economist Newspaper Limited, London; p. 179: extract from 'Don't criticise exams ...' © Daily Express, 28.09.2000, reproduced with permission; p. 189: extract from article 'Making the best of a good job', by Peter Baker, *The Guardian* 7.11.1999, © Peter Baker, reproduced with permission; p. 189: extract from article 'Testing...testing...testing' by Will Woodward, *The Guardian* 20.05.2000, reproduced with permission of *The Guardian*.

For permission to reproduce cartoons: p. 176: *How To Be Polite* (postcard No.2) and *Asking The Way* (postcard No.12) reproduced with permission of Lee Gone Publications. For permission to reproduce book jackets: Cambridge University Press for p. 177: *Cambridge International Dictionary of English, Cambridge Learner's Dictionary, Cambridge Schools Shakespeare: Romeo and Juliet, Hamlet, King Richard II.* For permission to reproduce magazine covers: p. 22 Emap Magazine/Grazia, Express Newspapers and OK Magazine, Time Out Group Ltd. For permission to reproduce photographs: Alamy/Todd Banner p.110 (br); © Apple; Catherine Ashmore p. 103 (D, E, F); © Associated Press p. 99; DEP65969 *Bowl of Pears*, 1991 by Lara Geffen (20th century) Private Collection/Bridgeman Art Library p. 118 (bl), TOP73590 *The Painter's Daughters Chasing a Butterfly*, c. 1759 by Thomas Gainsborough (1727-88) National Gallery, London, UK/Bridgeman Art Library p. 119 (r); Camera Press/Richard Stonehouse p. 88 (cr), /SUS p. 116; Corbis/Gareth Brown p. 110 (tl), /Terry W Eggers p. 13 (tl), /Ole Graf/Zefa p.110 (tr), /Manuela Herrmann/Bilderlounge p. 110 (cl), /Hulton-Deutsch Collection p. 64, /Bob Thomas p. 110 (bl), /Patrick Ward p. 58 (tl); Corbis Stock Market/© Ronnie Kaufman p. 121 (t); Greg Evans International Photo Library/Greg Balfour Evans pp. 13 (bc, br), 19, 65 (tr), 79 (br), 109 (A), 154 (br), 160 (utr, lbl), 166 (lc, ucr), 178 (cr), 187 (cl); © Hilary Fletcher p. 13 (bl); Format/© Jacky Chapman p 177 (tr); Gettyone/FPG International/B.P. p. 160 (ubr), /Larry Bray p. 177 (br), /Ron Chapple p. 160 (ltr), /Doug Corrance p. 154 (bl), /Rob Gage pp. 109 (C), 178 (br), /Michael Malyszko p. 154 (tr), / p. 13 (tl), /Miao China Tourism Press, Wang p. 161 (l), /Antonio Mo pp. 106 (tr), 187 (tc), /Friedhelm Thomas p. 79 (tl), /V.C.L p. 65 (tl), V.C.L/Nick Clements p. 187 (bc); Gettyone Image Bank/Cesar Lucas Abreu p. 94 (tl), /David W.Hamilton p. 109 (E), /Carol Kohen p. 23, /Ghislain & Marie David de Lossy p. 16 (c), Real Life p. 187 (bl), /Nicholas Russell p. 16 (br), /Henry Sims p. 46 (l), /Ken Tannenbaum p. 177 (bl), /David Vance p. 106 (bl), /Andrew Yates Productions p. 40 (r); Gettyone Stone/Martin Barraud p. 92, /Elie Bernager p. 94, (br), /John Blaustein p. 106 (bc), /Paul Chesley p. 130 (tl), /Stewart Cohen p. 46 (r), /Mary Kate Denny p. 94 (bl), /Julie Fisher p. 106 (br), /Jules Frazier p. 119 (tl), /Margaret Gowan p. 13 (tr), /Walter Hodges pp. 65 (c), 118 (tl), /Ed Honowitz p. 37, /Chronis Jons p. 154 (tl), /Alan Klehr p. 94 (tr), /Bob Krist p. 133, /Mark Lewis p. 160 (lbr), /Laurence Monneret p. 121 (b), /Ben Osbourne p. 79 (bl), /Penny Tweedie p. 166 (b), /Art Wolfe p. 160 (lc), /Gary Yeowell p. 10 (tl); © Granada; Ronald Grant Archive p. 103 (A, B, C), / © 20th Century Fox/Paramount p. 82; Sally & Richard Greenhill/ © Richard Greenhill p. 65 (bl); Impact/ © Alain Le Garsmeur p. 161 (r); Katz Pictures/IPG/Richard Baker p. 118 (r), /Marleen Daniels/REA p. 187 (cr), /Jeremy Nicholl p. 119 (bl), /Richard Smith p. 178 (bl); Life File/Arthur Jumper p. 166 (lcl), /David Kampfner p. 73 (c), /Ken McLaren p. 127 (r); Magic Carpet Theatre, The Magic Circus, www.magiccarpettheatre.com p. 92; Encarta box shot reprinted with permission from Microsoft Corporation p. 177 (cl); Photofusion/ © Peter Olive p. 88 (cl); Pictor pp. 10 (bl, tr, br), 38, 46 (c), 49 (b), 58 (b), 79 (tr), 88 (l,r), 106 (tl), 109 (B, D), 130 (bl, r), 160 (lbl), 166 (t), 166 (lcr), 178 (t, cl), 187 (tl); Popperfoto/Reuters pp. 39, 136 (tr), 136 (br), 149; Powerstock Zefa pp. 16 (tr), 73 (left), 160 (utl), /APL p. 127 (tl), /Benelux Press p. 73 (br, B), /A.Gin p. 10 (bc), /Index p. 58 (tr), /Ian Lishman p. 187 (tr), /Sharpshooters Dream pp. 136 (cl), 154 (c), /Visual Medi Fastforwards pp. 16 (l), 73 (br A), /Visual Medi Wild p. 160 (tc); Rex Features/Edward Webb p. 49 (t), /SIPA Press p. 136 (cr), /Ray Tang p. 22 (b); Punchstock/Stockbyte p. 136 (tl); Science Museum/Science & Society Picture Library p. 40; © John Walmsley p. 65 (br), 96, 187 (br); (c)Wildlife Matters p. 127 (bl). The following pictures were taken on commission for CUP: Trevor Clifford pp. 34, 61, 85.

Permissions research and picture research by Hilary Fletcher.

The recordings which accompany this book were produced by James Richardson at Studio AVP, London.

Development of this publication has made use of the Cambridge International Corpus (CIC). The CIC is a computerised database of contemporary spoken and written English which currently stands at over one billion words. It includes British English, American English and other varieties of English. It also includes the Cambridge Learner Corpus, developed in collaboration with the University of Cambridge ESOL Examinations. Cambridge University Press has built up the CIC to provide evidence about language use that helps to produce better language teaching materials.

The publisher has used its best endeavours to ensure that the URLs for external websites referred to in this book are correct and active at the time of going to press. However, the publisher has no responsibility for the websites and can make no guarantee that a site will remain live or that the content is or will remain appropriate.

Map of Objective CAE Student's Book

	TOPIC	GENRE	MAIN EXAM SKILLS	GRAMMAR	VOCABULARY
Unit 1 **Getting to know you** 10–13 People and places		Introductions	Speaking and Listening	Conditionals	Collocations Adjective-noun, adverb-verb, adverb-adjective
Exam folder 1 14–15			Paper 3 Use of English: 1 Multiple-choice gap fill		
Unit 2 **Keeping in touch** 16–19 Making contact		Informal letters	Writing and Speaking	Prepositions and adverbs	Multiple meanings
Writing folder 1 20–21			Informal letters		
Unit 3 **The real you** 22–25 Career paths		Interviews	Speaking	*Wish* and *if only* *It's time, would rather/sooner*	Idioms Verb + *the* + object
Exam folder 2 26–27			Paper 3 Use of English: 2 Open gap fill		
Unit 4 **Acting on instructions** 28–31 Memory techniques		Instructions	English in Use	Modals: *may, might, can, could*	Prefixes and suffixes
Writing folder 2 32–33			Essays		
Unit 5 **Dear Sir or Madam** 34–37 Dream jobs		Formal letters	Writing and Listening	Relative clauses	Connotation Positive, negative and neutral
Units 1–5 Revision 38–39					
Unit 6 **Speak after the tone** 40–43 Communications technology		Phone messages	Speaking	Phrasal verbs	Collocations *Have, do, make* and *take*
Exam folder 3 44–45			Paper 3 Use of English: 3 Word formation		
Unit 7 **Running a successful business** 46–49 The world of work		Reports	Writing	Cause and effect	Multiple meanings
Writing folder 3 50–51			Formal letters		
Unit 8 **Best thing since sliced bread** 52–55 Inventions		Describing objects	Reading, Listening and Speaking	Modals: *must, should, ought to, shall, will, would*	Positive and negative adjectives
Exam folder 4 56–57			Paper 3 Use of English: 4 Gapped sentences		

TOPIC	GENRE	MAIN EXAM SKILLS	GRAMMAR	VOCABULARY
Unit 9 **You live and learn** 58–61 Further study	Academic texts	Writing and Speaking	Participle clauses	Word formation
Writing folder 4 62–63		Reports and proposals		
Unit 10 **I have a dream** 64–67 Social change	Speeches	Listening	Future forms	Metaphors and idioms
Units 6–10 Revision 68–69				
Unit 11 **Read all about it** 70–73 Fashion	Magazine and newspaper articles	Listening and Speaking	Direct and reported speech	Collocation
Exam folder 5 74–75		Paper 3 Use of English: 5 Key word transformations		
Unit 12 **In a nutshell** 76–79 Dreaming	Short stories	Writing	Past tenses and the present perfect	Adjectival order
Writing folder 5 80–81		Reviews		
Unit 13 **Leaf through a leaflet** 82–85 Leaving home	Information pages	Listening	*-ing* forms	Verbs with the *-ing* form
Exam folder 6 86–87		Paper 1 Reading: 1 Themed texts		
Unit 14 **Views from the platform** 88–91 Language development	Lectures	Listening and Use of English	The passive *To have/get something done*	Word formation
Writing folder 6 92–93		Information sheets		
Unit 15 **If you want to know what I think ...** 94–97 Family life	Expressing opinions	Speaking	The infinitive	Agreeing and disagreeing
Units 11–15 Revision 98–99				
Unit 16 **Raving and panning** 100–103 The arts	Reviews	Speaking	Articles and determiners	Collocation
Exam folder 7 104–105		Paper 1 Reading: 2 Gapped text		
Unit 17 **Do it for my sake** 106–109 Persuasion	Proposals	Writing and Speaking	Language of persuasion	Multiple meanings
Writing folder 7 110–111		Set texts		

TOPIC	GENRE	MAIN EXAM SKILLS	GRAMMAR	VOCABULARY
Unit 18 **May I introduce ...?** **112–115** White lies	Small talk	Writing and Speaking	Cleft sentences and other ways of emphasising	Collocations and longer chunks of language
Exam folder 8 116–117		Paper 1 Reading: 1, 3 and 4 Multiple choice and multiple matching		
Unit 19 **Feeding the mind** **118–121** Food, pictures and science	Talks	Listening and Writing	Emphasising	Word formation
Writing folder 8 122–123		Articles		
Unit 20 **Answers on a postcard** **124–127** Mini sagas	Competition entries	Writing	Hypothesising	Idioms
Units 16–20 Revision 128–129				
Unit 21 **Travel broadens the** **mind 130–133** Trips and travel	Travel writing	Writing and Speaking	Range of grammatical structures	Word endings
Exam folder 9 134–135		Paper 2 Writing: 1 and 2		
Unit 22 **Under the weather** **136–139** Climate change	Interpreting facts and figures	Reading and Speaking	Linking devices	Collocations
Writing folder 9 140–141		Descriptive writing		
Unit 23 **I'm afraid I really must** **insist 142–145** How to complain	Formal letters	Listening, Writing and Speaking	Phrasal verbs	Language for complaining
Exam folder 10 146–147		Paper 4 Listening: 2 Listening for specific information		
Unit 24 **News and views 148–151** Stories in the news	Investigative journalism	Listening	Linking devices	Homophones
Writing folder 10 152–153		Formal writing		
Unit 25 **Powers of observation** **154–157** Research methods	Academic texts	Writing and Speaking	Complex sentences and adverbial clauses	Formal and informal language
Units 21–25 Revision 158–159				

TOPIC	GENRE	MAIN EXAM SKILLS	GRAMMAR	VOCABULARY
Unit 26 **Natural wonders** 160–163 Beauty spots	Travel articles	Writing	*Like, alike, as, so* and *such*	Idioms
Exam folder 11 164–165		Paper 4 Listening: 3 and 4 Sentence completion Multiple choice and multiple matching		
Unit 27 **The open window** **166–169** Personality traits	Fiction	Reading and Listening	Emphasising	Chunks
Writing folder 11 170–171		Informal writing		
Unit 28 **Weighing up the pros** **and cons** 172–175 Air transport	Discursive articles	Writing, Reading and Listening	Adverbials expressing opinion	Word formation
Exam folder 12 176–177		Paper 5 Speaking: The whole paper		
Unit 29 **A testing question** **178–181** Education	Debates	Reading	Gerunds and infinitives	Collocations
Writing folder 12 182–183		Descriptive, narrative and discursive articles		
Unit 30 **Why should we employ** **you?** 184–187 Job interviews	Interviews	Writing and Speaking	Using a range of structures	Using a range of vocabulary
Units 26–30 Revision 188–189				
Grammar folder 190–207				
Self-study folder 208–288				

 When you see this icon in the book it means that this language area has been identified in the Cambridge Learner Corpus (CLC) as an area in which learners often need extra practice. The CLC is a collection of over 100,000 exam scripts from Cambridge ESOL providing over 28 million words of data, and it shows the real mistakes candidates have made in their exams. The mistakes the authors focus on are typical of learners at this level and that is why this book provides further practice in using these features of the language accurately.

Content of the CAE Examination

The Cambridge Certificate in Advanced English examination consists of five papers, each of which is worth 40 marks. It is not necessary to pass all five papers in order to pass the examination. There are five grades: Pass – A, B, C; Fail – D, E. As well as being told your grade, you will also be given a statement of your results which shows a graphical profile of your performance on each paper.

Paper 1 Reading 1 hour 10 minutes

There are four parts to this paper and they are always in the same order. Each part contains one or more texts and a comprehension task. The texts used are from newspapers, magazines, journals, books, leaflets, brochures, etc.

Part	Task Type	Number of Questions	Task Format	Objective CAE Exam folder
1	Multiple choice	6	You read three short texts relating to the same theme and have to answer two multiple-choice questions on each. Each question has four options, A, B, C and D.	6 (86–87)
2	Gapped text	6	You read a text from which paragraphs have been removed and placed in jumbled order after the text. You decide where the missing paragraphs fit in the text.	7 (104–105)
3	Multiple choice	7	You read a text followed by multiple-choice questions with four options.	8 (116–117)
4	Multiple matching	15	You read a text preceded by multiple-matching questions. You match a prompt from one list to a prompt in another list, or match prompts to elements of the text.	8 (116–117)

Paper 2 Writing 1 hour 30 minutes

There are two parts to this paper. Part 1 is compulsory as you have to answer it in 180–220 words. In Part 2 there are five questions, two of which relate to set texts. You must write an answer of 220–260 words to one of these five questions.

Part	Task Type	Number of Tasks	Task Format	Objective CAE Exam folder
1	article report proposal letter	1	You are given a situation and some information which you need to respond to. You may be given two different pieces of material which you need to use in your answer.	1 Informal letters (20–21) 3 Formal letters (50–51) 4 Reports and proposals (62–63) 8 Articles (122–123) 10 Formal writing (152–153) 11 Informal writing (170–171)
2	article report proposal letter review information sheet competition entry contribution to a longer piece (only the first four from this list used for set text tasks)	Choose 1 from a choice of four tasks.	You are given a choice of tasks which specify the type of text you have to write, your purpose for writing and the person or people you have to write for.	As for Part 1 but also: 2 Essays 5 Reviews 6 Information sheet 7 Set texts 9 Descriptive writing 12 Descriptive, narrative and discursive articles **Exam Folder 9** (134–135): Writing, 1 and 2

Paper 3 Use of English 1 hour

There are five parts to this paper, which test your grammar and vocabulary.

Part	Task Type	Number of Questions	Task Format	*Objective CAE Exam folder*
1	Multiple-choice gap-fill mainly testing vocabulary	12	You choose which word from four choices fills each of 12 gaps in a text.	1 (14–15)
	Open gap-fill, mainly testing grammar	15	You fill each of 15 gaps in a text with one word each.	2 (26–27)
3	Word-formation	10	You form an appropriate word, using the given prompt word which has the same root, to fill each of the gaps in a text.	3 (44–45)
4	Gapped sentences	5	You are given sets of three sentences, each of which has a one-word gap. For each set you have to think of one word which can be used appropriately in all three sentences.	4 (56–57)
5	Key word transformations	8	You read a given sentence, and then complete a second sentence so that it has a similar meaning to the first one. You can use between three and six words, including one word which is given.	5 (74–75)

Paper 4 Listening 40 minutes

There are four parts to this paper. All the listening texts are heard twice. The texts used are a variety of types. In some parts you hear just one speaker; in others more than one speaker.

Part	Task Type	Number of Questions	Task Format	*Objective CAE Exam folder*
1	Multiple choice	6	You hear three short extracts and have to answer two multiple-choice questions on each. Each question has three options, A, B and C.	10 (146–147)
2	Sentence completion	8	You hear a text and have to write a word or short phrase to complete sentences.	10 (146–147)
3	Multiple choice	6	You hear a text and have to answer multiple-choice questions with four options.	11 (164–165)
4	Multiple matching	10	You hear a series of five short extracts. There are two matching tasks focusing on the gist and the main points of what is said, the attitude of the speakers, and the context in which they are speaking.	11 (164–165)

Paper 5 Speaking about 15 minutes

There are four parts to this paper. There are usually two of you taking the examination together and two examiners. This paper tests your grammar and vocabulary, interactive communication, pronunciation and how you link your ideas.

Part	Task Type	Time	Task Format	*Objective CAE Exam folder*
1	Three-way conversation between the students and one examiner	3 minutes	The examiner asks you both some questions about yourself and your interests and experiences.	12 (176–177)
2	Two-way interaction between students	4 minutes	You are each given a choice of three pictures. You choose two of these and you must talk about it for about a minute. You will be expected to make a brief response to what your partner says when it is their turn to speak.	12 (176–177)
3	Two-way interaction between students	4 minutes	You are given some visual prompts for a discussion or problem-solving task and you discuss these prompts with your partner.	12 (176–177)
4	Three-way interaction between students and one of the examiners	4 minutes	The examiner asks you questions relating to topics arising from Part 3.	12 (176–177)

1 Getting to know you

Genre Introductions

Topic People and places

Speaking and Reading

1 Look at the photos. Where would you see the landmarks?

2 Read the extracts (a–e) and then match each one with a city from the box below.

a
Situated amid the rural countryside, it is one of the most beautiful and romantic cities. The residents, students of the university and visitors have the best of all worlds: the combination of the romantic medieval image and an up-to-date city. Its unique setting on the banks of the River Cam and the magnificent architecture of the university buildings all combine to make it a place which will linger long in your memory.

b
I walked out for a good view of the world-famous building. The Broadwalk, a promenade surrounding the Opera House, led me along to splendid vistas: to the west, that magnificent structure, the Harbour Bridge, to the east, a bay with the Manly hydrofoil ferry charging in on plumes of spray.

c
It is March, a mild late-summer day here in the Southern Hemisphere. I have spent a glorious morning hiking up Table Mountain through deep green forests, up rocky ravines and finally out into wide-open moorland at the top.

d
The twin streams of history converge just below the delta, where the greatest city in the Islamic world sprawls across the Nile towards the Pyramids, those supreme monuments of antiquity. Every visitor comes here.

e
The background music in the café sounds like a distant Fellini film score; a poster of Carlos Gardel, tango idol of the thirties, winks down from the wall. Croissants are stacked along the blond wood bar. Outside the traffic has reached total gridlock, but no one is honking.

Buenos Aires, Argentina   Cairo, Egypt

Cape Town, South Africa   Cambridge, UK   Sydney, Australia

3 Read the quiz below. With a partner, choose the best response in each situation. Give your reasons for rejecting the others.

1 You are in a room with a number of people. Someone who is very near you but is not looking in your direction accidentally drops some money on the ground. You want to catch their attention in order to tell them they have dropped it. What do you say?

a Look out! You're dropping money all over the place!

b Excuse me. I think you might have dropped something.

c I hope you don't mind my mentioning it but I think you've dropped something.

2 You are in a crowded bus and, by accident, bump into someone, slightly upsetting their balance. What do you say?

a Why don't you look where you're going!

b I'm so dreadfully sorry. It was entirely my fault. I do hope you can forgive me.

c Sorry.

3 You are in a crowded bus and, by accident, bump into someone, slightly upsetting their balance, but on this occasion, you have clearly caused the person some pain. What do you say?

a I'm really sorry.

b Actually, it was the driver's fault, not mine.

c It doesn't look as though you need an ambulance so there's no need to look at me like that!

4 What does the person on the bus say as they experience the pain?

a Yippee!   b Yuk!   c Ouch!

5 Someone you do not know very well is talking to you. The person doesn't know that you have a train to catch and are desperate to leave. What do you say when you cut short the conversation by interrupting?

a Must go. Got a train to catch.

b Well, it's been lovely talking to you … .

c I know you're going to think this terribly rude of me and I must apologise in advance, but I'm afraid I have to leave you now.

6 What do you say when you answer the phone?

a Hello.

b I am (your name).

c The (family name) residence.

10   UNIT 1

4 With a partner, discuss the questions below.

a If you met someone from a different country who speaks a different language, which language would you communicate in and why?

b How many different languages do you think you need to know and why?

c When you meet someone for the first time, how does your language vary according to whether they are the same age as you, or older or younger than you?

d Which questions do you think it is impolite to ask the first time you meet someone?

Ⓔxam spot

In the first part of the CAE Speaking test (Paper 5) you and your partner will only have about three minutes to talk about yourselves. You may be asked to talk about where you come from, your leisure activities, your hopes for the future and so on. Make sure you use a good range of grammar and vocabulary as well as clear pronunciation.

5 Work with a different partner and discuss these questions.

a How do you begin a question when you are not sure if it is polite to ask it?

b When you are listening to someone, what sort of body language, sounds and phrases do you use to show you are interested and you are listening to them?

6 Look at the Exam spot above. Prepare some questions to find out more about your partner. Now ask your partner the questions.

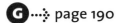 Ⓖ ⋯⋗ page 190

⊙ Conditionals

1 Look at this example of the second conditional from Speaking and Reading 4.

If you met someone from a different country who speaks a different language, which language would you communicate in and why?

Now complete the table about the four basic types of conditional.

Type	Tense – *if* clause	Tense – main clause	Use
zero		present simple/ continuous	
first			
second	past simple/ continuous	*would* + infinitive without *to*	to talk about a situation which is hypothetical or very unlikely to happen
third		*would have* + past participle	

2 Now look at these examples of conditional sentences. With your partner, discuss how you could express these using the conditional structures from the table above.

a Should you experience any difficulties, I'll be available to help you.

b Had it not been for Jane's intervention, the meeting would have gone on far too long.

c I'll turn on the air conditioning if it will make you feel more comfortable.

d If you would take your seats, ladies and gentlemen, the concert will begin.

3 Look at the words below which are often used in conditional sentences.

given	if so	unless	otherwise	provided

Now complete this text about advice for visitors to Japan using the words in the box.

How not to embarrass yourself in Japan

Before you go to any country where the culture is quite different, you should get to know something about the country, **(1)** .... you might end up embarrassing yourself and those around you. **(2)** .... that for most Europeans Japanese culture is very different, there are a few tips you might like to take note of. You could be invited to a Japanese home. **(3)** .... , remember that you should take your shoes off when you enter the house or flat. Don't wear your normal outdoor shoes inside **(4)** .... you really want to offend your host. **(5)** .... you follow a few basic house rules, both you and your hosts should have a mutually interesting time.

Reading

1 You are going to read an extract from a book which examines the similarities and differences between varieties of English. Before you read the extract, discuss these questions with a partner.

   a Have you ever visited a foreign country? If so, what cultural differences did you notice?

   b What might a visitor to your country perceive to be the biggest cultural difference?

   c What is culture shock? Have you ever experienced this?

2 Now read the text below and answer the questions.

Close encounters of the British kind

An underlying principle of cultural behaviour which is closely reflected in the language is the need to avoid face-to-face conflict. Even though the British may appear unpleasantly blunt when compared with some Asian cultures, they are on the whole concerned to offer a way out whenever a potential conflict between individuals occurs. This may be compared with public confrontations in large committees or parliament where much more confrontation goes on. Some cultures are, by way of contrast to the British, much less concerned to avoid conflict in private or personal encounters.

Perhaps there is a principle of 'aggression management' here: every culture has developed some ways of letting off steam, has some areas in which people are allowed to express their true feelings.

The immediate linguistic consequence of open conflict-avoidance is that you need to know what to do and what to say, for example, when someone takes a position in a queue in front of you, accidentally stands on your toe in a bus or disagrees with you in a public gathering. In the public gathering, depending on the nature of the meeting, the British reaction may be to confront disagreement openly and respond vigorously. In the other more personal situations, the same individual may work hard at taking a middle route between doing nothing and engaging in open conflict. In doing so, he or she will expect a similar cooperative response from the other person, such as an apology like, 'Oh, sorry, I didn't realise …'. In other cultures, behaviour might well be the opposite – a great effort to reduce conflict in a public meeting and robust responses in the private situations. Within our own cultures, we understand the conventions and know when people are being normally polite or normally outspoken. The difficulties come when we make errors in an unfamiliar environment.

   a What differences are there in the way many British people handle potential personal conflict and public confrontations? Would you say this is the same or different in your country?

   b Which phrase in the text means *expressing anger*?

   c When might a British person say, 'Oh, sorry, I didn't realise …'?

3 Discuss these questions in small groups.

   a What are the dangers of making general statements about the characteristics of certain nationalities?

   b What generalisations are made about your national characteristics? Do you agree with them?

Vocabulary

Vocabulary spot

It is important to know which words collocate (which words commonly go together) and a good dictionary will tell you this. When you see good examples of collocation, underline or highlight them in the text.

1 Look at these examples of collocations from the reading text.

an underlying principle (adjective and noun collocation)
closely reflected (adverb and verb collocation)
unpleasantly blunt (adverb and adjective collocation)

Go through the text and highlight some more collocations to remember.

2 Complete these word 'forks' with a word which collocates.

EXAMPLE: *to make*
to reach *a decision*
to come to

a supply a noun to make a compound noun
.... binder
.... finger
.... road

b supply three different verbs
to ....
to .... permission
to ....

c supply an adjective
.... weather
.... criticism
.... flavour

d supply three different adjectives
....
.... thanks
....

e supply a verb
to .... an ambition
to .... assets
to .... a dream

f supply three different verbs
to ....
to .... pain
to ....

Listening

Exam spot

In Part 4 of the CAE Listening test (Paper 4) you listen to five short extracts. There are two multiple-matching tasks in Part 4. In the test there are eight choices in each task and you match the correct five.

1 🎧 You will hear five speakers talking about meeting people. Look at the pictures below. As you listen, match the speakers to the pictures.

2 🎧 Listen again and match the speakers (1–5) to the topic headings (A–G). There are two topic headings which do not fit.

Speaker 1   **A** testing friendships
Speaker 2   **B** exchanging cultures
Speaker 3   **C** no way to get to know a lady
Speaker 4   **D** sharing experiences strengthens friendships
Speaker 5   **E** business and pleasure
          F strangers are not so strange
          G sharing delights of the environment

3 Which of the speakers did you find interesting to listen to and why?

Exam folder 1

Paper 3 Part 1 Multiple-choice gap fill

In Part 1 of the Use of English test (Paper 3) you must choose one word from a set of four (A, B, C or D) to fill a gap in the text. The focus is on vocabulary so you have to think about the meaning of the word. You also have to check whether the word fits the grammatical context of the sentence and the text as a whole.

Below are some examples of the types of words that are tested in this part of the paper.

Expressions
I .... sight of an old friend of mine when I went to the bank yesterday.

A saw   **B** caught   **C** set   **D** gained

B is the correct answer. The expression is *to catch sight of someone or something*.

Collocations
All that was left for breakfast were some .... rolls and tea.

A stale   **B** rotten   **C** sour   **D** rancid

A is the correct answer. We say *stale* bread, *rotten* fruit, vegetables or meat, *sour* milk and *rancid* butter.

Phrasal verbs
With all his experience he intends to .... up a computer business with his brother.

A put   **B** lay   **C** get   **D** set

D is the correct answer. The phrasal verb is *to set up* meaning to establish a company or business.

Linking words
He decided to go .... his family begged him not to.

A although   **B** despite   **C** otherwise   **D** if

A is the correct answer. *Despite* would require the construction *despite his family begging him not to* or *despite the fact that his family begged him not to*. *Otherwise* means *or else* and *if* does not make sense here.

Vocabulary
The child fell down and .... her knee.

A skimmed   **B** grazed   **C** rubbed   **D** scrubbed

B is the correct answer. *Graze* means to break the surface of the skin by rubbing against something rough. *Skim* means to move quickly just above (a surface) without, or only occasionally, touching it. *Rub* means to press or be pressed against (something) with a circular or up and down repeated movement. *Scrub* means to rub something hard in order to clean it.

Advice
- Read the title because it will help you predict the main topic of the text.
- Always read the whole text first to understand the gist of it.
- Read carefully not only the sentence where the gap is but also the sentence before and after the gap. Make sure that the word you write makes sense in the context of the text as a whole.
- Consider each alternative carefully, dismissing those which do not fit.
- Read through what you have written and see if it sounds right.

For questions 1–12, read the text below and then decide which word best fits each space. The exercise begins with an example (0).

Example:

0   **A** installed   **B** tied   **C** drawn   **D** retracted

C is the correct answer. We *draw* curtains or blinds.

Aunt Margaret's kitchen

The kitchen was quite dark because the blinds were (0) ......C...... . There was a smell of (1) .... cigarette smoke and some unwashed cups were (2) .... neatly in the sink, but the room was ferociously clean. It was quite a big room. There was a (3) .... dresser, painted dark brown, loaded with (4) ...., a flour jar, a bread-bin. There was a larder you could walk into. Melanie experimentally walked into it and (5) .... the door to on herself in a cool smell of cheese and mildew. What did they eat? Tins of things: they seemed particularly (6) .... of tinned peaches, there was a whole pile of tins of peaches. Tinned beans, tinned sardines. Aunt Margaret must buy tins in (7) .... There were a number of cake tins and Melanie opened one and found last night's currant cake. She took a ready-cut (8) .... of it and ate it. It made her feel more at (9) ...., already, to steal something from the larder. She went back into the kitchen, (10) .... crumbs.

There was a long table of (11) .... pine with a tablecloth (splashed with russet chrysanthemums, the sort of tablecloth you see through the windows of other people's houses as you walk by at teatime) folded back to cover crockery (12) .... out ready for breakfast, perhaps to keep mice from dirtying the cups.

1	**A** stale	**B** rancid	**C** ancient	**D** musty
2	**A** erected	**B** stacked	**C** ordered	**D** ranked
3	**A** built-up	**B** cornered	**C** walled	**D** built-in
4	**A** accessories	**B** crockery	**C** implements	**D** tools
5	**A** took	**B** pulled	**C** made	**D** put
6	**A** crazy	**B** loving	**C** fond	**D** likeable
7	**A** lots	**B** gross	**C** mass	**D** bulk
8	**A** slice	**B** rasher	**C** shaving	**D** remnant
9	**A** comfort	**B** place	**C** home	**D** rest
10	**A** sprinkling	**B** shedding	**C** sowing	**D** scattering
11	**A** grazed	**B** scraped	**C** bruised	**D** scrubbed
12	**A** sorted	**B** set	**C** done	**D** let

2 Keeping in touch

Speaking 1

1 With a partner, discuss these questions about keeping in touch with people.

   a Which method(s) of communication do you use with your friends – face-to-face conversation, telephone, email or letter? Which method do you think is best for different occasions?

   b Do you think it is necessary to see someone regularly, face-to-face, in order to remain friends?

   c How have recent changes in communications technology affected you? Do you feel that people are becoming more or less isolated because of these?

Ⓔxam spot

In the CAE Writing test (Paper 2), you may be asked to write an informal letter either in Part 1 or Part 2. Read the situation carefully and decide who you are writing to and why before you start the letter. Make sure you are consistent in your style of writing and that your purpose is clear.

Writing

1 Read the following letter. With a partner, discuss what the purpose of the letter is.

on holiday in beautiful Scotland
Midsummer

Hi Sarah

Well, here we are on the fantastic Isle of Skye - honestly, I can't begin to tell you how wonderful it is to spend some time away after my exams. As you know I'd been working so hard, I was beginning to think life would never be normal again (what's normal anyway?). Of course, it's the other extreme here - the only serious decision I have to make in any one day is shall I have smoked salmon for dinner or Scottish beef? Ha! What a life, eh?

Anyway, what I really wanted to say was a huge thank you for the present, it's the best present ever! The colours are just amazing and I love long T-shirts that I can wear for anything - even as a nightie - no, it's too good for that. Jack's been looking at it with envy so I'll have to keep my eye on it to make sure he doesn't swipe it. Really, a big thank you.

Tomorrow we're going to the north of the island, up along the coast road to an area that's known for wonderful walks and stunning views; I'll come back as fit as a fiddle. There's supposed to be a great pottery shop up there so I'll have a look at that too. Trouble is it's quite pricey now; ever since the potter featured in a national newspaper article some of his pots are now fetching astronomical sums in some trendy London gallery. Ah, well!

   Must dash, Jack's just come in and looks like a man hunting lunch!

   love

   Jane

PS I'll be back on Sun 8th, will give you a call then.

2 With a partner, discuss these questions about the letter to Sarah.

a What is unusual about the address and date in this letter? What are more common ways of writing them in informal letters?

b This letter begins with *Hi Sarah* and ends with *love Jane*. What other beginnings and endings can informal letters have?

c What do you notice about the type of vocabulary used? Give examples.

d What do you notice about the punctuation?

e Is it common to use contractions in informal writing?

f How did Jane add some information which she had forgotten?

g Write a key sentence for each paragraph which summarises the content.

3 An English friend of yours wrote to you some time ago asking about the possibilities of working in a hotel near where you live. Here is an extract from her letter.

> ... As you know I'm studying hotel management and as part of the course, I'm expected to get a holiday job working in a hotel. You mentioned once before that there are some great hotels near where you live. Could you let me know the name of one which you think would be good to work in? It would be even better if you could find out who I should contact ...

Unfortunately you have been very busy so you have not replied to her letter until now. Write to your friend to:

- apologise for the delay in writing back
- give information about a hotel and the person to contact
- suggest suitable dates for holiday jobs
- give some information about what has been happening in your life since you were last in touch with your friend
- ask some questions about your friend.

Write about 250 words and remember to think about the points raised in Writing 2.

Prepositions and adverbs

1 Look at this sentence from Writing 1.

*Well, here we are **on the fantastic Isle of Skye** – honestly, I can't begin to tell you how wonderful it is to **spend some time away** after my exams.*

Look at the words in bold. *On* is a preposition in this example. *Away* is an adverb in this example. Read through Jane's letter again and underline more examples of prepositions and adverbs.

2 Complete the following sentences by putting in any necessary prepositions or adverbs.

EXAMPLE: *Turn left the crossroads and then after two blocks, you will see the cinema the right.* ✗
*Turn left **at** the crossroads and then after two blocks, you will see the cinema **on** the right.* ✓

a It's your brother the phone.

b He got married Sarah when he was in his 30s.

c The noise of the storm prevented me sleeping.

d Who is that present?

e When I was my way to London, I realised I'd left my wallet home.

f I always suffer hay fever the summer.

g I think I was beginning to get stuck a rut in my home town.

h In the discount book shops near me you can get books next to nothing.

i You can find this chain of restaurants the country.

j I'm afraid you can't trust the trains to run time.

k Some of the students couldn't come the pub because they are age.

l Mary's got a job a teacher.

m Tom's a doctor and seems to be duty most weekends.

G⋯⟶ page 190

3 Read this extract from a book. In the extract, some family members are all sitting down together reading the letters which they have just received.

Look at the prepositions and adverbs in italics in the first paragraph. Then fill the gaps with a suitable preposition or adverb.

In the crisp, heady weather the family spent most of its time *on* the veranda, eating, sleeping or just simply arguing. It was here, once a week, that we used to congregate to read our mail which Spiro had brought *to* us. As we browsed *through* our letters we would frequently pass remarks *to* one another.

"Aunt Mabel's moved (**1**) .... Sussex. She says Henry's passed all his exams and is going to work (**2**) .... a bank. At least, I *think* it's a bank. Her writing is really awful, (**3**) .... spite of that expensive education she's always boasting (**4**) .... Uncle Stephen's broken his leg, poor old dear, and done something (**5**) .... his *bladder*? Oh, no, I see. Really, this writing – he broke his leg falling (**6**) .... a ladder. You'd think he'd have more sense than to go (**7**) .... a ladder (**8**) .... his age. Ridiculous. Tom's married one (**9**) .... the Garnet girls."

Mother always left (**10**) .... the last a fat letter, addressed (**11**) .... large, firm, well-rounded handwriting, which was the monthly instalment (**12**) .... Great-aunt Hermione. Her letters invariably created an indignant uproar (**13**) .... the family, so we all put (**14**) .... our mail and concentrated when Mother, (**15**) .... a sigh (**16**) .... resignation, unfurled the twenty odd pages, settled herself comfortably and began to read.

4 With a partner, discuss these questions about the extract.

   a How did the confusion over *bladder* and *ladder* arise?
   b How did the family members usually react to Great-aunt Hermione's letters?
   c The book paints a picture of life in the 1950s. In your opinion, has family life changed much since then? Do family members communicate with each other in the same way?
   d When do you tend to receive letters or cards? Will email replace letters written by hand?

Vocabulary spot

Some words in English have multiple meanings or are used in different ways depending on the context. In the reading text we saw *Henry's passed all his exams and is going to work in a bank*. Look at the use of *bank* in these sentences: *We had a lovely picnic yesterday on the river bank. I haven't got his details to hand but they'll be in the data bank.*
Whenever you look up a word in your dictionary, check to see how many different meanings and uses it has.

Vocabulary

1 Which word can fit all three sentences?

   a • I hurt my .... while I was climbing.
      • It's at the .... of the page.
      • I'll have to .... the bill.

   b • The .... I heard of him, he was living in Hastings.
      • She's awful, I hope we've seen the .... of her.
      • The rain is expected to .... all week.

   c • After the accident he was so shocked he lost the .... of speech.
      • It's not in your .... to cancel the project.
      • You need tremendous .... in your legs to be a good runner.

   d • Have we got time for another .... of drinks before we go?
      • There were 15 of us all .... the table.
      • It was disappointing to see the politician .... on his critics.

   e • She showed me a computer which might .... my particular needs.
      • Police are interviewing a man who is said to .... the description of the attacker.
      • Does anyone .... to the name of Devlan?

   f • Someone .... into the back of my car yesterday.
      • Halfway down the motorway we .... out of petrol.
      • Mr Jones .... the company single-handedly for many years.

Listening

1 You are going to listen to a conversation between two women, Rebecca and Amanda. Look at the picture of them. What do you think their hobbies may be and their dreams for the future?

2 🎧 Work with a partner. One of you will listen for Rebecca's answers and the other for Amanda's answers. Listen to the first part of the conversation and note down both the main idea and the extra information they give to develop the answer.

Question	Main idea	Extra information
Where are you from in England?		
Have you studied any foreign languages?		

3 🎧 Now continue to listen and make notes on Rebecca's or Amanda's answers. Make notes under the two headings.

Topic	Main idea	Extra information
hobbies		
future hopes and dreams		
living or working abroad permanently		
earliest memories of school		

4 Do you have anything in common with either Rebecca or Amanda?

Speaking 2

1 What do you think makes someone a good communicator?

2 In Listening 3 we heard Amanda develop her answer about her hobbies.

I've done a sort of Middle Eastern dancing. It's like an Egyptian belly dancing but it's not Egyptian, it's a kind of country form where your hips actually go down instead of upwards. And you're dressed in lots of clothes, you're not showing any stomach or anything. So, yeah, I did that for a little while but I get fed up with things really, get bored and move on. I did yoga and that annoyed me. It used to make me anxious.

With a partner, discuss ways of developing the answers to these questions.

a What do you enjoy about living in your city?
b Why are you studying English?
c What interesting things have you done lately?
d What are your plans for the future?

> **E xam spot**
>
> In the first part of the CAE Speaking test (Paper 5), you will be expected to talk about yourself and your life in an interesting way, showing a range of structures and vocabulary. Remember to develop your ideas by giving extra information.

3 Work in groups of three. Imagine one of you is the Examiner and the other two are candidates. The Examiner should ask the questions above and three more related questions. While the candidates are speaking, the Examiner should consider whether they are using a range of structures and vocabulary. Candidates should develop answers as fully as possible and make them interesting.

4 Apart from a range of structures and vocabulary, what other features are important when speaking?

Writing folder 1

Informal letters

1 Look at these extracts from letters. For each extract, decide who might have written it, who it was written to and why.

a

... Then for the last week I'll have a holiday and I'm going to spend it in Prague. I've got a friend who went there last year and she said it's great – a beautiful city, really friendly people and lots to do. What could be better after my holiday job? I'll tell you all about it when I get back.

b

... It's just brilliant, the best thing you could have got me. I'd tried to get that CD the other week but it wasn't in the shops then. I'll probably drive the whole family mad now playing it over and over again for days!

c

... It's a real shame you missed the party, it was great. You know that guy who goes to the sports club on Saturdays? Well, he was there – gorgeous or what! I got talking to him and he's just as nice as he looks. I hope you're feeling better now and ...

2 What are some of the features of informal letters? Complete the table below. One example has been given for the first two categories.

Choice of vocabulary:	*phrasal verbs, ...*
Grammatical features:	*reported speech, ...*
Length of sentences:	
Linking words:	
Punctuation:	

3 Look at this outline of an informal letter. What could go in each box?

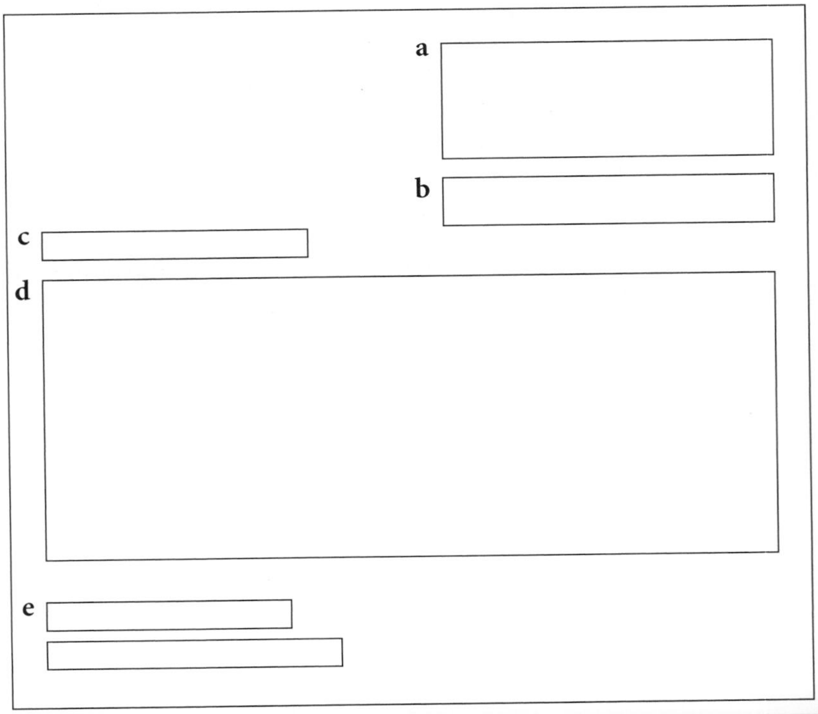

a

b

c

d

e

4 There are many set phrases which we can use in informal letters. Here are some examples:

Greetings
- referring to last letter: *It was wonderful to read all your latest news …*
- referring to time since last letter: *It's ages since I last heard from you. What have you been up to?*
- apologising for delay in replying: *I'm really sorry I've taken so long to get back to you but …*
- thanking for last letter: *Thanks for writing and telling me all about your plans for the summer holidays.*

Thanking
- for a present: *I really can't thank you enough for the book, it's just what I wanted.*
- for a party: *Thanks for the party, it was great. I met such a lot of new and interesting people!*
- for an invitation: *It's really kind of you to invite me to the wedding and I'd love to come.*

Now add at least two examples of set phrases to the following categories:

Refusing an invitation
Congratulating
Giving your opinion
Giving advice

Can you think of any other reasons for writing an informal letter?

5 Read the task below carefully.

A friend of yours is doing an interior design course at college and you have the same sort of taste. You have decided to redecorate your bedroom and you have saved some money to spend on it. Write a **letter** to your friend asking for his/her advice.

Now start planning. Work with a partner and discuss:

- the content – what main points do you want to include?
- the language – which phrases are appropriate for the letter?
- the organisation of the content – how can you organise the content into different paragraphs?
- linking devices – how will you link clauses, sentences and paragraphs?
- the style – remember the style features from 2.
- the opening and closing of the letter – choose an opening phrase and a closing phrase from 3.

Write a first draft of the letter. Exchange first drafts with another student and comment on the points made above.

Advice

When you check through your writing use this checklist.

- errors
- natural use of language
- good range of vocabulary
- spelling
- good range of structures
- full completion of task
- use of linkers
- appropriate and consistent style
- content – nothing relevant should be left out

The purpose of the letter should be clear and it should have a positive effect on the reader. This is what the examiners are looking for.

3 The real you

Speaking 1

1 With a partner, discuss these questions.

a Look at the magazine covers. What would you expect to read about in these magazines?

b Which magazines or TV programmes do you know where famous people are interviewed? Do you like reading or watching interviews?

c What sort of people make good guests on TV chat shows?

d Why do you think famous people appear on chat shows or do interviews for magazines?

e Who would you most like to interview? How would you approach the interview to encourage the person to give full and honest answers?

Reading

1 You are going to read an interview with a model, Helena Christensen. What questions do you think the interviewer will ask?

2 Read the interview to check if any of your predicted questions were asked.

Interviewer: Considering you belong to one of the glitziest professions there is, along with showbiz, you seem to have your feet pretty much on the ground.

Helena: I truly believe that who you are is because of your family, you know, the way that you were brought up, the love that you get from your family, the discipline from them. It all goes back to childhood no matter what happens later in your life. And also, probably, coming from Denmark has kept me very grounded because there's not too much fuss going on there and nobody really cares too much about fame, the same way that other countries are obsessed with it. In Denmark it's who you are and you shouldn't think you are more than anybody else. And, all in all, I would really say that it has helped me coming from a country like Denmark.

Interviewer: You have a really good reputation in the industry for being very professional; you come in, you do the job, you go home. There's no baggage, no tantrums and tempers.

Helena: Well, that's nice to hear, but, for me, that was the only way to deal with the job because it's such a strange job. If I didn't do it that way, if I created problems for myself, not just coming in, showing up, doing the job and leaving, if I thought too much about it, then I don't know if I would've been able to do this job. I think the only way to do it was just actually doing it that way.

Interviewer: I know it's a difficult question but why do you think you rose to the top? Was it a mixture of talent and luck, being in the right place at the right time?

Helena: It was a mixture of all of that. You know, you can't really define your look or why your look was perfect for the time. But I was really lucky. When I went to Paris for the first time I didn't really have any intentions of working as a model. I came down to eat, basically because I was invited to a weekend of good food, and it was the show week that week, and I went to see some clients and met some of the most amazing people in the industry. But it was not really that important to me. It wasn't what I wanted to do at that time.

Interviewer: What did you want to do?

Helena: I wanted to travel the world and take photos. Most people think I'm starting photography now, but actually, I did it before and did a bit of modelling in between.

Interviewer: Did a bit of modelling in between! That's one way of putting it. Do you think that all those years that you spent in front of the cameras make you a better photographer?

Helena: Obviously, working with some of the most amazing photographers in the world, you soak it all in and get a bit of their experience. And I'm very curious about everything I see in life.

Interviewer: What kind of photographs do you take, is it glamour shots or do you tend to go more for the real person as it were, showing them as they really are, warts and all?

Helena: I'm definitely more into taking portraits of people as they really are, getting something from them deep inside out through their faces. And it's an amazing thing taking photographs, portraits, as every time it's such an intimidating sensation when you take portraits of someone, and I know it makes me feel a little shy and

3 Work with a partner and answer these questions.

a Which two factors in particular have influenced Helena's personality?

b How did she deal with modelling?

c How did she get into modelling?

d What had she intended to do instead of modelling?

e How does she relate her own experience of being photographed to being a photographer?

f What other business is she involved in and what is her role in it?

g What does she say about the way men react to a female model?

---

nervous, and it also makes the person that you do portraits of feel a little strange about it because it's a very naked feeling to be that close to someone, and sometimes I don't even know the people that I do portraits of. But you get to know so much about them by just looking at them through your lens.

Interviewer: And now you've really branched out, got your own magazine …

Helena: Well, we started with four issues the first year and now we're on the second year and it's ten issues.

Interviewer: Ten issues, and you're doing quite a lot of the photographs for that yourself?

Helena: Yeah, I mean the idea from the beginning was that I was the creative director, but more than anything, I write and take photographs, so it's definitely what I'm most into.

Interviewer: Now, as you are Helena Christensen, super model, how easy was it for you to meet guys, to meet men? Weren't they intimidated by you?

Helena: Well, I think it does intimidate men, and I wish it didn't, to meet women from this strange profession, because it intimidates me. It's such a strange thing, I've never gotten used to doing this job really. But it really only comes down to talking to people and then as soon as you open your mouth and speak, then people are totally fine because they realise there's nothing there that's too weird. It's not what I thought it would be, which is, I guess, one of the problems with having been in the media so much. People get a kind of different perspective of you unless you really come across as the person you really are. But I haven't really had a problem with the men thing.

Interviewer: I'm sure you haven't!

---

4 Work with a different partner and discuss these questions.

a What is the stereotypical image of a female model? Does Helena fit this image?

b What did you think of the way the interviewer and Helena interacted?

c Do you think Helena develops her answers sufficiently and appropriately for this magazine interview? Give examples to support your opinion.

d Is there anything else you would have asked her if you had been the interviewer? Are there any questions you would have left out?

e What do you think of magazines and newspapers which carry a lot of stories about famous people's past and personal lives?

Listening

1 You are going to listen to an interview with David Burns, a soap opera star. In it, he talks about his troubled past. What sort of skeletons do you think there are in his cupboard?

2 🎧 Listen to the interview and tick the areas of his life that he talks about.

brothers and sisters	☐	his working relationship with a director	☐
school life	☐	his marriage	☐
hobbies	☐	his relationship with his parents	☐
a person who helped him	☐	his daughter	☐
fans	☐	his future acting roles	☐

3 🎧 Listen to the interview again for the expressions below. Tick the ones you know the meaning of. Put a question mark next to the ones you are not sure about. Put a cross next to the ones you do not understand and cannot guess the meaning of from the context.

a the public eye
b a bully
c a taunt
d downward spiral
e tuned into me
f playing villains
g an edgy person
h it can turn nasty
i obsessed
j I was hogging the limelight
k my lips are sealed

4 Try to find other students who can tell you the meaning of the phrases you do not know. If no one can help, ask your teacher or look the phrase up in a dictionary.

5 Look again at Listening 2 and discuss with a partner the ways in which David Burns has had a troubled past.

6 To what extent do you think people's childhood experiences affect them in later life?

Wish and *if only*

When people are interviewed, it is common for them to talk about their wishes and regrets. In Reading 2, Helena Christensen said *I wish it didn't*, meaning *I wish meeting famous women didn't intimidate men*. This is just one of the structures that can be used after *wish* or *if only*.

1 Work with a partner and complete these sentences with the correct form of the verb.

 a I wish I .... (start) photography earlier.
 b I wish I .... (have) more time to spend with my family.
 c I wish my parents .... (come) to visit me more often.
 d I wish .... (inform) you of our decision.
 e We do not wish the sum of money .... (disclose)
 f If only that .... (be) true!
 g If only the weather .... (brighten up)
 h I wish you .... (ask) such personal questions.
 i If only I .... (know) what it would be like before I started this job!

2 What do you think David Burns wishes? Think about his past, present and future.

 EXAMPLE: *Perhaps he wishes he hadn't been bullied at school.*

It's time, would rather/sooner

1 Which phrases can be used to complete the sentences?

It's time …	**a** to go home.
I'd rather/sooner …	**b** go home.
	c going home.
	d we go home.
	e we went home.

2 Read the text below and put the verbs in brackets into the correct form.

> I wish magazines (**1**) .... (have) more in-depth interviews with people. They always seem to focus on the same things, any skeletons in the cupboard and a person's love life. I'd sooner (**2**) .... (read) about their beliefs, aims and ambitions. It's time magazines (**3**) .... (wake) up to the fact that the general public has had enough of media invasion into people's privacy. If only I (**4**) .... (be born) with the necessary talent and expertise, I'd start a magazine for the company where I work. It's time (**5**) .... (do) something instead of complaining about other magazines.

3 Work with a partner and give your opinions on magazine and radio or TV interviews with famous people. What do you wish they were like or what would you rather hear about?

G ⋯⁖ page 191

Exam spot

Sometimes candidates lose marks simply because they do not speak clearly enough for the examiner to hear them. Make sure you do not lose marks in this way. In the role play for Speaking 2 in this unit, make sure all the other students can hear you loud and clear.

Vocabulary spot

In Listening 2, David Burns said *I was hogging the limelight*. This is an idiom with the form: verb + *the* + object. When you learn phrases with the same pattern, try saying the phrases out loud. The repetition of the rhythm may help you to remember them. Why not try it with the phrases in the following section?

Vocabulary

1 Work with a partner and match the verbs (a–f) with the objects (1–6). You may have to look these idioms up in a dictionary to help you. How do you look them up? In the idiom *to hog the limelight* for example, do you look under *hog* or *limelight*? Check in a dictionary.

a to take	**1** the water
b to test	**2** the shots
c to deliver	**3** the gap
d to call	**4** the biscuit
e to bridge	**5** the light
f to see	**6** the goods

2 Complete this text with four of the idioms from Vocabulary 1.

She was a complete unknown when she went to Hollywood but despite her obvious beauty, film directors were unsure of her acting ability. She was given a bit part in the movie *Braveheart* so that the director could (1) .... to see if she would be a viable commercial proposition to take on for future movies. She more than (2) .... , she was an overnight success. From then on, she was the one who (3) .... Whatever part she wanted, it was hers. And at first she accepted every role that was offered. After years of working all hours and after being involved in some rather mediocre films which dented her image, she (4) .... and learnt to accept only those films which would enhance her career.

3 Which method of finding out the meaning of idioms do you prefer and why?

 a guessing
 b looking them up in a dictionary
 c asking classmates
 d asking the teacher for an English paraphrase
 e asking the teacher for a sentence using the idiom
 f asking the teacher for a translation into your language

4 Another form of idiom is prepositional phrase + *the* + object.

EXAMPLE: *to be in the dark* = to know nothing about something.

Match the idioms (1–5) to the definitions (a–e).

 1 to be over the hill
 2 to be on the spot
 3 to be in the running
 4 to be up to the mark
 5 to be under the weather

 a to have a reasonable chance
 b to feel ill
 c to be considered too old
 d to be as good as the usual standard
 e to be at a place where an event is happening or has just happened

Speaking 2

1 Look back at Speaking 1e. Work with a partner and think of a famous person you both know about. You are going to role play an interview with that person.

2 Decide which role you are going to play. One of you is the interviewer and the other is the interviewee. Prepare some questions and answers together. In the interview, you must not say who the famous person is because the other students are going to guess.

3 Role play the interview for the class. Can the other students guess who the famous person is?

4 Now decide which interview you really liked and why. Which of your classmates do you think would make good interviewers?

Exam folder 2

Paper 3 Part 2 Open gap fill

In Part 2 of the English in Use test (Paper 3) you must complete a text by writing the missing word in the gap. You can use only one word. The focus is on structure, so you have to think about structure and meaning to fill the gaps. Check whether the word fits the grammatical context of the sentence and the meaning of text as a whole.

1 Look at these sentences and decide what kind of word would fit the gap. Is it a verb, a preposition, a determiner or a pronoun, for example? Which word completes the sentence?

  a This rolling of the letter 'r' is typical .... some Scottish accents.

  b The cold grey morning was far from welcoming and Janis pulled her dressing gown tightly round .... as she went downstairs.

  c Some people believe the only way to learn a language is to go to the country where it is spoken .... others would recommend learning the basics at home first.

  d Our teacher used to give us a vocabulary test .... single day of the week.

  e It is true that our policy may .... reviewing in the light of recent technological developments.

  f It was an epoch .... produced a true flourishing of the arts.

  g Jack was not sure .... his proposal would be accepted or not.

  h Each classroom has .... own display area, computer work station and quiet corner.

  i Anne hadn't set .... to cause such a disturbance among her colleagues.

  j .... John had had considerable success in his previous job, the new one was causing unexpected challenges.

2 With a partner, discuss what you understand by the title of the text opposite. What do you think you might read about in the text?

3 Give some examples of jargon and discuss when it might be useful and when it might cause problems.

4 Read the whole text without filling in any of the gaps. Then discuss the main ideas of the text.

5 Go through the text and decide which kind of word (verb, preposition, etc.) fits the gap. Check the sentences before and after the gap to find clues.

6 Complete the text.

EXAMPLE: 0 everyone

Jargon – the up side

The reality is that **(0)** ......*everyone*...... uses jargon. It is an essential part of the network of occupations and pursuits **(1)** .... make up society. All jobs have an element of jargon, which workers learn **(2)** .... they develop their expertise. All hobbies require mastery of a jargon. Each society grouping has **(3)** .... jargon. The phenomenon **(4)** .... out to be universal – and valuable. It is the jargon element which, in a job, can promote economy and precision of expression, and **(5)** .... help make life easier for the workers.

(6) .... we have learned to command it, jargon is **(7)** .... we readily take pleasure in, **(8)** .... the subject is motorcycling, baseball or computers. It **(9)** .... add pace, variety and humour to speech – as when, with an important event approaching, we might slip **(10)** .... the related jargon. We enjoy the mutual showing off which stems **(11)** .... a fluent use of terminology, and we enjoy the in-jokes which shared linguistic experience permits. **(12)** .... , we are jealous of **(13)** .... knowledge. We are quick to demean anyone who tries to be part of our group **(14)** .... being prepared to take on its jargon. And we resent it when some other group, sensing our lack of linguistic awareness, refuses to **(15)** .... us in.

Advice

- Remember you must write only **one** word.
- You are never required to write a contraction. If you think the answer is a contraction, it must be wrong, so think again.
- Decide what sort of word fits the gap.
- Try to justify your answer grammatically and with regard to the meaning by referring to the text.
- Check the spelling. The spelling must be correct to get a mark in the exam.
- Try reading the sentence out to yourself to see if it sounds right.
- In the exam always write something. You never know, you might be lucky even if you are not sure of the answer!

4 Acting on instructions

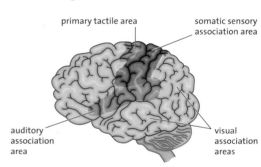

Genre	Instructions
Topic	Memory techniques

Listening 1

1 Have you ever been in situations like the ones in the pictures?
   What problems did you have?

2 🎧 Listen and follow the instructions.

3 Here is an example of an instruction from the listening:
   Hold for three seconds and then breathe out.
   Which grammatical structure is used? How else could you give this instruction?

Speaking

1 Look at these pictures which illustrate how to make an omelette.
   Put them into the correct order.

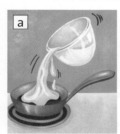

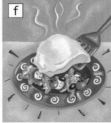

2 Now tell another student how to make an omelette.

Reading

primary tactile area

somatic sensory association area

auditory association area

visual association areas

1 You are going to read some tips on how to improve your memory. Before you read, discuss these questions with a partner.

   a How would you rate your memory? What evidence do you have for this?
   b To what extent do you think it is possible to improve your memory with techniques or exercises? Have you ever tried to improve your memory?
   c Do you think it is true that people's memory gets worse as they grow older? Why should this be the case?

2 Now read the tips below on how to improve your memory. Then with a partner discuss which recommendations you think are the most effective and why.

a Make sure you are alert and attentive before trying to memorise anything.

b Understand the material rather than merely memorising, if it is the type that requires deeper comprehension.

c Look for larger patterns or ideas, and organise pieces of information into meaningful groups.

d Link the new bits of knowledge with what you already know. Place what you learn into context with the rest of your knowledge, looking for relationships between the ideas.

e Engage your visual and auditory senses by using drawings, charts or music to aid memory.

f Use mnemonics – devices such as formulae or rhymes that serve as memory aids. For example, use the acronym 'HOMES' to memorise the Great Lakes in North America (Huron, Ontario, Michigan, Erie and Superior).

g Repeat and review what you have learned as many times as you can. Apply it or use it in conversation, as continual practice is the key to remembering things in the long term.

3 Which of the techniques would you like to try out?

4 You are going to read about three memory techniques which are recommended for language learning. Divide into three groups. Everybody should read the introduction.
Group A should read 1 (*The Linkword Technique*), Group B should read 2 (*The Town Language Mnemonic*) and Group C should read 3 (*The Hundred Most Common Words*).

Introduction

Learning foreign languages

Foreign languages are the ideal subject area for the use of memory techniques: the process of learning words is essentially a matter of association – associating what is initially a meaningless collection of syllables with a word in a language that we understand.

Traditionally this association has been carried out by repetition – saying the word in one's own language and the foreign language time and time and time again.

The whole tedious way of acquiring vocabulary can be eliminated by three good techniques.

---

1 The Linkword Technique

The Linkword Technique uses images to link a word in one language with another word in another language. For example, if an English person wanted to learn the French word for carpet – *tapis*, he might imagine an oriental carpet where a **tap is** the central design. **Tap is** has the same spelling as *tapis* so he will remember the French for carpet.

The technique was formalised by Dr Gruneborg. Linkword books have been produced in many language pairs to help students acquire the basic vocabulary needed to get by in a language (usually about 1,000 words). It is claimed that by using this technique the basic vocabulary can be acquired in just 10 hours.

---

2 The Town Language Mnemonic

The fundamental principle rests on the fact that the basic vocabulary of a language relates to everyday things: things that are typically found in a small town, city, or village. The basis of the technique is that the student should choose a town that he or she is very familiar with, and should use objects within that place as the cues to recall the images that link to foreign words.

Adjectives in the park

Adjectives should be associated with a garden or park within the town: words such as green, smelly, bright, small, cold, etc. can be easily related to objects in a park. Perhaps there is a pond there, a small wood, perhaps people with different characteristics are walking around.

Verbs in the sports centre

Verbs can most easily be associated with a sports centre or playing field. This allows us all the associations of lifting, running, walking, hitting, eating, swimming, diving, etc.

Remembering genders

In a language where gender is important, a very elegant method of remembering this is to divide your town into two main zones where the gender is only masculine and feminine, or three where there is a neutral gender. This division can be by busy roads, rivers, etc. To fix the gender of a noun, simply associate its image with a place in the correct part of town. This makes remembering genders so easy!

Many languages, many towns

Another elegant spin-off of the technique comes when learning several languages: normally this can cause confusion. With the town mnemonic, all you need do is choose a different city, town or village for each language to be learned. Ideally this might be in the relevant country; however, practically it might just be a local town with a slight flavour of the relevant country, or twinned with it.

---

3 The Hundred Most Common Words

Tony Buzan, in his book *Using your Memory*, points out that just 100 words comprise 50% of all words used in conversation in a language. Learning this core 100 words gets you a long way towards learning to speak in that language, albeit at a basic level. It is argued that if you start learning a foreign language by learning the words which occur most frequently, then your learning will be effective. However, critics of this method point out that these words alone would not allow a speaker to make sentences as the words are mainly articles, adverbs and prepositions. In order to communicate we need a range of different types of words so that we can make sentences. On the other hand, there is a lot to be said for learning useful words rather than the specialised words for some particular bird or scientific process.

The first 20 basic words

The first 20 out of a list of 100 basic words used in conversation are shown below.

1. a, an	2. after	3. again
4. all	5. almost	6. also
7. always	8. and	9. because
10. before	11. big	12. but
13. (I) can	14. (I) come	15. either/or
16. (I) find	17. first	18. for
19. friend	20. from	

5 Regroup and tell the others about what you have read.

6 Would you use the technique you read about? Why?/Why not?

⊙ Modals: *may, might, can, could*

Modal verbs tell us something about the attitude of the speaker. Look at these examples from Reading 4.

*If an English person wanted to learn the French word for carpet – **tapis**, he might imagine an oriental carpet where a **tap is** the central design.*

Words such as green, smelly, bright, small, cold, etc. can be easily related to objects in a park.

In these examples, *might* expresses probability and *can* possibility.

1   Match the meaning of the modal verb *can* with its use in each of the sentences below.

> ability   negative certainty
> offer   order   permission
> request   theoretical possibility

a   Can this camera take panoramic shots?
b   Can I get you something to drink?
c   That can't be the answer. It doesn't fit.
d   Can you help me with this bag?
e   You can collate the statistics while I phone the new customers.
f   The school can take 1,000 pupils.
g   Can I borrow your camera until tomorrow?

2   Explain the difference in meaning between these sentences.

1   a   I could get into the house by the back door.
     b   I was able to get into the house by the back door.
2   a   She may get here by 10 if she catches the 8.30 train.
     b   May I use the office photocopier to make a copy of my passport?
3   a   She might get here on time if she leaves work early.
     b   Might I make a suggestion?

3   Look at these pictures and speculate about what might have happened to the people in them or what they might be doing.

EXAMPLE: *The man in picture a might have fallen into a river.*
The woman in picture e might be studying for an exam.

G ···⁝ page 191

Writing

1   Write a set of instructions using imperatives and modal verbs. Choose one of the subjects below or one of your own.

How to:
- stay safe while travelling
- make a good cup of coffee
- follow a healthy diet
- make a study plan
- stay cool when you're feeling stressed out
- learn vocabulary in a foreign language.

Listening 2

Press 2 now · Please hold · You are 6th in the queue to be answered · Please be patient

1 🎧 When you phone a company, you often hear a set of instructions which tell you what to do in order to speak to a particular department. Listen to the instructions and answer the following questions.

  1 *Phoning the cinema*
    What should you do if
    a you want to make a booking for *Cast Away*?
    b you want to see a different film, not *Cast Away*, and you know what time it starts and how much it costs?

  2 *Phoning an airline*
    What should you do when
    a you want to book a flight?
    b you want a special deal?
    c you check in for a PanAir flight?

  3 *Phoning a telephone and Internet provider*
    What should you do if
    a you want information about STL's Internet service?
    b you have a problem with any STL service?
    c you do not use STL yet and would like information about their services?

2 How do you feel about hearing recorded instructions on the phone? Does it provide efficient customer service? Has the personal touch been lost?

Vocabulary

A prefix is a letter or group of letters added to the beginning of a word to make a new word. In Reading 2g you saw *Review what you've learned as many times as you can*. The prefix *re-* adds the meaning *do again*.

1 Put these words under the correct heading according to the prefix they take. Some words can go under more than one heading.

> appear iron believable lead logical prison mature accessible polite resistible regular continue sensitive material smoker literate trust timely expected conclusive

dis-	il-	im-	in-	ir-	non-	mis-	un-

2 Complete these rules for the use of *im-*, *il-* and *ir-*.

  a We often use .... before words beginning with *m* and *p*.
  b We often use .... before words beginning with *l*.
  c We often use .... before words beginning with *r*.

A suffix is a letter or group of letters added to the end of a word to make a new word. Suffixes fall into two categories:

- those connected with the grammatical form of the word, for example, *-ly* (for an adverb), as in *carefully*, or *-tion* (for a noun), as in *recommendation*
- those connected with meaning, for example, *-less* meaning *without*, as in *careless*.

3 Put these words under the correct heading according to the suffix they take. Some words can go under more than one heading and you may have to change the spelling slightly.

> photocopy count judge time emerge emancipate rude employ dramatise frequent argue calm recommend speech deceit care point respect tend rely

-able	-ation	-ency	-ful	-ly	-less	-ment	-ness

4 You are going to play suffixes bingo. Your teacher will give you a set of cards with suffixes written on them. Follow your teacher's instructions.

Writing folder 2

Essays

An essay written for a teacher or tutor very often requires you to give your opinion and support it with examples. Its purpose is to persuade the reader to agree with the opinions or to show reasons for a particular point of view.

Organisation of essays

1 What is the purpose of each feature in the *Content* column? Choose from the following list and write it in the *Purpose* column.

- To explain what is understood by some key words/concepts
- To underline the writer's point of view
- To express important ideas
- To tell the reader what you intend to cover in this essay

- To introduce the reader to the topic
- To remind the reader of the key ideas
- To support ideas with examples

Stage of essay	Content	Purpose
Introduction	General statement Definition(s) – optional Scope of essay	1 2 3
Body	Arguments Evidence	4 5
Conclusions	Summary Relate the argument to a more general world view	6 7

2 Look at this essay title and sample essay. In the table above, tick the purposes which have been included.

'Advances in technology will result in a growth in unemployment.' Discuss.

There has been considerable debate in the national press with some experts claiming that we are heading for a decrease in the number and type of jobs available while others insist that we are about to see a surge in job opportunities. However, when we look at the situation from a global perspective, we see increasing opportunities for work for those who are willing and able to travel.

On the one hand, there are those who believe that with the advent of new technology, such as automation and the use of robots, the number of jobs for people will decrease. In addition, these advocates of gloom argue that globalisation will mean that 'our' jobs will be taken by others in other countries where, for example, the labour cost is lower. On the other hand, the more optimistic among us view the future as a golden age when more people, architects and the like, will be able to enjoy jobs which are intellectually interesting because the dull monotonous jobs will have been automated. Advanced technology will enable us to travel and work almost wherever we like in the world and that means a global economy will work to our advantage.

In my opinion, having considered both sides of the argument, I believe that there will be more job opportunities, the workforce will be more mobile and jobs will be more rewarding. Moreover, this will be the case for an increasing number of people as the economy of the world as a whole continues to prosper.

Linking words and expressions

In any piece of extended writing or speaking we need to link our ideas so that we produce coherent and logical language.

3 Highlight the linking words or expressions in the essay on page 32. Are most of them formal or informal? Which ones are followed by a comma?

4 Make a plan for the following essay by answering the questions and completing the table.

In your English class you have been discussing the reasons why people study English. Your teacher has asked you to write the following 250-word essay: 'If everyone spoke one language, English for example, it would lead to better international relations.' Discuss.

- Who is the reader? ....
- Style – formal/informal? ....
- Length? ....

Stage of essay	Content	Purpose
Introduction		
Body		
Conclusion		

Brainstorming vocabulary

When planning the main body of your essay, write down all the main points you want to include. When you do this, it is a good idea to brainstorm vocabulary and key phrases connected with the topic. For example, if you have an essay title which requires you to discuss advertising, you could have a vocabulary box as follows:

Vocabulary resource: Advertising
1 Techniques: catchy slogan/jingle, celebrity endorsement, eye-catching packaging
2 For: raise awareness of product, encourage healthy competition between rival companies, creative/entertaining/stimulating
3 Against: make false claims, raise unrealistic expectations, intrusive, create materialism, create false needs

5 Read the following essay title and add to the vocabulary and key phrases.

'Our appearance, the way we dress, etc., reflects who we are. It is therefore important to be consistent in the style we adopt throughout our lives.' Discuss.

Styles: *hair style,* ....
For consistency: *suggests a trustworthy person,* ....
Against consistency: *dress to reflect different moods,* ....

Tips for essay writing

6 Look at the list of tips for essay writing and then add two more tips of your own.
- Highlight the key words in the question.
- List the points you want to include.
- Plan carefully.
- Give examples or reasons for your views.
- Link ideas.
- Present a balanced argument.
- Use formal/neutral vocabulary.
- Use a range of grammatical structures.
- ....
- ....

7 Using the title in 5, write an essay for your teacher following the tips and the suggestions for organisation and brainstorming vocabulary.
Write approximately 250 words.

5 Dear Sir or Madam

Speaking

1 With a partner, discuss the following questions.

a Have you ever written a formal letter? Who did you write to and what was the purpose of the letter?

b Do you find it easier to write formal or informal letters? Why do you think that is the case?

2 Read these extracts from formal letters and say what the purpose of each letter is.

a On behalf of everyone, I send you best wishes for a speedy recovery.

b Please accept our sincere apologies for any distress this situation may have caused you.

c You may have overlooked this payment but we ask that you give it your prompt attention.

d Please confirm in writing if you wish to accept this offer and when you will be in a position to commence work.

e Ms Wright is currently involved in a project which might be of interest to you and she will be contacting you soon to arrange a meeting.

f If you could forward the details of the Nile Cruise, I would be most grateful.

3 Look at this outline of a layout of a formal letter in English. Complete each box with the missing information (a–g).

a 20th March 2008
b Yours faithfully,
c 221 Cherry Drive
   York YK3 2FG
d Dear Sir or Madam,
e (signature)
   Dr C.R. Roberton
f The University Hotel
   65 Park Parade
   Durham DH6 8HY
g I am writing in connection with a recent visit to your hotel from the 12th to 15th March. My wife and I stayed in room 368. Unfortunately, our otherwise enjoyable visit was spoilt by the loss of some articles from our room during our stay. This loss was reported immediately upon our discovering it to the receptionist who, in turn, contacted the duty manager. The items lost were …

4 In the letter, *Dear Sir or Madam* is the opening phrase and *Yours faithfully* closes the letter. Imagine we had opened the letter with *Dear Mrs Simmons*. How would we close it?

Reading

1 **Read through the text and match the headings (a–h) to the 'secrets' (1–8).**

a Be Professional
b End with an Action Step
c Get to the Point Early
d Never Write in Anger
e Put Yourself in Your Reader's Place
f Start from the End
g Say it Plainly
h Use Active Verbs

THE SECRETS OF WRITING BUSINESS LETTERS

1 Decide what the result of your letter ought to be. List things you'd like to say, and review them. Good letters have a strong sense of purpose.

2 Don't delay. You should state your main purpose in the first paragraph.

3 If the letter came to you, how would you respond? Be pleasant; try to turn negative statements into positive ones.

4 Phrases like "in compliance with your request" and "enclosed herewith" are stilted. Write as you talk – naturally. Express just one idea per sentence. Sentences longer than two typed lines are suspect.

5 Passive voice is weak and confusing. "A decision has been reached by the committee" is inferior to "The committee has reached a decision." Also, readers can sense your evasiveness if you write: "Your order has been misplaced" instead of "I misplaced your order."

6 Emotion will evaporate; a letter won't. Devise a way to handle problems in an upbeat manner. Your chances of success will multiply tenfold.

7 The end of a letter should suggest the reader's next move, or your own.

8 The most well-written letters can't survive bad presentation. Use a clean, logical format for your letter. A crowded or over-designed page distracts from your message.

2 **Work with a partner and discuss which points you agree with and which points you disagree with. Support your opinions with reasons.**

Writing

E xam spot

You may be asked to write a formal letter in the CAE Writing test (Paper 2). You do not need to write any addresses in the exam. Remember:
- follow the conventions of formal letters
- use formal vocabulary
- make sure that the style is consistent
- show clear organisation
- do not use contractions
- make sure the purpose of writing is clear
- consider the effect the letter will have on the reader.

1 **Work with a partner. Read the advertisement for a Business Travel Coordinator and underline all the qualities and skills the company is looking for.**

BUSINESS TRAVEL COORDINATOR

Attractive salary

Our client requires an experienced travel professional to provide a planning and arrangement service for all their business travel needs.

Advising personnel on the most economical, safe and practical way to travel, you will make all the necessary arrangements and provide a proactive approach to passports, vaccinations and foreign currency. Your up-to-date knowledge on all travel options will enable you to advise the most economical travel plan, whilst with your excellent organisational skills you will manage our corporate database of travel and related medical/personal details and all liaison with external travel and hire car agencies.

As well as a thorough knowledge of the travel industry, you will need to be IT literate, including email and Internet, have good communication skills, be self-motivated, organised and have the ability to work to deadlines. You will be working with a set travel budget, therefore good numeracy is required.

2 **Now plan the content of the job application.**

3 **Talk about your plan for the letter with another pair of students and combine the best ideas from both.**

4 **Write a first draft of the letter (approximately 250 words). Pay attention to organisation of ideas and formal vocabulary.**

Then ask another student to read your draft and give you feedback on clarity of purpose, layout, letter conventions (opening/closing), use of formal vocabulary, sentence structure and errors.

You should comment on their first draft in the same way.

5 **Write the final draft.**

6 **Would this type of job appeal to you? Why?/Why not?**

Vocabulary

ⓥocabulary spot

Connotation is the feeling or idea that is suggested by a particular word. For example, *slim* has positive connotations suggesting *attractively thin*, whereas *skinny* has negative connotations, suggesting *unhealthily thin*.

1 Read the extract below about Dian Fossey and decide if these statements are true or false.

   a Dian had her appendix removed because she was ill.
   b She lived alone with the gorillas.
   c She spent all her time collecting data for research.
   d She had no formal qualifications.
   e She enjoyed a positive relationship with the game wardens.

Fossey, Dian 1932–1985

Six weeks after leaving hospital minus her appendix, Dian Fossey received a letter from the famous anthropologist, the late Louis S. B. Leakey. 'Actually,' he wrote, 'there was really no dire need to have your appendix removed. That's only my way of testing applicants' determination.' Louis Leakey had only somewhat facetiously suggested she have her appendix removed, but of course, he was so convinced of her determination that he offered her the job and invited her to begin field work in 1966. She lived alone on the damp misty slopes among the mountain gorillas in the Democratic Republic of the Congo until civil war forced her to escape to Rwanda. She established the Karisoke Research Centre (1967), alternating her time between her field work there and obtaining a PhD based on her research (Cambridge University Press, 1974), and writing her best-selling book, *Gorillas in the Mist* (published 1983). She was considered the world's leading authority on the physiology and behaviour of mountain gorillas, and portrayed these animals as dignified, highly social, "gentle giants" with individual personalities and strong family relationships. Her active conservationist stand against game wardens, zoo poachers, and government officials who wanted to convert gorilla habitats to farmland caused her to fight for the gorillas not only via the media, but also by destroying poachers' dogs and traps. She was found hacked to death, presumably by poachers, in her Rwandan forest camp in December 1985.

2 Look at the following words and phrases and put them under the appropriate heading. Some words can go under more than one heading.

Positive	Negative	Neutral

shack, mansion, house
evaluation, judgment, praise
modern, state-of-the-art, new-fangled
nosy, inquisitive   courageous, foolhardy
innocent, gullible, naive

3 Choose the word with the more positive connotation to complete this text.

Leakey's judgement was (**1**) *flawed/sound* when he chose Fossey as a field researcher. She had a (**2**) *steely/feeble* character and a natural empathy with the gorillas. She would sit for days in (**3**) *solitude/loneliness* in the mountains with the animals, making (**4**) *wordy/detailed* notes about the gorillas' every move. She was a (**5**) *keen/careless* observer. But still the (**6**) *dull/intriguing* question remains: why did she give up a life of luxury in the West?

Relative clauses

1 Look at these sentences about Dian Fossey. Which type of clause is the subordinate clause: a defining relative clause or a non-defining relative clause?

   a Her active conservationist stand against game wardens, zoo poachers, and government officials who wanted to convert gorilla habitats to farmland caused her to fight for the gorillas not only via the media, but also by destroying poachers' dogs and traps.
   b Her book, *Gorillas in the Mist*, which was published in 1983, became a bestseller.

2 Explain the difference in meaning between these two sentences.

   a Her stand against government officials, who wanted to convert gorilla habitats to farmland, became her overriding aim.
   b Her stand against government officials who wanted to convert gorilla habitats to farmland became her overriding aim.

3 Write four sentences, two with defining relative clauses and two with non-defining relative clauses, using the ideas below.

   • Leakey – give job to – person – show determination
   • Fossey's PhD – Cambridge University – based on her research in Africa
   • Fossey – live with gorillas in area – mountain slopes of the Democratic Republic of the Congo
   • Fossey – spend several years in Africa – met her untimely death there

4 Explain the omission of the relative pronoun in this sentence.

This is the region I like best.

5 If the relative pronoun is not necessary in any of these sentences, cross it out.

a Dian lived in a hut which had no electricity.

b The film of the story of her life made an impact that many people will never forget.

c The story which she told in the film made Dian Fossey a household name.

d The clothes that she wore in the jungle were old and worn.

e The place where she grew up has a different sort of beauty.

f The place that she grew up in is known to few, even in the USA.

g The people who made the film about Dian immediately realised the remarkable effect that her story has on whoever sees it.

h She had an inspirational quality which defies analysis.

i Her animals were often the only 'people' that she talked to for days on end.

j Dian had an intimate relationship with the land, which to a large extent determined the way that she lived.

6 In formal or academic English we tend to put the prepositions before the relative pronoun instead of at the end of the sentence, e.g. *There's the man to whom you were talking.* We use *which*, not *that*, to refer to things, and we use *whom*, not *who/that*, to refer to people when they are the object of the main clause. Rewrite the following sentences in formal style.

a This is the area of research that he is working on.

b Here are some new statistics that you'll be interested in.

c Is this the advertisement for the job you're applying for?

d Is this the experiment that you were reading about?

e Is this the person who you've entered into correspondence with?

f She received a reply from the editor that she sent her paper to.

g Social Sciences is the category that his work falls into.

h The college has cancelled the conference that you wanted to enrol for.

G ⋯⋟ page 192

Listening

1 With a partner, discuss these questions.

a How do you feel about dangerous sports like Formula One?

b Do you think there is too much money involved in sports these days?

c How do you think fame and money can affect a young person?

> **E** **xam spot**
>
> In Part 2 of the CAE Listening test (Paper 4), you will be asked to complete sentences. When you have written your answers, reread the whole sentence to make sure that it makes sense and is grammatically correct.

2 You are going to listen to an interview with James Warton, a successful Formula One driver. What word or words do you think might complete the sentences below?

a James's mother does not like facing a .... whenever she goes out.

b James's father believes that because James has a .... character, he will be a winner.

c In Australia, James was in .... place when his car developed mechanical problems.

d James remembers the time when his father did not have enough money for ....

e According to the interviewer, there are many .... who would love to get James to sign a contract with them.

f The next thing James would like to buy is a .... even though he knows he may be criticised for it.

g Most of James's former school friends are now ....

3 🎧 Listen to the recording and check your predictions.

4 James has been successful in both his professional and personal life. Work in small groups and discuss all the things in your life that you have been successful at or can do well.

Units 1–5 Revision

Topic review

a Which countries in the world would you most prefer to visit and why?

b If you went to stay with a British family, what would you take them as a gift from your country?

c How do you prefer to contact friends? By email, phone or by sending a text message?

d Is the art of letter writing dead?

e Would you rather work as a nurse or an artist?

f If you could have three wishes, what would they be?

g What is your earliest childhood memory?

h How may technology help you to learn a language?

i What would be your dream job?

j How interested are you in ecological issues?

Grammar

1 Read this letter from a friend who is not having a very good holiday. Fill the gaps with a verb in the correct form.

Hi Anita,

Well, I wish I (1) .... that I was having a wonderful time but that's far from the truth. For a start, it was a mistake to come here at Easter; it's too crowded, you can't move. And the second thing is I wish I (2) .... here with my sister. She's driving me mad. She always wants to go shopping and I'd sooner (3) .... for long walks along the cliffs. If only you (4) .... with me instead, it would have been so much better. As you know we're staying in a self-catering cottage and she never lifts a finger. I do all the cooking, clearing up, everything! It's time she (5) .... up and stopped acting like a baby. I don't know what to do because I don't want to have a row with her. Supposing you (6) .... with us, what would you do?

Oh well, from now on I'm going to do what I like. I'm not going to have my holiday ruined by her!

Hopefully some more cheerful news next time I write.

Lots of love
Carol

2 For questions 1–12, read the text below and decide which word best fits each space. The exercise begins with an example (0).

Example:

0 **A** provided **B** offered **C** enabled **D** presented

0	A	B	C	D

Kiwi Surprise

When a work project (0) ......B...... me the opportunity to return to New Zealand, I spent several weeks (1) .... a country I had left in my early twenties. I'd forgotten about the petrol stations where men in smart uniforms (2) .... to you. They fill your tank, (3) .... your oil and still (4) .... you less than one third of the British price for fuel. And the people rush to your assistance if they see you (5) .... over a map. Or the blissful (6) .... of tips. Locals simply cannot understand why anybody should (7) .... to pay extra for friendly efficient service.

Given that New Zealand has about 3,000 kilometres of coastline, it should come as no (8) .... that social life revolves around the sea. When Auckland office workers leave their desks at the end of the working day, they don't (9) .... home. Instead they (10) .... a beeline for the marina and spend the evening under sail on the Hauraki Gulf. There are more yachts in Auckland than in any other city in the world – no wonder it's called the City of Sails. Even those who can't afford a (11) .... of their own will always know someone who has one, or at the (12) .... least, will windsurf the offshore breezes at speeds that make the commuter ferries appear to stand still.

	A	B	C	D
1	regaining	recapturing	refamiliarising	rediscovering
2	assist	attend	supply	serve
3	control	measure	check	calculate
4	charge	ask	require	demand
5	pointing	doubting	clamouring	puzzling
6	absence	shortage	removal	neglect
7	accept	insist	expect	respond
8	wonder	surprise	amazement	news
9	move	aim	head	divert
10	have	do	get	make
11	vehicle	hull	vessel	receptacle
12	simple	single	hardly	very

Vocabulary

1 Complete these 'forks' with a word which collocates.

a to ....
   to .... an exam
   to ....

b to   a room
   to .... a competition
   to   information

c the ....
   the .... of nature
   the ....

d a ....
   a .... thinker
   a ....

e to ....
   to .... debts
   to ....

2 Choose the correct form of the word in brackets to complete these sentences. Each new word will be formed with either a prefix or a suffix.

a It was thought that the lawyer had .... the jury into believing the accused had been in trouble with the police on a previous occasion. (lead)

b This type of .... windscreen enables the driver to have a clear view even when it is smashed. (shatter)

c The manager's .... can be put down to his people skills. (popular)

d Andrew's .... was idyllic, as he was brought up in a tight-knit family with three sisters, a doting mother and caring father. (boy)

e I can't eat this steak, it's .... I don't like seeing the blood in it. (do)

f A great deal of work has been done to .... land from the sea in order to build a new airport. (claim)

g That was a .... remark to make. I'm sure you've hurt Suzanna's feelings. (heart)

3 With a partner, discuss how you would express the words in the box in a negative way.

simple	house	eat	assertive	evaluation

How would you express the words below in a positive way?

a problem	cheap	nosy	childish	gullible

4 Write a paragraph about someone you know or a place you know in either a positive or negative way. Make your attitude very clear.

5 Read this extract from a biography about Michael Flatley, who is famous for his modern interpretation of Irish dancing, and fill the gaps with a suitable word.

Flatley, Michael

At the 1994 Eurovision Song Contest, held at the Point Theatre in Dublin, the most successful act was not even entered **(1)** .... the competition. An intermission entertainment entitled *Riverdance*, starring American dancer Michael Flatley, captivated the audience **(2)** .... a modern interpretation of traditional Irish dancing. His arms flying, Flatley leapt **(3)** .... the stage, transforming Irish dance **(4)** .... a rigid, tradition-bound art form that placed a premium **(5)** .... discipline and control into an expressive, buoyant celebration. The jubilant response **(6)** .... the seven-minute performance was overwhelming, and the producers of *Riverdance* soon expanded it **(7)** .... a feature-length spectacle that thrilled audiences in London and Dublin. Following a bitter creative dispute **(8)** .... the show's producers, however, Flatley was fired **(9)** .... October 1995. His response was to develop *Lord of the Dance*, a spectacular Las Vegas-style Celtic dance show that featured Flatley **(10)** .... his most flamboyant.

Flatley was born **(11)** .... July 16, 1958, in Chicago **(12)** .... Irish immigrant parents. Flatley, whose grandmother was a champion Irish dancer, began taking dancing lessons **(13)** .... the age of eleven. His first teacher told him he had started too late to achieve real success, but Flatley persevered. When he was seventeen, he became the first American to win the all-world championship **(14)** .... Irish dancing. Flatley was also a Golden Gloves boxer and a champion flute player. None of these skills, however, seemed likely to help him earn a living, so he went to work **(15)** .... his father's contracting business and performed with local Irish dance groups in his spare time.

6 Speak after the tone

Speaking 1

1 With a partner, discuss these questions.

a What is the difference between an answering machine and voice mail? How do you feel about recording a message on a machine? How do you think that suddenly having to speak to a machine affects the way you express yourself?

b Do you have an answering machine? If so, do you ever leave it on when you are actually at home? If so, why?

c List the advantages that answering machines and voice mail offer.

d A lot of additional telephone services and equipment are available now. What are each of the following and when are they useful?
- a mobile
- a videophone
- text messaging
- a ring back service
- the speaking clock
- a bleeper
- a WAP phone
- a call waiting service
- dialling 1471 in the UK or *69 in the USA or 10 # in Australia

e Add to the list any other examples of telephone services or new communications equipment that you can think of.

Listening

1 🎧 Listen to this anecdote which mentions the speaking clock and answer the questions which follow.

a Why did the woman want revenge?

b How did she take revenge?

c Was it an effective way of taking revenge? Why?

2 🎧 You are going to hear six messages on an answering machine. Complete the notes below.

1 For:
  From   Name:
         Number:
  Message:

2 For:
  From   Name:
         Number:
  Message:

3 For:
  From   Name:
         Number:
  Message:

4 For:
  From   Name:
         Number:
  Message:

5 For:
  From   Name:
         Number:
  Message:

6 For:
  From   Name:
         Number:
  Message:

Phrasal verbs

1 Your teacher will give you the tapescripts of the phone messages. Note down any phrasal verbs that you find in them.

2 Look at the sentences below which contain phrasal verbs that can be useful when phoning people. Which particle is needed to complete each sentence?

   a You have to stop talking to someone from a public phone box if your coins run ....

   b Sometimes it can be difficult to get .... to distant or remote places on a mobile phone.

   c If you can't hear the person you are trying to talk to, you may ask them to speak ....

   d You ring a large business and the receptionist there will put you .... to the person you want to speak to.

   e You ring a friend but he wants you to wait a moment while he answers the door bell. He may ask you to hang ....

   f You ring home and talk to your dad for a while. After a few minutes, he says, 'I'd better pass you .... to your mum now'.

   g If you ring someone from a mobile and the signal begins to disappear, you may say, 'Oh dear, we're breaking .... '.

   h You were making a phone call and suddenly you lost contact with the person at the other end of line; in other words, you were cut ....

   i When you have finished talking to someone on the phone you ring .... or you hang ....

3 Match a sentence from A with one from B.

A says:	B says:
a I can't hear you very well.	1 I'll just put you through.
b Can I speak to the Finance Department, please?	2 OK, I'll try to speak up.
c We're going to have to stop talking soon. My money's about to run out.	3 Yes, we're going through a tunnel. I'll ring back in a few minutes.
d Well, I guess I'd better go. It's getting late.	4 No problem.
e Hang on a moment. I'll just turn the TV off.	5 That'd be great. I'll check with my parents and call you back.
f Is it easy to get through to Beijing from here?	6 Would you like me to call you back?
g I hate to say goodbye to you, darling.	7 No, don't ring off now – there's something I've got to tell you first.
h What's happening? We seem to be breaking up.	8 OK, bye then. Thanks for ringing.
i I think we've only got a few seconds left. We're going to be cut off in a moment.	9 Me too. You hang up first. Please.
j Do you want to come round to my house this evening?	10 It's usually OK but I had some problems last night.

G ···> page 193

⊙ Vocabulary

1 Put the words in the box under the correct headings, *have, do, make, take,* and *both have and take.*

a baby   a bath   a cake
a chance   a go   a mistake
a nap   a party   a phone call
a photo   a shower   an effort
an excuse   dinner   fun
hold of   part   the cooking
someone a favour   your best
someone seriously
someone's word for it
the housework   your homework

2 Choose one of the collocations from Vocabulary 1 to complete the following sentences.

   a Just .... your best at the interview. No one can ask for more than that!

   b It's easy to .... mistakes when you're tired.

   c My grandfather always .... a nap after lunch.

   d I have to go and .... some important phone calls.

   e I don't remember you giving me back the money you borrowed but I suppose I'll have to .... your word for it.

   f That looks like a great game. Can I .... a go?

   g You must .... your homework before you go out with your friends.

Speaking 2

1 Read the tapescript below of the anecdote about revenge from Listening 1.

> Oh, talking of revenge, I read about a great one once. There was this girl, she'd been dumped by her boyfriend, cos he'd decided he'd gone off her and he told her to move her things out of his flat before he got back from a business trip. I think he was going to the States for a month or something. Anyway, she moves her stuff out straightaway but before she leaves, she picks up the phone and dials the speaking clock. Then she leaves the phone off the hook while the clock goes on speaking the time to an empty flat. 'At the third stroke, it'll be ten twenty-five and thirty seconds...' So the boyfriend finds it when he returns four weeks later. You can imagine what the bill was like after a solid month of phone calls. Even at local rates, it'd be huge! That must have been really satisfying for the dumped girl!

a Highlight all the schwas.
b Listen to the recording again to check your answers.
c Practise reading the text aloud, taking care to pronounce all the schwas as the speaker did.

Reading and Speaking

1 Read the article opposite from a newspaper and answer the questions below.

a Why is the first paragraph written in such a strange way?
b What had the writer intended to write in the first paragraph?
c What sort of new technology does the writer tell us that he has and how does he feel about it?
d How has communications technology changed in the writer's lifetime?
e Why do you think capital letters are used for the phrase *a Very Long Telephone Lead*?
f What drawback does the writer see to these advances in communications technology?
g What is the point of the story about President Carter?

2 With a partner, discuss these questions. Then compare your answers with those of other students.

a In what ways might modern communications technology make people feel more harassed? List as many examples as you can.
b What do you understand by the expression *information overload syndrome*? Have you had any personal experience of it?
c At the beginning of the unit you considered the uses of a number of other developments in communications technology. Can you think of any disadvantages that each of these might also have?
d Can you give any examples from your own experience of people using sophisticated communications technology for trivial ends?
e What sorts of things do you think people spend most time talking about these days? List as many popular topics as you can.
f Do you think the topics you have listed are equally popular with men and women? Discuss what differences you think there are between male and female communication.
g In what ways do you think what people talk about has/has not changed over the last 100 years?
h All things considered, do you think modern communications technology has improved our quality of life?

Hello, this is me calling to say hi

Life in the Information Age leaves less and less time for thought, thinks Michael Bywater.

I AM wroting tgis on the train. I am wruting this, not jyst on thr train, but on ny telepjone on thr train. My teleohone is sumiltameously pixking up ny email and I habe just orderwd a book frim the Cambrudge Iniversity Librart, via their websute. All on ny trlrphone! Ism't techmology winderful?

I am not on the train any more. I am at home, on my new Macintosh PowerBook G3, which is also wonderful. I emailed the first paragraph of this column to myself, from my telephone, on the train, and it all worked perfectly. Admittedly the keyboard on my telephone is a bit small, as you can probably tell, but the idea of a telephone even having a keyboard is so exciting that I feel strangely proud of myself.

Actually, I am old enough and vulgar enough still to be impressed by the idea of a telephone that works on a train at all. When I was a child, telephones were made of black Bakelite, and had a dial, and a little drawer which slid out to reveal a small piece of card on which there was plenty of room to write down the telephone numbers of everyone you knew who had a telephone. Far from being able to take your telephone on the train, you couldn't even take it out of the room; if you wanted to make calls somewhere else in the house, you had to call in a GPO engineer and wait a month or two for him to turn up, whereupon he would drill huge holes in the walls and run transatlantic-style cabling around the place, and install a whole other telephone somewhere else on a very short cord, in case you had the un-English idea of walking round the room while making phone calls. Those were the days when a Very Long Telephone Lead was the height of sophistication; rich men had them in American films but they weren't for the rest of us.

As for the calling process itself, there were three possibilities. (1) The other person answered and you had your conversation. (2) Nobody answered and you tried later. (3) The line was engaged and you tried later.

Now we save time and keep in touch and, above all, communicate. My mobile telephone-cum-fax-cum-Internet-cum-diary-cum-notebook has even decided it's not a telephone at all: it is a Nokia Communicator. But do we really have that much more to communicate — and to communicate now — than our grandfathers did? And are we really saving time and being more efficient?

No; and no. Most of our hi-tech communications are communicating nothing more than the fact that we are communicating ("Hello? Hello? I'm on the train"). And as for time-saving and efficiency, well, isn't the greatest source of stress nowadays caused by the sense that none of us have any time?

Time is like computer memory: the more we have, the more stuff rushes in to fill it. In the communications game, we have overshot. "Personal productivity tools" haven't made us more productive, just more harassed.

A journalist told me, some years ago, that he had been sent to interview former President, Jimmy Carter. He worried about Carter at first; every time he asked a question, there was a long silence. Had Carter's mind started to fail? Then the journo realised. Carter was doing something extraordinary. Every time he was asked a question, Carter was stopping to think about it.

Perhaps that's the secret of surviving the Communications Era. Ensure brain is engaged before setting mouth in motion. I promise to give it a try but only if you do, too.

Exam folder 3

Paper 3 Part 3 Word formation

In Part 3 of the Use of English test (Paper 3), you are given a text. Most of the lines in this text contain one gap. At the end of the line is a word in capitals. You have to form a word from the same root as the word in capitals to fit the gap in that line.

EXAMPLE : *India gained its .... from Britain in 1947.* **DEPEND**
It should be clear from the context that the gap has to be filled by a noun, i.e. *dependant, dependence* or *independence*. In this case, the noun required is an abstract noun with a negative prefix. The answer is, therefore, *independence*.

1 Look at the gaps in the text. What part of speech is needed to fill each gap – a noun, a verb, an adjective or an adverb? When you have identified the parts of speech, can you suggest what the missing words might be?

THE school where pupils once fought and (**1**)..................... attacked a teacher during a visit by senior inspectors has been transformed and is now in the top 12 per cent for its teaching. Pupils were described as "polite, (**2**)..................... and helpful" by the latest (**3**)..................... of inspectors to visit The Ridings school in Halifax, West Yorkshire. Four years ago the Government (**4**)..................... an emergency inspection after a teachers' (**5**)..................... voted to back members refusing to teach its (**6**)..................... pupils. Union leaders described a school descending into chaos and said the situation could be (**7**)..................... only by the permanent exclusion of around one in 10 of the 610 (**8**)..................... .

2 Bear in mind that sometimes the words will need to have a prefix added to them. Add a negative prefix to the words below.

Verbs	Adjectives	Nouns
wrap	safe	appearance
ice	loyal	security
spell	sane	ease
tie	comfortable	comfort
entangle	European	mobility
understand	responsible	balance

3 List as many words as you can based on the words below.

a law ....
b hope ....
c act ....
d press ....
e centre...
f head ....
g office ....
h spoon ....
i place ....
j broad ....

4   Here is some more of the article from question 1. Fill each gap with a word related to the word in capitals at the end of the same line.

An **(1)** .... of the school carried out in 1996 was disrupted by   **INSPECT**

pupil **(2)** .... In their subsequent report the inspectors said   **VIOLENT**

poor teaching and weak **(3)** .... by the then head teacher had   **LEAD**

contributed to the poor behaviour. In 1997 "the **(4)** .... and   **OUTRAGE**

(5) .... behaviour of a few pupils" was said to create a hostile   **CONTROL**

atmosphere. A **(6)** .... report blamed the local authority for   **LATE**

failing to support its schools **(7)** .... and highlighted political   **PROPER**

interference by local **(8)** .... After that, the head of a   **COUNCIL**

(9) .... school in the same local authority was brought in to turn   **SUCCESS**

around the failing school. No **(10)** .... teaching was observed   **SATISFY**

by the most recent team of inspectors who were **(11)** ....   **REMARK**

impressed by the rapid turnaround the school has undergone.

5   Here is a different text for you to practise with. Again, fill each gap with a word related to the word in capitals at the end of the same line.

Nine years ago Philip Fletcher was a normal, **(1)** ....   **HAPPY**

married man with three children working as a highly **(2)** ....   **SKILL**

chemical worker. Then an accident changed his life beyond **(3)** ....   **RECOGNISE**

He was plunged into a surreal and **(4)** .... world as a head   **FAMILIAR**

(5) .... meant he could remember nothing of the previous   **INJURE**

15 years. In the accident a metal pole became **(6)** .... and   **LODGE**

fell on his head. He survived only thanks to his **(7)** .... helmet.   **SAFE**

He was **(8)** .... from hospital after only 4 hours. He seemed   **CHARGE**

normal at first but was soon having **(9)** .... He suffered   **CONVULSE**

for a number of years but his **(10)** .... breakthrough came   **PSYCHOLOGY**

when he learnt to accept his own **(11)** .... A few years ago he   **LIMIT**

and his wife accepted that their **(12)** .... could no longer continue   **MARRY**

but, **(13)** .... , they have both succeeded in building new lives.   **FORTUNE**

Running a successful business

Genre	Reports
Topic	The world of work

Speaking 1

1 You are going to read a report about research into young people's attitudes to work. Before reading, discuss these questions in groups.

   a In what ways do you think your own experience of work differs (or will differ) from that of your parents' or grandparents' generation?
   b Do you think your attitudes towards work differ from those of your parents?
   c List three advantages and three disadvantages of being an employee in a large company and of running your own business.
   d If you could run any business of your own, what would it be and why?

Reading

1 Read the report and then answer these questions.

   a Who exactly was studied in the research?
   b What factors were found to lie behind young people's enthusiasm to set up their own businesses?
   c What problem is identified at the end of the report?
   d What is the significance of the different words written on the brain in the picture in the article?

2 Now read the report again and fill the gaps with a suitable word.

The psychology of success

The need to be challenged. The need to be valued. A desire (1) .... financial independence. These are all powerful motivating factors for young people, an increasing number of (2) .... are setting up their own businesses and (3) .... a success of it.

But (4) .... drives young entrepreneurs? The Industrial Society has researched the views of 10,000 young people, aged 12 to 25, on attitudes on (5) .... from work to the family. Its study, published under the Society's 2020 Vision campaign, found a number of factors.

The first is the legacy of the buoyant 1980s where people (6) .... encouraged to take risks. The youngest people in our surve[y] will have only caught the tail end of Thatcher's Britain but will have grown up watching (7) .... elders strike out on their (8) .... A second factor is the change in the nature of work – the decline (9) .... long-term employment prospects and the rise in contract and freelance work. No more jobs for life. Many people have realised that the few real advantages of 'employment' – occupational pensions, sick pay, company cars – are (10) .... eroded. They have seen people around them struggle to adjus[t] (11) .... their lives in line with their changing work circumstances. And they have felt the pain it causes.

Ironically, the targeting of 'youth' culture by everything from drinks companies to Nike is also influencing their attitudes. Young people are realising that they are the (12) .... placed people to exploit these media and leisure markets because they are living in them – they are in the thick of it. Some of the most successful young entrepreneurs exemplify this – they own companies which have grown out of their hobbie[s] and leisure activities, (13) .... as computer games.

We also identified a new 'work ethic'. It appears that many young people don't believe (14) .... buckling down to trade their time and skills for pay; they are unwilling to make someone (15) .... rich. They have a broader definition of 'work' which includes doing something productive or beneficial. And for many young people their 'ethic' includes not exploiting others. Yes, there (16) .... those who make their money from drugs – but there are far more who want to build a business doing something they enjoy.

They will put (17) .... with initial hardship in the hope that they will reap the benefits (18) .... a later stage. They are driven by their belief in their enterprise, their love of the industry or field in (19) .... they work, and their determination to have more control over their lives than they (20) .... as an employee.

It's time business realised that the very people it needs in order to compete and surviv[e] – creative, entrepreneurial youngsters – are choosing to work on their own, because they prefer it and because they can.

Words on brain image: ambition, ethics, risk, challenge, value, success, cash, drive, indepen-dent, fun, compete, create, hard work

3 Mark each of the following statements true or false. If the statement is false, change it so that it is true.

   a The report says that one reason why young people start up their own businesses is that they want to make a lot of money.
   b The survey was carried out by the Industrial Society and investigated young people's attitudes to work.
   c The 1980s was a time when it was particularly risky for people to start up their own businesses.
   d Before the 1980s, many people were attracted to being employed rather than self-employed because of the security it provided.
   e Large companies have tended to ignore the existence of young people and their interests.
   f Young people's moral values are also one reason why they prefer to be in charge of their own working lives.
   g Young people don't mind it being tough at first if they believe in what they are doing.
   h The report says that established businesses ought to realise that new businesses founded by young people are going to provide serious competition for them.

⊙ Vocabulary

Vocabulary spot

Many words in English have more than one meaning. For example, the word *field* is used in the text to mean area of interest but it can also mean an area of land on a farm, a category of sporting event or a category in a computer database program. It can even be a verb meaning to catch or retrieve a ball in a game like baseball or cricket, or to deal cleverly with difficult questions.

1 One word can be used to fill the gaps in each of these pairs of sentences.

   EXAMPLE: *The farmer has decided to sell off the large* **field** *next to the wood.*
   The Prime Minister successfully managed to **field** *most of the interviewer's questions.*

   1 • .... the table before dinner is the children's daily task.
     • Streaming and .... are used by some schools as ways of dividing pupils into able or less able groups.

   2 • Most computers have at least two .... – one for a hard disk and one for CDs and DVDs.
     • The boss .... his workers very hard, begrudging them even a coffee break.

   3 • Worsening conditions for the work force led to a major .... last year.
     • Did anything .... you as strange about Hilary's behaviour last night?

   4 • I'm afraid I am going to have to .... your invitation.
     • Letters to newspapers regularly complain about a .... in standards of English.

   5 • A lot of young people would like to go on the .... but it is a very risky career.
     • I'd like to leave this question now and return to it at a later .... in my lecture.

   6 • Her success owes at least as much to .... as to talent, as she has never shirked hard work.
     • Rod's main aim is to get a job in the film .... and he really doesn't mind what he has to do.

2 Some words in the reading text are used not so much with a different meaning as with a metaphorical meaning. Here are the literal and metaphorical meanings of some of the words used in the text. Which words are being defined?

   1 • money or possessions that a person is left after someone's death
     • something that remains as a result of something that happened previously
   2 • floating on water
     • going through an effortlessly successful time
   3 • worn away by the weather (e.g. of rocks)
     • gradually reduced or destroyed (e.g. confidence)
   4 • aiming at something with a gun or a bow and arrow
     • aiming at something with an advertising campaign
   5 • fastening something down with a metal clasp
     • starting to work hard
   6 • cut and collect crops
     • receive something as the benefit of your own actions

⊙ Cause and effect

1 Read the text below about Pat and her business success. Underline any expressions that relate to the language of cause and effect.

What do you think is the reason for Pat's success?

Well, I think there are many reasons why she has done so well. Firstly, her boss had a profound influence on her. More importantly perhaps, her years of hard work have resulted in considerable financial rewards. Recently, her increased sales could be said to be a consequence of an improved marketing campaign. I think her interest in retail stems from a childhood passion for playing shops. It may also have its roots in her ancestry as both her grandfathers were shopkeepers.

2 Now read the rest of the text and fill each of the gaps with a suitable word.

It was Pat's sister who inspired her (1) .... open her own outlet although her teachers also encouraged her (2) .... a career in sales. Her experience in a Saturday supermarket job while she was still at school had a considerable effect (3) .... her later approach to selling. Studying for an MBA brought (4) .... a change in her attitude to business. She started a mail order service so (5) .... to gain a wider customer base. Many potential customers had complained that, because (6) .... work commitments, they could not get to her shop during opening hours. (7) .... a result of this new mail order service, her sales tripled. All these factors taken together then probably explain (8) .... Pat has been so successful in business.

3 🎧 Here are some more common words and expressions which can be useful to talk about cause and effect. Listen to someone talking about why he became an actor. Tick the expressions from the list that he uses.

(as a) consequence	accordingly	affect	aim	basis of
be based on	consequently	correspondingly		explanation
generate	give rise to	grounds for	lead to	motive
objective	originate	outcome	owing to	produce
purpose	reason	repercussion	so	thanks to	therefore

G····⊹ page 193

Writing

1 Read the report below. It was written by a group of 17-year-olds who took part in a work experience programme organised by a local supermarket during the summer holidays. Their head teacher asked for the report to find out whether it was worth encouraging similar programmes in the future.

2 Now answer the following questions.

a List the main points of each paragraph.

b Are the headings for each paragraph appropriate and useful? Do you think that this report follows a standard pattern?

c Underline all the words and expressions in the report which are used to link ideas within the text.

d Write headings for a report about a work, study or holiday experience that you have recently had. Your report should be for the benefit of someone who is considering embarking on a similar experience.

Work experience programme

Ten students took part in this year's work experience programme, which took place from July 4th to August 4th. We were all employed in the main branch of the supermarket and had the opportunity to experience different types of jobs; during our four weeks there we spent a week each as checkout cashier, shelf stacker, office junior and kitchen hand.

Usefulness of the programme

We all found the programme useful in a number of ways. Firstly, we learnt a great deal about what life is like behind the scenes in such a large supermarket. None of us had any previous experience of shop work and we found it much more demanding than we had expected. By the end of the month, we all felt that we had gained much more respect for people who do the routine tasks required in such an organisation and feel confident that we will never again get impatient with a slow checkout cashier. Secondly, we enjoyed the chance to learn about the supermarket business as a whole. We had two days' induction before starting work and this taught us a great deal about the complexities of

Exam spot

Looking at models of good writing (writing which is well set out in terms of organisation, has a clear layout and uses a good range of vocabulary and structures) can provide you with models to base your own writing on for the CAE Writing test (Paper 2).

the international operation of which this supermarket is part. Thirdly, we believe that we have benefited from the experience in that it served to highlight the importance of being able to deal effectively with the general public and people of all ages and backgrounds. Finally, and perhaps most importantly, we feel that we gained a lot of confidence from the opportunities we were offered. At the beginning of the month we thought that we would never be able either to do the jobs expected of us or to fit in with the regular staff, but we quickly managed both to get to grips with our duties and to make friends. We now feel much more prepared for life in the 'real world'.

Drawbacks to the programme

At times we felt as if we were being exploited as cheap labour by the supermarket. We worked at least as hard as the regular staff but only received about a quarter of their wages. Nor were we allowed any of their discounts on purchasing supermarket products. Moreover, although we enjoyed the experience, we all finished the month convinced that we never want to work in a supermarket again. We felt that it might have been even more useful if we could have had the opportunity to work in the kinds of environments that we hope to be in one day ourselves. Might it not be possible, for example, to arrange work experience in the health service for pupils who plan to become doctors or nurses or in hotels for people planning a career in tourism?

Conclusion

In conclusion, we would recommend continuing with this programme. However, we would also like the school's work experience programme to be expanded to include a wider variety of job opportunities in a range of different organisations.

Speaking 2

1 Look at these jobs. Which of them do you think are most valuable to society?

airline pilot	astronomer	car mechanic
chef	computer programmer	dentist
English teacher	footballer	lawyer
newsreader	plastic surgeon	plumber
poet	pop singer	Prime Minister
refuse collector	psychiatrist	soldier
stockbroker	vet	waiter/waitress

2 Work with a partner. Choose the three jobs which you think are most valuable and the three which you think are least valuable and put them in order. Be prepared to justify your choices and your ordering.

3 Regroup so that you are now working with a different partner. Compare your decisions.

4 Here are some features which might attract people to particular jobs:

being your own boss	occupational pension
company car	opportunity for creativity
flexitime	opportunity to travel

Work with a partner and add at least eight other things to this list.

5 Take one aspect of work from the list and prepare some questions to conduct a survey about this aspect of work. Keep notes of the answers which each student gives you.

6 Present the information which you collect to the rest of the class.

7 Discuss how you would present the information gained in your survey in the form of a report. What headings would you use? What kind of language would be appropriate?

Listening

1 🎧 Listen to eight people talking about their jobs.

a Which job is each person talking about? How do you know?

b What does each person like and dislike about their job?

c Why is the speaker in each job?

2 Which of the jobs described appeals to you most? Why?

Writing folder 3

Formal letters

1 Here are some statements about writing letters. If the statement refers to formal letters, write F. If it refers to informal letters, write I.

   a You write your own name and address in the top right hand corner of the page.

   b You write the addressee's name and address on the left hand side of the page above the salutation.

   c You begin the letter *Dear* (*name*).

   d You indent each new paragraph or put a line space between paragraphs.

   e You use contracted forms (*I'm, you'd,* etc.).

   f You end the letter *Love from.*

   g You sign your name by hand and then print it in brackets underneath in case your signature is illegible.

2 Much of the skill of writing formal letters is being able to use the typical phrases of such letters accurately and appropriately. Here are some examples of typical sentences from formal letters with some words missing. The first letters of the missing words are provided to help you. Complete the sentences.

   a I a_ _ _ _ _ _ _ _ for the d_ _ _ _ in r_ _ _ _ _ _ _ to your letter of 15th May.

   b I s_ _ _ _ _ be g _ _ _ _ _ _ _ if you c_ _ _ _ send me f_ _ _ _ _ information about …

   c Please could you a_ _ _ _ _ _ _ _ _ _ the r_ _ _ _ _ _ of this letter.

   d I e_ _ _ _ _ _ a s_ _ _-a_ _ _ _ _ _ _ _ envelope.

   e I w_ _ _ _ very much a_ _ _ _ _ _ _ _ _ an early r_ _ _ _ _ _ _ to my letter.

   f I look f_ _ _ _ _ _ to h_ _ _ _ _ from you at your e_ _ _ _ _ _ _ c_ _ _ _ _ _ _ _ _ _.

3 Writing formal letters at CAE level often requires you to be firm while remaining tactful and diplomatic. Grade the sentences below in accordance with the key.

> **Key**
> ✗ likely to antagonise reader
> ✓ firm and tactful
> ? might be OK but could be improved (if so, how?)

   a Your hotel did not live up to the claims made in the brochure.

   b Someone as stupid as you should never be allowed to run a hotel.

   c Your newspaper is usually full of rubbish but today it outdid itself.

   d Unfortunately, there were a number of errors in today's article on …

   e You must give me full compensation for all the inconvenience.

   f I feel that some compensation would be appropriate.

4 Look at tasks A and B and choose which one to respond to.

A You recently went on the holiday advertised below. However, many of the promises made in the advert did not match the reality of the holiday. There were a number of problems with the accommodation and some of the excursions offered were not available. Write a **letter** to the holiday company, putting your case for some kind of compensation.

Spend the best holiday of your life in our

NEW HOLIDAY VILLAGE

Comfortable self-catering chalets sleeping up to 6 people
On-site restaurants, shops and large swimming pool
Many excursions available from the village:

to the mountains

to the historic city of Oldtown with its well-preserved medieval centre and its magnificent shops

to the splendid beaches on the west coast

to the stunning historic castles for which the region is justly famous

B This article recently appeared in a British newspaper about the town where you live. There are a number of things that you object to strongly in the article. Read the article, then plan a **letter** to be published in the newspaper so that readers are not left with a false impression of your town.

. . . is the town which I had the misfortune to visit last week. Although I had heard and read many good things about the beauties and facilities of this town, it was an extraordinary disappointment to me. There was nothing historic or architectural that seemed to me to be of any interest. The nightlife was poor and I certainly didn't find a restaurant that I could recommend. In short, if you have the chance to go there, don't bother!

5 Now write your letter, which should be firm but tactful. Exchange your letter with a partner. If you were the person to whom the letter was addressed, would it have the desired effect on you? Tell your partner how you feel.

8 Best thing since sliced bread

Genre	Describing objects
Topic	Inventions

Speaking 1

ⓔxam spot

Inventions are sometimes the topic of a text in the CAE Reading or Listening tests (Papers 1 and 4) and you may also be asked to write or speak about them.

1 Look at the pictures. Then, with a partner, name each object, put the objects in the order in which they were invented and name the correct decade in which they were invented. There is one invention for each decade of the twentieth century.

Reading

1 Work with a partner. Which of these inventions do you think is the best and which is the worst? Give each invention a mark out of ten (10 = great, 0 = terrible).

a **A glove** for courting couples who wish to maintain palm-to-palm contact while holding hands. It has a common palm section, but two separate sets of fingers.

b **A ladder** to enable spiders to climb out of the bath. It comprises a thin flexible latex rubber strip which follows the inner contours of the bath. A suction pad is attached to the top edge of the bath.

c **A horse-powered minibus**. The horse walks along an endless conveyor belt treadmill in the middle of the bus. This drives the wheels via a gearbox. A thermometer under the horse's collar is connected to the vehicle instrument panel. The driver can signal to the horse using a handle, which brings a mop into contact with the horse.

d **An umbrella** for wearing on the head. The support frame is designed so as not to mess up the wearer's hair.

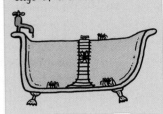

e **A portable seat** which you wear on a waist-belt. The seat cushion is pivotable between a stowed position and a seating position in which it hangs down so that you can sit on it.

2 Why do you think the inventors thought these inventions might be successful?

3 Why do you think each invention failed to catch on? Can you suggest any ways in which each of these objects might be changed to make them more successful?

Vocabulary

1 Answer these questions about the vocabulary used in the texts.

a What do you think these words mean? In each case, the context should give you some clues.

courting	contours
suction pad	treadmill
mop	pivotable

b What is the significance of the prefix *mini-* in *minibus*? Give more examples of nouns using this prefix.

c What is the significance of the suffixes *-able* (in *pivotable*) and *-less* (in *endless*)? Give more examples of adjectives using these suffixes.

d Suggest opposites for these words as they are used in the text.

common	flexible
inner	drives
mess up	stowed

Ⓥocabulary spot

Words can suggest whether the speaker or writer has positive or negative feelings about what is being described. If you called one of the inventions *brilliant*, it would be obvious that you admired it, whereas calling it *ill-conceived* would show that you thought it was inadequate in some way.

2 Put the adjectives below into the appropriate column.

absorbing	breathtaking	brilliant	delightful	enchanting
engrossing	grotesque	hackneyed	hideous	ill-conceived
impractical	ingenious	inspired	monstrous	pointless
ravishing	repulsive	ridiculous	stunning	trivial

Positive	Negative

Which of the words above could be used to describe any of the inventions in the reading texts?

3 Choose the best word to complete each sentence.

a The view from our hotel window was *inspired/ engrossing/ breathtaking*.

b I saw her grandmother in town wearing a *pointless/ ridiculous/ ill-conceived* hat.

c This is a very *enchanting/ ingenious/ ravishing* device for crushing garlic without having to peel it first.

d This kind of painting is very *hackneyed/ grotesque/ monstrous* – there's nothing original about it at all.

e Esther was wearing a(n) *absorbing/ stunning/ inspired* scarlet dress and jacket.

f I find films with gratuitous violence totally *trivial/ impractical/ repulsive*.

g Although the basic plot of the film is rather *ill-conceived/ brilliant/ hideous*, the locations are *delightful/ trivial/ engrossing* and the acting is first class.

Listening

1 🎧 You are going to listen to a radio programme in which people discuss things they could not live without. Which of the things in the pictures are mentioned by each speaker? Which other things are mentioned?

Speaker 1: ....
Speaker 2: ....
Speaker 3: ....
Speaker 4: ....

2 List the positive and negative adjectives used by the speakers.

⊙ Modals: *must, should, ought to, shall, will, would*

1 Underline the modal verbs in these sentences.

a Someone really ought to invent a machine to do the ironing for you.

b This key ring bleeps when you whistle – that should help you next time you lose your keys.

c You must get yourself a mobile phone – they're invaluable.

d My hair dryer's missing – my flatmate must have borrowed it again.

e You should have kept the instructions for the DVD recorder!

f He submitted his request for a patent ages ago – he must be going to hear from the department soon.

g You shouldn't have pressed that button before switching the power off.

h The design has been approved and we should be starting production next week.

i Even when he was still at school, he would spend hours in the shed designing weird and wonderful inventions.

j You will accept this design or else.

k We must light a fire somehow but no one's brought any matches – what shall we do?

2 What do the modals in these sentences convey? Choose from the possibilities in the box.

advice	deduction	obligation
offering	past habit	requesting

a You must help me.

b Will you help me?

c You ought to help him.

d She must be in her fifties.

e I think you should help him.

f Shall I answer the door?

g They must have left by now.

h He would walk down to the river every day.

i Would you close the window?

j You should consult him first.

3 Complete the sentences below using the modals in the box.

> must   mustn't   must have   ought to
> ~~shall~~   should   shouldn't have
> should have   will   would

EXAMPLE: ***Shall** I carry some of your heavy bags for you?*

a All pupils .... wear school uniform at all times in school and on their way to and from school.

b We're going to be doing a lot of hill-walking and so you .... bring strong outdoor shoes.

c I wonder where they can be. They .... got here by now. They .... missed their train.

d After school we used to go to the sweet shop on the corner where everyone .... buy a penny's worth of sweets or liquorice.

e You .... smoke in the garage forecourt.

f He's always late for work. He .... catch an earlier train.

g .... you take this man to be your lawful wedded husband?

h Jo looked very upset. You .... criticised her in public like that.

4 What kind of invention would you like an inventor to design for you? Write some instructions for the inventor, using modals.

EXAMPLE: *I'd like you to design a machine which will do the ironing for me. It must be able to recognise what type of material the clothes are made of and it should be able to adjust the temperature accordingly. It shouldn't cost more than £500 but it must be totally reliable …*

Exam spot

When someone is speaking to you, you need to show that you are listening and appreciating what is being said. In other words, you need to have a range of exclamations and fillers to use in different circumstances.

G ⋯⟶ page 194

Speaking 2

1 Below is a list of common exclamations.

a Absolutely!
b Fantastic!
c How extraordinary!
d Oh dear!
e So do I!
f That's terrible!
g Brilliant!
h What a coincidence!
i Me too!
j Poor you!
k Surely not!
l What a surprise!
m What a shame!
n You must be joking!

Match the exclamations (a–n) with the appropriate language function from the box below.

> expressing agreement   expressing admiration
> expressing surprise or disbelief   expressing sympathy

2 Which of the exclamations do you think would be appropriate responses to the following?

a I've been offered a fantastic job in New York but if I take it, I have to start next week!

b I've failed my driving test. Again!

c Jackie and I turned up at the party wearing identical outfits!

d I'm going to have to have a small operation next week.

e Would you like these free tickets for tonight's concert?

f I'm sure the government will hold on to power at the next election.

g I love that amazing painting!

h I don't think we're going to be able to come to your party at the weekend.

Exam spot

Fillers such as *Yes, Right* and *Mm* are also useful to indicate that you are listening attentively as someone is telling you something. They can be said with different intonation in order to convey different reactions.

3 🎧 Listen to some snippets of speech on the tape. Respond in an appropriate way to each of them.

4 Can you think of any other useful fillers? Practise saying the fillers using different intonation to indicate enthusiasm, doubt and surprise.

5 Tell a partner about an interesting experience that you have recently had. Your partner should use some of the exclamations and fillers practised in this section while listening.

Exam folder 4

Paper 3 Part 4 Gapped sentences

In Part 4 of the Use of English paper you have to find one word which fits in a gap in three different sentences. For example, which word would fit in this set of sentences?

There was a .... in the local paper about the Town Council's plans for the new bus station.
I'm sorry to ask you to do this work at such short ....
If things don't look up at work soon, I'm going to hand in my ....

The answer is *notice*, which, like many words in English, has a number of different meanings in different contexts.

1 Work with a partner. What meanings can the following words have? How would you translate them into your first language?

bar	flat	mean	put on	figures

2 Here are some examples of the five words used in different contexts. Which word fits in each sentence?

1 I've never met anyone so .... He never buys his round if we go out together after work.
2 I hated maths at school because I was never any good at working with ....
3 It's freezing outside. .... your scarf and take some gloves with you too.
4 I love staying in my sister's .... It's on the top floor and has some great views over London.
5 Next summer the local amateur dramatic society is planning to .... a play written by one of its own members.
6 The boss has decided to .... all staff members from using the company car park at weekends.
7 .... rainfall for the three winter months here is about ten centimetres.
8 I always treat myself to a .... of chocolate after I've been to the swimming pool.
9 The surface of an ice rink should be perfectly ....
10 Material goods .... nothing to her.
11 At the supermarket checkout they use a scanner to read the .... codes on the items that people are purchasing.

12 We've been .... out at work all week and I'm totally exhausted.
13 This style of dress will look good on most ....
14 If we decide to catch that train, it will .... getting up very early.
15 When I came out of the restaurant I discovered that someone had let down my tyres – they were all completely ....
16 Suzie .... a wonderful meal for her future in-laws.
17 We agreed to meet at his hotel in the ground floor .... later that evening.
18 If you look at .... A and B on the next page you will see some different trends.
19 Getting his book finished in such a short time was no .... feat.
20 It can be hard to .... a happy expression when you are feeling miserable.
21 Waltzes have three beats in each ....
22 You need to tune the bottom string of your violin – it sounds a bit .... to me.
23 That actor's name .... in the list of nominees most years but he has never actually won.
24 This is the best restaurant in the town .... none.

25 Do you mind if I .... some music?

26 After all the excitement of preparing for the wedding, life inevitably feels a little .... now it is all over.

27 Politicians and other public .... have to be careful how they behave in their private as well as their public lives.

28 I .... far too much weight during the holidays and need to go on a diet now.

3 Find some different meanings for these words:

> set fair wind stay

Write three possible sentences for each word, with gaps like those in Exercise 2. Work with two or three other students. Take it in turns to read out a sentence to each other. The others must say which word is needed to fill the gap in your sentence.

4 In preparing for Part 4 of the Use of English test, be aware of how many words do have different meanings and uses in English. Note any interesting ones that you come across in your vocabulary notebook. Look at the examples of inventions on page 52. In each of the five descriptions (a–e), can you find a word that has more than one distinct meaning in English?

5 Look at the Advice box. Then find one word only which can be used appropriately in all three sentences in each set.

a I wouldn't .... on Geoff for any kind of support.
As we approached the airport the plane began to .... quite steeply.
I'd .... the money as soon as possible – it's not safe having it lying around the house.

b I must have read a .... of books on the subject but I still don't understand it.
I'll return the money next week so there's nothing to worry about on that ....
What was the final .... in the rugby match?

c I don't think I can .... this job a day longer.
Keep stirring the sauce or it'll .... to the pan.
As we can't agree on where to go for our holiday, why don't we just .... a pin in the map?

d I try to do my shopping early in the morning to .... the rush.
It won't taste as good if you don't .... the eggs thoroughly before adding them to the mixture.
You can't .... a nice cup of hot tea when you're feeling cold and miserable.

e Their house was in the .... of the storm and was completely destroyed.
Could you cast your .... over this report for me, please, and let me know if you notice any problems?
She still does a lot of embroidery but her sight is so bad now that she needs help getting a thread through the .... of her needle.

Advice

When you are doing this task in the test there are two important pieces of advice:

- Don't spend too long puzzling over the first gap. Read all the sentences as the last one may make the answer suddenly obvious.
- Check that the word that you have thought of for one gap fits the other two sentences as well.

You live and learn

Speaking 1

Reading

1 The extracts opposite come from textbooks about economics, history, law, sociolinguistics and psychology.

   a Match the extracts with the subjects above.
   b Match each extract with one of the pictures.
   c Suggest a heading summarising each text.

ace of hearts

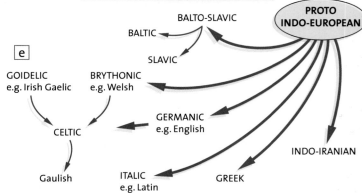

PROTO INDO-EUROPEAN

BALTO-SLAVIC

BALTIC

SLAVIC

e

GOIDELIC e.g. Irish Gaelic

BRYTHONIC e.g. Welsh

GERMANIC e.g. English

CELTIC

INDO-IRANIAN

Gaulish

ITALIC e.g. Latin

GREEK

1 With a partner, discuss the following questions.

   a Have you ever used English to study another subject? If you have, how easy did you find it?
   b Some people say that one of the best ways of learning English is to study another subject through English. Do you agree with this? Why?/Why not?
   c How likely do you think you are to use English for studying other subjects in the future?

1

Recent work in sociolinguistics has raised once again a long-standing question: can linguistic change be observed while it is actually occurring? In modern linguistics, the answer to that question has usually been a resounding negative. Following the example of two of the founders of the modern discipline, de Saussure (1959) and Bloomfield (1933), most linguists have maintained that change itself cannot be observed; all that you can possibly hope to observe are the consequences of change.

2

As a further symbol of his determination to haul Muscovy kicking and screaming into the eighteenth century, the Tsar refused to let his boyars kow-tow to him in traditional oriental style, and took scissors, cutting off their beards and snipping the capacious sleeves of their traditional robes as a prelude to making shaven chins and European dress obligatory for all Russian gentry and officials. Along with robes and beards, the ancient title of boyar was soon to disappear as well. Peter also greeted the eighteenth century by adopting the Julian Calendar, an important symbolic change since Muscovy had hitherto reckoned time from the notional beginning of the world. For so backward a state to have been, as it were, 6,508 years ahead of western Europe was absurd, and the Julian Calendar put it, more appropriately, eleven days in arrears.

3

The immediate crisis of 1968 soon passed and the marketing experts dismissed it as a spasm, an intellectuals' fantasy. Students went back to business schools, consumers went on consuming and the car – with the help of gadgetry, computers and improved engineering – soon became once again an object of glamour, status and sexiness. East Asians did their bit to promote Western spending by producing gadgetry, music-machines and glamorous electronics which could be replaced by still more novelties every year; while their own spending power created new opportunities at home. 'I don't think saturation will ever happen,' Akio Morita of Sony told me, 'because our technology can create new products which give new joy to the public.'

4

English law now fixes the age of majority at eighteen, all persons below that age being minors. A minor attains his majority on the day of his birthday – not, as formerly, on the beginning of the day before his birthday. A minor is incapable of holding office as a Member of Parliament or a Local Authority. He cannot be a priest or deacon, or a barrister or solicitor. Minority is no defence in an action in tort – that is for a wrong done independently of contract. Where an undergraduate, who was a minor, had hired a horse for riding, on the express condition that it was not to be used for jumping, but took it out with a friend to whom he lent the horse, and allowed it to be used for jumping various fences and ditches with the result that the horse staked itself on a fence and was fatally injured, he was held to have committed an 'independent tort' for which he was liable to the owner apart from any question of contract, just as if he had ridden the horse without hiring or the leave of the owner.

5

Experiments on both these lines have shown that both clairvoyance and telepathy must be presumed to exist. It has also been found that, while many people who possess the one type of ability tend to possess the other, this is by no means necessary and in certain cases individuals may obtain high scores by telepathy but not by clairvoyance and vice versa. The great majority of experiments, however, do not attempt to differentiate between these two abilities and must simply be taken as evidence of some all-round parapsychological or extra-sensory perception capacity on the part of individuals.

2 Academic language often uses rather unfamiliar vocabulary. Match the words and phrases (a–l) from the texts with their meanings in the box.

a a resounding negative (text 1)
b as a prelude to (text 2)
c hitherto (text 2)
d in arrears (text 2)
e spending power (text 3)
f saturation (text 3)
g attains (text 4)
h formerly (text 4)
i leave (text 4)
j obtain (text 5)
k vice versa (text 5)
l differentiate (text 5)

before	behind	a firm no
get	make a difference between
permission	previously (×2)
reaches	spare money
stage where nothing more is needed
the other way round

3 Choose one of the words or phrases from list a–l in Reading 2 to fill the gaps in the following sentences.

a It is estimated that the demand for mobile phones will soon reach .... point in this country.
b People who are colour blind cannot always .... between shades of red and green.
c Student A should look at Student B's composition and ....
d You cannot go out of the school during the day without getting .... from the head.
e I am afraid you are .... with your mortgage payments.
f These nineteenth century stamps are almost impossible to ....
g Mr Peter Tomlins, ... Sales Manager at XYZ Ltd., joins us on April 1st.
h Teenagers these days tend to have much greater .... than used to be the case.

⊙ Vocabulary

1 Many words used in academic texts are of Latin or Greek origin. They are often part of a set of words formed from the same root. Complete the following table based on words used in the reading texts.

Verb	Noun	Adjective
occur		
	founder	
✗	consequence	
		obligatory
disappear		
	glamour	
	authority	
		various
presume		
	perception	

2 Rewrite the sentences using the word in brackets.

a All pupils must wear school uniform. (obligatory)

b There are a great many different animals which are indigenous to Australia. (variety)

c Burglaries happen every day in this part of town. (occurrence)

d Most people think that the mountaineer must have died in the blizzard. (presumed)

e Giving up work to bring up a child and the loss of income which happens as a result is difficult for many women. (consequent)

f What is the opinion of people in your country on the role of the United Nations? (perceive)

g Cambridge University Press has been in existence since 1534. (founded)

h Modern films tend to make violence seem more glamorous than it really is. (glamorise)

⊙ Participle clauses

Participle clauses are clauses beginning with either a present or past participle. Look at these examples from the texts.

Following the example of two of the founders of the modern discipline, de Saussure (1959) and Bloomfield (1933), most linguists have maintained that change itself cannot be observed …

the Tsar … took scissors, *cutting off their beards and snipping the capacious sleeves of their traditional robes* …

Participle clauses can be expanded to make full clauses. This may be done by forming clauses beginning with conjunctions like *when, if, because* or *and* or forming relative clauses beginning with *who, which* or *that.*

1 Expand the underlined clauses in the examples above.

2 Here are some more examples of participle clauses. How can each of these sentences be expanded?

a Hoping to gain a speedy victory, the army invaded.

b They killed many people living in the border areas.

c It being a Sunday, most of the shops were shut.

d Generally considered a weak king, Charles I was eventually beheaded.

e Having previously learnt their language, Picton was able to communicate with the tribe.

f Having measured the wood carefully, cut as indicated.

3 Rewrite these sentences using a clause beginning with a present or past participle.

a While I was walking round the exhibition, I caught sight of an old school friend at the far end of the gallery.

b Because Marti had made so many mistakes in her homework, she had to do it all over again.

c As she is only a child, she can't fully understand what is happening.

d As Jack didn't know anyone in the town to spend the evening with, he decided to have an early night.

e When all the inequalities of life before the revolution are considered, it is surprising that a revolution did not happen sooner.

f When you have climbed to the top of the church tower, be sure to walk right round and admire the view from each of the four sides. (Use two participles here.)

g We set off at midnight and hoped to avoid the rest of the holiday traffic which would be heading for the coast. (Use two participles here.)

h When he saw me, he stood up and knocked his glass to the floor. (Use two participles here.)

4 Work with a partner and complete the sentences below. Compare your sentences with those written by other students.

   a Having been a major news item last week, …
   b Having become successful at quite a young age, …
   c Being one of the largest cities in our country, …
   d Not daring to interrupt him, …
   e Starting this CAE course, …
   f Having worked hard all his life, …

   G ⋯⫶ page 194

Speaking 2

1 Read the dialogues and underline the words which Speaker B would be most likely to stress.

   1 **A** Did you go to the cinema last night?
     B No, but I went to the theatre.
   2 **A** Did you go by bike to the theatre last night?
     B No, Marco was using my bike last night.
   3 **A** Did you go to the theatre by bus last night?
     B No, I went to the theatre by taxi last night.
   4 **A** Did you go home by taxi last night?
     B No, I went home by taxi two nights ago.
   5 **A** Anne's wearing a lovely green dress.
     B It's a green blouse and skirt, actually.
   6 **A** Did you have a good time at the party last night?
     B Yes, we had a brilliant time.
   7 **A** Are you hungry yet?
     B I'm not hungry, I'm starving.
   8 **A** Are you hungry yet?
     B I'm not hungry but Tina is.
   9 **A** Are you tired?
     B Yes, I'm exhausted!
  10 **A** Are you feeling a bit cold?
     B Yes, I'm freezing!

2 🎧 Now listen and check whether your predictions were correct.

3 Practise reading the dialogues with a partner.

4 Write three more two-line dialogues like those in exercise 1.

5 Look at the pictures below and notice the differences between them. Work with a partner taking turns to suggest sentences about them. Make sure that you use contrastive stress in the appropriate way.

   EXAMPLE: *There's a **red** fountain pen in picture **a** and there's a **blue** fountain pen in picture **b**.*

Writing folder 4

Reports and proposals

1 With a partner, discuss these questions.

 a Name five possible kinds of reports or proposals, e.g. *A scientific report of an experiment*.
 b Have you had any experience of writing reports or proposals?
 c What do you think is going to be characteristic of the format and language of a report or proposal?
 d How is an article about some interesting scientific research likely to differ from a report of the same research?

Reports and proposals are similar in many ways. They both aim to set out information in a formal and clear way, often so that someone else can take a decision based on the information provided.

The differences between a report and a proposal are largely:
- a report looks backwards while a proposal looks forward
- a proposal always presents the writer's viewpoint whereas a report focuses more on facts; although a report may have a persuasive element to it, this is not always the case.

2 Work with a partner and choose one of these pairs of tasks that interests you.

A Write a **report** for your teacher on the work experience and aspirations of other students in the class.

Write a **proposal** for your college principal in which you ask for money to travel to an English-speaking country to gain some work experience there. Explain what you would like from the college and why it would be of benefit to you.

B Write a **report** for your teacher on the most popular Internet sites among the class. Describe what they are and why they are popular, and comment on any trends that you observe.

Write a **proposal** to your college principal suggesting that your college set up its own website. Explain why it would be a good idea and what it should contain.

C Write a **report** for your teacher on the physical fitness activities done by the students in your class. Describe what people do and how much time they spend on it, and comment on any interesting tendencies that you observe.

Write a **proposal** for your college principal about improvements to your college's sports provisions. Describe what you would like and give reasons why it would be of benefit to the college.

---

3   With a partner, discuss the questions below.

   a What information do you think it would be useful to include in the
       report you have chosen?
   b What questions will you ask the other students in the class in order
       to get the information you need?
   c What trends do you think you might observe from the information
       you collect?
   d Why do you think your requests in the **proposal** would be
       a good idea?
   e Remember that the college principal is likely to be more concerned
       than you are about costs, potential organisational problems and
       college prestige. How will you address these issues in your **proposal**?

4   Collect the information you need for your **report**.

   a Ask the other students in your class the questions you prepared in 3b.
   b Discuss the information you collected with a partner. Did you
       observe the trends you predicted in 3c? Did any other particularly
       interesting points emerge from your questions?
   c What headings would it be appropriate to use for your report?

5   Discuss the presentation of your **proposal**.

   a It is important to open with a clear statement of what the proposal
       contains. How will you do this in your proposal?
   b It is also important to close effectively. How will you do this in
       your proposal?
   c What headings are appropriate to use for your proposal?

6   In pairs, decide which of you should write the **report** and which
     the **proposal**.

   a Write the report or the proposal.
   b Give your work to your partner for comments and suggestions.
   c Make any improvements suggested by your partner.

I have a dream

Genre	Speeches
Topic	Social change

Speaking 1

1 Who makes speeches? On what occasions? Have you ever had to make a speech? If so, why, and how well did the speech go?

> **E**xam spot
>
> You are not asked to write or to make a speech in the CAE exam. However, you might hear an extract from a speech in the CAE Listening test (Paper 4). You can learn from studying famous speeches, as they use language in a clever and powerful way. This can help you to write more effectively yourself.

2 Who is the man in this photo? What do you know about him? How do you think the other people in the picture are feeling?

3 Have you heard of a famous speech which is often referred to as *I have a dream*? If so, what do you know about it? Who made it, when and why?

Five score years ago, a great American, in whose symbolic shadow we stand today, signed the Emancipation Proclamation. This momentous decree came as a great beacon light of hope to millions of Negro slaves who had been seared in the flames of withering injustice. It came as a joyous daybreak to end the long night of their captivity.

But one hundred years later, the Negro still is not free. One hundred years later, the life of the Negro is still sadly crippled by the manacles of segregation and the chains of discrimination. One hundred years later, the Negro lives on a lonely island of poverty in the midst of a vast ocean of material prosperity. One hundred years later, the Negro is still languished in the corners of American society and finds himself an exile in his own land. So we have come here today to dramatize a shameful condition.

In a sense we have come to our nation's capital to cash a check. When the architects of our republic wrote the magnificent words of the Constitution and the Declaration of Independence, they were signing a promissory note to which every American was to fall heir. This note was a promise that all men, yes, black men as well as white men, would be guaranteed the unalienable rights of life, liberty, and the pursuit of happiness.

It is obvious today that America has defaulted on this promissory note insofar as her citizens of color are concerned. Instead of honoring this sacred obligation, America has given the Negro people a bad check, a check which has come back marked "insufficient funds". But we refuse to believe that the bank of justice is bankrupt. We refuse to believe that there are insufficient funds in the great vaults of opportunity of this nation. So we have come to cash this check – a check that will give us upon demand the riches of freedom and the security of justice. We have also come to this hallowed spot to remind America of the fierce urgency of now. This is no time to engage in the luxury of cooling off or to take the tranquilizing drug of gradualism. Now is the time to make real the promises of democracy. Now is the time to rise from the dark and desolate valley of segregation to the sunlit path of racial justice. Now is the time to lift our nation from the quicksands of racial injustice to the solid rock of brotherhood.

Reading

1 Read the first part of the speech. Which of the sentences (a–e) sums up each paragraph? There is one extra sentence that you do not need to use.

a A century after their emancipation, black Americans are still not truly free.

b America has behaved unjustly to its black people.

c Black people must fight to be treated equally.

d Lincoln brought hope to Negro slaves with his proclamation of emancipation in 1863.

e The march has come to Washington to claim the rights that all were promised.

2 How do you think people felt when they were listening to this speech?

Listening

1 🎧 Now listen to the rest of the speech. Which of the techniques below does Martin Luther King use to help to create a powerful effect on the audience? Tick all the appropriate techniques.

- repetition
- mixing short and long sentences
- shouting
- addressing the audience directly
- humour
- making use of metaphor
- drawing attention to the location where the speech is taking place
- exaggeration
- quoting famous lines
- alliteration
- making analogies or comparisons
- asking rhetorical questions
- making dramatic pauses
- appealing to the audience's emotions
- appealing to the audience's senses
- using gestures or visual aids
- presenting interesting or surprising facts

2 🎧 Listen to some more extracts from speeches. What do you think the occasion was in each case? Match the speakers (1–5) with the pictures (a–e).

3 🎧 Now listen again and note down any examples of the techniques referred to in Listening 1.

Vocabulary

Martin Luther King makes powerful use of metaphor in his speech. The metaphors are often based around the themes of light, heat, punishment, economics and the natural environment.

1 Here are some examples of metaphors he uses. Match each one to the appropriate theme.

a The life of the Negro is still sadly crippled by the manacles of segregation and the chains of discrimination.

b It came as a joyous daybreak to end the long night of their captivity.

c This momentous decree came as a great beacon light of hope to millions of Negro slaves …

d We have come to our nation's capital to cash a check.

e … who had been seared in the flames of withering injustice.

f We refuse to believe that the bank of justice is bankrupt.

g Now is the time to rise from the dark and desolate valley of segregation to the sunlit path of racial justice.

h Even the state of Mississippi, a state sweltering with the heat of injustice, sweltering with the heat of oppression, …

i … will be transformed into an oasis of freedom and justice.

> **Ⓥocabulary spot**
>
> Sometimes metaphors are so commonly used that they become fixed as idioms. People no longer notice the metaphorical associations of the expression and think of the idiom simply as a fixed expression in its own right.

2 Here are some idioms based on the five metaphorical themes listed in Vocabulary 1.

- light: *shed light on; light dawns*
- heat: *go up in smoke; get your fingers burned*
- punishment: *be tied up; be pilloried*
- economics: *foot the bill; put your money where your mouth is; in debt*
- the natural environment: *feel (all) at sea; common ground*

Choose one of the idioms above and use it to complete the sentences (a–k) below. Make any necessary changes, such as putting the verb into the correct form.

a The washing machine is broken but we're hoping our landlord .... for a new one.

b Hopes of union and management reaching agreement finally .... yesterday.

c I .... all day but could meet you in the evening, if you like.

d I hate the first day in a new job, ...

e Thank you for .... this very complex issue for us.

f Jack was teasing her but it was ages before .... !

g We found some unexpected .... at the meeting with the opposition.

h The MP .... by the press for the foolish remarks he made in his speech.

i I am .... to my first schoolteacher for the invaluable advice she gave me.

j If the government is interested in improving the health service, it should ....

k You .... if you go on trying to interfere in their private lives.

⊙ Future forms

Look at this sentence from Martin Luther King's speech.

One day even the state of Mississippi, a state sweltering with the heat of injustice, sweltering with the heat of oppression, will be transformed into an oasis of freedom and justice.

In this sentence the future is conveyed by the word *will* and the sense is of a confident prediction.

1 Identify the words used to express the future in the sentences (a–j) and match them to the uses (1–10) below.

a What are you doing this evening?

b What will you be doing this time tomorrow?

c What are you going to do for your next holiday?

d What are you going to do when this course finishes? (two uses)

e What will you do if you pass the CAE exam?

f What would you do if you passed the CAE exam?

g What time does this English lesson finish?

h Which student in the class do you think is most likely to be very successful in business?

i Is there anyone in the class who might eventually become internationally famous, in your opinion?

j What do you hope you will have achieved by the time you are 60?

1 focus on one moment in future time

2 focus on looking forward to the future in order to then look back

3 future probability

4 future after time conjunction

5 intention

6 plan (with stated time)

7 something fixed by a timetable

8 talking about the future using the first conditional

9 talking about the future using a less confident, more hypothetical conditional

10 tentative prediction

2 Choose the best form for each of these sentences.

  a *I go/I'm going/I'll go* to the cinema on Saturday to see that new Brad Pitt film.
  b I'll call you as soon as I *get/will get/will have got* home.
  c This time next week *we're going to lie/we'll lie/we'll be lying* on a tropical beach.
  d If he got the job, *he'll leave/he'd leave/he'll have left* for Paris next month.
  e Melissa is very likely *getting/to getting/to get* a good job as she is fluent in three languages.
  f My flight *is going to leave/leaves/is leaving* at 10.20 tomorrow morning.
  g When we *will be/are going to be/are* in London, *we are spending/we spend/we are going to spend* the first day doing a sightseeing tour.
  h If Penny *gets/will get/is getting* a place at Oxford University, *she's studying/she's going to study/she studies* philosophy and politics.
  i In ten years' time perhaps people *set foot/are going to set foot/will have set foot* on Mars.

3 Work with a partner asking and answering the questions in Future forms 1. Make sure you answer using the correct verb forms.

4 Think back to the speeches in Listening 2. Work with a partner and write about what the future holds for Johnny and Megan, baby Maria and Fiona.

What do you think will happen to them in the short term and the long term?

EXAMPLE: *This morning Johnny and Megan got married. In a few moments, everyone is going to drink a toast to them. Then first thing tomorrow they fly off for their honeymoon in Greece. So this time tomorrow they'll be swimming in the Aegean. Let's hope that by the time they get back they'll have got over the stress of planning the wedding.*

Compare your ideas with those of other students.

G ⋯⟩ page 195

Speaking 2

1 Work with two or three students. Choose an issue that you all feel strongly about. Use the words below to help you.

canteen food

homework   local transport

the environment   taxes

leisure facilities

2 Now discuss the following questions.

  a Why do you feel strongly about it? List as many points as you can think of.
  b What would you like to be changed? Be as precise as you can.
  c Who would you need to persuade for changes to be made?
  d How would you try to persuade them to make the changes? What action could you take and what arguments could you use?

3 You are going to report your discussion back to the rest of the class. How could you do this? Decide what to say and who should say it.

4 Listen to each group's reports of their discussions in turn. Write down how many changes each group proposed and briefly note what each of these changes were.

5 After listening to each speech, discuss with a partner which of the changes would be for the better and which for the worse.

Topic review

a Which telephone services do you use most?

b How do you feel when someone hangs up on you?

c What factors can give rise to an increase in unemployment?

d What are possible grounds for sacking an employee?

e Which modern invention could you not live without?

f Do you think wearing cycling helmets ought to be compulsory?

g What are some of the rewards and challenges of studying abroad?

h What subject have you always wanted to study?

i What do you hope you will have achieved by the year 2020?

j How do you feel about public speaking?

Grammar

1 Think about last year and next year and answer the questions below. Write at least one full sentence in answer to each of the questions.

a What changes are going to take place in your life next year?

b What must you try to do next year?

c What special things did you have to do last year?

d What should you do next year if you possibly can?

e What should you have done last year but were unfortunately unable to?

f What do you think will have happened by the end of next year?

g Think about something that happened last year and the effects it has had or is likely to have. Write a sentence to link what happened with its effects or likely effects.

EXAMPLE: *Last year there was an election and this has resulted in more money being spent on the health service this year.*

h Now write a sentence using a participle clause about the events from last year that you thought about above.

EXAMPLE: *Having won last year's election, the Labour Party now has to try to implement its pre-election promises.*

Reading

1 What is teleworking? With a partner, discuss what you think would be its advantages and disadvantages.

E xam spot

Part 2 of the CAE Reading test (Paper 1) tests your ability to see how paragraphs hang together in a text. The following exercise helps you to see what kinds of links there often are between paragraphs.

2 The article below about teleworking has the paragraphs (A–G) in the wrong order. With a partner, put them in the right order and discuss what clues there are in the text to help you do this.

WHEN THE OFFICE IS YOUR BEST BET

A He likes to tell the story of the painter Magritte, whose studio was at home. Each morning Magritte would rise and put on his suit. He would then go out through the front door of his house, walk once around the block, re-enter the house and enter his studio, where he would change into his artist's smock and spend the day painting. At the end of the day he would change back into his suit, leave the house again and go once round the block in the opposite direction, and return home for the evening.

B My score: zero out of three. Dedicating a room to work is not feasible in a small flat, and has all sorts of complicated tax implications anyhow. I didn't have a separate business line. And although I had a separate fax line, my fax machine, like my computer, was squeezed into a corner of the living room, which made drawing a line between home and work even harder: even when I was relaxing, all that equipment would be glowering at me from across the room. I'd pick up my e-mail in the evening, and half of it would be work-related.

C Technology makes it easier than ever to work from home, but unless you know what you're doing, it's still a terrible idea. Like Superman and kryptonite, home and work are meant to be kept apart.

D John, a friend who used to work from home, had a separate phone line, but he didn't have a separate room, so he couldn't get away from his work either. "At one stage," he says, "I had to go through my 'office' to get to the loo."

E I look back on my days spent working at home with mixed feelings. Sure, it was great not to have to fight through the rush-hour throng to get to my desk. The trouble was, once I'd started working, I couldn't stop. When there was more work to do, I just kept doing it. Then I spoke to Alan Denbigh of the British Telecottage Association, who explained the three laws of teleworking.

F "First of all, you should ensure that you have a self-contained office," he said. "Next, you should have a separate phone line, both from a business point of view and also from a psychological point of view. And you need to keep your work and your home life apart."

G Magritte probably didn't have a separate phone line. But it seems he had the right ideas about working from home successfully. Unless you can stick to the three laws, stick to the office.

3 Think of one word only that can be used appropriately in all three sentences.

a My little sister thinks it's not .... that girls are usually discouraged from playing football.
You should use plenty of sun-screen as your skin is so ....
I managed to do a .... amount of work last night but there is still a lot left to finish.

b They're an excellent band and they always manage to .... a large crowd.
Most men start to .... their pension when they reach 65.
I hope the teams don't .... again this year. It always feels like a bit of an anti-climax.

c It's a good idea to re-read an email before you .... the Send key.
The singer was dreadful – he couldn't .... the high notes at all.
Production this year was badly .... by the industrial action in the spring.

d We'd better .... out soon if we want to get there on time.
After reading the documents Jack .... light to them so that no one else would every know what they had contained.
Don't forget to .... your alarm for 6.30 tomorrow or we'll never get to the airport in time to meet Grandma's flight.

e It's difficult for Sally to have to .... so much responsibility at such a young age.
.... left when you get to the crossroads.
I'm afraid that none of these trees ever .... any fruit.

f After each jump the .... was raised a little higher.
Let's meet after work in that new little coffee .... on the corner.
Why don't you produce a .... chart? That would illustrate the figures very clearly.

4 Make a word from one of the words in the box below in order to fill the gaps (1–10). The first one has been done for you as an example.

late	extend	cover	obsess
proud	expense	survive	edit
~~happy~~	addict	alphabet	

Objects of desire

A BOY THING

WHAT is it about boys and toys? Men will spend hundreds of pounds and waste hours fiddling so that they can, say, dictate letters to their PCs, or they will (0) ..happily.............. spend a whole weekend putting their CDs in (1) .... order – or, worse, typing their titles into a database. This (2) .... behaviour is reflected in an ever-increasing number of men's magazines that combine buying advice with techno-fetishism and a dash of new laddism. More and more (3) .... is being given to gadgets in an attempt to satisfy men's (4) .... to gizmos. "Men love gadgets – it's an (5) .... of their manliness," says Adam Porter, Net (6) .... of the lads' magazine *Loaded*. "Gadgets are toys – men can't buy Action Men when they are 30, so they go and buy something electronic and a lot more (7) ...." James Lawrence, editor of *FHM* magazine's hardware section, agrees: "There is a macho male (8) .... in gadgets – it's like it's my toy, and I know how to use it, and if you ask me nicely then I just might show you how to use it. Women don't seem to need that kind of one-upmanship." Andy Clarke, editor of *Stuff*, the (9) .... men's glossy to hit the shelves, thinks it has something to do with the much-hyped male (10) .... instinct. "Men feel like Indiana Jones, like they are out there in the wilds if they've got a gadget in their pocket," he says.

Read all about it

These trousers will make your hips look big!!!

| Genre | Magazine and newspaper articles |
| Topic | Fashion |

Speaking 1

1 Discuss these questions with a partner.

a How often do you read a newspaper? When do you read it? Which parts do you read first?

b Do you think people read newspapers more or less often than before?

c Do you ever read newspapers or magazines on the Internet? Which do you think is better, reading 'real' newspapers or newspapers on the Internet? Why?

d Look at these front-page headlines and decide what sort of newspaper you think each one is.

BOOST YOUR METABOLISM FOR LIFE!

First pupils sent home for lack of teachers

HUMAN CLONING IS CLOSER THAN YOU THINK

EXCLUSIVE: What the public really thinks of the Royal Family

Manchester United back on form

2 What sorts of articles do you enjoy reading and which articles do you avoid reading?

Reading

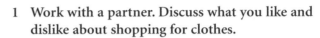

1 Work with a partner. Discuss what you like and dislike about shopping for clothes.

2 Read the newspaper article below and choose which of the paragraphs opposite (A–G) fit into the gaps (1–6). There is one extra paragraph which does not fit in any of the gaps.

Talking clothes get our measure

They could be the trousers that will not belt up. Customers in some of Britain's top clothing stores may soon find their prospective purchases telling them whether they would be a good fit.

The system, which can also be applied to jackets, skirts and almost any other garment, is heralded as the most exciting innovation in retailing in years. It could cut the hours spent trying on clothes that will never fit and, once perfected, could mean the end of the changing room.

`1`

A version of the technology is already being worked on by Marks and Spencer, whose next big sizing survey, the first in more than 10 years, will make use of the latest three-dimensional scanning technology. M&S will use the information to determine the shapes of its future clothing and to run a trial in which selected customers can use the cards to order bespoke suits and other clothes.

`2`

The technology has already been taken further in the United States, with smart cards holding an individual's scan details being designed to plug into a portable device that shoppers carry round the store with them.

`3`

The beauty of scanning systems, as opposed to conventional tape measures, is that they detail an individual's shape as well as their size. "A tape measure may tell you that a lady's hips are 36 inches, but it tells you nothing about where on her hips the bulk of those inches lies," said Jerry Dunleavy, specialist clothing manager at M&S. "With a scanner you can see exactly."

`4`

"The most likely scenario, and one which is already possible, is that the shopper, once scanned, would be given a smart card holding all the information about their body type," said Stephen Gray, head of the computer clothing research centre at Nottingham Trent University.

`5`

According to Gray, it will be possible for shops to go a step further and allow customers to use their smart cards to order made-to-measure clothing. "Translating three-dimensional images into two-dimensional clothing patterns is a skill we have lost as traditional tailoring has disappeared," said Gray. "However, it is something clothing manufacturers are going to have to relearn and then automate."

`6`

Instead of loudspeakers, customers can opt for a small ear-piece, so that their potential trousers, suit or even underwear would not need to talk. They could just whisper softly in the ear.

3 How did you select the missing paragraphs?

A

As they pass racks of clothing, tags programmed with a selection of pre-recorded responses interact with the device and talk to the customer, advising on the garment's likely fit.

B

By doing so, the device will also enable customers to shop by mail order more satisfactorily. This is something which customer groups have been pressing for.

C

Any garment, from a top-of-the-range suit to underwear, could be programmed to chat to its buyer, with warnings such as "This is nice but not quite right for you" or encouragements along the lines of "I'm a perfect fit" or "Suits you, Sir".

D

"That card could then be used to guide the customer automatically to the clothes which fitted them best."

E

For some customers the prospect of successive pairs of trousers – in sizes that once might have fitted – loudly announcing that they are far too small could turn shopping into a humiliation – but the system is likely to be designed with them in mind.

F

Customers who agree to take part will be led to a scanning booth by M&S staff, who will ask them to strip off and stand still while intense beams of white light are played over their bodies. A computerised scanner will turn the results into a "virtual reflection" – an electronic recording of their exact shape.

G

He expects scanning booths about the size of a normal changing room to become available to all his customers in the next five years.

Vocabulary

1 Use the words in the box to complete the text below.

aubergine	browsing	fake	wear	look
pencil	sleeveless	slim	suede	tailored

What's in store?

Wool, fur and tweed, new lengths and simple shapes were all over the international catwalks but have they found their way to a shop near you? Sarah McDonell previews the season's shopping.

Phew! After months of waiting, the fashion faithful here welcome the Spanish label *Mango* and rejoice in the great good fun to be had in an afternoon (1) .... through rails of clothes that combine edginess and classic, continental looks. Sharp, (2) .... trouser suits; tunics; (3) .... tops; straight (4) .... skirts in plum and (5) .... and grey. For weekend (6) ...., twinsets and T-shirts; (7) .... leg trousers; (8) .... and leather, shoes and bags. Even evening wear with (9) .... fur and lace finish, all brilliantly priced so a total (10) .... is easy to achieve.

Listening

1 Do you have a dress code where you work or study? If you do, are you happy with it? If you do not have a dress code, would you like one?

2 You are going to hear the manager of a company. She is not at all happy with the way some employees dress. What do you think she is going to mention?

3 Listen to the recording. Complete the sentences (a–i) with the missing information.

a The manager first singles out those who work in .... for criticism.

b Men in this department have to wear ....

c Clients may come in to see .... at any time so dress is especially important for them.

d The dress code is relaxed on what is called ....

e When the dress code is relaxed, the style of clothing accepted is referred to as ....

f The manager is particularly unhappy about the way employees dress when they are on ....

g The manager was appalled to hear that a man had worn .... when he went to a management college.

h The manager recognises that some employees may complain on the grounds that this is a .... issue.

i She suggests employees take further complaints to the .... department.

4 What do you think of the company's dress code and the way the manager addresses the staff?

⊙ Direct and reported speech

1 Change these sentences from Listening 3 into reported speech. Start each sentence with the words given.

EXAMPLE: Now, it's been brought to my attention that certain members of staff have been flouting the dress code.
She said that *it had been brought to her attention that certain members of staff had been flouting the dress code.*

a I want to make it crystal clear to everyone just exactly what's expected in terms of attire.
She clarified ....

b Those of you who work in reception must be businesslike, at all times.
She insisted that ....

c Don't forget in many people's eyes sloppy clothes means sloppy work.
She reminded ....

d I'm not at all happy about the way some people dress for training days.
She pointed out that ....

e It seems as though some of you have got the idea into your head that when you're on a training day you can dress like a student.
She said that ....

f I've even heard remarks about a certain man who turned up to a management college wearing a nose ring.
She criticised someone ....

g What I want to emphasise is that it's a matter of professional pride, the way you dress.
She stressed that ....

h You have to toe the line.
She said ....

i If anyone feels particularly aggrieved by any of this, all I can suggest is that you take it up with the Human Resources department.
She said ....

j I hope I won't have to refer to this again.
She hoped ....

2 You are going to interview your partner about fashion. Here are some questions to ask. Add another two questions of your own.

a Where do you buy most of your clothes?
b Do you prefer dark or light colours?
c Have you ever bought something quite expensive which you later regretted buying?
d Do you prefer going shopping for clothes alone or with a friend?
e Have you got any brothers or sisters? Do you borrow each other's clothes?

Now interview your partner and make notes of the answers.
Write a summary of what your partner said, using reported speech.

3 Match the verbs (a–n) with the appropriate structure (1–4). More than one structure may be possible.

a He promised
b She suggested
c We agreed
d They told
e She asked
f He offered
g She advised
h He recommended
i He denied
j She invited
k They warned
l I insisted
m He threatened
n I regretted

1 doing it
2 to do it
3 me (not) to do it
4 that I (should) do it

4 Choose the correct alternative to complete these sentences.

a She suggested *to buy / buying* the black jeans.
b He suggested *us another style / another style to us.*
c *I promised myself / I promised to myself* that I would save more money.
d Your assistant promised *us to refund / that she would refund* the money.
e He agreed *on being / to be* the one to make the speech.
f I asked her what *was her name / her name was.*
g You asked if *I was / was I* the owner of the red car.
h It is *recommended / recommend* to book well in advance.
i I recommend *you to pay / that you pay* by credit card.
j He offered *to help me / to me to help.*
k I can recommend *to you the Isa Hotel / the Isa hotel to you.*

G ⋯⋗ page 196

Speaking 2

1 In order to compare (find similarities) and contrast (find differences), you will need to use appropriate linking devices. Add as many words or expressions as you can to these lists.

Comparing	Contrasting
similarly	*whereas*
both pictures show	*but*

2 Look at these plans for comparing and contrasting two photos.

Plan A Compare the photos in general terms and then in detail. Contrast the photos in general and then in detail.

Plan B Start in the foreground of each photo and compare and contrast each point as you come across it. Work towards the background.

Plan C Make a general comment about the photos being mainly similar or different. Then compare and contrast each point you find in the picture.

3 🎧 Look at these pictures and listen to two students, Angela and Luciano, doing a speaking activity.

a Which plan does Angela use?

b Tick the linking devices you hear Angela use.

| but | and | on the other hand | then | in contrast | whereas |

c What does Angela think about the suit the man is wearing in picture a?

1 it's conventional 2 it's flamboyant 3 it's inappropriate

d What does Angela think might be the job of the man in picture b?

1 a banker 2 a naturalist 3 a teacher

4 Sometimes one of the hardest things to do when you have to speak on your own is to get going. If you have some phrases that you can use to start with, you will feel more confident. Here is an example you might be able to use. Add to it by thinking of other opening lines Angela could have used to talk about her photographs.

EXAMPLE: *Well, obviously both pictures have the same theme: fashion.*

5 Work in groups of three. One of you is the Examiner and should ask the Examiner's questions, one is Student A and one is Student B.

a Examiner's question for Student A: Look at the two pictures and compare and contrast them, saying what sort of people follow fashion.
Examiner's question for Student B: Do you think that young people follow fashion whereas older people don't?

b Examiner's question for Student B: Compare and contrast two students in the class, saying what their clothes tell us about their personalities.
Examiner's question for Student A: Do you think your choice of clothes reflects your personality?

Exam folder 5

Paper 3 Part 5 Key word transformations

In Part 5 of the Use of English test (Paper 3), there are key word transformation tasks which test your vocabulary and grammar. There are eight pairs of sentences and you have to complete the second sentence using the word given. These are the key points:

- Complete the second sentence using the word given.
- You cannot change the word given in any way.
- The second sentence must be as close in meaning to the first sentence as possible.
- You must use between three and six words, including the word given, to complete the second sentence.

EXAMPLE:
I was about to leave school when I saw George.
point
I was .... when I saw George.

Answer: *on the point of leaving school*
To answer this question you have to know *to be on the point of + -ing.*

1 Complete the second sentence using the word given.

   1 The essay impressed me a lot.
     made
     The essay...
     .... me.
   2 Sarah would only speak English with the visitors.
     on
     Sarah ....
     English with the visitors.
   3 The price of petrol went up a lot last month.
     sharp
     There was a ....
     the price of petrol last month.
   4 I saw the postman for a minute as he passed my window.
     caught
     I .... the
     postman for a minute as he passed my window.

2 Why are these answers not correct? Correct them.

   1 Each new generation is told the secret recipe.
     down
     The secret recipe *is handed down* each new generation.
   2 I hadn't expected the present at all.
     came
     The present *comes as a complete surprise* to me.
   3 The child's mother became very emotional when he was found.
     overcome
     The child's mother *was overcome with emmotion* when he was found.
   4 Could you possibly help me with this suitcase?
     hand
     Could you possibly *help my hand* with this suitcase?

Fixed phrases

In this part of the Use of English test, it will help you if you know a wide range of fixed phrases, e.g. *to be at a loose end*, which means *to have nothing in particular to do.*

3 Match the phrases in A with the equivalent phrases in B.

A		B	
1	I had no idea	a	There was no sign of him
2	I was shocked	b	He drew my attention to
3	He pointed out to me	c	I was unaware
4	He'll feel much better	d	He was made redundant
5	I couldn't see him anywhere	e	It came as a complete surprise to me
6	He lost his job	f	It'll do him good

Adjectives/verbs/nouns + prepositions

When you learn an adjective, verb or noun, make sure that you also learn whether you need to use a preposition after it; and if you do, what that preposition is.

4 Complete these sentences with a preposition.

1 She takes pride .... her work.
2 He's proud .... his daughter's achievements.
3 I was prevented .... entering the competition because of my age.
4 They specialise .... making furniture out of local wood.
5 You could trust him .... your life.
6 There's been a huge increase .... the number of students going to university.

Always learn the preposition in a sentence, because an adjective, verb or noun can have different prepositions after it, depending on the meaning. For example:

He applied to Cambridge University.
He applied for the job.

Know your grammar

Sometimes the transformation will require you to think about grammar, e.g. passives, conditionals, reported speech, etc.

5 Complete the following sentences with three to six words, including the word given.

1 Unless we can get the 8 am train, we won't get there for lunch.
   mean
   If we don't get the 8 am train, ...
   .... missing lunch.
2 They say Italian football players get paid the most.
   highest
   Italian football players are ....
   salaries.
3 'I'm sorry I forgot to email you the details earlier,' said the tour operator.
   for
   The tour operator ....
   emailing the details earlier.
4 I don't think the advice your accountant gave you is very good.
   should
   Your accountant ....
   better advice.

Practice

6 Complete the second sentence so that it has a similar meaning to the first sentence, using the word given.

1 I didn't have to provide a medical certificate to get my USA visa.
   required
   A medical certificate ....
   my USA visa.
2 The island has a lot of natural resources.
   rich
   The island .... natural resources.
3 Gina complains all the time.
   nothing
   Gina .... complain.
4 The candidate answered the questions honestly.
   honest
   The candidate ....
   the questions.
5 The tennis court was so wet the match was cancelled.
   been
   If the tennis court .... ,
   the match wouldn't have been cancelled.
6 I'd support you even if you weren't my friend.
   side
   I'd .... even if you weren't
   my friend.
7 He wouldn't help me no matter how much I pleaded with him.
   flatly
   He .... help me.
8 Could you get some fruit as you're coming home?
   way
   Could you get some fruit ....
   .... home?

In a nutshell

Genre	Short stories
Topic	Dreaming

Speaking 1

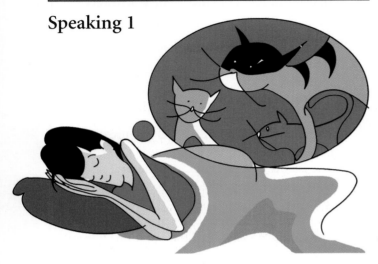

1 Work in small groups and discuss these questions.

   a Why do you think we dream?
   b Do you believe dreams carry significance?

2 According to the book *Dreams and their Meanings,* dreams do have significance. Match the dreams (a–f) to their possible significance (1–6).

Dream	Significance
a cage full of birds	1 an omen of success
b lightning	2 difficulties to overcome before arriving at your goal
c cats	
d apples	3 solutions to your money problems
e milk	
f going barefoot	4 be careful who you trust
	5 good luck
	6 health, prosperity and rewarding work

3 Have you ever heard of someone having a premonition in a dream? Do you believe in premonitions?

4 If you dreamed of something that you thought was an omen of good or bad luck, would you change your life accordingly?

Reading 1

1 Read the first part of this story and answer the questions.

   a Why was the narrator in Vladivostok?
   b How did the narrator get into conversation with the Russian?
   c What impression do you get of the Russian?
   d What do you think the narrator's profession might be?

The Dream

It chanced that in August 1917 the work upon which I was engaged obliged me to go from New York to Petrograd, and I was instructed for safety's sake to travel by way of Vladivostok. I landed there in the morning and passed an idle day as best I could. The trans-Siberian train was due to start, so far as I remember, at about nine in the evening. I dined at the station restaurant by myself. It was crowded and I shared a small table with a man whose appearance entertained me. He was a Russian, a tall fellow, but amazingly stout, and he had so vast a paunch that he was obliged to sit well away from the table. His hands, small for his size, were buried in rolls of fat. His hair, long, dark, and thin, was brushed carefully across his crown in order to conceal his baldness, and his huge sallow face, with its enormous double chin, clean-shaven, gave you an impression of indecent nakedness. His nose was small, a funny little button upon that mass of flesh: and his black shining eyes were small too. But he had a large, red, and sensual mouth. He was dressed neatly enough in a black suit. It was not worn but shabby; it looked as if it had been neither pressed nor brushed since he had had it.

The service was bad and it was almost impossible to attract the attention of a waiter. We soon got into conversation. The Russian spoke good and fluent English. His accent was marked but not tiresome. He asked me many questions about myself and my plans, which – my occupation at the time making caution necessary – I answered with a show of frankness but with dissimulation. I told him I was a journalist. He asked me whether I wrote fiction and when I confessed that in my leisure moments I did, he began to talk of the later Russian novelists. He spoke intelligently. It was plain that he was a man of education.

2 Find words in the text which mean the following:

a quite fat and solid-looking, especially around the waist

b a fat stomach, especially on a man

c yellowish and looking unhealthy

d looking old and in bad condition because of lack of care

e boring or annoying; causing a lack of patience

f concealment of the truth

Listening 1

1 You are going to listen to the next part of the story. What do you think will happen?

2 🎧 As you listen, note down any new information you find out about:

a the Russian
b the Russian's wife
c the narrator's reactions to the Russian

3 What are the significant words in this sentence? *She was, however, of a jealous temperament and unfortunately she loved me to distraction.*

4 How do you think the story will continue?

Reading 2

1 Read on and then discuss these questions with a partner.

a What new information do we find out about the Russian's wife?
b How would you describe the relationship between the Russian and his wife?
c What do you think is the significance of the dream?
d How do you think the story will end?

'I do not pretend that I was faithful to her. She was not young when I married her and we had been married for ten years. She was small and thin, and she had a bad complexion. She had a bitter tongue. She was a woman who suffered from a fury of possession, and she could not bear me to be attracted to anyone but her. She was jealous not only of the women I knew, but of my friends, my cat, and my books. On one occasion in my absence she gave away a coat of mine merely because I liked none of my coats so well. But I am a man of an equitable temperament. I will not deny that she bored me, but I accepted the acrimonious disposition and no more thought of rebelling against it than I would against the bad weather or a cold in the head. I denied her accusations as long as it was possible to deny them, and when it was impossible I shrugged my shoulders and smoked a cigarette.

'The constant scenes she made did not very much affect me. I led my own life. Sometimes indeed, I wondered whether it was passionate love she felt for me or passionate hate. It seemed to me that love and hate were very near allied.

'So we might have continued to the end of the chapter if one night a very curious thing had not happened. I was awakened by a piercing scream from my wife. Startled, I asked her what was the matter. She told me she had had a fearful nightmare, she had dreamt that I was trying to kill her. We lived at the top of a large house and the well round which the stairs climbed was broad. She had dreamt that just as we arrived at our own floor I had caught hold of her and attempted to throw her over the balusters. It was six stories to the stone floor at the bottom and certain death.

Listening 2

1 🎧 You are going to listen to the end of the story. As you listen, make notes to answer the questions below.

a In what way did the dream prey on the Russian's mind?
b Had the Russian previously thought of murdering his wife?
c Did the dream change his wife's behaviour?
d What was the second dream about?
e Why do you think the Russian was sweating when he told the story?
f According to the Russian, how did his wife die and who found her?
g What caused the narrator to doubt the Russian's story?
h How do you think the Russian's wife died?

2 Did you enjoy this short story? Why?/Why not? Do you prefer short stories to have clear happy endings or do you prefer mysterious endings so that you have to come to your own conclusion about what happened?

Writing folder 5

Reviews

In the CAE Writing test (Paper 2) you may be asked to write a review in question 5 in relation to one of the set texts. You might also have the opportunity of writing a review in one of the other questions. This will probably be a review of something other than a book, e.g. a film, a play, a computer game, a CD, a restaurant. Whatever kind of review you are writing, you need to be able to describe accurately and concisely and to convey your opinion in a clear and interesting fashion.

1 What is the purpose of a review? Choose from this list.

a to interest and entertain the reader
b to describe the subject of the review to the reader
c to convey the writer's opinion about the subject of the review

d to promote the subject of the review
e something else

2 Read the film review below. As you read, think about whether you would like to see this film (if you have not seen it). If you have seen it, think about whether the review seems to be fair. Then make notes under these headings.

• Facts about the film
• Phrases that convey the writer's opinion of the film
• Things included to interest and entertain the reader

Shortly before Mission: Impossible *2* opened in the United States, the Wall Street Journal ran a front-page story about an editing genius who was called in at the last hour to reorganise the film. Seemingly, the critics were concerned that John Woo's highly anticipated sequel to Brian de Palma's unbelievably complicated but hugely entertaining Mission: Impossible was a bit hard to follow. Now that the finished product has been released, it's possible to report that the sequel, at the very least, has a story line that makes sense. It's klunky, it's goofy, it has holes big enough to drive the entire United States Marine Corps through, but at least it can be followed. Thank heavens for small mercies. And industrious editors.

M:I 2 is the kind of movie that intelligent, self-respecting critics (there are seven of us, globally) hate to review. Because it's a summer blockbuster, because it's already a mammoth hit in the United States, and because, despite its faults, it's quite an engaging film, it seems almost churlish to say anything negative about it. Thus, let me preface my remarks by stating that, while M:I 2 is not nearly as good as the original, it isn't a dud.

This time out Ethan Hunt (Tom Cruise) is forced to abbreviate a rock-climbing vacation in order to save the world in general and Australia in particular from a lethal virus that has fallen into the hands of fiendish villains. Well, in fact, the fiendish villains, though very, very cruel, are such ninnies that they have only secured one half of the virus and need the other half in order to bring the world to its knees. In exchange for returning their half of the virus, or all of the virus, or some combination thereof, the villains are demanding the nice round sum of £37 million.

It is a little unclear why the unspeakable forces of pure, unadulterated evil are asking for a measly £37 million when £3 billion and complete domination of New South Wales seems a more reasonable asking price.

But never mind.

It's a great relief when the tangled threads of the plot finally coalesce. In a way it's almost a shame that Woo had to even bother with a plot since all anyone really wants to see in a John Woo movie is some good-looking guy – or John Travolta – cavorting on a motorcycle, plunging through plate glass windows, just generally raising hell.

3 Is the title of the review an effective one? Why?/Why not?

4 Is there anything else about the language of the review that you think in some way reflects the content of the film?

5 There are a lot of strong collocations in this review. Pick three that you would like to learn. Did you select the same ones as other students in the class?

6 Reviews often use emphatic language. This can be done by using adverb + adjective combinations such as *unbelievably complicated* and *hugely entertaining*.

Find two collocating adjectives for each of these adverbs:

		1	stupid
		2	disappointing
		3	dull
a	bitterly	4	cold
b	deeply	5	grateful
c	intensely	6	irresistible
d	highly	7	regarded
e	utterly	8	irritating
f	perfectly	9	entertaining
		10	suited
		11	formed
		12	personal

7 Now try this exam task.

An international arts magazine is preparing a feature on TV programmes that viewers find particularly original or unusual.

Write a review in which you:

- outline the programme you choose
- explain why you consider it original or unusual
- discuss what you believe the aims of the programme makers were
- comment on whether you felt the programme achieved its aims successfully or not.

Write your **review** in 220–260 words.

Leaf through a leaflet

Genre	Information pages
Topic	Leaving home

Speaking 1

1 Work with a partner and answer the questions below.

a Match the words in the box to the pictures (a–d).

> a leaflet   a flier   a brochure   a prospectus

b What exactly is a leaflet? What different purposes can a leaflet have?

c Do you think a leaflet is an effective means of communication?

2 With a partner, discuss these questions.

a Have you seen the film *Titanic*? If you have, what do you remember about it?

b Where do you think most of the passengers on board the *Titanic* were going and why?

c What do you think it was like to emigrate to a new country in 1912?

Reading

1 Read the leaflet about the Titanic Trail. Are the following statements true or false?

a You can go on the Titanic Trail at any time of the year.

b Michael Martin built the Heritage Centre.

c The full-day *Titanic* tour allows you to reflect on the final sight of dry land that the passengers would have had.

d Sea angling is included in the traditional Wake Special.

e The *Titanic* sank in 1911.

Titanic Trail

Titanic Trail

**Cobh (Queenstown), Ireland
"Last Port of Call" RMS Titanic**

Guided Tours

Guided walking tours covering the main features of the 1¹⁄₂ mile trail take place daily at 11 am from the Commodore Hotel, Cobh.
Afternoon tours arranged on request.

Special arrangements can be made for bus tours and other groups.
Whenever possible the tour will be introduced by **Michael Martin, author and creator of the Titanic Trail, Cobh.** Additional activities such as boat trips to the anchorage, traditional wakes and evening entertainment can be arranged for groups. See below. www.titanic-trail.com

TITANIC TRAIL OPTIONS

CULTURAL AFTERNOON Ref. No. CA 10
A guided walk of the Titanic Trail with Irish Coffee being served in an authentic emigrant pub. This is followed by a visit to the Queenstown Story at Cobh's beautiful Heritage Centre.

TITANIC FULL DAY EXPERIENCE Ref. No. TF 21
A morning boat trip to the area of Cork Harbour where the Titanic anchored on the morning of April 11th, 1912. Experience for yourself the last images of Ireland that passengers would have seen from the decks of the great ship. This is followed by a cultural afternoon.

ACTIVITIES AND ATTRACTIONS IN OR NEAR COBH

- Marlogue Woods
- Fota Wildlife Park
- Barryscourt Castle
- The Old Middleton Distillery
- Blarney Castle (40 minutes' drive)
- Waterford Crystal (1¹⁄₂ hours' drive)
- Lakes of Killarney (2 hours' drive)
- Tralee, Co. Kerry (home of the Rose of Tralee, 2¹⁄₂ hours' drive)
- The Famine ship, Blennerville (2¹⁄₂ hours' drive)
- Horse riding
- Sea angling

- Golf
- Bird watching
- Sailing
- Windsurfing

TRADITIONAL WAKE SPECIAL

Day 1 Arrival and check in to accommodation. Introduction to Cobh and guided tour of Cobh's famous Titanic Trail with Irish Coffee being served in authentic emigrant establishment
Dinner

Day 2 Breakfast
Boat trip in Cork Harbour to area of Titanic anchorage
Afternoon shopping
Dinner
Evening in authentic rural Irish bar where you can experience first hand the fun, sadness and music of a typical party afforded to the parting emigrants.

Day 3 Breakfast
Visit Queenstown Story at Cobh Heritage Centre, reliving the history of the 4 million Irish emigrants who departed this port

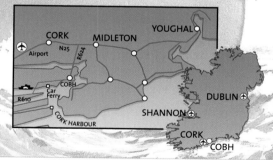

2 Answer these questions about the leaflet.

  a What information is provided in the leaflet?
  b What is the purpose of the leaflet?
  c How does the layout contribute to the communication of the information?
  d How does the writer try to interest the reader? Do you think he succeeds?
  e How would you describe the style of the leaflet?

3 What would you include in a leaflet for visitors to your town or a famous town in your country? Choose three points to write about. Give each paragraph a heading and write a contribution to the leaflet.

Listening

1 You are going to listen to a recording for visitors to the Titanic Heritage Centre. Tick the words from the list below which you think you will hear.

a	embarked	g	quay
b	microchip	h	data
c	crew	i	setting out
d	berthed	j	diesel fuel
e	hi-tech	k	on board
f	iceberg	l	struck

🎧 Now listen and check your answers.

2 🎧 Listen again and complete the sentences below.

   a The leaving party for those emigrating was known as ....

   b The building of the .... made Queenstown an easy place to reach.

   c At the height of emigration, ... people left Queenstown every week.

   d A .... was an immigration requirement.

   e Local goods, such as .... , were taken to the liners to be sold.

   f In total the number of people on board the *Titanic* was ....

3 In what ways would living in a different country from the rest of your family be easier now than in 1912?

⊙ -ing forms

In the listening text, you heard some examples of the use of -ing forms.

EXAMPLE: *Passengers on the Titanic were no doubt looking forward to **travelling** on the brand-new luxury liner.*

1 There are several different uses of the -ing form. Match the sentences (a–g) to the statements (1–7) about the use of the -ing form.

   a Learning keeps the mind active.
   b I avoid travelling on a Monday morning if possible; the trains are so crowded.
   c I'm interested in seeing the new Heritage Centre.
   d If you keep on searching the Internet, you're bound to find some information on the *Titanic*.
   e It's worth making a detour to the west coast; it's spectacular.
   f I hope you don't mind my asking but …
   g I can't imagine being paid that much money.

   1 We can use the -ing form after phrasal verbs.
   2 We can use the passive -ing form.
   3 The -ing form can be the subject of the sentence.
   4 We can use the -ing form after some common expressions.
   5 We can use the -ing form after certain verbs.
   6 We use the -ing form after prepositions.
   7 In formal English, possessives are used with the -ing form.

2 You are going to read an extract about a family who emigrated to the USA in the middle of the nineteenth century. The first and last sentences are in the correct order, but the other sentences have been jumbled up. Put the sentences (b–f) in the correct order, then underline all the -ing forms.

   a I often recall the delightful stories my grandmother used to tell of the days when our family crossed the plains to seek a new life in the West; how must she have felt?
   b He never tired of tending the horses and encouraging us all with wondrous images of our destination.
   c Travelling West must have been a great adventure for the children but a tremendous undertaking for the parents.
   d She told us how grandfather packed the wagon and then left without even taking one final glance back; he was so convinced that it was worth making the trip.
   e Although she conjured up vivid pictures of the trip, I can't really imagine setting out in 1864 with six children and all your worldly possessions on a wagon.
   f My grandmother remembered feeling a sense of excitement tinged with concern.
   g My grandmother said that towards the end of the trip she used to look forward to waking up in a bed in a house, knowing that that day she didn't have to move on.

3 Correct the sentences (a–j) if necessary.

  a He burst out laughing when I told him what had happened.
  b Since he started his new job, he's got used to get up very early.
  c Have time to spend talking with friends is very important.
  d I'm looking forward to see you soon.
  e I can't help thinking this is all a waste of time.
  f It's no use to tell me now that you can't finish the report. You should have told me last week.
  g What I miss is not to be able to have lunch with all my family every Sunday.
  h I'll look into replacing the existing computers with something more up-to-date, but don't hold your breath!
  i I'm fed up with not to have all the facilities I need to do the job properly.
  j Having a positive outlook on life is very important.

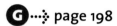 **page 198**

Speaking 2

Here are two ways of linking spoken English.

Type 1
When a word ending in a consonant sound is followed by a word beginning with a vowel sound, the words run together. *Get up* is pronounced /getʌp/.

Type 2
When a word ending with a vowel sound is followed by a word beginning with a vowel sound we insert the sound /j/ or /w/. We insert /j/ as in *he is* (/hiːjɪz/) when the mouth and lips are in a spread position.

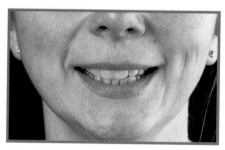

We insert /w/ as in *do it* (/duːwɪt/) when the mouth and lips are in a rounded position.

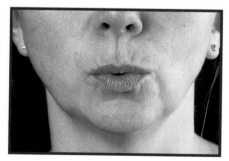

1 Which linking sounds can be used in the phrases below?

  a start off
  b she eats
  c blue ink
  d here at the centre
  e We are leaving the quay at 9 am.

🎧 Now listen and check your answers.

2 Write /w/ or /j/ as necessary in the place in these sentences where linking occurs.

  EXAMPLE: *I'm going to /w/ Ireland next week.*

  a If you are part of a group, it's much more fun.
  b So I'm going to start off by telling you about the conditions on board.
  c You'll see it in the film.
  d When I'm asked about that, it's difficult to answer.
  e You can do it too.
  f Book through our agency, which is open from 9 am to 6 pm.

🎧 Now listen and check your answers.

Exam folder 6

Paper 1 Part 1 Themed texts

In Part 1 of the Reading test (Paper 1) there are three short texts which are thematically linked. Each text is followed by two multiple-choice questions and there are always four options. Reading and understanding of the text are crucial. The questions may focus on understanding detail, opinion, purpose, main idea, implication, etc.

You are going to read three texts which are all linked by the word *kiss*.

1 Read the following extract from a novel and answer these questions.

   1 What made the people believe that they had seen a kiss?
   2 What sort of event were the people attending? How do you know this?

Chapter one

When the lights went off the accompanist kissed her. Maybe he had been turning towards her just before it was completely dark, maybe he was lifting his hands. There must have been some gesture, because every person in the living room would later remember a kiss. They did not *see* a kiss, that would have been impossible. The darkness that came on them was startling and complete. Not only was everyone there certain of a kiss, they claimed they could identify the type of kiss: it was strong and passionate, and it took her by surprise. They were all looking right at her when the lights went out. They were still applauding, each on his or her feet, still in the full throes of hands slapping together, elbows up. Not one person had come anywhere close to tiring.

Advice

- Read the title of the text. It will help you know in advance what type of text it is and what the subject is.
- Read the whole text quickly to get an impression of the content.
- Think about the question (perhaps without looking at the options) and find the answer in the text.
- Read the question again with the options and select the correct answer.
- To confirm, underline the part of the text which contains the answer.
- Think about why each of the other options is not correct so that you can justify your choice.

2 Now look at these two questions which test the same ideas. Which of the multiple-choice options is correct?

   1 People believed they had witnessed the kiss because
     A they knew of the close relationship between the couple.
     B it was what they all wanted to believe.
     C everyone described seeing it in the same way.
     D there was a barely perceptible indication that it would happen.
   2 The audience was attending
     A a musical event.
     B a play.
     C a surprise party.
     D a film.

Focusing on the question rather than the options is a good way to train yourself to find the correct answer to multiple-choice questions.

3 For questions 3 and 4, choose the answer (**A, B, C** or **D**) which you think fits best according to the text.

Arts review
Ballet's opening night

Darcey Bussell's status at London's Royal Ballet has been a privileged one, yet ironically it was never in the company's signature works that she was at her most comfortable. Her radiant and great physique was given more freedom in some of the minor productions and one senses that choreographer Alastair Marriott, whose new work *Kiss* was created for her, understands that it is in her expansiveness that Bussell's dance is at its most appealing. Her limbs have a gorgeous plush, her legs especially seem to unfold in a swelling *legato*, her back melts at the very touch of air – Bussell is big, her dance is big and Marriott has offered her choreography which is undoubtedly big in gesture. Yet somehow it seems to be at odds with the conceit (and the length) of the work which is inspired by the quiet and intimate love of the sculptor Auguste Rodin and his muse Camille Claudel: the whirling drama offered by Bussell and her partner William Trevitt crescendos towards a somewhat frenzied kiss which then rather bathetically diminuendos into nothingness. All of this takes place under the intense and surgical glare of the stage lights and seems too large-scale for the intimacy implied in the tender artistic expression of Rodin's *Kiss*.

3 In his new work, the choreographer Alastair Marriot's aim is to
  A allow the principal ballerina some freedom to interpret her role.
  B create a work which is appropriate for a prestigious ballet house.
  C provide a role for the principal ballerina to excel in.
  D bring a more modern work to an established ballet house.

4 The writer criticises this ballet by saying
  A the style of dancing and the theme are incongruous.
  B it is too long to support such a simple theme.
  C the finale, the kiss, does not make an impact.
  D more advanced technology is needed for the set.

4 Underline the parts of the text where you found the answers.

5 For questions 5 and 6, choose the answer (**A**, **B**, **C** or **D**) which you think fits best according to the text.

Advice for family doctors

The KISS Principle in Family Practice: Keep It Simple and Systematic
A clear, deliberate, consistent approach will beat the alternative every time.

Family doctors make many important contributions to patient care with their pragmatic approach and their individualised attention to the needs of each patient they see. Their tendency to follow the classic admonition of KISS ("Keep it simple, stupid") is an important counter to the tendency of specialists to devise unnecessarily complicated and costly approaches to patient care. However, these positive characteristics of family physicians can also get them into trouble.

By focusing so intently on individual patients and pragmatic solutions, family physicians often miss the broader solutions that could improve care for entire panels of patients. Their individual mind-set also causes them to practise in isolation – even when they belong to a group – and to do things their own way, rather than the best way, which limits their abilities to provide safe, effective, efficient patient care. In many ways, they are just working harder, not smarter, and the collective results are not what they want.

5 According to the writer, the problem with specialists is
  A they do not treat the patient as an individual.
  B they are better at theory than practice.
  C they offer more than is required.
  D they are unaware of cost implications.

6 The writer believes family doctors could improve their patient care by
  A having a broader overview.
  B getting wider experience.
  C working in larger teams.
  D sharing their knowledge.

Views from the platform

Genre	Lectures
Topic	Language development

Listening and Reading

1 🎧 Listen to Speakers 1–4 and match them to the speech (a–d) they are giving.

Speaker 1	**a** a sermon
Speaker 2	**b** a eulogy
Speaker 3	**c** a summing up
Speaker 4	**d** an official statement

2 What is the difference between a lecture, a seminar, a talk, a presentation and a briefing? Match the words (a–e) to the definitions (1–5).

a a lecture   **d** a presentation
b a seminar   **e** a briefing
c a talk

1 the information that is given to someone usually just before they do something
2 a formal talk on a serious or specialist subject given to a group of people, especially students
3 a talk which presents information often with audio-visual aids
4 a speech to a group of people
5 an occasion when a teacher or expert and a group of people meet to study and discuss something

Exam spot

In the CAE Listening test (Paper 4), you may be asked to listen to a talk, lecture or speech. The more you understand about the style and delivery of these forms of speaking, the easier it will be to answer questions about the speaker's standpoint and attitude.

Listening

1 You are going to hear a lecture on evolutionary factors of language. Before you listen, see how many of these questions you can answer.

1 When do you think human beings began speaking?
  a 1.3 million years ago   **b** 50,000 years ago
  c 6,000 years ago
2 Why do you think humans developed language?
  a The population expanded.
  b They needed to communicate more effectively.
  c It is an innate ability.
3 Human babies need their mother and other adults to look after them for quite a long time compared with other animals. Why do you think this is?
  a Human babies are more complex.
  b The gestation period of humans is half that of other animals.
  c The father provides food for the mother and baby.
4 What physical features of human beings enable them to speak?
  a They have fewer teeth than other animals.
  b The human tongue is more flexible.
  c The larynx is simpler.

How do you think children learn their first language?

2 🎧 Listen to the first part of the lecture and complete the notes.

a People began writing .... years ago.

b It is estimated that people began speaking between .... and .... years ago.

c Tools from .... BC show people recognised the concept of space.

d Tools .... years old show people were capable of abstract thought.

e People first used .... to communicate.

f Pettito and Marentette concluded that manual language (sign language) is more .... , ... and .... than spoken language.

g People may have stopped communicating with sign language because they started using .... and wanted to communicate ....

Now let's turn to the biological constraints.

If we assume that all humans are able to speak a language, a number of biological facts fall into place, suggesting that the human body is partially adapted to the production of language.

Human teeth are different to those of other animals – being even and forming an unbroken barrier, they are upright, do not slant outwards and the top and bottom set meet. This is not necessary for eating. Yet evenly spaced equal sized teeth which touch are useful for the articulation of the sounds /s/, /f/, /v/, /ʃ/ and /θ/ as well as several others.

Human lips have well-developed muscles which are more intricately interlaced than those of other primates. The mouth is small and can be opened and closed rapidly, allowing the sounds /p/ and /b/ to be made.

The human tongue is thick, muscular and mobile. This means that the size of the mouth cavity can be varied, allowing a range of vowel sounds to be produced.

The human larynx is simpler in structure than that of other primates; air can move freely past and then out of the mouth without being hindered by other appendages. The 'stream-lining' of the larynx may be a sign of adaptation to speech – however, a disadvantage of this is that we cannot breathe while we eat, unlike monkeys. If food becomes trapped in our windpipe we could choke to death.

Our breathing is well adapted to speech; during speech we are able to alter our breathing rhythm without noticing discomfort.

Humans have a prolonged childhood compared to other animals – if factors like size, lifespan and gestation are taken into account, compared to other animals humans appear to be born prematurely; for humans to conform to the general trend, they would have to have an 18 month gestation period. Thus, with other factors taken into account, the human gestation period is only half as long as the gestation periods of other animals. This means that less information is inherited genetically. In effect the genes are given more opportunity to 'ask the questions' and the environment provides the answers. Perhaps humans are biologically disposed towards language, but they need the environment to make use of the structure of their brains.

Reading

1 Now read the next part of the lecture and answer the following questions.

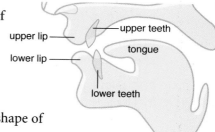

upper lip — upper teeth
tongue
lower lip —
lower teeth
larynx —

1 The importance of the shape of human teeth is that they
  A form a barrier to the throat.
  B allow certain sounds to be produced.
  C make chewing food easier.
  D allow the lip muscles to develop.

2 The structure of the human larynx means
  A the mouth cavity has space for the tongue.
  B it blocks air exiting from the mouth.
  C humans cannot breathe and swallow at the same time.
  D breathing requires effort in humans.

3 Why is it suggested that the human gestation period is so short?
  A to allow humans to learn more from the environment
  B to limit the size humans grow to
  C to take full advantage of our genetic make-up
  D to ensure children learn speech

2 Work in small groups and discuss these questions.

a Did you learn anything new from the lecture? If so, what?

b Do you think animals 'talk'? Give examples of how animals communicate.

c Do you think humans are more intelligent than other animals? Why? / Why not?

d Why do you think it takes such a long time for babies to learn their first language and for adults to learn a foreign language?

⊙ The passive

1 In Listening and Reading 1 you heard the following phrases:

Goods were taken from the warehouse.
The theft was discovered by Mr White when he arrived on the morning of February 15th.
His fingerprints were found on the window.

How is the passive formed?

It is common for the passive to be used in statements, lectures and so on because the action is often more important than the person who carried it out. The passive is also commonly used when we do not know who did something.

2 Match the sentences (1–9) to the statements (a–i) about the form and use of the passive.

1 A man has been arrested.
2 The lecture will be given by Dr Tomlinson.
3 Delegates will arrive at the centre at 6 pm.
4 The lecture room ought to be air-conditioned.
5 The lecturer should have been given more time.
6 He enjoys being recognised in the street.
7 She was awarded an OBE for her services to the community.
8 It is considered impolite to jump a queue.
9 Several people are said to have been injured in the accident.

a Passive constructions can be made with *it* + passive + clause.
b Intransitive verbs cannot usually be made passive.
c When a verb has two objects, it is more usual to make the 'person object' the subject of the passive verb than the 'thing object'.
d This is an example of the passive *-ing* form.
e We use the passive when the action is more important than the agent or the agent is unknown.
f We can use the construction subject + passive + *to* + infinitive.
g This is an example of the passive of a past modal.
h We use *by* + the agent when this provides useful information.
i Modals can be followed by the infinitive passive.

3 Rewrite the underlined sentences in this lecture in the passive.

Recent studies have revealed three important areas in the study of the evolutionary factors of language. 90% of humans are right-handed and have language in the left hemisphere of their brain. The second is that humans freed their hands in order to make and use tools, which meant having to find a method of communication other than sign language. Thirdly, syntax developed which increased the quality and quantity of the message.

People say that we can teach chimps to speak but there are several biological factors which make humans more predisposed to speech. You should note that the form of the human teeth, lips, tongue and larynx are all important when it comes to speech.

4 Look at these two pictures. Picture a shows a sitting room before a burglary and Picture b shows the same room after the burglary. What has happened?

EXAMPLE: *The painting above the fireplace has been stolen.*

To have/get something done

We use *to have/get something done* when we talk about arranging for things to be done by other people. The past participle has a passive meaning.
I'm going to have my car serviced at that new garage down the road.

1 Look at these pictures and say what the person has had done or is going to have done.

2 Work with a partner.

   a Explain the difference in the use of *had* and *got* in these two sentences:
     I had my handbag stolen while I was on holiday.
     She got her fingers trapped in the door.

   b Explain the use of *won't* in this sentence:
     I won't have you staying out so late at night.

   c Explain the meaning of the second sentence:
     Put your money somewhere safe. We don't want it stolen.

G ···⟶ page 199

Vocabulary

Vocabulary spot

When you learn a word, you can increase your vocabulary even more by learning all the forms of the word, e.g. the noun, verb, adjective, and adverb. This will help you in the CAE Use of English test (Paper 3) where in Part 3 you need to fill each gap in a text with the correct form of a given word, as in the exercise below.

1 In the extract below, use the words in capitals on the right of the text to form a word that fits in the gap.

Oral communication

Effective oral communication is an important
– but often (1) .... and   **LOOK**
(2) .... – skill in scientific   **PRACTISE**
and academic endeavours. This tutorial has
been developed to serve as an
(3) .... guide and general   **INTRODUCE**
(4) .... for use when formulating   **REFER**
a talk. The principles should be applied
whenever you are faced with making a public
presentation, whether it's an informal or a more
formal talk, such as a conference presentation
or interview. There are very few people who
have a natural talent for delivering
(5) .... presentations. On   **EXCEL**
the other hand, foresight, hard work, and
practice can carry most of the rest of us into
the 'very good' level of presentation skills.
The standards for public speaking in the
(6) .... and academic   **SCIENCE**
realms are (7) .... low,   **RELATE**
so a good presentation is often
(8) .... I've attempted to compile   **MEMORY**
a short summary of skills needed to make a
good presentation so that a user can learn these
skills, then apply them in professional settings.

Speaking

1 You will be given a card with information about a topic. You are going to give a short talk about this topic. On the card there is one piece of information which is not correct. Read your card and check with your teacher which piece of information is incorrect. Prepare your talk.

2 Work in groups of three. One person in the group gives their talk and the others listen and note down the piece of information which they think is incorrect.

3 After each talk, check which piece of information was incorrect.

Writing folder 6

Information sheets

1 Look at these extracts from different types of information sheets. Discuss who they are designed to attract and which techniques are used to attract the readers.

a

Cambridge Drama Centre

Events for Children

January – April

book now on 01223 322748

Saturday 29th January   Age 5 – 11

Magic Carpet Theatre: The Magic Circus

The Magical Ringmaster has planned a show full of acrobats, elephants, and tightrope walkers ... but the acts have disappeared and the Clowns have taken over! As you might expect they make a fantastically messy job of it. Packed full of audience participation, this is a colourful, exciting and funny show full of crazy circus capers and marvellous magic. Another hit from the company who enthralled us with **Mr Shell's Seaside Spells**.

11 am at Cambridge Drama Centre £3.75 (£1.75 unwaged)

3.30 pm at Impington Village College £3.50 (£1.50 unwaged)

Running time: 70 minutes

b

Lloyds TSB online wherever you are

at your *leisure*

Wouldn't it be useful to be able to pick up the phone and know how much you have in your account, be able to transfer money between accounts or confirm if a payment has gone through?

These are just some of the ways PhoneBank Express, our telephone banking service, can make everyday banking more convenient – wherever you are.

c

SOUTH WEST TRAILS

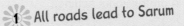

1 All roads lead to Sarum

A journey through 5,000 years of history from Stonehenge, following the footsteps of the Celts, Romans, Saxons and Normans at Old Sarum, then on to the superb medieval cathedral at New Sarum – Salisbury.

◎ Stonehenge, 2m W of Amesbury on the junction of A303 and A344/A360

2 Battlements and boats

A memorable tour of Devon's most historic towns, Totnes and Dartmouth, linked by a river cruise through the beautiful scenery of the Dart Valley.

◎ Totnes Castle, on hill overlooking the town.

3 Forts and ferries

Explore the coastal fortifications that protected the Fal estuary for 450 years.

2 Which of these features do you think we are **not** likely to find in information sheets?

- catchy slogans
- jargon
- rhetorical questions
- imperatives
- very formal language
- encouragement to buy/do something
- long sentences
- headings and subheadings
- lots of adjectives

3 In the CAE Writing test (Paper 2), you may be asked to write a contribution of approximately 250 words to a leaflet, brochure or other type of information sheet. Look at the examination questions below and underline the key parts of the writing tasks. Think about who the leaflet/brochure is for, the nature of your contribution and what you are required to include.

A Most tourists who come to your country only visit the same few overcrowded places. Consequently, the Tourist Board is trying to encourage people to spend holidays in the countryside, and it is planning a new brochure called *The Undiscovered Countryside*. You have been asked to write a contribution to the brochure. You should include information about what can be done on a countryside holiday, what kinds of accommodation are available and what the weather conditions are likely to be.
Write your **contribution**.

B You have been asked to write an information sheet for visitors to your company. You should give a brief history of the company, describe its main activities and plans for the future and mention any other points that you think are important.
Write your **information sheet**.

C In a London museum there is to be an exhibition of some items of great interest from your country, and you have been asked to assist with the publicity. Write a contribution to the museum guide which outlines the history of the items and explains their importance within and outside your country.
Write your **contribution**.

4 Now read the question below. With a partner, underline the key parts of the question and decide on content, style and headings.

Your town would like to attract a greater range of visitors, from young people to older people. You have been asked to write a contribution to a new brochure, issued by the Tourist Board. You have been asked to make sure you mention activities or visits for young people and older people. It is also important that there is a balance of fun activities and more intellectual activities for the different age ranges.
Write your **contribution**.

5 Write a first draft of your contribution then give this to another student and ask for comments. Revise your first draft by checking through the Advice box.

Advice

- Make sure you have answered the question.
- Make sure you have covered all the points in the question.
- Use special techniques/features to attract the reader.
- Check that your contribution is clear.
- Use a range of adjectives, adverbs and grammatical structures.
- Check for spelling and grammar mistakes.

If you want to know what I think ...

Genre	Expressing opinions
Topic	Family life

Speaking 1

1 Work with a partner and match the photographs (a–d) to the speakers (1–4).

1 *At home mum would never let us choose what we had for dinner but now I really miss all that home cooking.*

2 *It's lovely having the children here but it's also nice when they go home to their mum when they've tired me out!*

3 *They're always nagging me to tidy my room and do chores round the house.*

4 *I'm so thankful mum and dad live nearby; they've been a real help since the twins were born.*

2 What kinds of things do you and your family tend to talk about?

3 Among your family and friends, who manages to get their opinion across the most forcefully? How do you think they do this?

Reading

1 You are going to read a newspaper article in which a father gives his opinion about bringing up his three children. What do you think he might say about discipline?

2 Read the article and answer the questions.

1 Jonathan wants to be like his father in that he would like
   A to have the same profession.
   B his children to be proud of him.
   C to teach his children how to get on in life.
   D his children to feel secure.

2 Why is Jonathan strict with his children?
   A He is trying to set a standard in his community.
   B He is teaching his children where the limits of behaviour are.
   C He is making time to spend with his wife.
   D He is moulding his children according to his beliefs.

3 Jonathan fears society may influence his children so that they
   A cannot come to their own decisions.
   B will not cope with life's challenges.
   C will grow up far too quickly.
   D resent their parents' authority.

4 Why did Jonathan finally buy Jacob a Nintendo?
   A Jacob felt his father was being unfair.
   B Jacob was behaving well.
   C Jacob had waited a year.
   D Jacob was being made fun of at school.

5 Jacob has been having some difficulties at school because
   A he cannot play football.
   B his top-of-the-form position is hard to keep.
   C he is seen to be a swot.
   D demands on him are becoming unbearable.

3 Work in small groups and put the following things in life in order of importance. Support your opinions with reasons.

love	fun	living up to family expectations
food	health	job status	strong moral sense
money	friends	security	family

4 When you were a child, were your priorities different? How/Why?

WHAT THESE KIDS NEED IS DISCIPLINE

Jonathan Myers tells Ann McFerran why he has decided to be as strict with his children as his father was with him

I'm a very old-fashioned and strict parent, like my own father. He wanted me to become a barrister, like him, but I used to say to him that he'd made me secure enough not to worry about having a proper job. He was very disappointed when I said I was going to be a writer, but I think that was out of anxiety: he didn't know how I would survive in the world.

As a child I was really proud of my father. I have an image of him, 6ft 5in and broad-shouldered, wearing a smart suit and tie and behaving maturely – an image I feel I should live up to. My father had status in other people's eyes. I worry that I didn't give my children that. They don't see me wearing a suit and going out to work or having status: they see me slobbing around at home in shorts and no shoes.

I think children want to feel proud of their parents because it makes them feel secure in a Darwinian sense. The one time that my children knew how to rate my professional life was when I was nominated for an Oscar for my adaptation of *The Canterbury Tales* – my lucky break. Briefly, I was elevated in their eyes. When I didn't win I felt that I had let them down, which is ridiculous. I had one little cry because I felt I had failed.

I have inherited from my father a strong sense of the importance of doing the right thing. And, like him, I am strict, even though I lack the sort of authority bubble he had around him. In the right context, my children are allowed to be rude to me – they might call me 'fat face' in a jokey way, when I would never have dared.

But I'm also very authoritarian: I believe strongly in proper bedtimes, that chores have to be done and that certain times of the day – when Julie and I have an evening drink – are reserved for adults, which the children are not allowed to interrupt.

Some parents of our children's friends have told Julie that their children are scared of me because I am so strict with my own children. I know I have quite a demonic image in a few families' eyes. But I want to make my children into the sort of children I want them to be.

We live in a terribly liberal age when people feel they should take a back seat in making moral decisions. I don't think that children should make up their own minds – and saying that is about as unfashionable as you can get. But if you don't influence them, they will only be influenced by others.

I don't believe in reasoning with my children. They do what mummy and daddy say. If you say to a child, 'Would you like to go to bed now?' no child in his right mind will agree, and if he does, he needs to be seen by two psychiatrists immediately.

Julie and I don't let our children watch television after 6pm, ever. It's important to think through why a programme is being made. If it's fun, that's fine, but I can't stand all those Saturday morning programmes that are really just to promote the latest pop records and to persuade people to buy accessories. Our children watch it for an hour after school and then it goes off. They never ask to turn it on again.

I think it's a parent's job to preserve childhood as long as possible – which is also terribly unfashionable. We are proud of the fact that Jacob, at 10, still likes cuddly toys.

In our house we never buy toys which are fashionable crazes, such as Furbies. We held out against getting a Nintendo for a year, even though everyone else in Jacob's class had one. But I cracked when he said, 'I don't understand why, if I'm good and I do all my homework and I do everything right, I don't have a Nintendo and all the bad boys do.' I thought that was a very strong argument.

Jacob could not believe it when we got him a Nintendo for his birthday. But we still lay

down rules about its limited use, which he has never argued with because that is the atmosphere in the house.

I am strict about homework and achievement. Our children will work hard until they finish university, and I think they will thank me for the rest of their lives. If they do drop out, at least they will have made a conscious choice.

At the moment the older two are doing well at school and sometimes I try to raise the amount of homework they are given. Jacob protests because I make him take it into school, which makes him look clever. He is already at the top of his form – and that in itself is very difficult for him.

I don't watch football, so nor does Jacob. That is also hard for him. Last year he had a tough time at school in terms of low-intensity bullying. Had he been interested in football, he would have had a *lingua franca* with the others in his year. I was not prepared to change, however. I don't like the attitudes in football.

Speaking 2

1 How far do you agree or disagree with Jonathan's opinions? Complete these sentences.

EXAMPLE: I don't really feel that *Jonathan's ideas on raising children match my own.*

a In my view, ...
b What I think is ....
c As I see it, ...
d If you ask me, ...
e The way I see it is ....

> ## Ⓔxam spot
>
> In Part 3 of the CAE Speaking test (Paper 5) you are given a visual or written prompt for a decision-making task. You have to work with your partner and you may be asked to sequence, rank, compare and select, for example. During this task you are expected to invite the opinions of your partner and express your own.

2 It is a good idea to have a selection of phrases ready for starting the tasks in the Speaking test. Look at these phrases and decide which would be appropriate and which would be inappropriate.

1 A Would you like to start or shall I?
  B You start.
2 A I don't know what to say.
  B OK, so we have to talk about each of these goals and say which is closest to our opinion. Well, this …
3 A Shall we go through all the goals first and then decide which is closest to our opinion?
  B OK, a quick look through and then decide; simple!
4 A I think it's obvious that this is the best.
  B What do you think about this idea here?

3 Here are some pictures illustrating parents' goals for their children. With a partner, talk about the different types of goals and decide which two are closest to your own opinion.

I would like my children to …

4 How did you start the discussion? Which phrases did you use to give your opinion? Did you support your opinions with reasons?

⊙ The infinitive

The infinitive in English is the base form of the verb. We call it the full infinitive when *to* is used before it and the bare infinitive when there is no *to*.

EXAMPLE: *I think children **want to feel** proud of their parents because it makes them feel secure in a Darwinian sense.*
*My children **are allowed to be** rude to me.*
*I don't think that children **should make up** their own minds.*

1 Underline the sentences which use the infinitive in the article. Which take the infinitive with *to*? Which take the infinitive without *to*?

2 Correct the sentences below if necessary.

   a I don't want that you think I'm doing this as a punishment.
   b You are not to use the computer after 10 pm.
   c I must to go home before I miss the last bus.
   d In my opinion parents should not let their daughters to wear make-up until they are over 16.
   e No wonder he's proud of his son, he seems to win every school prize there is!
   f I was helped to get on in my career by one of my lecturers from university.
   g I'm writing the address down so that you don't forget it.
   h It was fantastic see so many young children enter the competition.
   i The school made students do their homework on a computer.

3 Do you agree or disagree with the following statements?

   a Having their mother at home all day with them makes children feel more secure.
   b Children should be set high educational goals by their parents.
   c Children from large families seem to do better at school.
   d Children want to be the same as their friends and different from their parents.
   e Parents should let their children begin to make their own decisions from the age of eight.

G ···⟩ page 199

Listening

1 Do you watch more or less television now compared to when you were a child? Do you and your family/friends have the same taste in television programmes?

2 🎧 You will hear five short extracts in which people give their opinions about TV programmes. As you listen, match the speakers (1–5) to the programmes (A–H).

Speaker 1
Speaker 2
Speaker 3
Speaker 4
Speaker 5

   A *Naturally Yours*
   B *Elizabeth*
   C *Food and Drink*
   D *Sci-fi Season*
   E *Walking with Dinosaurs*
   F *The Cops*
   G *Wind-down-for-bedtime*
   H *I Love the 80s*

3 🎧 Listen again and match the speakers (1–5) to the opinions (A–H).

Speaker 1
Speaker 2
Speaker 3
Speaker 4
Speaker 5

   A The programme's normality was what appealed.
   B I'm not sure all the facts are correct.
   C I can't imagine why original pieces weren't used.
   D I think the focus of the programme was all wrong.
   E I don't think the title reflects the programme's content.
   F I admit to being a bit of a nostalgia fan.
   G The jokey undertones and use of special effects made it.
   H The music was inappropriate.

4 Work in small groups and discuss the questions below.

   a Why do you think some people find horror films so exciting while others cannot watch them?
   b What makes a good comedy? Is it the characters the actors play, the story line or the language?
   c Do you think westerns are losing their appeal?
   d What sort of people like action programmes? Do they appeal to the lazy or the dynamic?

Genre	Reviews
Topic	The arts

By George, they've done it!

Unaccustomed as you are to public speaking, this will sort you out

THE BLACK PRINCE ALMOST SCORES

144 levels of fun

Ensnared by love – you'll be caught too

Speaking 1

1 Look at the headlines above which are all from reviews.

 a What do you think they might be reviewing?

 b Can you tell from the headline whether the review is mainly praising or criticising?

2 Work with a partner and answer the questions.

 a What is the significance of the title of this unit?

 b List as many things as possible that may be reviewed in the media.

 c What sorts of things do you read (or listen to) reviews of?

 d Has a rave review or a panning ever affected you?

Reading

1 Read the extracts opposite from the reviews (A–E) and note what kind of thing is being reviewed and whether the critic's opinion is basically favourable or unfavourable.

2 Look at the statements below. Are they true, false or is the information not given in the extracts?

 1 a The writer had planned to stay at The George.

  b The George is near a place called Aviemore.

  c The George is very expensive.

 2 a Howard's story is partially autobiographical.

  b It is a detective story.

  c It tells how a seemingly intelligent middle-aged woman was deliberately deceived by a man.

 3 a Grag and Thog are troll brothers.

  b They are super-intelligent.

  c The game is not too difficult to complete.

 4 a Nick Cave's music has changed style.

  b Nick Cave has a very powerful voice.

  c This new album consists largely of happy love songs.

 5 a The website gives advice about public speaking.

  b It contains a lot of anecdotes suitable for including in speeches.

  c The website was only partially complete when the review was written.

A

I stumbled on The George one holiday when I drove the family mad dragging them everywhere searching for my McPherson roots – there's an area near Aviemore with lots of family connections. It's set on a huge loch with water so deep it looks black and it's framed by charcoal blue mountains and looks like a mock Venetian folly. I had a fabulous night there talking to a genealogist who charges Americans £500 to chart their family tree. I've been back there since on the pretext of doing a documentary about the McPhersons for TV but I never made it out of The George. It's that kind of place.

B

Have you ever wondered how an intelligent woman could fall for a callous con man? Here, with icy inevitability the process is laid bare. Howard examines predator and prey, exposing the workings of both minds as the trap is gently laid and we sit back, transfixed, to watch the kill. This subtle romance of late middle age reads more like a thriller – with the added piquancy of knowing there are parallels with the author's own life. Prepare to be seduced.

C

POOR OLD GRAG AND THOG. The two brothers don't have a care in their pea-sized brains until an earthquake opens the way for hordes of pesky creatures from the surface to invade their troll homelands deep within the bowels of the earth. Due to a little misunderstanding, the brothers manage to volunteer themselves to expel the invaders and so begins their quest to clear all twelve realms of the underworld. Veteran gamers may notice that this game is based on the arcade classic, Mario Bros. It has 144 standard levels divided into 12 themed worlds. Dogs, wasps, spiders and other critters emerge at the top of the levels and proceed across the screen, dropping through holes in the platforms. Grag and Thog won't stretch your new iMac to the limits but they will provide you with hours of light-hearted entertainment.

D

After years playing the darkest, most haunted princeling in all rock's gothic underworld, Nick Cave's finest moment came when he abandoned morose noise-mongering for the quiet piano balladry of 1997's *The Boatman's Call*. With *No More Shall We Part*, Cave takes half a pace backwards towards his anguished past. While songs like *Love Letter* maintain the contemplative style of *Into My Arms*, the record also comes loaded with smoking guns, darkening days and 'black trees bent to the ground'. It's as if, after reflecting on the pain and profundity of love, Cave is rediscovering his anger at the world.

E

Is one of your worst nightmares having to stand up in front of an audience and 'say a few words'? If so, sweat no more. Speechtips.com is a concise guide to speech-writing for every occasion. In easy steps, it teaches you the basics of planning (the occasion, the audience, their expectations), writing (the correct structure) and delivery (notes or memory). Its common-sense advice should be compulsory reading for many would-be orators. Unfortunately, the practical section of Speechtips ('speech guides' e.g. weddings, eulogies, retirement, school, awards ceremonies) was still under construction as we went to press.

3 Now read the reviews in more detail and complete the table below. Identify the words and expressions that tell you about the subject of the review and those which indicate the critic's attitude.

Text	Words identifying the topic	Positive words and expressions	Negative words and expressions
A	*The George – it's set – had a fabulous night there – that kind of place*	*fabulous*	*nothing negative in the piece*
B			
C			
D			
E			

4 To what extent would you like to try out each of the things reviewed?

Speaking 2

1 You are going to work on some expressions that a producer of a play uses when trying to decide how to organise a production. Fill the gaps with a suitable word. The first letter of each missing word is provided.

  a Why d..................... we hire costumes?
  b I'd suggest g..................... Jackie Brown the lead
    – she was the strongest person at the auditions.
  c We might as w..................... have the dress rehearsal
    on the Sunday before the first performance.
  d So am I r..................... in saying that the theatre
    will be available for rehearsals every morning?
  e In other w..................... , we should have plenty
    of opportunity to rehearse on the stage itself.
  f Isn't it mainly a m..................... of careful
    planning?
  g I'm not entirely c..................... that we should
    cut that bit you suggest from the second act.
  h I agree with you on the w..................... but there
    are a couple of things I'd like to t.....................
    you up on.

2 Look again at the sentences above and underline the expressions that are useful for giving opinions and making suggestions.

3 Work in groups. You are going to plan the reviews section for a class magazine. As you work, try to use some of the language for giving opinions or making suggestions.

  a Discuss what you are going to review, e.g. restaurants, films, books, plays, TV, music, websites, local facilities and so on.
  b Discuss what guidelines the reviewers need to be given, e.g. how many words to write, whether they should aim to give a strong opinion or to be more balanced and what exactly you would like from them.
  c Present your plans to the other students. How are they different?
  d Now write your reveiw (approximately 250 words).

Articles and determiners

1 Look at the reviews in Reading 1 again and underline all the articles and determiners used in them. Answer the following questions about their use.

Review A
  a Why is it *The George*?
  b Why is it *a huge loch* and not *the huge loch*?
  c Why is it *Americans* and not *the Americans* or *some Americans*?

Review B
  a Why is the indefinite article used in the first sentence?
  b Why is it *the process* in the next sentence?
  c Why is it *the author* at the end of this review?

Review C
  a Why is it *their* rather than *the* before *pea-sized brains*?
  b Why is it *the* rather than *an arcade classic*?

Review D
  a Why is it *the* before *quiet piano balladry*?
  b Why is it *the* before *ground* and *world* in the last two sentences?

Review E
  a Why is it *a few words* and not *few words*?
  b Why is *the* used in the first two sets of bracketed notes but not in the third set?

2 These sentences illustrate some of the most common mistakes that advanced learners make with articles in English. Correct the sentences and then explain what the rule is in each case.

  a The life is hard!
  b Life of the poor in a country with no welfare state is very hard.
  c My brother is biochemist in London.
  d Jack broke the leg skiing.
  e He's only 18 but he already has the own business.
  f Maria's on a business trip to People's Republic of China.
  g Do they sell fruit in the USA by kilo or pound?
  h Since they built the tunnel, fewer people are using a ferry.

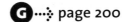 page 200

Listening

1 Look at these pictures. What kinds of film or show do you think they come from?

EXAMPLE: *I think the first picture must be from a cowboy film. You can tell by the costumes and the location!*

2 Which of the types of films or shows in the pictures do you like best and which do you like least?

3 🎧 Listen to two people discussing films they have recently seen and answer the questions below.

   a What is being discussed?
   b List all the facts that you learn about the films.
   c What words and expressions do the speakers use to make their feelings clear?

4 Choose two of the categories in the box. Choose one example from each of these categories that you would recommend to a partner and one that you would not recommend. Explain your choices to your partner.

film	website	novel	theatre production
computer game	CD	restaurant	hotel

Vocabulary

1 Here are some collocations from the reviews you have read and listened to. Match the first half of the collocation (a–l) with the second half (1–12).

a	have	1	mad
b	breathing	2	age
c	drive someone	3	the way
d	family	4	letter
e	lay	5	reading
f	middle	6	bare
g	open	7	entertainment
h	light-hearted	8	guns
i	love	9	tree
j	smoking	10	nightmare
k	worst	11	reservations
l	compulsory	12	space

2 Choose a collocation from Vocabulary 1 to complete the sentences.

   a Is there any .... to do before the history course you're doing this summer?
   b Many people can only do three or four generations of their ....
   c In the attic I found some bundles of old .... tied up in pink ribbon.
   d When do you think .... begins? 45? 50?
   e It's not a profound film in any way – it's just good ....

3 Work with a partner to add to the sets of collocations below.

   a family .....*tree*.............................
   b to drive someone .....*mad*..........
   c love ....*letter*..............................
   d middle ......*age*...........................
   e to lay .....*bare*.............................

Exam folder 7

Paper 1 Part 2 Gapped text

Advice

- Read the whole of the text first.
- Read through all the paragraphs and notice the difference between them.
- Pay careful attention to linking devices throughout the text and paragraphs, as well as at the beginnings and ends of paragraphs.
- Read the whole of the text again when you have completed the task.
- Don't rely on matching up names, dates or numbers in the text and paragraphs just because they are the same or similar.
- Don't rely on matching up individual words or phrases in the text and the paragraphs just because they are the same or similar.

1 Choose which of the paragraphs (A–G) fits into the numbered gaps (1–6) in the article below. There is one extra paragraph which does not fit any of the gaps.

2 Now go back and mark the words and phrases which help you to decide what fits where.

Don't be fooled: *the Queen is not speaking our language*

A deeply fascinating piece of academic research from Australia has managed to ruffle a few feathers. It's really a dispassionate observation of a particular fact, but it can hardly seem anything other than disrespectful to the point of *lèse-majesté*. An expert in linguistics has examined the Queen's Christmas broadcasts, from the earliest to the most recent, and has observed that, in the course of her lifetime, her vowels have shifted from the front of her mouth toward the back.

[1]

If you wanted to track the changes in linguistic usage in a single individual over the course of a long lifetime, you could not possibly find a better subject for your research than the Queen.

[2]

The Queen's vowels, from her first broadcasts, don't strike us as unusually forward in the mouth; they strike us as almost unimaginably posh. "But", "bet" and "bat" all sound very much the same. "House" really does sound like "hice".

[3]

We generally like to assume that the speech of individual classes is a fairly stable thing, but I doubt that is the case. The upper-class dropping of the final "g" is much rarer than it used to be, for instance – something that would aggrieve one famous lady, of whom it was said that she was so grand, she dropped the final "g" from words that didn't have it. In general, the speech of the members of a particular social class tends to sound rather more vulgar than that of its parents.

[4]

And now, the young of the upper classes rarely talk in what we normally think of as an upper-class accent. The upper-class socialite, Tara Palmer-Tomkinson, sounds like Eliza Doolittle before Professor Higgins got his hands on her. A real cut-glass accent, in anyone under 40, is invariably rather an aspirational middle-class thing, acquired by someone who taught himself to stop saying "toilet" and "settee". Middle-class London children, now, always sound appallingly common to their grandparents, but their way of talking is quite distinct from that of real working-class London children.

| 5 | |

In short, pronunciation is in a constant state of change, and individuals' pronunciation is as prone to alteration as anything else. Only people isolated from their linguistic community are unlikely to alter their accent at all; old Indian expats do still talk in the accent of their youth. The rest of us are not going to carry on talking as we did as children, and that includes the Queen.

| 6 | |

What is surprising, however, is that it demonstrates that she has, after all, been listening to other people all these years.

A What is entirely idle is to draw the conclusion that the Queen is now talking in the accents of the lower classes. She is talking exactly as a woman of her class and generation might be expected to in the year 2000, and it is no surprise whatsoever that that does not much resemble the ways of talking of her youth.

B Accents in English have always suggested something about a person's class as much as about their geographical origins and the Queen is no exception. It is very hard to change your original accent unless you have the help of a professional expert like the famous fictional Professor Higgins who taught the Cockney flower-girl Eliza Doolittle (in Bernard Shaw's *Pygmalion*, made into the musical and film *My Fair Lady*) to pass herself off as a lady.

C A very interesting and valuable observation. The Queen is a particularly good subject for such observation, since there are so many recordings of her speech, and they cover such a long period of time. From the famous wartime recording to the children of the Empire – "Come on, Margaret!" – to the present day, there is a record of her speech for practically every year of her life, and there is probably no other speaker of English for whom that is the case.

D All the same, it is difficult to describe such things in a neutral way, and perhaps the researchers might have made a sensible decision to refer to her, in scientific manner, as Elizabeth R. The point about her pronunciation is that the shape of vowels has definite social connotations, and the unarguable shift in her vowels certainly seems like a shift down the social scale.

E Middle-class English of half a century ago, as typified by an announcer on the BBC, tends to sound to us like aristocratic speech. The pre-war novelist Virginia Woolf's accent, which was probably fairly typical of the London upper-middle class, now sounds almost incomprehensibly grand.

F So, the distinctions that the Queen has learnt to make over the years, to the point where she now has more than one vowel to her name, don't seem merely like a neutral linguistic change; they sound as if she has become distinctly more common. Certainly, that was the interpretation widely placed on this fascinating and undoubtedly accurate research, and the Palace greeted the news that the Queen has embraced estuary English – a useful though rather broad linguistic category – with the sort of sniffy response it generally reserves for paparazzo shots of the Duchess of York.

G The accents of the working classes change as much as anything. It's quite rare, now, to hear the old London accent that pronounces "catch" as "ketch"; it has been altered by all sorts of new influences, and particularly by black English, which have turned it into what would probably seem quite a new accent. The Cockney accent of 50 years back, though still familiar from old films, is in reality as dead as that of Sam Weller from *The Pickwick Papers*, which routinely interchanged Vs and Ws.

17 Do it for my sake

Genre Proposals

Topic Persuasion

Exam spot

You may be asked to write a proposal in the CAE Writing test (Paper 2) and you may also have a negotiating or discussion task in the Speaking test (Paper 5). This unit helps you with the language needed for such tasks.

Speaking 1

1 Read the adverts (a–d) below and decide which of the people in the photos might be most likely to apply for each one.

2 With a partner, discuss the travel grant (a). Where exactly would you go and what would you do there? What would you need the money for?

3 Now discuss any other one of the adverts you might like to respond to. What project or course would you want the money for? List all the specific things that you would need to spend the money on.

Reading

1 Imagine that you and your friends are considering applying for the travel grant (a). What would you need to do before you write your proposal to give it a better chance of success?

a

Calling all students who wish to travel to further their studies:

Money is available for:
* travel and living expenses
* computers, books and other relevant study equipment
* fees for appropriate courses.

Phone our office for information about what you may and may not be entitled to and for instructions as to how to submit your proposal.

b

Have you got a good business idea but no funds to put it into practice?

We can offer set-up grants to people with original and viable ideas.

All proposals must be submitted by the end of this month.

c

The local council has money available for projects that would benefit the local community.

Have you got a suggestion for something that would improve the quality of life for local residents?

Call us and we'll arrange an appointment to discuss your proposal.

d

BORED WITH YOUR LIFE? TIME FOR A CHANGE? WHY NOT RETRAIN?

Grants available for deserving applicants who would like to do one of a wide range of retraining courses at a number of local further education colleges. Send us a one page proposal explaining what you would like to do and why.

2 Now read the guidance below. Tick any of the points that are relevant to your travel grant proposal. Mark with a cross any of the points that you do not think would be relevant to your proposal.

Tips on Preparing a Successful Proposal

The following is a list of tips or advice by project reviewers and others familiar with proposal development and review.

- **Be realistic:** what can reasonably be accomplished in the scope (time and resources) of this grant?

- **Be factual and specific:** don't talk in generalities or in emotional terms. Be able to substantiate all statements in your proposal, otherwise don't make them.

- **Use language anyone will understand:** no abbreviations, initials, or jargon. Don't assume the reader will understand your acronyms or abbreviations.

- **Read the guidelines carefully!** Make your proposal fit the funding requirements. Don't ask for things that are outside of the intent of the grant.

- **Choose a format that's clear and easy to read:** readers are overloaded with proposals and appreciate legible, attractive proposals.

- **Stick to the specified number of pages:** extra pages or attachments may be removed before the proposal is read, or may disqualify your entire proposal from the reading process.

- **Do it yourself:** teach your own staff about proposal writing. But if you hire a development person or a consultant, stay on top of it; proposals exclusively written by development people usually don't make sense because that person isn't familiar with the project.

- **Give details about who will do what:** think of all the details, such as ordering materials, cataloguing and managing them, arranging for staff development, etc. Make sure someone is assigned to manage each step of the project.

- **Be clear** about the type and amount of staff development required, and the amount of time necessary for staff to feel confident about implementing the project. Be realistic!

- **Check** current prices of hardware, software, and materials you plan to purchase for this project. Also include staff development costs: consultant fees, substitute fees and associated materials costs.

- **Give evidence of district or school site support:** if there are matching funds available, or your site or district has a demonstrated commitment to this project, describe the commitment.

- **Call** if you have questions, but realise that many others will be calling as well. Don't wait until the last minute.
- *Read the directions.*
- *Read the directions.*
- *Read the directions.*

Listening

1 With a partner, discuss these questions.

  a List any situations when you have had to persuade someone to do something.

  b How did you persuade them to do what you wanted? How easy was it to do so?

  c When is it particularly difficult to persuade someone to do something?

  d What sorts of techniques can be used to try to persuade people to do things that they are reluctant to do?

2 🎧 Listen to eight people trying to persuade others to do different things. As you listen, complete the table.

Speaker	What speaker wants others to do	How speaker tries to persuade them
1		
2		
3		
4		
5		
6		
7		
8		

3 Work with a partner and take it in turns to try to persuade each other to do some of the things below. Use language from Listening 2 where appropriate.

- go on a scary roller coaster ride
- fly to an exotic place for a weekend break with you
- sell you one of their treasured possessions (perhaps a bike, a favourite computer game, CD or piece of jewellery)
- help you move a piano up some stairs
- teach you a skill (e.g. to drive a car or play the violin)
- lend you a large sum of money
- go with you to a social function that they really do not want to go to
- have their hair dyed
- change their job

Language of persuasion

There are often several ways of saying the same thing that are all grammatically correct. One may, however, fit a particular set of circumstances better because it conveys a slightly different nuance of meaning. For instance, it may sometimes be better to be more tentative and polite whereas sometimes it may be better to be more direct.

1 Look at the different ways below of persuading someone to do something. Which would be the better alternative to use in the situations outlined?

  1 A new employee thinks his boss has not been as thorough as she should have been in a report.
    a Are you absolutely certain that you've taken everything into account?
    b This is rather careless work.
  2 A teenage girl wants her father to change his mind and let her go to an all-night party.
    a Are you quite sure you won't reconsider?
    b Just this once. Please!
  3 A husband is trying to persuade his wife that they should take part in a marathon.
    a Please, just do it for my sake.
    b How can I convince you of the sense of what I'm suggesting?
  4 The manager of a sales department is trying to persuade his staff to work longer hours.
    a Couldn't you be persuaded to give it a try?
    b Come on, just do it for me.
  5 A father is trying to persuade his young son to swim the length of a pool.
    a Oh come on, have a try. It's not as hard as it looks.
    b It's in your own best interests to do what I suggest.
  6 A woman is trying to put an end to a small quarrel with a friend.
    a Surely the most sensible thing would be to take some independent advice?
    b Don't be like that. Please!
  7 A businessman is trying to persuade fellow workers at a meeting about what the company should do.
    a You're a load of idiots if you can't understand what I'm driving at.
    b The best course of action would be to survey our markets for their reactions.

2 Complete the table in an appropriate way, using formal and informal expressions.

Persuading someone to	Formal	Informal
help you check some written work	Could you possibly find time to check through this report for me, please?	Cast your eye over this for me, will you?
change their mind		Come off it! You're being really stubborn.
lend you some money	I'd be really grateful if you could possibly lend me ten pounds until Monday.	
do something a little dangerous		Come on. Don't be scared. You'll be OK.
change their appearance in some way	Madam would look wonderful if her hair had highlights put in it.	
learn some new computer skills		

3 Work with a partner.

  a Write a dialogue in which a teenager tries to persuade a parent to let them do something. There should be at least eight exchanges in your dialogue.
  b Write another dialogue in which a manager tries to persuade a member of her staff to do something that they are reluctant to do. Again, there should be at least eight exchanges in the dialogue.

G ···⟶ page 201

⊙ Vocabulary

Many words in the texts you have been working on in this unit have multiple meanings. For example, in the title *Tips on Preparing a Successful Proposal*, *tips* means advice, but *tip* can also mean:

- an extra payment for a service
- the pointed end of something like a pencil
- a place for depositing rubbish
- to make something not straight.

Proposal here means a formal, written suggestion but it can also mean an offer of marriage.

1 In each of the sets of sentences below, one word from the reading text can be used to complete the three gaps. Which word fits each set?

1 • I even managed to save money from my student ....
   • Sarah's a good writer, I .... you.
   • His request that they .... him asylum was rejected.

2 • University .... tend to be shorter than school ones.
   • Be sure to read all the .... of the agreement before signing anything.
   • Sam always speaks of his boss in glowing ....

3 • She forgot to .... a stamp on the envelope.
   • My grandma's got quite unsteady on her feet and usually uses a ....
   • I wish the speaker would .... to the point.

4 • I've got a terrible .... of direction.
   • Can you make any .... of what he's trying to say?
   • There's no .... in waiting here any longer.

5 • What's her .... address?
   • The strong .... makes it dangerous to swim here.
   • We'd better transfer some money into our .... account.

2 Here are some more words from this unit which have multiple meanings in English. Can you think of at least two senses for each word?

call	course	direction	fit	order	own	step	sum

Speaking 2

1 Work in small groups. You are going to go on holiday as a group. Each group should choose a different kind of holiday.

a Discuss ways to persuade the other groups that this would be the best type of holiday for you all to go on.
   Think also of the objections that the other groups might raise and of how you could counter those objections.
   You may need to consider these aspects of the holiday:

activities	accommodation	cost
fun	learning experience	weather

b Regroup and take it in turns to present the holiday you have been thinking about. Try to persuade the others that your idea is the best one. Raise as many objections as you can to other suggestions that are made.

c At the end, vote on which holiday you think your group should go on. You are not allowed to vote for your own suggestion.

d Feed back to the class as a whole, saying which holiday your group voted for and why.

Exam folder 8

Paper 1 Parts 1, 3 and 4 Multiple choice and multiple matching

In Parts 1 and 3 of the CAE Reading test (Paper 1), you have to answer multiple-choice questions.

1 Following the Advice box below, read the text and answer the questions which follow.

Advice

- Read the whole text very carefully before you begin to answer the questions.
- Read the whole of the question and all the options carefully.
- Read the text for inference as well as fact.
- Remember that the questions follow the order of the text.
- Remember that the final question may ask about the text as a whole.
- Don't rely on matching individual words or phrases in the options and the text just because they are the same or similar.

Where was I?

In nostalgic mood, I alight at Central Station, where, it has to be said, the prospects of catching a train are about the same as an encounter with little green men. That is why it is known to everybody except me by another name.

Despite this, the city has always been at transport's cutting edge. Just around the corner is a canal that, when opened in 1761, was something of a revolution: another, 36 miles long and far more impressive, was only completed in 1894. A little time after that, it was here that a one-time electrical engineer and an aviator first met and so it is home to what, at that time, was one of Britain's first municipal airports. And to bring the story right up to date, it is a place justly admired for a means of getting around that not so long ago was considered well and truly extinct. But I shun them all: shoe leather will get me to the city centre.

1 Which contradiction about the town does the writer bring out?
  A It is right up to date but at the same time historic.
  B It is famous for transport but it is difficult to get a train.
  C It has two different names.
  D It is the home of inventors and development.

2 The purpose of the text is to
  A promote rail travel.
  B provide a competition question.
  C inform the reader about transportation.
  D criticise today's facilities.

In Part 4 of the Reading test, you have to match questions or prompts to bits of text. There are two basic reading skills: scanning and skimming. Scanning means reading for specific information while skimming means reading quickly through a text to get a general impression of the content. You will need to make use of both these skills in this part of the Reading test.

Advice

- Read the subtitle to get a general idea of what the text is about.
- Read the questions before you scan for the information/opinions needed.
- Read the whole of each question very carefully.
- Skim the whole of the text before you scan for the information/opinions needed.
- Don't rely on matching up individual words or phrases in the question and the text just because they are the same or similar.
- Don't rely on finding all the information you need for a question in just one part of the text.

2 Now read the reviews below and answer the following questions.

a Which of these films does the reviewer like least?
b Which one is a serious drama?
c Which is a political comedy?
d In which two is the reviewer critical of the acting?
e Which one deals with the less glamorous side of the pop world?
f In which one does the director not use his full name?
g Which one relates to a type of film that was popular about forty years ago?
h Which one is the longest?
i Which two are the cheapest?
j Which one has a scene centring round a type of traditional British food?

new on video

★★★★★ Excellent   ★★★★ Very Good   ★★★ Good   ★★ Poor   ★ Give it a miss

1 Charlie's Angels ★★

Columbia Tristar, 15, 99 mins, 2000; rental, £19.99 (DVD)

As the first scene in-joke has it: "Not another film based on an old TV series?" Well, yes, but one that took £13m at the UK box office and that combines high-tech hyperactivity with arch camp. Plus, it has Drew Barrymore in a shell suit, not to mention the free-dancing, ever-grinning, good-meal-needing Cameron Diaz and foxy brainbox Lucy Liu. Hard to tell whether the name of the director, McG, indicates cool or embarrassment, for this is little more than a stunt-filled extended pop promo.

2 Yes, Minister: Party Games ★★★★

BBC, PG, 61 mins, 1984; £10.99 (VHS)

Not a bad time given the upcoming election to revisit Antony Jay and Jonathan Lynn's extended episode of *Yes, Minister*, first seen on December 17, 1984, detailing how Jim Hacker rises from ministerial nonentity to national leader via a Churchillian stand on the sanctity of the British sausage. Paul Eddington's minister not only narrowly survives a seasonal drink-driving charge, but uses his position as party chairman effectively to blackmail two more gifted but morally fragile colleagues, played by James Grout and Peter Jeffrey. It's worth noting that, in the old days, senior civil servants like Nigel Hawthorne's Sir Humphrey doubled up as spin doctors, thus saving a figure currently estimated at £80m a year.

3 Perfect Strangers ★★★★

BBC, 15, 237 mins, 2001; £19.99 (VHS)

A quick release by the BBC for Stephen Poliakoff's epic of the family just seen on TV, inspired by his own life and using photography as a way into those hidden parts and secret silences that form part of our individual and collective identity. Superbly cast, it stars Lindsay Duncan and Timothy Spall, who featured in its predecessor, *Shooting the Past*, as well as Michael Gambon and Matthew Macfadyen, in the pivotal role of Daniel. As a director, Poliakoff deliberately avoids the fast-paced cutting of today, which makes for languor and intimacy, but sometimes encourages the actors to strut their stuff at the expense of the whole. That said, it's remarkable.

4 Sugar Town ★★★

FilmFour/VCI, 15, 89 mins, 2000; £12.99 (VHS)

A sly and cynical comedy set amid the rock-music and showbiz world of Los Angeles, made by Allison Anders and Kurt Voss. It may interest fans of soap star Martin Kemp and Duran Duran's John Taylor. The former gets to say all the rude words he's not allowed to say on the soap, as a former 1980s rock icon reduced to dealing drugs. Meanwhile Taylor, of Duran Duran fame, makes his acting debut as another former legend of the mike, now short of a record deal and lumbered with a frustrated wife and a recently arrived angry kid whom he is said to have fathered. Also features Rosanna Arquette, Ally Sheedy and Michael DesBarres.

5 Hammer House of Horror: Vols 3 and 4 ★★★

Carlton, 15, 150/200 mins, 1980; £10.99 (VHS)

This television nostalgia classic may soothe those who long for a bit of good old-fashioned gothic. They were produced by the immortal Roy Skeggs, who worked on the original Hammer films, which became so renowned in the 1960s and 1970s that the name was franchised out for this series. It was famous for its theme tune, bad scripts, improbable manor-house settings, classic horror plot lines and obsession with car accidents. It also featured the likes of Denholm Elliot, Diana Dors, Pierce Brosnan and Julia Foster in performances that will not be written on their gravestones. Great fun, though.

19 Feeding the mind

Exam spot

Although you do not have to give a talk in the CAE exam, you do have to understand a monologue in the Listening test (Paper 4). You also have to organise your ideas in the Writing test (Paper 2) in ways that are similar to organising a well-structured talk.

Speaking 1

1   Look at the pictures above and discuss these questions with a partner.

   a How often do you eat out? Where do you like to go? Why do you like it there? Who do you usually go with? What are the advantages and disadvantages of eating out compared to eating at home?

   b Would you ever take a photograph of this kind? Would you choose either a photo or a painting of a still life for your wall?

   c How many ways can you think of in which science has affected food production?

Reading

1   Look at the pictures with the three texts opposite. Work with a partner. Take it in turns to give a sentence describing one of the pictures. Then do the same thing with the other two pictures.

2   Skim the three texts. One relates to each of the three discussion topics in Speaking 1. Which text goes with which topic?

3   Now read the texts more carefully. Which of the three texts does each of these titles best fit?

   a The influence of social background
   b Time flies
   c Inspired by nature

1

Frequent eating out in commercial premises is associated positively with having high household income, being highly educated, being younger, and being single, and negatively with being a housewife. Significantly, the same factors also operate, and even more strongly, in one sector of the communal mode, eating with friends. People with greater economic and cultural capital are most frequently invited to be a guest in someone else's home, while such characteristics are much less important in respect of kin. Happily, you don't have to be rich for mum to cook for you! Since there is a statistical association between restaurant going and entertaining, it is possible that the expansion of the former has encouraged the latter and even extended the habit of entertaining to a wider population than previously.

2

The first person to examine whether freezing food might delay its deterioration died in the process. In March 1626, Francis Bacon, lawyer, Member of Parliament, wit and philosopher, was passing Highgate in north London. Observing the snow outside his carriage he wondered whether snow might delay the putrefaction of living tissue. He stopped his carriage immediately, bought a hen, and, with his own hands, stuffed it with snow. But he was seized with a sudden chill which turned to bronchitis, and he died at the Earl of Arundel's house nearby on April 9th.

Some three centuries later, Clarence Birdseye, an American businessman, developed Bacon's speculation into a process for freezing food in small packages suitable for retailing. In 1912 and 1916, Birdseye travelled to Labrador in north-east Canada to trade fur. He noticed the natives froze food in winter because of the shortage of fresh food. The combination of ice, wind and temperature almost instantly froze fresh fish straight through. When the fish were cooked and eaten, they were scarcely different in taste and texture than they would have been if fresh. Birdseye, a former government naturalist, realised the fish froze too quickly for ice crystals to form and ruin their cellular structure. In 1924 he founded the General Seafoods Company, having patented a system that packed fish, meat or vegetables into waxed-cardboard cartons, that were flash frozen between two metal plates, under high pressure. His invention significantly changed eating habits.

3

This week's picture, *The Painter's Daughters Chasing a Butterfly*, is a loving depiction of carefree youth and innocence but a faintly troubling picture too, charged with feelings deeper than sentimentality alone. The two girls holding hands are radiant in their silk dresses of silver and yellow, but we find them in a dark wood, under a stormy sky, with dusk approaching.

The day is short and childhood quickly passes: a common enough feeling for any parent to have, but Gainsborough has caught it with absolute precision and authenticity. With an attentive father's keenness of observation, the artist notes the difference made by even the small gap of age that separates the two girls. Mary has already developed a certain air of circumspection and self-consciousness, implicit in her careful gaze, her restrained posture and the nearly adult, upright carriage of her head. Looking across from her to the more impetuous, instinctive figure of her little sister, Margaret, whose arms and legs seem somehow less tense and organised, and whose face still has a certain toddlerish chubbiness about it, one might almost be looking at a single girl at different stages of her life.

Gainsborough has also conveyed his own ambiguous attitude towards his daughters' growing up, paternal pride mingled with the sense that each new stage in life, each new level of maturity attained, also marks a kind of small death, the loss of a little person no less loved. Margaret reaches out towards a butterfly, traditional symbol of life's fragility and brief duration, with an expression of little girl concentration which seems tinged with melancholy.

4 Write a sentence summarising each of the three extracts.

5 Answer these questions about the texts.

Text 1
a What kinds of people are most likely to eat out in restaurants?
b Who is most likely to eat at friends' houses?
c What kinds of people tend to eat in the homes of other family members?

Text 2
d What do Francis Bacon and Clarence Birdseye have in common?
e Why did Birdseye succeed where Bacon had not?
f Why is freezing a successful way of preserving food?

Text 3
g In what ways is Margaret different from her sister?
h What general theme can be drawn from the painting?
i Do you think this painting is basically happy or sad?

6 Which of these three texts do you find most interesting and why?

Vocabulary

1 Look at this extract from the Gainsborough text. What part of speech is required to fill each gap?

2 Write one word in each gap.

This week's picture, *The* (1) ....'s *Daughters Chasing a Butterfly*, is a loving depiction of carefree youth and innocence but a (2) .... troubling picture too, charged with feelings (3) .... than sentimentality alone. The day is short and (4) .... quickly passes: a common enough feeling for any parent to have, but Gainsborough has caught it with absolute (5) .... and authenticity. With an (6) .... father's keenness of observation, the artist notes the difference made by even the small gap of age that separates the two girls.	**PAINT** **FAINT** **DEEP** **CHILD** **PRECISE** **ATTEND**

3 Identify the missing part of speech in these sentences. Then fill the gap with an appropriate word formed from the word in brackets at the end of each sentence.

a Fruit and vegetables have been .... proven to provide some protection against cancer. (science)

b You get a wonderful feeling of the magnificent .... of the artist's vision in this exhibition. (broad)

c Although the investigation was time-consuming and costly, the results were .... and we still cannot be sure whether our basic hypothesis is correct. (conclude)

d Nothing is more pleasant than spending a .... evening at a good restaurant with close friends. (leisure)

e The research wanted to .... the relationship between social background and eating habits. (clear)

f Although his paintings reflect great peace and tranquillity, the artist himself is said to have had a very obstinate and .... character. (argue)

g Would you like another .... of roast potatoes, Charlie? (help)

h It is very important that food should not be prepared in .... conditions. (hygiene)

i This drink is lovely and .... Do try some. (vigour)

j It's a good idea to .... the freezer every few weeks. (frost)

⦿ Emphasising

Notice the use of inversion in these sentences.

Never in my life have I had such poor service!

Little did he imagine what his discovery would ultimately lead to!

On no account should you add more than a pinch of salt to the mixture!

1 What might someone say in the sentences below? Begin your suggestions with the words provided.

a Little did I ....
b Never in my life have I ....
c Not until I got to the airport ....
d No sooner had I ....
e So engrossed ....

2 Use inversion to make these sentences more emphatic.

a I've never in my whole life tasted anything so awful!

b Credit cards are not accepted under any circumstances.

c We didn't find out about his research until much later.

d We only realised what had happened when we arrived back at the lab.

e We not only lost our passports but also all our money.

f We'd hardly got there when the fire alarm went off.

g He has little idea of what's in store for him.

h I only learned her secret after her death.

3 You are writing about food and restaurants in your country. Complete these sentences in any way that might be appropriate.

EXAMPLE: On no account *should you leave our town without sampling the speciality of the region.*

a Little ....
b Never ....
c Hardly ....
d Only after ....
e Under no circumstances ....
f Not until ....
g Not only ....

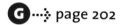 page 202

Listening

1 Listen to two talks in which people describe their favourite pictures.

2 What are the main points which each speaker is making?

Talk 1
a ....
b ....
c ....
d ....

Talk 2
a ....
b ....
c ....
d ....

3 Would you consider each of these a good talk in terms of content, delivery and use of language? Give reasons for your answers.

4 Prepare a brief talk on one of these subjects:

• eating out
• a favourite painting or photograph
• an influential scientific breakthrough.

5 Give your talk to other students in the class.

Speaking 2

1 Work in groups of four. Two students will act as Examiners and two will be candidates. Note that one of the Examiners simply listens while the other asks the questions and sets the tasks. After fifteen to twenty minutes you will change roles. The Examiners will become candidates and vice versa.

For Parts 1–4, your teacher will give the Examiner some instructions. Candidates should answer the Examiner's questions.

Here are the pictures for Part 2 of the test.

Here are some words for Part 3 of the test.

technology	transport	housing
education	health care	employment

Writing folder 8

Articles

1 With a partner, discuss what the differences are between articles and reports.
   Complete the following table. Some boxes have already been filled in to help you.

	Article	Report
Who it is usually written for	*a wide audience who you don't know and who will only read it if it catches their interest*	
What its aims usually are	*to interest, entertain or inform the readers*	
Any special characteristics of its layout		
Any special characteristics of its register		*unmarked or formal*
Any other special characteristics of its style		*must be absolutely clear and unambiguous in what it says; usually has a clear introduction presenting what it is going to say and usually comes to some distinct conclusion at the end*

2 Are the sentences below most likely to come from articles or reports?
   What are the clues in the sentences that make you choose your answers?

   a In conclusion, I would recommend that we go ahead with our plans for the event but that we take on board the suggestions made by the members of the public whose opinions we surveyed.

   b It was a beautiful balmy evening when the little boat chugged into the harbour and our holiday began in earnest.

   c Never in a million years would it have occurred to me to do what Janella then suggested.

   d The aim of the investigation was to ascertain local residents' attitudes towards the proposed developments.

   e Rowena (secretary, 25, from mid Wales) says that she would be quite 'cool' about the idea of going on a blind date although she admitted that she had never actually done so.

3 Remember that in Part 1 of the CAE Writing test (Paper 2) it is important to think about the content, language and register of your answers. You will lose marks if you do not write in a way that is appropriate to the genre or the target reader.

Look at this task.

You and ten other students from the college where you are studying English have just returned from an exchange programme where you spent a month at a school in London. You attended classes with the students and in the evenings did a variety of cultural activities. You lived with the families of the students at the school. You attended a debriefing meeting with the other students who went on the programme and made some notes on the feelings they expressed. You have now been asked to write an **article** about this for the magazine of the London school.

> _Journey_ all found it a bit tiring – any easier way to get there another time?
> _School_ great fun (though two or three found some lessons a bit boring and easy)
> _After-school activities_ varied (good theatre trips, e.g. to musical, fantastic end of month dinner in restaurant, interesting exhibition at National Gallery, cinema trips expensive and not very good, not much free time)
> _Accommodation_ some brilliant though two or three complaints – had to travel long way to school, very strict family, not enough food

First decide which bits of information provided in the notes would be appropriate to use in the article.

Now write your article for the magazine of the school in London, giving the students there your personal view of the exchange programme (180–220 words).

Exam spot

In the CAE Writing test (Paper 2) you may also be asked to write a contribution to a longer article or some other longer text. The style used for a contribution to an article should be the same as the style you would use for writing a complete article.

Answers on a postcard

Genre	Competition entries
Topic	Mini sagas

E xam spot

You are sometimes asked to write a competition entry in the CAE Writing test (Paper 2). All this means is that you have to try to write in a particularly interesting and effective way (in order to win a prize, i.e. a good grade!).

Speaking

1 With a partner, discuss these questions.

   a Have you ever entered any competitions?

   b What did you have to do?

   c Have you or any of your friends or family ever won anything in a competition? If so, what did you or they win and what for?

2 Here are some common competition prizes. Put them in your order of preference.

3 Here are some popular types of competitions. What are they? Do you ever do this kind of competition?

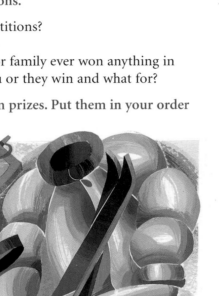

Reading

One popular competition was organised by a daily newspaper and invited readers to write a complete story in fifty words. These stories were called mini sagas.

1 Read these entries to the mini saga competition. Match the titles (1–5) with the sagas (A–E).

1 **Sophisticated management techniques are not always the panacea for a company's ills**

2 Like Mother, Like Son

3 **Perhaps there's something to be said for the three R's after all**

4 How To Deconstruct Everything You Were Taught in Your Creative Writing Class

5 Priorities

2 Find words and expressions in the mini sagas to match the meanings below.

Text A
a exceptionally good
b using words in a clever and humorous way
c a work of art

Text B
a conspiracy
b infection (colloquial)

Text C
a treat a weaker person in a cruel way
b try to keep cheerful

Text D
a improve
b bankrupt

Text E
a moulding
b thinking about something else

3 Discuss with a partner how you would summarise the point of each saga.

EXAMPLE: *Mini saga A: It is important to follow instructions.*

4 Discuss in small groups which story you would give the prize to. Give reasons for your choice. Compare your choice of winner with the choices of other groups.

A
At school he had been no good at maths but outstanding at writing and reading. But who needs arithmetic? He entered the competition with enthusiasm and produced a dazzling, witty, profound and paradoxical story. He was inspired. It was an absolute masterpiece. The judges sighed. Another one with 51 words.

B
The King died. A statement. Then the Queen died. A storyline. She died of grief. A plot? Or was it grief? A murder mystery. Then the Prince died, and the Princess, and the Princess's puppydog. All had been poisoned by an E Coli bug in the Royal Beefburgers. A mistake.

C
1955

Dear Mummy,
I hate this boarding school. Food awful, prefects bully me. Please take me home.
Love,
David

Dear David,
Nonsense. Chin up.
Mother

1997

Dear David,
I hate this home. Food awful. Nurses treat me like a child. Fetch me immediately.
Mother

Dear Mother,
Nonsense. Chin up.
David

D
The company was performing badly and morale was low. The board restructured the management and introduced a performance and appraisal system. They established multi-functional system-based audit teams, and people and quality initiatives. Structured systems analysis and design methodology were used to enhance information technology projects. The company went bust.

E
Intently, I crafted my fifty words. I carried them with me as I would a ball of plasticine in my pocket, shaping and squeezing them. Distracted, I ignored you when you called me.
Later, I brought them proudly to you, finished.
You'd left a note: 'Three words would have done'.

⊙ Vocabulary

In mini saga C we see the idiom *Chin up!*, which means *Try to keep cheerful!* There are many idioms in English based on parts of the body.

1 Complete the sentences (a–h) below, then match the cartoons (1–8) with the sentences.

a Jack is bound to know who we should ask about the matter – he's got a .... in every pie.

b Working with such a bright team of people certainly keeps me on my ....

c He's set his .... on becoming a ballet dancer.

d I'll give you a ....

e Do tell me what happened last night. I'm all ....

f She hasn't a clue what's going on. She's always got her .... in the clouds.

g Put your .... up for an hour or so and then you'll feel refreshed for the evening.

h Try and catch the waiter's ....

2 Here are some more idioms connected with parts of the body. Match each idiom (a–h) to its definition (1–8).

a to bite your tongue
b to be down in the mouth
c to keep your fingers crossed
d to be tearing your hair out
e to rack your brains
f to put someone's mind at rest
g to break someone's heart
h to fall head over heels in love

1 to be very anxious or upset about something
2 to make someone stop worrying
3 to make someone who loves you very sad
4 to hope things will happen the way you want them to
5 to stop yourself from saying something you want to say
6 to start to love someone passionately
7 to feel miserable
8 to think very hard

3 Choose one of the idioms from Vocabulary 1 and 2 to fill each of the gaps in the text below. Make any changes to the verb form that are necessary.

> As soon as John met Amanda, he
> (1) .... with her. They
> got to know each other when John
> noticed her loaded down with shopping
> and offered (2) ....
> Amanda is a bit of a dreamer and
> her mother always says she
> (3) .... Nevertheless,
> she has a very good position as an
> MP's Personal Assistant and she
> (4) .... on getting a job
> in the Prime Minister's office. She says
> that having to cope with the demands of
> life in politics (5) ....
> Amanda talks a lot about her job and at
> first John (6) ....
> But now he has to (7) ....
> to stop himself from telling her how
> bored he is with hearing about everything
> 'her' MP says or does. Today when
> I bumped into him in town, John
> (8) .... because
> Amanda had decided to go to a
> conference with her MP rather than on
> the holiday they had planned together. 'She
> (9) ....,' John said. 'I'm
> sure she likes her MP more than she
> likes me.' I (10) .... but
> I couldn't think of anything that would
> (11) .... All I could do
> was promise (12) ....
> for him.

☉ Hypothesising

Ⓔxam spot

The competition entries that you may have to write in the CAE Writing test (Paper 2) often involve an element of hypothesising. This language is, of course, also useful in a range of other situations.

Here is some language that is useful for hypothesising.

A	C
I wonder whether … *Suppose …* *What if …* *Just imagine …* *If only …*	*If I may speculate for a moment, …* *Speculating for a moment, …* *Let us take a hypothetical case: …* *On the assumption that …* *Provided (that) …* *Allowing for the fact that …* *Given (that) …*

B
Let us imagine … *Let us consider …* *Let us suppose …* *Let us assume …* *If we were to …* *Were we to …* *If we had …* *Had we …*

1 🎧 Listen to a dialogue in which two people, who were students together ten years ago, meet up. They are speculating about one of their classmates. Tick any of the expressions from box A that you hear.

2 Rewrite these sentences in which a head teacher is discussing, at a formal meeting, the benefits of employing a new deputy head.

  1 If we appointed a new deputy head, that would allow me to spend a lot more time in the classroom.
    a If we were to ....
    b Were we to ....

  2 Having more time in the classroom would give me more of a finger on the pulse of school life.
    a If I had ....
    b Had I ....

  3 I'd like you to think about how a deputy would use his or her time.
    a Let us imagine ....
    b Let us consider ....

  4 It is probably the case that a deputy would take over a lot of the day-to-day running of the school.
    a Let us suppose ....
    b Let us assume ....

3 🎧 Listen to a speech in which a politician is arguing for the introduction of a new law. What is he arguing for and what points does he make?

4 Now complete the sentences as if you were a politician discussing the introduction of any different law of your choice.

  a If I may speculate for a moment, …
  b Speculating for a moment, …
  c Let us take a hypothetical case: …
  d On the assumption that …
  e Provided (that) …
  f Allowing for the fact that …
  g Given (that) …

Ⓖ ⋯⫶ page 202

Listening

1 Here are the titles of three other mini sagas.

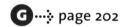
How Success Can Go to One's Head

A Moment in Venice

August When the Statue in Her Garden Gives Her Most Pleasure

Work with a partner to speculate about what each of the sagas might be about.

2 🎧 Listen to the mini sagas. Which title and which picture goes with which mini saga?

Units 16–20 Revision

Topic review

a What is the best film you have ever seen?

b Do you prefer to read reviews in a newspaper or a magazine or to trust your friends' opinions?

c Could you ever be persuaded to do a bungee jump?

d Would you employ someone with purple hair?

e Do you ever pretend to understand English when you really haven't?

f Someone who says they always tell the truth is a liar. Do you agree?

g Which country (apart from your own) has the best food?

h What do you prefer: home cooking or eating in restaurants?

i What would you do if you won a lot of money?

j Imagine you could choose between two prizes: a luxury holiday in the sun or two tickets to the World Cup football final. Which would you choose?

Writing

1 Insert all the necessary punctuation and capital letters into this paragraph.

Little lies, big mistake

1 now be honest most of us in the course of our working day tell the odd little fib we

2 may pretend weve nearly finished something when weve barely started it or say

3 someone is in a meeting when they dont want to take the call but its very easy for

4 white lies to turn into something more serious and the assumption that little

5 porkies are a necessary part of a secretarys role is a dangerous one most

6 secretaries and pas are used to telling white lies for the boss says ros taylor

7 business psychologist and author of the key to the boardroom if he asks you to

8 do something that is slightly more dishonest the easy thing is to assume that its

9 ok that he wouldnt ask you to do something illegal unfortunately that isnt always

10 the case last month a pa to a chief executive who was being tried for fraud

11 admitted in court that she had faked documents to smooth the passage of a huge

12 deal she argued that lying was standard practice in the city and that she was

13 simply trying to protect her boss but must secretaries sign up to a culture of

14 dishonesty what happens if you want to tell the truth ive done things that i know

15 are dishonest says kate matheson pa to the director of a large property company

16 its easy to feign ignorance ive shredded things that deep down i know should be

17 kept and been asked to change figures on documents that if i really thought

18 about it id know shouldnt be changed but my boss is top dog in a huge

19 organisation and im not about to say no to him ive always assumed that since im

20 doing what im asked it couldnt get me into trouble

21 this is a common misconception the fact is that any untruth even a seemingly

22 harmless white lie can lead to trouble and the best policy is to try to avoid

23 dishonesty from the start because ive done the odd thing that is a bit

24 questionable in the past its even more difficult to say no now says kate matheson

25 my boss can say oh well you did it last time what can I say to that

Grammar

1 Fill in each of the gaps in the text with one word. The first one has been done for you as an example.

Art's old masters draw the queues

It is enough (0) ......to...... make a pickled shark weep. In the new millennium, with contemporary art universally touted as the new rock'n'roll, a huge international survey shows that people may (1) .... know much about art, but they know (2) .... they like: old pictures.

The National Gallery director, Neil MacGregor, who emerged from the survey as organiser of (3) .... of the world's most popular exhibitions, saw no contradiction. "Old master paintings speak powerfully (4) .... a contemporary audience," he said yesterday.

In a survey by *The Art Newspaper*, in city after city, from Melbourne to Athens, from London to New York, the pattern was (5) .... same: the exhibitions people queued (6) .... the block to see were of old masters or of long dead craftsmen. The nearest to a contemporary artist in the international top 10 is Picasso.

Seeing Salvation is the most startling statistic from the survey. This exhibition, at the National Gallery, was not (7) .... by far the most popular exhibition in Britain, with more than 5,000 visitors a day, it was the fourth (8) .... popular in the world.

It was sponsored by a charity and admission (9) .... free. Within a day staff knew they had a phenomenon. People were queuing for hours to get in, moving (10) .... a snail's pace because visitors spent so (11) .... studying the works.

Mr MacGregor said "*Seeing Salvation* investigated (12) .... theme that has shaped western art through the centuries. This historical approach to familiar material clearly captured the public's imagination."

Reading

1   Choose which of the paragraphs (A–G) fill the numbered gaps (1–6) in the newspaper article below. There is one extra paragraph which you do not need to use.

Is honesty the best policy?

Lying is bad for your health, according to an American psychotherapist. But telling the truth is tricky, says Thea Jourdan.

'Does my bum look big in this?' said my friend. It had to happen. The question I had been dreading for the past few hours needed an answer. As she looked at me inquiringly, turning this way and that in an aquamarine micro-mini at least one size too small for her, I mentally steeled myself before replying in a whisper. 'Yes, I'm afraid it does.' Hopes for a jolly afternoon's shopping fell, along with her face. So much for telling the truth.

1 ☐

'We all lie like hell. It wears us out. It is the major source of all human stress,' says Brad Blanton, psychotherapist and founder of the Centre for Radical Honesty. The best-selling author of *Practising Radical Honesty: How to Complete the Past, Live in the Present and Build the Future with a Little Help from Your Friends* has become a household name in the States, where he spreads his message via day-time television talk shows.

2 ☐

Well, fibbing may be murderous, but honesty started becoming inconvenient for me just after breakfast, when I needed change for a parking meter. The cashier in the corner shop looked at my £10 note with a jaundiced eye. Did I really want the gobstopper or was I after change for the parking, he wondered? If so, the shop always had a policy of refusal. On a normal day, I would have lied. Traffic wardens in these parts show no mercy. Instead, I admitted everything and was shown the door, change-less.

3 ☐

The alternative, he believes, is the stress of living 'in the prison of the mind', which results in depression and ill health. 'Your body stays tied up in knots and is susceptible to illness,' he says. Allergies, high blood pressure and insomnia are all exacerbated by lying. Good relationship skills, parenting skills and management skills are also dependent on telling the truth.

4 ☐

'I have always believed that honesty is the best policy. Obviously, there are moral and ethical values in business. If you want to make deals, you have to have trust.'

5 ☐

Richard Wiseman, a psychologist at the University of Hertfordshire, says that lies can protect people as well as harm them. He is also certain that people will continue to tell them because human beings follow the law of survival of the fittest. 'I suspect Dr Blanton has devised an unstable strategy. If we all told the truth all the time, it would be fine, but the advantage would then go to the few who were prepared to lie.'

6 ☐

A   Dr Blanton, who lives in Virginia with his wife and two children, is adamant that minor inconveniences are nothing compared with the huge benefits of truth telling. 'Telling the truth, after hiding it for a long time, reopens old wounds that didn't heal properly. It hurts a lot. It takes guts. It isn't easy. But it is better than the alternative.'

B   Radical honesty therapy, as it is known in America, is the latest thing to be held up as the key to happiness and success. It involves telling the truth all the time, with no exceptions for hurt feelings. But, as I found out, this is not as easy as it might sound. Altruistic lies, rather than the conniving, self-aggrandising variety, are an essential part of polite society.

C   People who tell lies get so confused about what they have said to whom that they can sometimes get to the point where they no longer know what the truth is. This is very bad for their physical as well as their mental health and is one reason for the stomach complaints and headaches frequently reported by frequent liars.

D   By the end of my day of telling nothing but the truth, I definitely regretted my honest approach. Forget personal gain. My big-bottomed ex-friend decided to tell some home truths of her own. I still haven't quite recovered.

E   Honesty, according to Dr Blanton, brings many rewards, not least in business – and perhaps he is right. Gifi Fields, chief executive of Coppernob Communications, who has made tens of millions of pounds in a long career, insists that his own integrity has helped him succeed.

F   On the other hand, Anne McKevitt, an interior designer and television presenter, is happy to admit to frequent fibbing. She points out that the truth can sometimes be too painful. 'I think white lies are good,' she says. 'I tell them all the time.'

G   He certainly has his work cut out for him. In a recent survey of Americans, 93 per cent admitted to lying 'regularly and habitually' in the workplace. Dr Blanton is typically blunt about the consequences of being deceitful. 'Lying kills people,' he says.

Genre	Travel writing
Topic	Trips and travel

Speaking

1 With a partner, discuss these questions.

a Have you ever been on a holiday like the ones in the photographs? Did you enjoy it? Why?/Why not?

b What sorts of people might prefer a package holiday?

c What are the advantages and disadvantages of having a backpacking holiday?

d Would you agree that a holiday in a mobile home satisfies people's desire for freedom? Why?/Why not?

e Which is the most exciting part of travelling for you: the preparation before you go, the excitement of first arriving in a place or getting to know somewhere new?

f What is the strangest, funniest, best or worst thing that has happened to you while travelling?

Listening

1 You are going to hear three people talking about their travel experiences. Before you listen, look at the three pictures (a–c). What do you think each story is going to be about? Think of five words you are likely to hear for each picture.

2 🎧 Listen to the speakers, Alan, Simone and Mick, and number the words in the order they occur in the story. The first one has been done for you as an example.

Picture a: Alan

a France .... `1`
b an attendant .... ☐
c there's a strike .... ☐
d free vouchers .... ☐
e the train stopped .... ☐
f about twenty passengers ... ☐
g stuck at this platform ..... ☐

Picture b: Simone

a north of Queensland .... `1`
b big billboard .... ☐
c the beach was fantastic .... ☐
d start running .... ☐
e a river that cut off our side of the beach ☐
f a short cut .... ☐
g go for a walk .... ☐

Picture c: Mick

a in Greece for three years ... `1`
b they got the wrong pages .... ☐
c someone who spoke English ... ☐
d a phrase book .... ☐
e completely mad .... ☐
f start laughing .... ☐
g really cheap .... ☐

3 🎧 Listen again and complete the tapescript opposite.

4 Look at the words and phrases you used to complete the tapescript. Are they fillers, linking devices, words that show feeling or examples of direct speech?

5 Why do people use fillers when they speak? Which fillers do you use when you speak in English? Which fillers do you use in your own language?

6 Write down five nouns relating to your last holiday or the last time you travelled. Now add an interesting adjective to each noun.

7 What other techniques do people use when telling stories to make them more interesting or dramatic?

8 Tell your partner about the last time you travelled. Make your story interesting.

So we start walking through this river and you know, I'm thinking, it's only going to go up to my knees so it'll be OK. We get to the middle and it's up to our waist. And (1) ...., I'm thinking this was (2) ...., you know. (3) .... we'll walk nice and slowly, we'll get to the other side and we'll just have to sit in wet, wet clothes for about twelve hours while we're travelling south on the bus. (4) ...., what happened was, (5) ...., we got about half way through and suddenly my husband goes, 'Quick! Run!' And I said, (6) '.........................' And he said, 'Just run, just run'. So we start running and the water is literally in waves over our head and you know, we get to the other side, and I'm standing there with water dripping off my hair and everything is drenched at this point, and I'm going, er, 'And (7) ....' And he goes, 'Well, I just had a really bad feeling'.

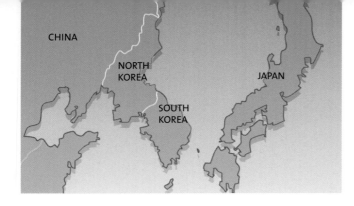

Reading

1 Read these extracts from an account of a trip
   around the Pacific Rim. Extract 1 describes arriving
   in South Korea by ship from Japan and Extract 2
   describes arriving at a hotel. Choose the best
   answer, A, B, C or D for the questions which follow.

Hakata to Pusan

Extract 1

Day 46 Pitch darkness. Rudely awoken by a thunderous rumbling roar
which sounds as though the ship is being disembowelled beneath me.
It's the anchor going down which means we must already have covered
the 140 miles of the Korea Strait to Pusan.

Dawn: Our ferry, the *Camelia*, stands off the rocky undulating coast
of South Korea, one of the queue of vessels waiting to pierce the hazy
brown veil of pollution that all but obscures the country's second
largest city. Several passengers are up on the deck exercising. I'm going
through my travel documents in an anxious pre-Customs and
Immigration way, ticking boxes to aver that I am not carrying 'guns,
knives, gunpowder, drugs, psychotropic substances or any items
harmful to the national constitution, public security or morals'.
(I always wonder what sort of person answers 'yes' to a question
like that.)

With a mournful blast of the horn, our ship moves slowly towards
the dockside. It's only 7.30 am. But South Korea is already at work,
making itself bigger. Cranes are swinging and concrete is pouring into a
vast land-reclamation project. Shoreline highways are choked with
morning traffic and a powerful array of multi-storey blocks bear
familiar names – Daewoo, Samsung, Hyundai.

Extract 2

The bus deposits us at the town of Kyongju, 55 miles north of Pusan.
At my hotel personal cleanliness is tackled with a vengeance. An
enormous communal bathing area offers just about everything you
might want to do with water. There are showers enough for a small
army; a hot tub and a semi-hot tub, a cold tub with high-pressure
waterfall simulator, several jacuzzis, a ginseng-flavoured steam room
and two capacious saunas. This palace of hydrophilia is filled with the
soft, the soothing sound of sloshing and scrubbing, spraying and
gurgling, swilling, slapping and lathering.

---

1 How does the writer feel as he prepares to get off
   the ship?
   A terrified by strange noises
   B irritated by the delays
   C nervous about formalities
   D suspicious of other passengers
2 What does the writer think about Pusan?
   A It is difficult to understand why it was built in
      a rocky area.
   B It has all the signs of a rapidly developing city.
   C He cannot identify with any aspect of the city.
   D He is surprised at the old-fashioned methods of
      working.
3 The writer's overwhelming impression of the hotel
   is one of
   A obsessive hygiene.
   B overcrowded facilities.
   C confusing traditions.
   D relaxing luxury.

Vocabulary

1 The words in italics in the sentences below come from
   Extract 2. They are all connected with water in some way.
   Match the words (in 1–7) with their definitions (a–g).

1 When you go round a corner, you can hear the
   petrol *sloshing* about in the tank.
2 He *scrubbed* the old saucepan clean and it looked
   as good as new.
3 Can you feel the *spray* from the garden hose?
4 The water went down the plughole with a loud *gurgle*.
5 The dentist handed me a glass of water to *swill* my
   mouth out with.
6 We could hear the *slap* of the waves against the side
   of the boat.
7 Most soaps won't *lather* in sea water.

a a liquid forced out of a special container under
   pressure so that it becomes a cloud-like mass of
   small liquid drops
b produce a pale mass of small bubbles when soap
   is mixed with water
c moving around noisily in the bottom of a container
   or causing a liquid to move around in this way by
   making rough movements
d flow around or over something, often in order to clean it
e flow with a low, uneven noise
f rubbed something hard in order to clean it, especially
   using a stiff brush, soap and water
g a noise made by quickly hitting something with a flat
   object

V ocabulary spot

Look carefully at the endings of words. Try to recognise patterns which tell you if a word could be an adjective, an adverb, a verb or a noun. For example, a word ending in *-ic* is usually an adjective, *-ly* an adverb, *-ise* a verb, *-age* a noun.

2   You are going to complete the text using the words provided in the box below. There is one extra word which is not needed. First read the text and decide which type of word goes in each gap.

My holiday

I was brought up in a little fishing (0) ....village.... so we didn't really have holidays as kids. The place was so (1) .... that the whole summer was like a holiday. We had a lot of (2) .... and we even had our own (3) .... boat. We used to go out in it for hours. I used to just sit in it and read books.

I find now that for my holidays I always (4) .... towards the sea, and I've realised that unless I can see the sea, I don't feel that I'm on holiday. Of all the places I've been to, I think India is the most (5) .... stimulating. Every little town we went through there was this (6) .... of colour – even the clothes hanging on the washing lines had an extraordinary (7) .... quality to them. I'd never been anywhere like it before. At the end of my holiday in India, we splurged out on an amazing hotel; it was like a (8) .... I love staying in interesting places when I travel.

3   Now look at the endings of these words and decide which are the adjectives, the adverbs, the nouns and the verbs.

aesthetic	fairy tale	freedom
gorgeous	gravitate	ocean
riot	rowing	visually

4   Now fill the gaps with the correct word.

Range of grammatical structures

E xam spot

In the CAE exam, you are expected to produce a range of structures when writing and speaking. This does not only mean a range of tenses but also the use of the passive form, modal verbs, gerund and infinitive and complex sentences.

1   Look again at the text in Vocabulary 2 and underline the different tenses and grammatical structures.

2   Complete this extract by putting the verbs (1–15) in an appropriate form.

Looking back on it now, it seems like a dream – my year off after university travelling the world. The best bit (0) ......was...... (be) definitely Indonesia. Intuition (1) .... (tell) me even before I left rainy England that Indonesia was where something special (2) .... (happen). A friend of mine (3) .... (cycle) through China with paintbrushes and a sketch pad and we (4) .... (arrange) to meet in Bali. We (5) .... (lie) on the beach for a day and then decided that what we (6) .... (need) was more of a cross-Indonesia adventure. So we (7) .... (set) off for the idyllic island of Lombok. And it was there that I (8) .... (see) him. He (9) .... (sit) with his back to me under the shade of a palm tree, (10) .... (look) out to sea. He (11) .... (turn) and (12) .... (smile), which at once (13) .... (render) me incapable of even (14) .... (think) of moving on to another island. And that is how I (15) .... (come) to stay for six months in the one place!

3   Incorporating one of the sentences below, write a paragraph which demonstrates a range of structures and a range of descriptive vocabulary.

- *But for the mosquitoes, it would have been pleasant to be perched on a wobbly wooden platform in an oak forest in …*
- *This is my first summit – but it seems I have made one glaring error. I have forgotten to bring the champagne.*
- *Our guide assures me we are lucky with the weather as at this time of the year we could just as easily be swirled in fog or soaked by rain.*
- *The following morning we were anxious to immerse ourselves as quickly as possible in the wonderful atmosphere of the city.*
- *Across the other side of the lake, an unmade, stony road runs along a gorgeous stretch of unspoilt coastline that reminds me of …*

4   Work with a partner and exchange your paragraphs. Read your partner's paragraph and highlight the interesting structures and vocabulary.

5   With your partner, discuss any improvements that could be made to the paragraphs you have written.

G page 203

Exam folder 9

Paper 2 Parts 1 and 2

1 How much do you know about the CAE Writing test (Paper 2)? Answer these questions.

- ⓐ How many parts are there in the Writing test?
- ⓑ Which question is compulsory?
- ⓒ How many questions do you have to answer in total?
- ⓓ How long is the Writing test?
- ⓔ How many words do you have to write in total?
- ⓕ Do the questions carry equal marks?
- ⓖ What types of writing might you be asked to write (e.g. formal letters)?
- ⓗ What is the assessment focus in Part 1?
- ⓘ What is the assessment focus in Part 2?

Advice

- Remember that in Part 1, you may need to select points to be mentioned; there may be some information in the 'input' that you do not need to use. You have to choose the information which is appropriate to the question.
- Spend plenty of time reading the question carefully and highlighting the points which you need to include in your answer.
- Spend time planning your work.
- Think about who you are writing for and why you are writing.
- Think carefully about how to paragraph your work in an appropriate way. Too many paragraphs may be just as unsatisfactory as too few.
- Allow time to check what you have written – and check not only the language of your answer but also that you have dealt with all the necessary parts of the question.
- Write legibly and make corrections as tidily as possible.
- Put a line through any work that you do not want the examiner to read.
- Don't waste time writing out your answers and then rewriting them.
- Don't copy language directly from the question paper – try to reword it in your own way, if possible.
- Don't attempt the set text question unless you have read the book or seen the film mentioned in the question.

2 Read the exam writing task below.

While studying English, you are helping to organise an after-class 'English Club'. You have just received a letter from your English teacher enclosing an article from an international magazine about young people's attitudes to learning English.

Read the magazine article, the extract from the letter, and the English Club programme with the notes you have made on it. Then, using the information provided, prepare to write the **article**.

Learning English
Why can't it be fun?

Sadly, most people learn English by attending rather traditional courses where the English taught does not meet the requirements of modern living. In a recent survey we discovered that most young people would like to learn English in a communicative way. They want to be involved with the language through watching films in the original language, listening to music, reading authentic articles from newspapers and magazines and having lively debates on 'real' international issues. So why is no one offering English language learners this motivating way of studying?

... so I knew you'd be interested in reading this. I think it would be interesting for the magazine and its readers to hear about our English Club. I think an article from you, a student, would be much better than an article from me, a teacher. You could make it clear that not all English language learning is traditional and boring. You could make this point by mentioning just some of the activities on our English Club programme and how successful the club is.

ENGLISH CLUB

PROGRAMME FOR JANUARY – APRIL

January: Film Evening

Post-Christmas and New Year blues? What you need is a thrilling evening watching *What lies beneath*, the latest, scariest movie. Discussion review with refreshments afterwards.

A great success!

February: Top of the Pops

A music evening where you listen (with video) to the latest pop music and then vote for the top ten tracks. Dance to the number 1 hit at the end of the evening.

12 new members!

March: Regional Food of Britain

Yes, you might be amazed by this gourmet evening. Regional dishes prepared by Club members. And recipes to take home!

Truly amazing.

April: Film Festival

As you know, many groups have been working on their 3-minute films to present at this award winning evening. You will vote for the winner. The winner will receive five DVDs of the latest English language films.

Hollywood, look out!

Now write your **article** for the international magazine (180–220 words).

---

3 Choose **one** of the following writing tasks. Your answer should follow the instructions given exactly. Write 220–260 words.

A A guidebook called *Off the Beaten Track* is being produced. It gives information about interesting parts of towns or cities which are rarely discovered by tourists. You have been asked to write a contribution recommending a weekend break in your town or city for visitors who want to do something other than see the usual tourist sights. Your contribution should include information about:

- the area in general and why it is interesting for visitors
- the route visitors should take and the new things they will be able to see and do
- the best time of year to go.

Write your **contribution to the guidebook**.

B You see the following advertisement in your local paper.

International Summer Camp

For the 10th year running we are organising our very successful Summer Camp for young people aged between 8 and 16. We are looking for energetic, creative people to help our kids have fun. Do you have:

- an outgoing personality?
- an ability to get on with youngsters from all over the world?
- a knowledge of foreign languages, including English?
- a knowledge of sports or games suitable for youngsters?

Write your **letter of application** for this job. You do not need to include addresses.

C An international magazine has asked its readers to send in a review of two different English dictionaries. Write a review for the magazine in which you compare and contrast **two** different English dictionaries, commenting on the following points:

- the layout and organisation
- the grammatical detail and examples of words in sentences
- value for money.

Write your **review**.

D Your English teacher has asked you to write an essay on either of the set texts, explaining why you feel or do not feel it is an appropriate book for English learners to study.

Write your **essay**.

Under the weather

Genre	Interpreting facts and figures
Topic	Climate change

Speaking 1

3 DAY FORECAST

TUE 80° WED 83° THU 8

Seasonal Affective Disorder –
connection with cosmic storms established
The mood of Alaskans may be related to cosmic
storms and the Northern lights, according to an
expert in the study of brainwaves. Depression in
the far north …

1   With a partner, discuss these questions.

   a What climatic area of the world do you live in?
   What are the features of this climate?
   b Do you think climate affects people's
   personalities? Give examples.
   c How is the local weather forecast presented on
   TV? Is the weather presenter glamorous/
   handsome or academic-looking?
   d What would be your idea of a perfect climate?

Reading

1   Have you ever experienced weather conditions
   similar to the ones in the photos?

2   Look at the diagram below. What does it tell us?

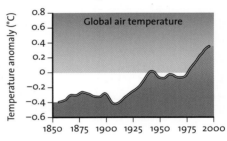

3   Read the magazine article opposite and discuss the
   questions below.

   a Would you say this newspaper article is mainly
   reporting fact, opinion or a mixture of both?
   b How many people or groups, apart from the
   journalist, are represented in the article?
   c What do they add to the basic statement that
   global warming exists?

4   Read through the article again and note down the
   words/phrases people use to express how sure they
   are that something is happening or will happen.
   Put *VS* for *very sure*, *QS* for *quite sure* and *NSS* for
   not so sure.

IPCC	could increase ... if	NSS
Dr Wainwright	have discovered seem to be adding	S NSS
Mark Gibson		

It's not if, its when

The world's scientists have given their starkest warning yet that a failure to cut greenhouse gas emissions will bring devastating climate change within a few decades. As droughts affect more areas for more prolonged periods, it is estimated that global food production will fall by 10%. Conversely, we are experiencing more powerful hurricanes which result in both human tragedy and costly damage to infrastructure. There are dire predictions of 80 million more people being exposed to malaria and 2.5 billion to dengue fever.

The 2007 report from the Intergovernmental Panel on Climate Change (IPCC) concludes that average temperatures could increase by as much as 6.4°C by the end of the century if emissions continue to rise at the present rate. However, they do concede that a rise of 4°C is more likely. The forecast is still higher than previous estimates because scientists have discovered that the Earth is less able to absorb carbon dioxide than previously believed.

What would a 4°C increase in temperature mean? According to the IPCC, it would wipe out hundreds of species, bring extreme food and water shortages in vulnerable countries and hundreds of millions of people would be displaced as a result of catastrophic flooding. As warming is likely to be more severe towards the poles, the melting of the Greenland and west Antarctic ice sheets would accelerate.

Dr Wainwright explained that the 2007 report painted a gloomier picture than the 2001 report because scientists have discovered 'feedbacks' in the global carbon cycle that seem to be adding to the amount of carbon dioxide in the atmosphere and producing a cumulative effect. She goes on to suggest that this could mean at least another 1°C should be added to present estimates. Moreover, Dr Wainwright concludes that there is little room for doubt that human activity is to blame for global warming.

However, Mark Gibson of Environment Watch goes to great lengths to point out that such an outcome is not inevitable. If there were a significant switch to clean and resource efficient technologies, we could cut expected temperature rises by half. He stresses that what is needed is international political commitment to take action – something which has been absent so far.

Vocabulary

1 Here are some more words related to the weather. Match a word from the list (a–i) with a word which collocates (1–9).

a	torrential	1	defences
b	high	2	freezing
c	ice	3	forecast
d	sea	4	gale
e	below	5	gusts
f	long-range	6	cap
g	squally	7	rain
h	ozone	8	tide
i	force nine	9	layer

2 Complete this weather report with some of the collocations from Vocabulary 1.

> It may be Easter in the UK but no one seems to have told the weather! The west coast is receiving a constant battering from a **(1)** .... which has ripped roofs from houses in Devon and Cornwall. What's more, this is bringing with it **(2)** .... which has caused flood alerts to be issued for some areas. This makes you really believe what they say about the **(3)** .... melting; floods seem to have been a much more common occurrence in the UK over the last year or so. Coastal areas are prone to flooding too as this spring sees **(4)** .... at record levels in the Severn estuary. In this area too **(5)** .... have been breached and waves rolled into town centres in some cases. As if all this wasn't enough, night temperatures have been **(6)** .... all week leaving gardeners bewildered as to what they should do with their spring plants.

Linking devices

A snapshot of the world's weather on 16th April					
Country	Argentina	Brazil	Greece	Japan	Sweden
City	Buenos Aires	Rio de Janeiro	Athens	Tokyo	Stockholm
Temperature	18°C	26°C	18°C	17°C	8°C
Humidity	84%	26%	53%	58%	38%
Wind speed	9 (NE)	4 (NE)	4 (NW)	4 (SW)	6 (SW)
Visibility	good	moderate	very good	n/a	n/a

When we interpret information in charts, graphs or statistics, we usually:

- make a general statement about the information
  This chart shows the main weather features of a number of cities on a particular day.

- comment on significant features of the information provided (often by comparing and contrasting data)
  It can be seen from this table that the warmest place was Rio de Janeiro whereas the coldest place was Stockholm.

- discuss the important features (often by providing examples or giving reasons)
  According to the information, visibility was very good in Athens; this is particularly important as there is often concern about the levels of pollution in large cities but, as we can see, this was not a problem in Athens.

- draw a conclusion.
  In conclusion, depending on your preferences, Rio de Janeiro or Athens might have been very pleasant places to spend that day.

> **E** xam spot
>
> You can adopt this strategy for the CAE Speaking test (Paper 5), where you have to compare and contrast pictures.

1   This text is about how the weather can affect your mood. Complete the text with linking devices from the box.

because   contrary to   however   on the other hand   whereas   indeed

On the one hand, some people say they feel dull and gloomy when the weather is grey. (1) .... others say they feel cosy and secure when they are inside on grey days, reading in front of the fire. (2) .... , it is true to say that higher levels of light do raise the spirits. You know yourself when you wake up and it's sunny, you feel brighter, (3) .... when you wake up and it's dull, you feel sluggish. Interestingly, recent research has shown that, (4) .... popular belief, people are more creative in colder climates. For example, more inventions have been made by people living in colder climates than in hotter ones. (5) .... , it could be that they stay at work longer (6) .... the weather is so awful outside!

2 Complete the words in the third column. They are all nouns which describe changes in quantity. The number of dashes tells you how many letters there are in the words. Indicate with an arrow if the change is upwards or downwards.

| There was/ has been a | minimal
slight
small
gradual
steady
marked
significant
steep
sharp
rapid
sudden | i _ _ _ _ _ _ _
r _ _ _
f _ _ _ _ _ _ _ _ _ _
d _ _ _ _ _ _ _
d _ _ _ _ _ _
r _ _ _ _ _ _ _ _
f _ _ _
d _ _ _ | in | temperature.
humidity.
rainfall.
hours of sunshine.
wind speed.
the number of storms.
the amount of damage.
night-time temperatures. |

3 These sentences all contain phrases for drawing conclusions. The words are jumbled up. Rewrite the sentences with the words in the correct order.

a conclusion the temperature over the couple in we world's has risen last of can say decades that significantly.

b whole weather experiencing the may are extreme conditions on be we more it said that.

c scientists following with interest increased are therefore concluded it that all changes climate be can.

d reduce the threat given that unless emissions is this be countries under climate carbon may deduced it.

G ⋯⋮ page 203

Listening

1 🎧 You will hear two friends, Tim and Wendy, giving their views on climate change. Listen and tick which aspects of climate change each speaker mentions.

Aspect of climate change	Tim	Wendy
El Niño		
Floods and droughts		
Global warming		
Greenhouse gas emissions		
Sea level		
Storms		

2 🎧 Listen again and make notes about each speaker's views.

3 Work with a partner and compare and contrast Tim and Wendy's views using linking devices where appropriate. Say whether you agree with them or not.

Speaking 2

1 Your teacher will give you some charts comparing daily life now and in the future. Your chart has some missing information.

Find out the missing information to complete your chart by asking your partner. As you do, discuss the information using linking devices. Make sure that you:

- make a general statement about the information
- comment on significant features of the information provided (by comparing and contrasting data)
- discuss the important features (by providing examples or giving reasons)
- draw a conclusion.

2 How do you think things will change in the future? Do you agree with the predictions in the chart?

Writing folder 9

Descriptive writing

1   Read the following CAE writing tasks and discuss whether there would be an element of description in your answer.

A You see the following announcement in an educational magazine.

Competition

The ideal school of the future
- What will the ideal school be like in 50 years' time?
- How will it be different from schools today?
- What subjects, technology and facilities will schools of the future have?

Write your **competition entry**.

B You have recently been to two music events and have been asked to write a review of these events for a music website. Your review should compare and contrast:
- the instruments and singers at each event
- the ability of the performers at each event
- the audiences' reactions.

You should also say which event you enjoyed more and why.

Write your **review**.

C You see the following announcement in an international students' magazine.

How to survive examination preparation

We would like our readers around the world to share their ideas and experiences.

Write an article suggesting how best to prepare for exams, and say what you should and should not do the night before the exam.

Write your **article**.

D Your department has recently asked for your offices to be refurbished. You have received the following memo from the Managing Director.

Re: your request for office refurbishment
I need more information before I can make a decision. Could you write me a report stating the problems with the present furniture, decoration and layout of the offices? Indicate how this refurbishment will improve working conditions and performance.

Write your **report**.

2   Here are some steps to go through when planning your answer to a writing task. Put them into a logical order. Write number 1 next to the first step and so on.

a think about sentence structure
b reorganise your brainstorming notes into a logical order
c think about the vocabulary
d write and edit the text
e think about your introduction
f think about your conclusion
g think about the reader
h read the question
i brainstorm the topic
j think about the layout, including the number of paragraphs

3 You are going to prepare a review in answer to question 1B.

   a Look back at question 1B and underline the key words.

   b Tell your partner about a music event you have been to (or seen on TV or in a film). What were your impressions of it?

   c Who is the intended reader of your description?
- a friend
- a music teacher
- people interested in music

   d What style of writing is appropriate?
- formal and factual
- lively and entertaining
- chatty

   e Brainstorm your topic again but this time complete the word webs as you go along.

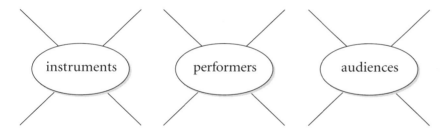

   f What are you going to include in each paragraph?

Introduction:

Conclusion:

   g Think about sentence structure. Which structures do you think you will be able to use in your description? Put ✓ next to the ones you are quite sure you will use, ? next to the ones you are not sure if you will use, and ✗ next to the ones you really don't think you will use.

- past simple
- past continuous
- past perfect
- past perfect continuous
- present perfect
- present perfect continuous
- present simple
- present continuous
- conditional forms
- passive forms
- gerunds
- infinitives
- relative clauses

   h Write your first draft. It is often useful to leave a generous margin and/or write on alternate lines so that you can make changes and corrections clearly.

   i Exchange your first draft with another student and edit their first draft using this code:

SP	spelling
X	unnecessary word
GR	grammar
WW	wrong word
P	punctuation
RW	repeated word
WO	word order

   j Write the final version of the task and check it again.

I'm afraid I really must insist

Speaking 1

1 Read these situations and discuss them with a partner. Choose A, B or C, whichever is closest to your opinion.

1 You are in a restaurant with a group of friends. The waiter is taking ages to come and take your order and now you've been waiting for 45 minutes. You are going to the cinema after your meal so you don't want to spend a long time waiting. The restaurant is very busy so you know it is not the waiter's fault. Do you

A walk out of the restaurant glaring at the waiter but saying nothing?
B go up to the head waiter and demand to see the manager?
C attract the waiter with your best smile, explain the situation and try to get what you want by being nice?

2 You paid a lot of money for a designer label T-shirt. The first time you washed it you followed the washing instructions carefully but still the colour ran and ruined some other clothes you washed it with. When it dried it was obvious it had shrunk. You think the material is of poor quality and does not represent the amount you paid for it. Do you

A throw it in the bin and vow never to go to that shop again?
B phone the shop and tell them that they are frauds and you're going to sue them?
C go back to the shop with your receipt and ask for your money back?

3 You went on a day trip to a beach with a tour company. The trip was advertised as using comfortable buses with experienced drivers. The trip took much longer than expected so you did not have much time at the beach. The coach was awful and the driver was reckless. Do you

A get a taxi back to your hotel and pay for it yourself?
B get a taxi back to your hotel and insist that the tour company pays for it and gives you £300 as compensation?
C mention to the driver that you are a nervous passenger and explain to the tour company why you are dissatisfied when you get back?

2 With a partner, discuss these questions about complaining.

a What sort of complainer are you? Do you just moan to your friends or do you complain calmly to the shop or company concerned?
b Do you get angry when you have to complain about something?
c If you had to complain about something in English, what do you think might be the best way to do it: face-to-face, by phone or by letter? Why?

Reading

1 Imagine a visitor to your country wants to complain about something. What is the best way to do this?

2 You are going to read an article called *How to complain*. With a partner, make a list of the pieces of advice you expect to read.

EXAMPLE: *Do not complain when you are feeling angry.*

3 Read the article and match the headings (A–H) to the paragraphs (1–6). There are two headings which do not fit.

A Who will I complain to?
B How can I get my money back?
C How do I feel?
D What are the facts?
E What do I do if I don't get satisfaction?
F What are my rights?
G How will I complain most effectively?
H What do I want?

4 Choose three pieces of advice in the article which you consider the most important.

How to complain

Most people love to complain, but while moaning to friends is a national pastime, when it comes to protesting to a retailer, for example, we often prefer to suffer in silence about faulty goods or services.

When we do decide to make our point, we can become aggressive, gearing up for battle and turning what should be a rational negotiation into a conflict.

To complain effectively, you need to be clear in your communication, specific about your problem and how you want it solved, and objective in the words you choose to make your point. Good negotiators tend to be calm and logical. You should first ask yourself:

Was the product faulty or are you complaining about rude service or a delay? Sift out feelings from hard fact. This will help you to be concise and to the point.

What will it take to put the problem right? Most complaints become negotiation and it's important to know what you'll accept. Do you want your money back, or the product replaced? Or will an apology be sufficient?

If the complaint is a serious one, you need to go armed with your legal rights.

Have you ever begun to complain with the words: "I know this isn't your fault, but ..."? Spouting hot air to the wrong person is a waste of time and energy. Start off by finding out exactly who you should be speaking to, and who has the authority to handle your problem. Take the name of the person who deals with your complaint.

In person, by letter, or over the phone? If face-to-face isn't possible or you feel you lack confidence, a phone call may be easier. Start by explaining the situation and stating your requirement clearly, without threat. If you are not satisfied with the response, remind the other person about the agreement that's been broken.

Most complaints prompt an emotional response, but being reasonable is more likely to get the positive result you want. If you feel angry or upset about what has happened, go ahead and tell the company, but do it calmly. Demonstrate that you understand the situation from the other person's point of view. "I appreciate that it might be difficult to arrange a special delivery, but I really need the order by tomorrow." Do state clearly the consequences of your request being ignored. ("I'm going to place the order elsewhere and cancel my account with you"), but never make a threat that you can't carry out.

G ⋯⋗ page 204

Phrasal verbs

1 Look at these examples of two-part phrasal verbs from the article. What do they mean?

- *When we do decide to make our point, we can become aggressive, **gearing up** for battle and turning what should be a rational negotiation into a conflict.*
- ***Sift out** feelings from hard fact.*
- *Start off by **finding out** exactly who you should be speaking to, and who has the authority to handle your problem.*
- *If you feel angry or upset about what has happened, **go ahead** and tell the company, but do it calmly.*
- *… never make a threat that you can't **carry out**.*

2 Correct the sentences below if necessary.

EXAMPLE: *They refused to enter any discussion into about the matter.* ✗
They refused to enter into any discussion about the matter. ✓
(*to enter into* = to start to become involved in something, especially a discussion)

a Before you go to the shop to complain, jot down the points you want to make.
b I looked the guarantee through but I couldn't find out how long it was valid for.
c The engineer's explanations as to why it doesn't work just don't add up.
d I didn't expect a problem to crop up so soon after buying a new computer.
e We don't hold much hope out, but we are still trying to get compensation.
f Trying to get a satisfactory answer to my queries took the whole morning up.
g If you had taken out an extended guarantee, the cost of the repairs would have been covered.
h I didn't really want to spend so much on a TV but Frank talked me it into buying.

3 Read the note below all the way through first to get a general understanding of what it says. Then fill the gaps (1–8) using phrasal verbs from the box.

get on with	make out	pluck up	put across
sink in	stick up for	take to	turn out

Hi Sandy
You know I'd been having problems with my noisy neighbours? Well, last week I couldn't (0) ...put up with... the din any longer so I (1) .... courage and went and knocked on their door. They live in the flat above me and I hear their music day and night. During the day it's awful because I can't (2) .... my studies, I can't concentrate, and in the evenings when I want to relax, I can hardly (3) .... a word from my own TV, theirs is on so loud. Anyway, I thought I've got to (4) .... myself and go and face them. This woman came to the door and I tried to (5) .... what I wanted to say as calmly as I could. She listened and then said how glad she was that I'd come to her and explained that it's her teenage son who has his music on so loud. She said she'd told him it would disturb the neighbours and he'd said it obviously didn't as no one had complained. She explained that once I'd complained, she'd have ammunition to confront him with and it might (6) .... that he can't behave as though he lived on a desert island. Funnily enough, I really (7) .... her and she asked me in for a coffee. So after being afraid of going to see my neighbour, it (8) .... that I've made a new friend.

Listening

1 **You are going to listen to someone giving advice about how to ask their boss for a pay rise. Before you listen, discuss these questions with a partner.**

a What sort of person would your ideal boss be and why?

b What do you think is the strongest reason for asking for a pay rise?

c If your boss was rather 'difficult', how would you go about asking for a pay rise? Which of these suggestions might be useful?

- Make sure you make a formal appointment with him/her to discuss the matter.
- Wear more formal clothes to work for some time before you ask for a pay rise.
- Go into his/her office frequently and drop hints about how much work you are doing and how good it is.
- Make a list of all the reasons why you should have a pay rise.
- Tell your boss how much better you are than other employees.

Ⓔxam spot

In the CAE Listening test (Paper 4), you will be asked to complete a multiple-choice task like the one opposite. Read all the questions before you start listening so that you are prepared to choose the right answer. You hear the recording twice.

2 🎧 **Listen to the recording and choose the best answer (A, B, C or D) according to what you hear.**

1 The key factor when asking for a pay rise is
   A voicing your demands in a convincing way.
   B making it clear you feel undervalued.
   C proving you are an asset in the business.
   D comparing yourself to the rest of the staff.

2 If you have any failings, you should
   A check that no one knows about them.
   B put them right gradually so that it is not too obvious.
   C accentuate your strengths, such as punctuality.
   D make sure your boss likes you as a person.

3 When preparing what to say in your salary negotiation,
   A put yourself in your superior's shoes.
   B do not forget that you really need that extra money.
   C make a list of all the points in your favour.
   D focus on what you can do for the company in the future.

4 What should you do if your boss raises objections to your pay rise?
   A pre-empt them by raising them yourself and giving a counter argument
   B make sure you can quote company rules to him or her
   C appreciate that your boss is only doing his or her job
   D accept any offer as it is better than nothing

5 During salary negotiations, it is important to
   A mention that the company is very successful.
   B ensure your boss is aware that you are taking these negotiations seriously.
   C arrange to see your boss early in the day when he or she is fresh.
   D try not to put your boss in an awkward position.

6 What should you do if you do not get a pay rise or as much as you wanted?
   A be prepared for a long drawn-out conflict
   B know that you might have to resign as a matter of principle
   C either have an alternative or ask for constructive criticism
   D either get a colleague to back you up or talk to your boss again soon

Writing

E xam spot

In the CAE Writing test (Paper 2), you may be asked to write a letter of complaint or an article complaining about something. Read the situation carefully and make the purpose of your writing clear.

1 Read the writing task below and then discuss the questions which follow with a partner.

> You recently bought a piece of electronic equipment from a shop. After a very short time it began to go wrong so you took it back to the shop where they said they would have it repaired. You waited four weeks to get it back and when you did, you discovered that it had not been repaired at all. If anything, it was worse. You took it back to the shop again and they took it again for repair, you waited three weeks and when you got it back it still did not work properly. You are annoyed because you have not been able to use your purchase for about two months and the shop has done nothing to repair it. You decide the only solution is either to have a new one or get your money back. You decide to write a letter to the manager of the shop.

a Which pieces of advice in the article *How to complain* might be appropriate to this situation?

b Plan your letter. Think about:

- the number of paragraphs you need
- the main content of each paragraph
- some formal phrases suitable for your letter
- some grammatical structures suitable for your letter
- the overall organisation of your letter.

2 Write your letter in 220–260 words.

Speaking 2

E xam spot

In the CAE Speaking test (Paper 5), one of the things the examiner is listening for is your interactive communication.

1 Getting your views across is all part of being a good communicator. Below is a list of suggestions as to what makes a good communicator. Tick the suggestions which you think are important.

A good communicator is someone who:

- listens actively and responds logically
- always starts speaking first
- can paraphrase and reformulate what they want to say
- can explain precisely what they want to say
- only says what is necessary
- uses body language to emphasise what they want to say
- doesn't interrupt others when they are speaking
- helps other people to finish their sentences
- summarises periodically what they have said so far
- has a large vocabulary
- makes few grammatical errors.

E xam spot

In the CAE Speaking test (Paper 5), you are given an activity which you discuss with your partner. Then the examiner will ask you some more general questions which relate to the topic of the activity. You will need to show that you can get your views across.

2 Look at these items that a company might offer as compensation for faulty goods or unsatisfactory service. Discuss with a partner which ones you would be prepared to accept.

Exam folder 10

Paper 4 Part 2

1 How much do you know about the CAE Listening test (Paper 4)?
Answer the questions below.

> **a** How many parts are there in the Listening test?
>
> **b** How many times do you hear each part?
>
> **c** What sorts of tasks do you have to do (e.g. sentence completion)?
>
> **d** Where do you have to write your answers?
>
> **e** How many marks can you get for each question?
>
> **f** Do spellings have to be correct?
>
> **g** How long is the Listening test approximately?
>
> **h** What percentage of the whole CAE exam is the Listening test?

2 You are going to hear part of a radio programme about blue jeans.
Before you listen, discuss the questions below with a partner.

a Do you know when jeans were invented and by whom?

b What sort of clothes were they intended to be? When do you think they became popular among young people?

c Do you think jeans should be blue or do you like wearing other colours?

d Who wears them these days?

Advice

- Read the title to find out what the context is.
- Read the questions carefully before you listen.
- Try to predict what sort of word(s) is/are needed in the gap. For example, is it a noun?
- Try to predict the answer using your knowledge of the context and your logic.
- Write down the word(s) you hear.
- Remember that the answers are short – one to three words – and very often concrete nouns.
- Check your spelling.
- Make sure you have made a grammatically correct sentence.
- When you listen the second time, check carefully.
- Always try to write something, even if you're not 100% sure it's the correct answer.

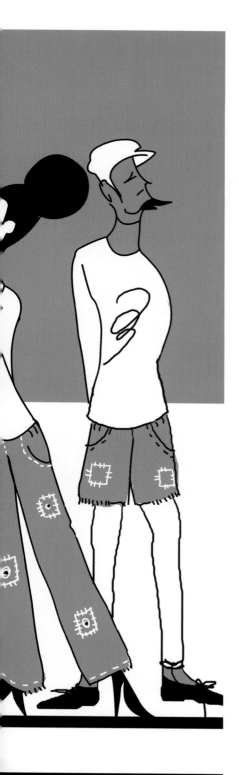

3 🎧 You are going to hear part of a radio programme about jeans. For questions 1–8, complete the sentences.

1 Young people in the 1950s started wearing jeans as a symbol of ....

2 As parents thought of jeans as .... , they disapproved of them being worn as 'going out' clothes.

3 Jeans became internationally popular because they are what the writer describes as .... , and they make everyone equal.

4 The .... of jeans and youth culture are in the United States.

5 Most jeans in Europe are imported from ....

6 Nowadays members of the establishment, for example ...., are seen wearing jeans.

7 You could still make an impact today if you wore jeans with .... to an elegant party.

4 Go through the Advice box and check all the points there.

5 🎧 Now listen to the recording again.

News and views

Genre	Investigative journalism
Topic	Stories in the news

Speaking

1 With a partner, discuss these questions.

   a How do you usually find out about the news?
   b What are the main purposes of broadcasting?
   c What do you think TV viewing will be like in the future?

2 What sorts of programmes do you think make ideal Saturday TV viewing? Work in small groups and match the types of programmes to the best times in the schedule.

Types of programmes

Sport   Chat show   Children's TV
Chart music show   Hospital drama
News and weather   Documentary
Lottery   Quiz show   Wildlife programme
Satirical comedy show   Film   Learning zone

TIMES OF SATURDAY'S PROGRAMMES

7.00 am
12.10 pm
12.15 pm
5.55 pm
6.50 pm
7.45 pm
8.55 pm
9.55 pm
10.15 pm
10.30 pm
11.40 pm

3 Form new groups and present your choice of schedule. Be prepared to support your choices with reasons.

E xam spot

In the CAE Listening test (Paper 4) you may be asked to listen to extracts from documentaries, news bulletins, sports reports or arts reviews. Watching television or listening to the radio will familiarise you with the style and language of these programmes.

Listening

1 🎧 You are going to hear the headlines from a world news broadcast. Listen and note down which news item in particular you would like to listen to.

2 🎧 Now listen to two short news items and complete the table.

	Where	Who	Topic
Item 1			
Item 2			

3 You will hear a broadcast called *Those who break the labour laws*. What do you think this story will be about?

4 🎧 Listen to the broadcast and answer the questions below.

a Is the problem of illegal employment confined to one country?

b What are the two types of illegal employment the journalist mentions?

c Give one reason why the employees do not complain.

d What sort of work is Janine doing?

e What happened when she said she might leave the job?

f Does the reporter think it is likely that she will go back to school?

5 Do you think that investigative journalism can actually improve conditions by exposing exploitation? Why?/Why not?

Vocabulary

A homophone is a word which has exactly the same pronunciation as another word but has a different spelling or meaning. For example, in Listening 3 you heard the word *steak*. *Stake* (which means *a thick strong stick or metal bar with a pointed end* or *a share or financial investment in something*) has the same pronunciation as *steak* but a different meaning and spelling. *Steak* (/steɪk/) and *stake* (/steɪk/) are therefore homophones.

Homophones are often used in newspaper headlines to catch the reader's attention.

1 What is the homophone for the underlined word in these headlines?

a
<u>RED</u> THE NEWS LATELY?
A new newspaper has decided to print not only pictures in colour but also text. *The Daily ...*

b
No <u>way</u>!
A health farm with a difference has recently opened. Guests are forbidden to jump on the scales and ...

c
WHO WOULD HAVE <u>GUESSED</u>?
Fellow visitors to a small seaside Bed and Breakfast were astonished to discover that Brad Pitt was booked in ...

d
<u>MALE</u> DELAYED
A woman who thought she was getting married to the man of her dreams had to wait ...

e
THE <u>HOLE</u> STORY!
A golfer who thought he had missed ...

f
A <u>minor</u>! But you're 55!
When Bert Smith filled out a form for the local government, his spelling got him into trouble ...

g
If bingeing on chocolate makes your trousers too tight, blame the <u>genes</u>
Chocoholics no longer need to feel guilty about their craving ...

2 Think of a homophone for the following words.

a won	e stairs	h where
b meet	f blue	i waste
c sell	g sail	j through
d so		

Reading

1 Newspaper headlines often proclaim a new scientific breakthrough or discovery. You are going to read an article about the 'sweet tooth gene'. Before reading, discuss these questions with a partner.

a Where do you get most of your information about new scientific discoveries from – newspapers, documentaries or your studies?

b Have you got a sweet tooth? Does this trait run in your family?

c If scientists could discover a sweet tooth gene, what could they do with this information?

2 Read the article and then decide if the following statements are true or false.

a Having a sweet tooth is an inherited trait.

b A drug has been developed which can put you off sweet food.

c The two teams of researchers used mice with the same DNA structure.

d The sweet tooth gene produces a protein.

e Aubrey Sheiham believes dieting is futile if you have the sweet tooth gene.

f It is natural for humans to be attracted to sweet foods.

g This discovery may lead to the production of a new type of chocolate.

3 What do you think about newspaper articles which herald new 'wonder discoveries'? Are you sceptical of them? Why?/Why not?

4 What scientific developments do you think we will see in the near future as a result of work on DNA?

IF BINGEING ON CHOCOLATE MAKES YOUR TROUSERS TOO TIGHT, BLAME THE GENES

CHOCOHOLICS no longer need to feel guilty about their craving. They are simply the victim of their genes, scientists have found.

The so-called 'sweet tooth gene' has been identified by separate teams of researchers and helps explain why some find it harder to resist chocolate bars and cream cakes.

It also raises the possibility of designing a drug which could 'switch off' the gene and help people resist sugary foods. Children, in particular, risk their health by eating too many sweets and chocolates.

To identify the gene, the research teams - based at Harvard Medical School in Boston and Mount Sinai School of Medicine in New York - conducted almost identical experiments using mice which have differences in their ability to taste sweet foods. They compared the DNA of the two types of mice and noticed differences in the gene called T1R3.

Dr. Gopi Shanker, of the Mount Sinai team, said: 'It contains information which produces a protein called the sweet taste receptor.

'This recognises the sweet content of food and initiates a cascade of events which signal to the brain that a sweet food has been eaten.' Dr. Shanker added: 'Exactly the same gene exists in humans, so it means that if your parents have a sweet tooth then you probably will as well.'

Research by the Harvard team has come to the same conclusion.

But Aubrey Sheiham, professor of dental public health at University College, London, said the results did not provide chocoholics with an excuse to give up dieting.

He said: 'We have always known that some people have a sweeter tooth than others. But it has also been proved that if you gradually expose people to less sugar, then the body becomes accustomed to less. They will be satisfied with a lower level of sweetness.'

Mr. Sheiham warned against any form of gene therapy which sought to deactivate the sweet tooth gene.

'We have produced this gene through evolution because sweet foods in nature are not poisonous and also give us energy. We all need to have some sugar in our diet.'

The U.S. researchers are using their discovery to develop artificial sweeteners without an aftertaste.

Linking devices

1 Fill the gaps (1–10) in the article below with the linking devices from the box. There are two linking devices which do not fit.

> and what's more as
> but because by then
> even despite
> provided resulted in
> so to cap it all then

30,000 runners take London in their stride

(0) ....No sooner.... had the gun sounded than we were all off, including me and my running flatmate, Fran, jostling for position (1) .... we crossed the starting line, which was awash with plastic bags, unwanted clothing, bottles and banana skins.

The real running began as Greenwich came into view and the crowds, which were already big, increased even further. People shouted at friends. Anyone with their name on their vest became public property (2) .... everyone wanted to be part of this event. Screams of encouragement mixed with brass bands and Beatles tribute bands.

The 12-mile point. I must have lived this part at least a dozen times from my armchair. I could hear a commentator murmuring about how plucky we all were.

(3) .... the halfway mark was within reach and it was getting tiring. Tower Bridge loomed, magnificent, with thousands of people screeching encouragement.

I knew what was coming. At 13 miles out I saw a small flag fluttering and annoying someone's ear and then the words: "There he is." My parents had spotted me. I stopped for a chat, and went on my way. (4) .... someone was watching after all.

(5) .... regularly ingesting isotonic fluid and strawberry and banana flavoured gels (350 calories a sachet), we were getting only fleeting benefits. Children were pressed to the barriers offering support and sometimes sweets.

Through a haze of discomfort Canary Wharf appeared. It went on forever. Things were flagging. Knees were sore, ankles pinching, (6) .... my arms were tingling. Twenty miles gone and it was agony. I guessed this was my wall coming. Tall and slippery with broken glass on the top. How I got past that point without hiring a cab I have yet to unravel.

Things worsened. The closer to home, the harder it became. My feet

were sticking to the floor. Fran was looking worried. We did not stop and walk (7) .... just ran at a walking pace.

The last mile felt like the first 13. Nothing was much fun. I was gone. (8) .... , I was hungry.

(9) .... , turning past Big Ben I saw a man holding an advert for McDonald's bacon double cheese burger. Unbelievable cruelty. (10) .... I would have eaten my hand if it was encased in a bun and covered in mayo with a couple of those gherkin-type things for relish. And I am a vegetarian.

The finish was in sight. Past Buckingham Palace and a couple of screeching friends and to the end. The fullstop finish, no more, never again. Around me people staggered, their faces covered in dry salt deposits from sweat, lips trembling, a few crying.

Strangers offered congratulations, touched our backs, smiled the brightest smiles, spoke the most beautiful words. I loved the world and it loved me.

2 Would you ever consider taking part in a marathon or similar event?

(G)···· page 204

Writing folder 10

Formal writing

1 The sentences below mean approximately the same thing. What is the difference between them?

 a Give us a ring soon.
 b We look forward to hearing from you at your earliest convenience.

Written English tends to be more formal than spoken English. You may have to write both formal and informal English in the CAE Writing test.

2 Here are some of the types of writing that you may need to do. Put them on a scale with the most formal at the top and the most informal at the bottom.

 • article for a student magazine
 • competition entry for an international magazine
 • contribution to a tourist guidebook
 • leaflet for a local sports club
 • letter of complaint to a newspaper
 • letter to a pen friend
 • proposal to a benefactor on how you would spend the money he might give you
 • report for your boss
 • review for an English Club newsletter

3 With a partner, discuss these pieces of advice relating to formal writing. If necessary, modify the pieces of advice to make them more appropriate.

 • Avoid verb contractions in formal writing.
 • Avoid phrasal verbs in formal writing.
 • Never use slang or colloquial expressions in formal writing.
 • Keep to formal layout conventions.
 • It is particularly important in formal writing to make the structure of what you are saying totally clear.
 • Use linking words and phrases to help clarify the structure of your writing.

4 These sentences all come from a report which should have been written in a formal style. Improve each one in any way that seems appropriate to you.

 a It was kind of difficult to collect as much data as we'd originally hoped.
 b The guys tended to express views that were a bit more conservative than those of the girls.
 c A number of our respondents brought up some very important things in response to our questions.
 d Interviewees' responses depended on how old they were and whether they were male or female, not to mention their occupation and educational background.
 e I'd like to go on a bit more about some important parts of the survey.

5 Replace the adjectives in italics in the sentences below with more interesting and appropriate adjectives.

 a Thank you for your *nice* letter. You have been doing a lot of *good* things!
 b The job you are advertising sounds very *good*, working with *nice* people.
 c In our restaurant you can enjoy a *nice* meal while admiring the *beautiful* view.
 d Club members have enjoyed a very *nice* programme this year.
 e The first interviewee for the position was a *beautiful* woman with very *good* qualifications for the post.

6   Add the linking devices in the boxes to each paragraph.

Secondly	Moreover	Finally	Firstly

a

The people present raised a number of objections to the plan for the club's yearly programme proposed by the committee. (1) .... they felt that the proposed programme did not contain enough to attract new members. (2) .... they considered that there were not enough meetings geared towards younger members. (3) .... several people made the point that the events suggested were not varied enough. (4) .... it was suggested that some new young members be co-opted onto the committee and a new programme be proposed as soon as possible.

So	However	Consequently	Although

b

Employed for five years in a small company in the remote town where she lived, my cousin knew that she ought to find herself a better job but she found it very hard to make the decision to leave. (1) .... she liked the job and she had enjoyed the company of her colleagues, the work itself was not very challenging. (2) .... she knew that it would make sense, from a career point of view, to look for something else before too many more years elapsed. (3) ...., the fact that her mother was in failing health made the decision a more serious issue for her. (4) ...., she realised she could not consider taking on a job in another town.

After that	Finally	because	especially
then	Firstly	when	Gradually

c

If you have only a couple of hours to spend in the countryside near our town, (1) .... this is the most valuable way to spend them. (2) ...., starting from the city centre, walk out of town along the river. Pay attention to the very interesting old industrial buildings that look quite different (3) .... viewed from the river. (4) .... you will move into residential areas where there are large expensive homes with long gardens stretching down to the river. You will see some very nice boats moored there. (5) .... you will be away from the town and will be able to enjoy magnificent views over the broad expanses of the local countryside. Keep an eye open (6) .... for bird life and for flowers (7) .... both are particularly rich in this area. (8) ...., you will come to an attractive pub on the river where you can enjoy lunch or a drink before catching the bus back to the city centre.

7   A benefactor is prepared to give a large sum of money to your college if a good case is put for how it will benefit the students there. Write your proposal, bearing in mind all the work on formal writing which you have done.

Units 21–25 Revision

Topic review

a If you could go anywhere in the world, where would you go?
b Would you like to be a travel journalist? Why?/Why not?
c Has the climate in your country changed since you were a child?
d Do you agree that people are to blame for the world's climate change?
e Have you ever taken anything back to a shop? If so, what happened?
f What characteristics do you find difficult to put up with in your neighbours?
g How much chocolate do you eat every week?
h Who should decide what children should watch on TV and when?
i How far can humans train animals to do different things?
j Have you ever taken part in a survey? If so, what for and what did the results show?

Grammar

1 Linking devices can be divided into the following categories: listing, concession and contrast, cause, result and summing up. Add more examples of the categories to the table below and mark formal words with F, neutral words with N and informal words with I.

Listing	Concession and contrast	Cause	Result	Summing up
first and foremost F	despite / in spite of N/F	because N	therefore F	in conclusion F

2 Look at this extract from a book. The linking devices are in italics. Which category does each linking device belong to?

Individual development

Effective teamwork seeks to pool the skills of individuals and to produce better results by so doing. *Whilst* the effectiveness of the team can be greater than the sum of the parts, it *also* follows that effective teams need to pay attention to the development of individual skills. Just as different societies have different views of the developed group, *so* throughout the history of man different societies and cultures have had different views as to what constitutes the developed and effective individual. *As* one obvious fact about teams is that they are a collection of individuals, *then* their effectiveness must in part be a function of individual ability.

Reading

1 In the following extract, the author suggests that different people take on different roles in group activities. Look at the list of different types of roles. What type of team member do you think you are?

the innovator	the challenger	the judge
the diplomat	the expert	

The challenger

Often seen as the 'maverick' of the team as s/he often adopts an unconventional approach. This is an individual who will look afresh at what the team is doing and why, and who will challenge the accepted order. Because of this, such an individual is often unpopular with those who prefer to conform and can be accused of 'rocking the boat'. The challenger provides the unexpected and whilst many ideas may prove to be worthless, some may become 'the idea of the year'. Without a challenger the team can become complacent, for it lacks the stimulus to review radically what the team is doing and how it is doing it.

The expert

We live in an age of ever increasing specialisation and the team may require several specialists whose primary role is to provide expertise which is not otherwise available to the team. Outside their area of specialisation, these people make little contribution; in meetings they assume the role of 'expert witness' giving a professional viewpoint which the rest of the team may need to evaluate in the light of other constraints and opportunities. The expert may be an accountant, engineer, marketing adviser, trainer, personnel specialist, corporate planner or any other specialist, whose primary role is to provide the team with the expertise required.

The judge

Like the judge in the courtroom this team member listens, questions and ponders before making a decision. This character tends to keep out of the arguments and does not see himself or herself as an advocate for any particular view or cause, but is concerned to see that ideas are properly evaluated and that the right decisions are made. A judge will not be rushed, preferring to pay the price of slow progress to make sure that the team follows the right path. Down-to-earth and logical, regarded by some as slow and ponderous, this person provides a balance and check on those who may be carried away by their own enthusiasm; like the courtroom judge seeking out the truth and seeing justice done.

2 Read the text quickly to get a general impression of the different roles people play.

3 For questions 1–9, match the statements with the types of team members. There may be more than one possible answer for some of the statements.

  1 This member realises the importance of support from further afield.
  2 If a team does not have this member, it may be satisfied with present results and not try harder.
  3 This team member can see a creative way through difficulties.
  4 Some team members find this person a destabilising influence.
  5 This person smoothes the process towards the result.
  6 This person makes sure the team is not swayed by someone's flights of fancy.
  7 Although this team member makes an invaluable contribution, their influence is limited.
  8 The whole team has to consider this member's advice in relation to the bigger picture.
  9 The overriding concern of this team member is to guide the team in a favourable direction.

4 With a partner, discuss these questions.

  a What type of team member do you think you are? Have you changed your opinion since reading the descriptions of the roles? Does your partner agree?
  b Which types of team members are indispensable and dispensable?
  c What do you think causes the most conflict in teamwork?

The innovator

Here is one who uses imagination to the full: an ideas person who is always proposing new ways of doing things. The innovator ensures that new ideas are evaluated, nurtured and developed and builds on the original ideas of others, visualising opportunities and transforming ideas into practical strategies. A fearless capacity to grapple with complex problems which demand new approaches provides the team with a rich source of vision, ingenuity, imagination and logic and can usually help the team to understand the unconventional and the new.

The diplomat

The diplomat is the team member who knows the diplomatic solution. This character generally has high influence within the team and is a good negotiator, and because of these skills plays a large part in the orientating of the team towards successful outcomes. Building alliances within and outside the team and trying to ensure that solutions are acceptable to all, the diplomat can sometimes be seen as 'papering over the cracks' in an effort to compromise, but is often dealing with the 'art of the impossible' rather than the ideal solution. Ways are found through difficult problems and in difficult times this is often the person who leads the team through dangerous ground.

Vocabulary

1 Complete all three sentences in each question with the same word.

  a • It would be silly to let things that have happened in the past .... a wedge between us now.
    • Of course, banning boxing will simply .... the sport underground.
    • You want £600 for that old car? You certainly .... a hard bargain.

  b • The .... to success is fraught with difficulties.
    • The Weather Service issued a warning to people in the .... of the hurricane.
    • They followed the .... until they came to a gate.

  c • The cart was pulled by a .... of oxen.
    • It was a real .... effort – everyone contributed something to the success of the project.
    • All the players perform well individually but they seem a little lacking in .... spirit.

  d • We put an advertisement about a nursery school in the newspaper to .... the water.
    • That lecturer really does .... your powers of endurance, he is so boring.
    • This machine is designed to .... people's hearing.

  e • After a .... of five years, Jennifer decided to go back to work full-time.
    • There is a .... in the magazine market which needs to be filled.
    • The children squeezed through a .... in the wall.

  f • The doctor promised that these pills would .... the pain.
    • If it will .... your mind, I'll speak to the boss for you.
    • At last the rain began to .... off.

26 Natural wonders

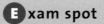

| Genre | Travel articles |
| Topic | Beauty spots |

Exam spot

You are quite often asked to write on the topic of travel in the CAE Writing test (Paper 2). Practise by using the language in this unit about your own country or another place that you know well.

Speaking

1 Work with a partner and answer the questions below.

a Do the pictures on the right remind you of the place where you live or anywhere that you have visited?

b How could you use the phrases in the box to describe the scenes in the pictures or a place that you know well?

> internationally recognised   outdoor restaurant
> complete range of   spectacular   the ultimate adventure
> perfect for   luxurious facilities   sumptuous lunch
> guided tours   luxury   diverse marine life
> once-in-a-lifetime experience

Listening

1 You are going to listen to a text that refers to one of the seven natural wonders of the world. Do you know what these are? Suggest what you think might be on the list and why they would deserve to be there.

2 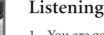 Listen and explain how the pictures on the left relate to what you heard.

3 🎧 Listen again. Are the following statements true or false? If they are false, correct them.

a Cairns is in south-west Australia.
b Cairns is on the Great Barrier Reef.
c Cairns has the fifth busiest airport in the southern hemisphere.
d Great Adventures is the name of a travel company.
e Green Island is 100 years old.
f It takes 45 minutes to fly to Green Island from Cairns.
g The pontoon is a kind of underwater capsule.
h You are only allowed to go to the pontoon once.

4 Work with a partner and list all the things that the destination described offers. Which three aspects of the destination appeal to you most?

Reading

1 You are going to read an extract from a book called *Running a Hotel on the Roof of the World*. What kind of place do you think the text is going to be about?

2 Read the first part of the text about two men, Dorje and Tashi, then complete the notes below.

Dorje had an interesting driving technique which involved keeping the car off the ground for as much time as possible. 'Terrible' Tashi called out whenever we were airborne, grinning from ear to ear and bracing himself for the inevitable impact whenever the Landcruiser would hit the tarmac again. It was hardly surprising that our car had practically no suspension.

Dorje had an advantage which would have made his taxi comrades in the city I had just flown from green with envy: visibility. In the pure rarefied air of Tibet, the view is not hindered by smog or pollution. Mountains which are tens of miles away appear crisp against the horizon. Apart from a few army trucks, the roads are free of traffic and the only limiting factor on Dorje's driving was how hard could he keep his foot pressed down on the accelerator pedal weighed up against the likelihood that at any moment one of the rattles could lead to the total disintegration of the vehicle.

Just visible through the vibrating windows were rectangular coracles setting out across the river. Tashi saw me trying to look at them. 'Yak-skin boats' he shouted over the roar of the Landcruiser engine. It seems that every part of the yak has a use. To make water-tight boats, the skins are stretched over a wooden frame, sewn together with wool made from yak hair and the joins are then sealed with yak butter.

Travelled by: ....
Driver's aim: ....
How Tashi felt about the journey: ....
Difficult aspects of the journey: ....
Good aspects of the journey: ....
Scenery: ....
What could be seen on the river: ....
Boats made of: ....

3 Now read the second part of the text. Imagine you wanted to paint a picture of the villages being described. Underline all the things the writer mentions which would help you with your picture.

Every now and then we would speed through a village lined with waving Tibetan children. Their villages looked wonderful and so inviting but Dorje was not showing any signs of slowing down. Small clusters of single and double storey buildings with walled-in courtyards jostled together in the foothills to gain maximum exposure to the sun. The houses looked solid, built to withstand the harsh environment. Walls were made of stone up to waist height and finished off with mud bricks to the roof.

Tin cans lined the window ledges, with the bright orange of marigolds in full bloom livening up the stark black and white of the houses. Branches of trees adorned with colourful prayer flags stood high into the wind from the top of the flat roofs. The auspicious blue, white, red, green and yellow colours of the fabrics stood out against the rich blue of the Tibetan sky. Each prayer flag carries a picture of *lungta*, the jewelled dragon-horse, who carries the owners' prayers up to the divinities every time the flag flaps in the wind.

The larger villages had a healthy copse of trees, usually willows or poplars which looked quite out of place in the generally treeless landscape. Wood is a precious commodity in the highland areas of Tibet and is never wasted. The few shrubs which grow wild on the hill-sides are harvested for use as brushwood and each courtyard wall is piled high with kindling gathered from the mountains.

4 Look at the picture of a Tibetan village. Which of the things you underlined are shown in the picture?

5 Now read the third and final part of the text and answer the following questions.

1 What problem is being discussed here?
   A getting rid of yak dung   B finding building materials
   C getting materials to burn   D looking after the yaks
2 Who does not seem to play a part in solving the problem?
   A young children   B older children
   C women   D men
3 Why is the dung mixed with water and barley straw?
   A to help make it into biscuits   B to make it look nicer
   C for the children to play with   D to make it more useful
4 Why is the dung put on walls?
   A to dry in the sun   B for decoration
   C to make the walls higher   D to help keep the homes warm

The lack of solid fuel in the shape of wood is of little consequence to the Tibetans who have an ingenious wood substitute: yak dung. The dung is collected during the day by young children who are out on the hills tending to flocks of sheep or yaks. What better way to spend the time when out on the hills than by collecting every piece of dung which can be found? It certainly sounds more attractive than being locked up in a school room.

When the children return in the evenings with their panniers of dung, it is usually the mother of the household, or an older sister, who has the task of mixing the raw material with a little water and, if available, some barley straw. This concoction is then made into attractive chocolate chip cookie shapes and slapped against the whitewashed walls to bake in the sun. Once dry, the cookies are stacked in rows on top of the walls to be used as fuel throughout the year.

Vocabulary

1 Tibet is described as being *on the roof of the world*. This simply means that Tibet is very high up. Below are some more idiomatic expressions which can be used to describe places, and explanations of the meanings of the idioms. Match each idiom (a–j) with its explanation (1–10).

a a black spot
b a tourist trap
c home from home
d no room to swing a cat
e picture-postcard
f a stone's throw from
g as the crow flies
h hit the road
i off the beaten track
j put a place on the map

1 attractive in a slightly artificial way
2 crowded place selling souvenirs, entertainment, etc. at high prices
3 make a place important or famous
4 place where you feel very comfortable
5 very small
6 a bit of road that has seen a lot of accidents
7 distance when measured in a straight line
8 leave a place, begin a journey
9 very close to
10 where not many people go

2 Choose one of the idioms above to complete each of the sentences below.

a I prefer to spend my holidays .... , far away from any other tourists.
b It's getting late and we've got a long drive home. It's really time we ....
c We stayed in a lovely .... village nestling in the valley.
d Take care on the drive across the mountains. There's a notorious .... just as you leave the main road to start the climb up to the pass.
e There was .... in our hotel room but the view we had was superb, so we didn't mind too much.

3 Which of the expressions in Vocabulary 1 would you be most likely and most unlikely to find in a tourist brochure? Why?

G ···:> page 205

⊙ *Like, alike, as, so* and *such*

1 Look at these sentences. What is the grammatical difference between *like* and *alike*?

The Scottish Highlands are very like the Southern Alps in New Zealand.
The Scottish Highlands and the Southern Alps are very alike.

2 Now look at these sentences. What is the grammatical difference between *so* and *such*?

Our holiday was so wonderful despite the fact that we had such terrible weather!
This is such a beautiful hotel. It is so beautiful here.
I had never been to so remote a place before.
I had never been to such a remote place before.

3 Now look at these sentences with *as* and *like*. What is the grammatical difference between *as* and *like*?

The mountain is rather like a cathedral spire in shape with a pointed top and steeply sloping sides.
The water in the mountain streams is as clear as crystal.
On this mountain, as on any mountain, you have to be careful.
Its peak was first reached, as were most of the peaks in the range, in the nineteenth century.
It looks like a mountain whose surface was smoothed by glaciation.
It looks as if its surface was smoothed by glaciation.

4 Now look at these sentences. What do they show you about the meaning of *as* and *like*?

As the highest mountain in the range, it is popular with both tourists and mountaineers.
Like the highest mountain in the range, it is popular with both tourists and mountaineers.

5 Change each sentence to use the word in brackets at the end. Your new sentence should mean approximately the same as the original.

a Oxford and Cambridge in some ways are like each other. (alike)
b The scenery we saw in the Himalayas was so amazing. (such)
c It was such a long way to the campsite. (so)
d Our holiday cottage and the one allocated to our friends looked alike. (like)
e She looks like someone who has just returned from a tropical holiday. (as)

Writing

1 Read the text below about a hotel. Some of the sentences are from an informal letter and others are from a holiday brochure. They have been mixed up to make one text. Can you separate them out to make the original two texts? There are three sentences from each.

The hotel has a magnificent location overlooking the broad spread of the gulf and most of the bedrooms enjoy sea views. It's a great hotel with loads of character. The bedrooms get a bit chilly at night and the uncarpeted corridors can be noisy but it's worth putting up with a few minor inconveniences as it has so much atmosphere in other ways. Each room has its own luxuriously-appointed en suite bathroom and is individually decorated with many original finishing touches. The superb restaurant offers a wide range of delicious dishes to suit all tastes. The food is fantastic and you can stuff yourself at breakfast so you don't need to eat again till the evening.

2 Read the following texts from a luxury holiday brochure. Which of the two places would you prefer to stay in?

a

The exuberance of the Canary Islands appears in all its splendour at the Hotel Botanico. Here, amidst an atmosphere of quiet elegance, every creature comfort is catered for by its 24-hour room service. The lavishly-appointed Ambassador rooms and magnificent top-floor penthouse suites combine private luxury with spectacular views and, for those in search of the ultimate in luxurious living, the Royal Suite exudes regal opulence with its antiques, original paintings and unique private terrace.

b

Cashel House offers its guests a charming confusion of cosy nooks and crannies, comfortable sofas, polished antiques and warm, welcoming fires. 32 guest rooms and 13 garden suites all enjoy that home-from-home feeling with pretty floral fabrics and views over the hotel's magnificent 10 acres of gardens. Gourmet dinners, with an emphasis on locally caught seafood, are served each evening in the delightful restaurant, whilst snack lunches are available in the bar. The hotel boasts its own equestrian centre with guided treks and other daytime pursuits, including tennis, shore-walks, sea fishing and golf.

Cashel House

3 Imagine you are spending a holiday in the Hotel Botanico. The hotel is just as good as **advertised**. Write a postcard to a friend describing it.

4 Imagine you are writing an entry for a guide book which simply presents the facts about hotels for its readers without making any subjective comments. Look at this description of a Brussels hostel from such a guide book.

Jacques Brel, Rue de la Sablonniere, Brussels 30, (tel. 218 01 87).

An official HI hostel – modern, with a hotel-like atmosphere. Facilities include showers in every room, bar, restaurant, meeting room. Beds in 6–12-bed dorms from 15.50 EUR, in double/twin rooms from 44.00 EUR and in 4-bed private rooms from 70.40 EUR. No access to rooms between 10 am and 3 pm. No curfew. Prices include breakfast. Sheets can be hired.
Métro stops – Madou, Botanique.

Write an entry in a similar style for Cashel House.

5 Imagine that you spent a very expensive week in one of the hotels and that two or three of the claims made in the advertisement for it proved to be false. Write a letter of complaint to the manager of the hotel, explaining what you are unhappy about and saying what action you would like to be taken.

Exam folder 11

Paper 4 Parts 3 and 4 Multiple choice and multiple matching

Both Part 1 and Part 3 of the Listening test (Paper 4) have multiple-choice questions. In Part 3, you listen to one long text and there are six multiple-choice questions, each with four options.

1 You are going to listen to an interview with a business woman. Before you listen, discuss these questions with a partner.

   a Can you find women in top business jobs in your country?
   b Are there any jobs which you consider to be exclusively male or exclusively female jobs?
   c When a company is run by women, do you think there are any differences in the way the company is run? What might those differences be?

2 Read through the questions below before you listen and think about what the answers might be.

3 🎧 Listen to the interview. For questions 1–6, choose the answer (A, B, C or D) which fits best according to what you hear.

   1 What did Julia instinctively do when she began her own company?
      A listened carefully to male colleagues' advice
      B made sure she came across as being professional
      C avoided bringing family problems to work
      D worked in cooperation with all the employees
   2 What did Julia learn from the work of Jennifer Alderton?
      A to make sure she was respected by all the staff
      B a concept of power that she found acceptable
      C the importance of persuading staff to do the right thing
      D that belief in what you are doing is essential
   3 According to Julia, companies that have command control management
      A waste productive time in dealing with conflicts.
      B work well in certain manufacturing industries.
      C do not offer their staff adequate facilities.
      D do not treat staff fairly when there are disputes.

4 Julia believes that by encouraging criticism in a company
   A the number of disagreements is reduced.
   B managers get more varied experience.
   C managers delegate more effectively.
   D opportunities for development are created.

5 Julia explains that the debate surrounding the work/life balance has been helped by
   A international barriers being broken down.
   B workers becoming more assertive in the way they communicate.
   C well-known people openly favouring time spent away from work.
   D an increasing number of women taking on top positions.

6 What is Julia going to be working on in the near future?
   A financially supporting small businesses
   B running communication skills courses
   C helping people come up with creative ideas
   D doing market research for small businesses

4 🎧 Compare your answers with a partner's and then listen again.

Advice

- Use the listening preparation time to read the questions and think about possible answers.
- Listen attentively to the first playing of the recording and lightly mark the answers you think are correct.
- Don't worry about missing a question; leave it and keep listening attentively.
- Listen to the second playing and confirm your answers.
- If you're not sure of an answer, guess. You have 25% chance of getting it right!
- In the exam transfer your answers to the answer sheet carefully in the time given at the end.

Part 4 of the CAE Listening test is a multiple-matching task. You hear five short extracts twice and there are two multiple-matching questions. You may be asked to identify the speakers, topics or opinions, to interpret what was said or to say what each speaker is doing when he or she speaks (e.g. apologising). There are eight options, so three options will not fit what you hear.

5 🎧 You will hear five short extracts in which different people at a party are explaining how they know the host, Sarah. Match the speakers (1–5) with their relationship to Sarah (A–H).

	A dentist
Speaker 1	B colleague
Speaker 2	C daughter's teacher
Speaker 3	D hairdresser
Speaker 4	E former employee
Speaker 5	F neighbour
	G old school friend
	H member of same gym

6 🎧 Now listen again. Match the speakers (1–5) with their opinions of Sarah (A–H).

	A She's competitive.
	B She gets on well with everyone.
Speaker 1	C She's efficient.
Speaker 2	D She's sympathetic.
Speaker 3	E She's eager to help.
Speaker 4	F She arranges things quickly.
Speaker 5	G She's changed from when she was a child.
	H She's keen to become successful.

🎧 Check your answers with a partner and then listen again for a final check. Don't forget that in the exam you will be expected to do both tasks as you listen to the recording twice.

Advice

- Use the listening preparation time to read the questions in both tasks so that you know what to listen out for.
- As you listen to each speaker try to answer the questions in both tasks.
- Remember that the answer to each tasks may come at the beginning , middle or end of what each speaker says, so listen attentively all the way through.
- Listen out for paraphrases of what is in the question or listen and decide if there is a sort of summary of what the speaker says in the question.
- There are five speakers and eight options so know why the ones that don't fit are wrong.

3 With a partner, discuss how you think the story might continue.

4 🎧 Listen to the next part of the story. As you listen, decide whether these statements
   are true or false.

   a Four men went shooting.
   b This is the third anniversary of the tragedy.
   c The bodies were discovered in a bog.
   d The men had a dog with them.

   e One of the men had a blue raincoat with him.
   f The aunt's brother always used to sing a particular
   song to tease his aunt.

5 Now read the next part of the story. What do you think will happen next?

She broke off with a little shudder. It was a relief to Framton when the aunt bustled into the room
with a whirl of apologies for being late in making her appearance.

"I hope Vera has been amusing you?" she said.

"She has been very interesting," said Framton.

"I hope you don't mind the open window," said Mrs. Sappleton briskly; "my husband and brothers
will be home directly from shooting, and they always come in this way. They've been out for snipe
in the marshes today, so they'll make a fine mess over my poor carpets. So like you menfolk, isn't
it?"

She rattled on cheerfully about the shooting and the scarcity of birds, and the prospects for duck in
the winter. To Framton it was all purely horrible. He made a desperate but only partially successful
effort to turn the talk on to a less ghastly topic, he was conscious that his hostess was giving him
only a fragment of her attention, and her eyes were constantly straying past him to the open window
and the lawn beyond. It was certainly an unfortunate coincidence that he should have paid his visit
on this tragic anniversary.

"The doctors agree in ordering me complete rest, an absence of mental excitement, and avoidance
of anything in the nature of violent physical exercise," announced Framton, who laboured under the
tolerably widespread delusion that total strangers and chance acquaintances are hungry for the least
detail of one's ailments and infirmities, their cause and cure. "On the matter of diet they are not so
much in agreement," he continued.

"No?" said Mrs. Sappleton, in a voice which only replaced a yawn at the last moment. Then she
suddenly brightened into alert attention – but not to what Framton was saying.

6 🎧 Listen to the end of the story. How far were
   your predictions correct? Why do you think Mr
   Nuttel and the niece each behaved as they did at
   the end of the story?

Vocabulary

1 Here are some chunks of language from the story.
   What are the missing words? Note that a–h come
   from the reading extracts and i–l from the second
   listening extract.

   a He doubted whether these formal visits would
   do much towards helping the nerve cure he was
   supposed to be ....
   b You will bury yourself down there and not speak
   to a living ....
   c Some of them, as .... as I can remember,
   were quite nice.

   d In this restful country spot tragedies seemed out
   of ....
   e The aunt bustled into the room with a whirl of
   apologies for being late in making her ....
   f They'll .... a fine mess over my poor
   carpets.
   g It was an unfortunate coincidence that he
   should have .... his visit on this tragic
   anniversary.
   h Framton .... under the delusion that total
   strangers are hungry for the least detail of one's
   ailments.
   i A tired brown spaniel kept close at their
   ....
   j He dashed off without a .... of goodbye
   or apology.
   k One would think he had seen a ....
   l Romance at short .... was her speciality.

2 Here are some more chunks of language from the story. The words in italics could each be replaced by three of the words from the box. Which words can fit? Note that changing the word may result in a big change in meaning.

a long time	avert	chatted
confidence	droned	escape
harped	head	his salary
laugh	mind	most of his income
prevent	sigh	smile

a She broke off with a little *shudder*.
b She *rattled* on about the shooting
c A cyclist had to run into the hedge to *avoid* imminent collision.
d He had to spend *the night* …
e It was enough to make anyone lose their *nerve*.

Emphasising

Look at this sentence.

Romance at short notice was her speciality.

Here are some ways of making this statement more emphatic.

Romance at impressively short notice was her speciality.
No one was better at romance at short notice than she was.
Romance at short notice was her most particular speciality.
What she did best was romance at short notice.
What a talent she had for romance at short notice!
Romance at short notice was such a speciality of hers!
Never could she be bettered as far as romance at short notice was concerned.

1 What has happened in each of the variations above to make the statement more emphatic?

2 Now write each of these statements in a more emphatic way.

a You can't draw reliable conclusions about people's characters from their appearances.
b The girl's behaviour surprised me.
c She shocked me with her next words.

G ⋯⋙ page 206

Writing

1 Which of these techniques does the writer use to hold the reader's attention? Where appropriate, find one example of each technique in the reading texts.

- direct speech
- describing the scene in an interesting way
- describing people in an interesting way
- a striking opening
- an effective ending
- combining general statements with specific examples
- using language of emphasis
- dropping hints about what may happen later
- humour

2 Think of an incident where someone you know (or thought you knew) did something unexpected. Describe the situation to your partner. If possible use some of the techniques listed above.

3 Write an article in response to the announcement below. Try to use as many as possible of the techniques worked on in this section.

TRUE STORIES MAGAZINE

We are looking for articles in which readers describe how they were once surprised by a friend or relative's unexpected behaviour. The best articles will be published and will win a gift voucher.

Writing folder 11

Informal writing

If you are not sure whether it is appropriate to write in an informal register or not, it is better to write in a neutral style. Below is part of a letter of reference for a friend who had applied for a holiday job on a cruise liner. A letter of reference should be written in a neutral to formal style, but the extract below is too informal.

1   Underline all the parts of the reference that are too informal.

2   Rewrite the reference, replacing everything you have underlined with more appropriate equivalents.

> I've known Ted for donkey's years – in fact, ever since we were kids at school together – and he's a really nice guy, one of the best. I'd give him the job like a shot if I were in your boat (excuse the pun!). Don't be put off by the fact that he can sometimes seem a bit bossy – that's just because he's such a well-organised bloke himself, he can't stand it when other people are slow to get their act together. He's got loads of experience of working with other people and he can be relied on to get things going. Go for it and give him the job – you won't regret it.

3   Sometimes students lose marks in the CAE Writing test because they do not use register in a consistent way. They use both formal and informal words in the same sentence in an inappropriate way. In the sentences below, mark the words which are inappropriately formal or inappropriately informal.

   a   It's daft to alight from a bus while it is moving.
   b   Jack lives in a flat adjacent to the local chippie.
   c   Julia always wears very snazzy apparel.
   d   John's life was torn asunder by the death of his missus.
   e   When talking to the fuzz, it behoves you to be polite.
   f   Jenny's birthday bash ceased at midnight.
   g   The deceased man left all his clobber to his nephew.
   h   You must give the office a bell if you intend to change your domicile.
   i   Lawrence dwelt in a remote village in Tibet for yonks.
   j   Richard is an erstwhile mate of my husband's.

   Now rewrite each sentence twice. One sentence should be consistently formal and the other consistently informal.

Exam spot

In the CAE Writing test (Paper 2) you will probably only need to write in an informal style when you are writing a letter to a friend. You might also choose to use a slightly informal style if you are writing an article for a more informal type of publication, e.g. for a student newspaper.

4   One of the most noticeable characteristics of informal writing is its use of colloquial or slang words. Match the words (a–s) below with their neutral equivalent (1–19).

a	argy-bargy	**1**	friend
b	brat	**2**	insane
c	chuck	**3**	lively
d	broke	**4**	insect
e	crabby	**5**	badly-behaved child
f	mega	**6**	large amount
g	bubbly	**7**	disagreement
h	crony	**8**	hard work
i	barmy	**9**	information
j	higgledy-piggledy	**10**	mixed up
k	jumpy	**11**	bad-tempered
l	beastie	**12**	nervous
m	chomp	**13**	customer
n	info	**14**	steal
o	oodles	**15**	throw
p	pinch	**16**	chew noisily
q	punter	**17**	very good or very big
r	slog	**18**	without money
s	grand	**19**	thousand pounds or dollars

5   Choose one of the words (a–s) above to complete each of the sentences (a–i) below.

a There's no need to hurry – we've got .... of time.

b Sally's a lovely .... girl – I'm sure you'll have a great time with her.

c Last Saturday I decided to .... out all my old school books – I've made a lot of extra space in my cupboard.

d I wish she wouldn't .... like that when she eats.

e The party was ....! Everyone was there!

f Her bedroom is always untidy with clothes lying .... all over the place.

g The problem with picnics is all the .... that crawl over you and the food.

h I can't possibly go away for the weekend – I'm ....!

i It was quite a .... but I managed to get my assignment finished on time.

6   You receive this email from a friend. Underline all the informal words and expressions in the email, then write a reply to your friend. Your reply should be in informal English.

You'll never guess what's happened! My boss is going to send me on a business trip to your town! So get ready for me to drop by some time next week. Hope we can hit the town together one evening. What do you reckon we should do? I'm really into folk music at the moment – is there anywhere we could go and have a bite or a drink and listen to music at the same time? But I'm open to other suggestions if you don't fancy that. Also, could you just let me know about a few other things:

What's the weather like at the mo, i.e. what sort of clothes should I bring with me?

I've got to take a prezzie for some friends of my boss (he's arranged for me to crash with them). What do you think might be good for a middle-aged couple? Here we'd usually take chocs or a bottle but maybe things are different with you?

What's public transport like in your town? I'm trying to decide whether it's worth hiring a car or not. Have to be travelling quite a bit during the week – am not wild about the idea of driving on the right but may have to brave it.

Looking forward to hearing from you and to seeing you soon,

Sammy

⊙ Vocabulary

1 The table below contains some more words from the article. Fill in the meanings and three phrases for each word in the third column.

Words from the text	Meaning	Other words from same root (in typical phrase)
stressful	causing worry and anxiety	a stress-free environment; to feel stressed; stresses and strains
agree		
undeterred		
excessive		
concede		
forcibly		
frequent		
compensation		
correlation		

2 Complete each sentence with a word derived from the word in brackets at the end.

a Air traffic control is said to be one of the most .... jobs of all. (stress)

b I found him very unpleasant and .... and I hope that I never have to spend another evening in his company again. (agree)

c Some people claim that nuclear bombs actually prevent wars as they act as a .... (deter)

d There are severe penalties for .... the speed limit. (excessive)

e The government has slightly relaxed the tax regulations as a .... to small businesses. (concede)

f It is very hard to .... speed restrictions on the roads here. (force)

g After administering the questionnaire, the sociology student had to classify the answers according to their .... (frequent)

h There is a direct .... between being depressed and being in debt. (correlate)

i If your train is delayed by more than one hour, you may be able to claim .... (compensate)

⊙ Adverbials expressing opinion

1 Look at these sentences from the text.

a *As yet, **sadly**, no airline seems to agree that children should be screened and not heard.*

b *Instead, to reduce delays, most airlines are **rightly** imposing stricter limits on the size or weight of bags that can be carried on to planes.*

c ***Understandably:** if you put luggage in the hold, you have to wait ages for it at the other end – if it shows up at all.*

What do the words in bold tell you about the opinion of the writer?

2 Here are some more adverbials which can be used to express opinion.

apparently	evidently	fortunately
indisputably	inevitably	ironically
predictably	surprisingly	
unbelievably	undoubtedly	

Think of each of these adverbials in the sentence *Mark and Susanna have got married* and then answer the questions below.

Which of the adverbials tells you that the speaker …

a is pleased about their marriage?

b is not totally sure that they did actually get married? (2 possibilities)

c is absolutely sure that they did get married? (2 possibilities)

d would have expected them to marry? (2 possibilities)

e would not have expected them to marry? (2 possibilities)

f finds something slightly amusing or curious about the fact that they got married?

3 Choose the most likely adverbial from the options provided to complete each of the sentences below.

a *Fortunately/Undoubtedly/Ironically*, no one was hurt in the accident.

b After having eaten so much, I *surprisingly/inevitably/evidently* began to feel rather sleepy.

c *Predictably/Unbelievably/Undoubtedly* Jack passed his exam with flying colours – he always does do well in exams.

d I didn't see it happen myself but *ironically/apparently/indisputably* she fainted in the heat.

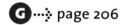 page 206

Listening

1 You are going to listen to some people talking about three different forms of transport: plane, train and bicycle. What do you think they might say about the advantages and disadvantages of each of these means of transport?

2 Now listen and list the advantages and disadvantages of flying, rail travel and cycling that are mentioned in the conversation.

3 Listen again and note the discourse markers that you hear. What functions do they serve?

> **V**ocabulary spot
>
> Using discourse markers when you speak and write helps to clarify the structure of what you want to say – as long as you use them appropriately. When you read or listen to English, pay attention to the discourse markers that are used and try to use them in similar ways in your own speaking and writing.

Speaking 2

1 Complete the dialogue with expressions from the box.

| as I was saying   certainly   I know   I suppose |
| just my luck   so   stupidly   then   you mean |

Brian: Well, anyway, (1) .... , I left home at the normal time but the traffic jams were terrible.

Jill: Mm, (2) .... , it's got a lot worse recently.

Brian: Yes, (3) .... I was a bit late when I got to the station and (4) .... you should have seen the queues there. There was no chance that I'd be able to buy a ticket before the train left, so I (5) .... decided to take a risk and just get on the train without one.

Jill: What, (6) .... a ticket inspector actually got on the train?

Brian: Yes, (7) .... The first time in months that I've seen one.

Jill: You had to pay a fine, (8) .... ?

Brian: Yes, twice the price of the fare. I (9) .... won't do that again!

2 Work with a partner. Write a brief dialogue using some of the discourse markers you heard in the listening text.

3 Perform your dialogue to the other students. If possible, do it from memory rather than reading it. While listening to each dialogue, the other students in the class should note down the discourse markers which they hear.

Exam folder 12

Paper 5 Speaking

The CAE Speaking test (Paper 5) is quite short and so it is important not to waste time with unnecessary silences. Don't worry too much about making mistakes – the important thing is to show that you can communicate in English both with the examiner and with your partner.

Advice

- Smile at the examiners as you greet them – it will relax you and create a pleasant first impression.
- Try to relax – imagine you are talking to a new friend.
- Answer the examiner's questions fully, not just with one-word answers.
- Listen carefully to the instructions and do what you are asked.
- If you did not understand or do not remember all the instructions, it is fine to ask the examiner to clarify or repeat something.
- Speak clearly and loudly enough for both examiners to hear you.
- Give your partner a chance to speak too.
- Talk to your partner – you get marks for interacting, so ask each other questions, and react to what your partner says (as in a normal conversation) but try to do so without interrupting.
- When you ask questions, try not to use an intonation which rises too much as this can sound aggressive.
- Try not to repeat what you or your partner has already said – add something new.
- Don't worry about making mistakes – you will get marks for communicating your ideas and not just for accuracy.
- In Part 1, give reasonably full answers to the examiner's questions.
- In Part 2, you should simply listen to each other and not speak until the examiner asks you to.
- In Part 3, you will have more to say if you do not simply agree with your partner but react either by taking their ideas a step further or by disagreeing – remember you don't have to tell the truth in the exam, so you may find more to say if you deliberately disagree a bit.
- In Part 4, as with all the other parts, it is above all important to listen carefully to what the examiner asks you to do.

1 Imagine you are talking to someone you have never met before. Introduce yourself and talk about your own experience of learning languages. What do you enjoy and what do you find most difficult?

2 Look at these cartoons. Describe them and comment on what points they are making.

3 Work with a partner. You are going to set up a self-access centre for people who want to learn English and other languages in the place where you live. Discuss which of the resources in the pictures it would be most important to include in your self-access centre and why. In what ways (if at all) do each of these things help people to learn languages? Is there anything else that you would want to include in your self-access centre?

4 If, for reasons of cost, you could only have three of these resources in your self-access centre, which three would it be and why?

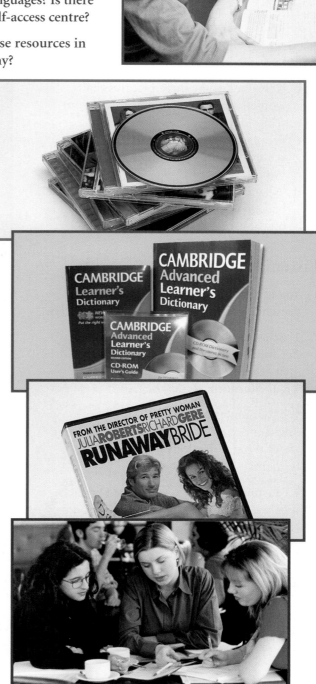

A testing question

Genre	Debates
Topic	Education

Speaking 1

1 Work in groups and answer the following questions.

   a Which (if any) of the pictures remind you of your own schooldays?

   b Describe two or three pictures that would sum up your memories of your schooldays.

   c People sometimes say that your schooldays are the best days of your life. Would you agree?

   d What do you think is the main educational issue in your country at the moment and how do you feel about this?

Listening

1 You are going to hear three people presenting the case for these points of view:

   1 Schoolchildren are tested too much.

   2 Children do not spend enough time at school.

   3 All education should be free.

   What arguments do you think they might make in favour of these points of view? What objections might they raise to them?

2 ⌒ Listen to the three speakers. For each speaker, note down the main arguments. Note also the points against these arguments made by other speakers.

3 Would you vote for or against each of the three points of view? Give reasons for your answers.

Reading

1 Look at the title of the text. What do you think it is going to be about and what points do you think it might make?

DON'T CRITICISE EXAMS:
They're a lesson in life

George Marsh, head of posh Dulwich College Preparatory School in London, probably thought he was doing kids and parents a favour with his rousing speech at the annual prep school conference this week.

He spoke of the pressures facing young people, who need to be nurtured during difficult pre-teen and teenage years. Above all, he said, we had reached a stage where the obsession with passing exams was 'killing the fun' of school.

We've all read this before. We've heard of the burnout kids, pushed by ambitious parents until they're at the end of their tethers, and gasped at the stories of the hothouse flower children who wilt in the real world. We've seen the headlines. 'Pressures of work too much for our teenagers,' they scream. Now we have Mr Marsh's contribution about too many horrid exams spoiling the school's broth.

In our child-obsessed society, the worst sin of all is to stop a child having 'fun'. It is right up there

with smacking in the new millennium book of bad parenting. Children must be endlessly indulged, treated with kid gloves, escorted to amusement parks, given computer games and showered with pocket money.

They must never have a minute when they're neither protected nor enjoying themselves. Heaven forbid that they should be told to study, strive and compete – words which seem to have taken on the quality of blasphemy.

But whoever said school was meant to be fun? Yes, school is a place where a child develops and a rounded curriculum is vital. Our children should play sport, do drama, join choirs, hang out at playtimes. The rest of the time, however, they are there to learn and to achieve some basic qualifications that will, whether they want to accept it or not, cushion them when life gets really hard. Yet, in the current climate, saying that exams matter is tantamount to saying that our

children should spend their teenage years at an Army boot camp.

This is the same mentality that dictates there should be no winners at sports day in case other children get upset by coming second. It's the same misguided attitude that drives parents to spray their kids with antiseptic to protect them from all known germs when actually they only end up sickly because their immune system never develops. Cosseting children in cotton wool does them few favours in the long run.

Mr Marsh is right when he says that we should shelter our children from the pressures of growing up too soon but there is a difference between sheltering and smothering.

If he really wanted to do us all a favour in his speech, he should have told parents to get real. School can be tough and exams always are but then so is life – and it's best that children learn that particular lesson as early as possible.

2 Answer these questions about the text.

a Who is George Marsh?
b What are the main points he is making?
c To what extent do you think that other people agree with his views?

3 These words and expressions from the article all have strong positive or negative associations. Divide them into two groups, positive and negative, and explain what each word suggests.

rousing	nurtured	burnout	hothouse flower children
wilt	scream	sin	showered
blasphemy	rounded	cushion	boot camp
misguided	cosseting	sheltering	smothering

4 To what extent do you agree with the views that George Marsh is putting forward? How far do you think his opinions would be generally accepted in your country?

Vocabulary

1 Match the two parts of these collocations used in the reading text.

a	to do someone	1	a stage
b	a rousing	2	a qualification
c	to reach	3	run
d	at the end of	4	climate
e	the real	5	your tether
f	to treat someone with	6	speech
g	pocket	7	world
h	the current	8	money
i	to achieve	9	a favour
j	in the long	10	kid gloves

2 Now match the completed phrases from Vocabulary 1 to their meanings.

a to be very polite and careful in your behaviour towards someone

b the way things are at the moment

c to get a certificate showing you have taken courses or passed some exams

d how things are rather than how we might like them to be

e very upset or anxious

f looking to the distant rather than the immediate future

g a talk that stirs the audience

h cash or notes given to someone on a regular basis to help them pay for their everyday needs

i to do something nice for someone

j to get to a particular point of development

3 Now choose which of these collocations best fit each of the sentences below.

a It's a lot of hard work now but I'm sure you'll feel it's worth it ....

b I wonder if you could .... and get me a newspaper when you're in town.

c When she rang me last night she was .... and so I thought I'd better go round at once and see if I could do anything to help.

d It's taking a bit of a risk to give up a steady job in ....

e There's no need .... ; I won't bite your head off.

f Now she's left university she's going to have to get used to life in ....

g The building work has now .... where we can begin to imagine how things will eventually look.

h How much .... did your parents use to give you?

☉ Gerunds and infinitives

1 Look at these sentences from the text and underline all the uses of the gerund and the infinitive in them. Why is the gerund or the infinitive used in each of the cases you underline?

a The rest of the time, however, they are there to learn and to achieve some basic qualifications that will, whether they want to accept it or not, cushion them when life gets really hard.

b It's the same misguided attitude that drives parents to spray their kids with antiseptic to protect them from all known germs when actually they only end up sickly because their immune system never develops.

c Mr Marsh is right when he says that we should shelter our children from the pressures of growing up too soon but there is a difference between sheltering and smothering.

d If he really wanted to do us all a favour in his speech, he should have told parents to get real.

2 Complete these sentences about the rules for the use of gerunds and infinitives. Fill in the gaps with either *gerund* or *infinitive*.

a You always use the .... (or a noun) after a preposition.

b When the word *to* is used as a preposition as in *be used to*, *look forward to*, *object to*, it is followed by a(n) ....

c The .... can be used to express purpose. For example, you might use one to give an answer to the question *Why are you studying English?*

d Phrases like *It is impossible/easy/nice for Mary/me/the children* are usually followed by the ....

e *It's not worth / There's no point / It's no use* are usually followed by the ....

3 Put the verbs in the box into one of the two columns below.

mind	feel like	promise	deny	enjoy
refuse	arrange	risk	suggest	tend	give up
offer	expect	decide	agree	manage

Verbs followed by a gerund	Verbs followed by an infinitive
enjoy	*decide*

4 Now put the verbs from the box below into one of the following groups, A, B or C.

forget	start	intend	permit	advise
regret	allow	go on	begin	remember
forbid	continue	try	can't bear

A can be followed by either (with a change of meaning) e.g. remember
B can be followed by either (with no change in meaning) e.g. begin
C can be followed by either (depending on the grammar of the sentence) e.g. allow

5 Rewrite each sentence using the words in brackets in an appropriate form.

a Jack said it would be a good idea to go to the new Chinese restaurant. (suggest)
b No eating is allowed in the classrooms. (permit)
c The police officer wouldn't let anyone into the building. (forbid)
d Could you possibly open the window? (mind)
e Melinda said she would paint my son's portrait. (offer)
f I hope you remembered to buy some apples. (forget)
g I'm really sorry that I wasted so much of my time at school. (regret)
h Despite his injury, he continued to play his violin. (go on)
i Everyone is sure that he will do well in his exams. (expect)
j Passengers are not permitted to smoke on any of that airline's flights. (allow)

G ···÷ page 206

Speaking 2

When you are presenting an argument in a more formal way, it is usually most effective to be brief and to the point. This is particularly important when you are summarising something.

1 🎧 Listen to this speaker talking to children about how to pass exams. Complete the notes below.

> Aim of exams:
> Types of examinees:
> 1
> What to do if you are one of these:
> a
> b
> 2
> What to do if you are one of these:
> a
> b

What other things did the speaker mention that you did not include in your notes?

2 Think about how you might summarise what the speaker said for someone who missed her talk. What can you leave out from the original? How can you modify the rest of the language used? Summarise the main points made by the speaker.

3 With a partner, discuss how to get the best possible marks in the CAE exam. Think about the following points:

- before the exam
- during the exam
- general advice for all the papers
- Reading test (Paper 1)
- Writing test (Paper 2)
- Use of English test (Paper 3)
- Listening test (Paper 4)
- Speaking test (Paper 5).

When you have discussed this fully, talk about how you would summarise the discussion.

Present the summary of your discussion to the rest of the class.

Writing folder 12

Descriptive, narrative and discursive articles

1 Look at these exam-type writing tasks and answer the questions below.

   a In each case, what do you have to describe, what (if anything) do you have to narrate and what do you have to discuss?
   b In one of the tasks, a narrative element would not be appropriate. Which one is this and why is it inappropriate?

A Many students in the college where you are studying complain that they have to live in conditions which make it difficult for them to study. Write an article for the local students' magazine in which you outline the conditions that many students have to put up with, including examples from your friends' experiences. You should also suggest ways in which students can make the best of the situations they are in.

Write your **article**.

B You see this announcement in an international magazine.

COMPETITION

Modern methods of communication have transformed our world. What means of communication do you personally find most useful? Email? Mobile phone? Fax? Texting? Something else? Choose ONE means of communication and explain exactly how you use it. Then comment on how it has changed your life, pointing out ways in which it has had negative as well as positive effects.

Write your **competition entry**.

C As a college student, you recently took part in a week's work experience in a company. You learned a great deal from the programme and found it an enjoyable experience on the whole. However, there are a number of ways in which you feel it could be improved, so that next year's participants would benefit even more from the experience. Write a report for the college committee that organises work experience placements, in which you summarise your personal experience and make suggestions for improvements.

Write your **report**.

D A large international sports company is considering donating money for sports facilities in a number of different areas of the world. To apply for money, it is necessary to send the company a proposal in which you outline what facilities are already available and then propose one specific facility which your area needs, explaining why it is necessary and what benefits it would bring your community.

Write your **proposal**.

E This is part of a letter which you receive from a pen friend in the United States. Write a reply to the letter.

We are doing a project on punishments and rewards used in schools in different countries. Can you write and tell me what sorts of punishments and rewards are used in schools in your country? What experiences have you personally had of punishments and rewards at school? What do you think is good about this system and what is bad? What changes would you like to introduce if you were a head teacher or a Minister of Education and why?

Write your **letter**.

2 Think about the descriptive parts of writing tasks A–E. With a partner, discuss how you could make each of the descriptive parts more interesting. Consider the questions below and make notes on how you could proceed with each of the tasks.

  a In Task A, what specific living conditions are you going to describe? Note down some good expressions that you could use in order to convey these living conditions vividly.

  b In Task B, what general points are you going to make about how you use the means of communication you choose? Think of one or two specific examples.

  c In Task C, you will need to invent a specific situation if you have never had any real experience of a situation like this. Could you base what you describe on your parents' workplace, or something you have seen on TV? Remember that it is more important to write in an accurate and relevant way than to write about an experience you have actually had.

  d In Task D, think about what the sports company needs to know. Is it relevant here to give personal anecdotes? What sort of situation is likely to inspire the company to give money? How could you slant your description to strengthen your case?

  e In Task E, make a list of all the punishments and rewards you can think of that are used in schools in your country. Beside each one, note down a typical kind of behaviour that would result in that punishment or reward. An anecdote might be relevant here. Note down some good words and expressions you could use in this letter.

3 Think about the narrative parts of these tasks. Note down some ideas that you could include for the narrative parts of questions A, B, C and E.

4 Think about the discursive parts of each of the tasks. For each one, prepare a mind map using the information below to help you.

  a For Task A, your mind map should be based on the aspects of living conditions which you have described. At least one solution should relate to each of the problems identified.

  b For Task B, your mind map should centre on the means of communication chosen, indicating the changes it has enabled and noting its good and bad effects – the map might possibly culminate in some kind of overall conclusion.

  c For Task C, your mind map should indicate both the good and bad points in the experience with at least one solution relating to each of the bad points indicated.

  d For Task D, your mind map should focus on the proposed facility with a set of supporting ideas which will help to argue the case for that facility.

  e For Task E, your mind map should have areas devoted to good and bad points and your suggested changes.

5 In some tasks containing descriptive and discursive elements, it will be appropriate to deal with all the description first and then to move on to the more discursive parts of the task. In other tasks, the descriptive and discursive tasks are likely to be interwoven. With a partner, discuss which approach would probably work best for each of the five tasks, A–E.

6 Write an answer to two of the five tasks worked on in this Writing folder.

Why should we employ you?

Genre	Interviews
Topic	Job interviews

Speaking 1

1 Discuss these questions in groups.

a Can you identify all the jobs in the pictures?

b Have you ever had a job interview? If so, describe to the other students in the group what happened and how you felt before, during and after the interview. Describe the experience in as much detail as you can.

c What advice would you give to an interviewee about dress and body language?

d What else can an interviewee do in order to create the best possible impression at the interview?

Reading

1 Below are some typical interview questions.

a Do you like routine tasks / regular hours?

b Why do you think you would like this type of work?

c What is your general impression of your last company?

d How interested are you in sport?

e Do you make your opinions known when you disagree with the views of your supervisor?

f What kinds of decisions are most difficult for you?

g What is your greatest strength?

h Do you prefer working with others or alone?

With a partner, discuss how you think it would be appropriate to answer these questions if you were at an interview for a job:

• in middle management in a supermarket chain
• as a driving instructor
• as a chef
• of the kind that you would like to apply for.

2 Look at the possible answers opposite. Match the answers (1–8) to their questions (a–h).

3 Do you think the advice provided is appropriate for the kind of job that you might consider applying for?

❶ Always answer positively. Keep your real feelings to yourself whatever they might be. Your answer is 'Very good' or 'Excellent'. Then smile and wait for the next question.

❷ Your answer in part might be: 'I believe in planning and proper management of my time and yet I can still work well under pressure.'

❸ A trick question. The interviewer knows from experience that most recent graduates are hopeless employees until they come to terms with such facts of life. You could say: 'There's no problem there. A company expects to make a profit, so the doors have to be open for business on a regular basis.'

❹ If you can, state that you come from an environment where input is encouraged when it helps the team's ability to get the job done efficiently.

❺ A recent survey of management personnel found that the executives who listed group sports among their extracurricular activities made an average of £3,000 a year more than their sedentary colleagues. Don't you just love football suddenly?

❻ This question is usually asked to determine whether you are a team player. Before answering, however, be sure that you know whether the job requires you to work alone.

❼ You are human, admit it, but be careful what you admit. If you have ever had to fire someone you are in luck, because no one likes to do that.

❽ This is a deceptively simple question because there is no pat answer. It is usually asked to see whether you really understand what the specific job and profession entail on a day-to-day basis.

Listening

1 🎧 Now listen to two different job applicants answering the same interview questions. Complete the table with notes on each applicant's response.

Question	Mr Higgins	Miss Smith
Why should we employ you?		
Are you willing to take calculated risks?		
Which of the jobs you have held have you liked least?		
In what areas do you feel that your last boss could have done a better job?		

Which applicant do you think gives the better answer to each question and why?

2 🎧 Here are some phrases used by one or other of the job applicants. Which applicant uses each phrase and in what context? Listen again and complete the table.

Phrase	Used by	Context
better suited		You won't find anyone better suited to this job than I am.
badly need		
take the instructions		
I wonder if		
good and bad points		
which is why		
it's hard to know		

3 Overall, which of the two candidates would you offer the job to?

Using a range of structures

E xam spot

To get good marks in the CAE exam, you need to show that you can handle a range of structures in English. This is particularly important in writing although you will also gain extra marks when speaking if you use a variety of structures.

1 Here are some situations in which you might find yourself having to write something in English. How could you use each of the verb forms listed under the topic in such a situation?

a giving advice to someone, e.g. about ways of economising

conditionals
modals
inversion
present simple

b reminiscing, e.g. about your early years at school

used to
would
past simple
present perfect

c telling a story, e.g. about a difficult situation you had to face

past simple
past continuous
past perfect
inversion

d hypothesising, e.g. about how your life would have been different if you had been born the other sex

conditionals
wish
indirect questions
inversion

2 Fill the gaps in the situations below. You need one word for each gap.

a giving advice

> You could save quite a bit of money if you (**1**) .... to work instead of taking the bus. I think you (**2**) .... also try to spend less on food. In your position, I would try to eat out less often. Growing your own vegetables also, of course, (**3**) .... many people a lot of money.

b reminiscing

> I think the first years at school were the best in many ways. I (**1**) .... to stay for school dinners. As most of the kids (**2**) .... home for lunch, we school dinner kids had a lot of time to play and we (**3**) .... invent all sorts of games. I've always (**4**) .... good at making up games and I'm sure it's because of all the practice I (**5**) .... at primary school.

c telling a story

> It was a very difficult decision to take. I could either stay in a dull but secure job or I could take the chance I was being offered to travel the world. I (**1**) .... worked in the same job for ten years and had many good friends there so it was not an easy decision. However, one day as I (**2**) .... sitting at the computer writing yet another tedious report, I (**3**) .... that I had to get out or it (**4**) .... be too late. No sooner (**5**) .... I made up my mind than I (**6**) .... on my way to hand in my letter of resignation.

d hypothesising

> I sometimes wonder (**1**) .... my life would have been different if I (**2**) .... been born as a boy. First of all, I (**3**) .... not have (**4**) .... the opportunity to wear such interesting clothes. (**5**) .... I (**6**) .... male, I think I'd also (**7**) .... felt more pressure to get a secure job. My brother sometimes says that he wishes he (**8**) .... a girl, as we (**9**) .... things easier and I must say that I think I (**10**) .... inclined to agree.

3 Look at A and B below, both of which are grammatically correct. Improve them as much as you can.

A
> I am very much against the proposed new factory. Firstly, building it will involve cutting down a lovely wood. Secondly, it will cause additional traffic problems in the area. Last but not least, it will lead to increased air and water pollution in our area.

B
> It was an excellent film. I liked the way in which the main actress presented her character. I also liked the way in which the plot was developed. I loved the camerawork and the music too.

E xam spot

If you want to get more practice in spoken English, you should take every opportunity to speak to other people in English and to watch films and TV in English whenever you have the chance. You might even try talking to yourself in English!

G ⋯⋮ page 207

Vocabulary

V ocabulary spot

It is important to try to use a range of vocabulary when you are answering a question in the CAE Writing test (Paper 2).

1 Replace the words in italics below with as many alternatives as you can think of. How do the different words you suggest affect the meaning of the sentences?

a I was *surprised* by the writer's account of his adventures in Peru.

b I spent my first evening in the town where I would spend the next five years of my life *walking* round the city streets.

c My brother *said* that he would always support me if I needed help.

d My first day in my new job turned out to be very *interesting*.

e There was a *man* sitting opposite me reading a newspaper.

f You can *get* a variety of souvenirs at the market.

2 Look at the two sets of verbs below. For each set, match the verbs (a–d) with the person (1–4) most likely to behave in this way.

A

a	tiptoe	1	a drunk person
b	lurch	2	an arrogant person
c	strut	3	someone who has no special aim
d	wander	4	someone who is anxious not to wake others up

B

a	yell	1	someone who feels very strongly that something should be done
b	murmur	2	a nervous person
c	stammer	3	an angry person
d	insist	4	someone who wants only one person to hear

3 What other verbs can you add to the two lists (A and B) and what shades of meaning do these words provide?

4 Think of two different adjectives to describe the following:

- everything that you can see from the window of the room you are in at the moment
- everything that you have in your pockets or handbag.

Speaking 2

1 Are the following good or bad pieces of advice for the CAE Speaking test (Paper 5)?

a Look down at the ground when you are speaking.
b When you are talking to your partner, it is more important that your partner should hear you than that the examiner should hear you.
c You will sound more natural if you talk very quickly.
d It is a good idea to shout at the examiner in case he or she is hard of hearing.
e Speak very slowly and clearly and pronounce each word as distinctly as you can.
f English intonation patterns go up and down quite a lot and so using a very flat intonation will sound unnatural.
g Keep eye contact with the examiner at all times.
h Speak a little bit indistinctly so that the examiner will not realise if you make pronunciation mistakes.

2 Now turn any of the bad pieces of advice from Speaking 1 into a positive recommendation.

EXAMPLE: ~~Look down at the ground when you are speaking~~ – *Keep your head up and speak directly to the examiner and/or your partner as fits the part of the test.*

3 Work in groups of four. Take it in turns to be the pair of candidates and the pair of examiners. One pair should look at the pictures in Task A and the other pair should look at the pictures in Task B. After each pair of candidates has completed their task, the examiners should comment on the candidates' performance.

Task A (Examiner's questions)
Which two of the jobs below would you like to do least and which two most? Why?

Task B (Examiner's questions)
Discuss the different ways below that a school principal could use to choose a new teacher. Which procedure do you think would be most useful? Which would be least useful? Why?

Units 26–30 Revision

Topic review

a What is your favourite place in your country?

b How is your country like Great Britain? How is it different?

c How far do you think people judge by appearances?

d What did you think of the short story in Unit 27?

e How do you feel about flying?

f An increasing number of people are going on walking holidays. Why do you think this is?

g Which do you prefer: tests or continuous assessment? Why?

h Does wrapping children up in cotton wool protect them or harm them?

i When people are nervous in job interviews, how do they show it?

j What did you use to want to be when you were a child?

Vocabulary

1 For each of the sentences below, fill the gap with a word based on the word in brackets at the end of each sentence.

a The mountainous .... in Switzerland is particularly spectacular. (scene)

b The gardens were all south-facing to gain maximum .... to the sun. (expose)

c The Grand Canyon was created by millions of years of .... (erode)

d .... , her father wasn't too pleased when she said she'd scratched his new car. (predict)

e I was absolutely taken aback by such .... behaviour from him. (expect)

f From the airlines, you only get a small sum in compensation for lost luggage, ... of the value of the contents of your suitcases. (regard)

Reading

1 Answer these questions about the text. Choose the correct option, A, B, C or D.

1 What did interviews tend to be like more than five years ago?
   A friendly conversations
   B either very relaxed or deliberately stressful
   C accompanied by a cup of tea or lunch
   D a police interrogation

2 How do modern companies want to save money?
   A by not inviting so many people to interview
   B by interviewing people from a distance
   C by not choosing unsuitable employees
   D by using scientific interview techniques

3 Which part of the selection process now has most influence on who gets a job?
   A interview
   B aptitude test
   C personality questionnaire
   D evaluation at assessment centre

4 What is the main aim of interviews these days?
   A To check that you have the necessary skills for the job.
   B To discover whether your past experience is relevant for the job.
   C To determine whether you really want the job.
   D To establish that your values match those of the company.

5 What is special about a structured interview?
   A It includes psychological tests.
   B All candidates are asked the same questions.
   C Questions vary to match individual candidates.
   D It asks candidates what they would do in specific situations.

6 Why are interviews in some ways more relaxed now than they used to be?
   A Candidates talk more when they are relaxed.
   B Offices have simpler furniture these days.
   C Work hierarchies have no importance now.
   D The interview is seen as a meeting of equals.

7 How successful are modern interviews in helping employers to choose the right candidate?
   A very successful   B quite successful
   C not very successful   D of no use at all

8 This article was probably published in
   A a magazine for employers.   B a psychology journal.
   C a general interest newspaper. D a magazine for students.

Making the best of a good job

Today's applicants need to run the gauntlet of modern interview techniques. Peter Baker reports.

If your last job interview took place five or more years ago, you could be in for some big surprises when you re-enter the employment market. Interviews are now much less likely to take the form of a cosy fireside chat. Neither, at the other extreme, should you expect an intimidating interrogation supposedly designed to test your ability to cope with stress. These traditional approaches have gone the way of tea-trolleys and two-hour lunch-breaks.

As lean modern companies have learned the costs of making bad appointments, interviews have become part of a multi-layered quasi-scientific selection process, and are increasingly likely to be conducted by managers trained in complex psychological techniques. They are also becoming high-tech: before too long, candidates can expect many interview panels to include at least one member who participates by means of video-conferencing technology from another site or even overseas.

One thing has not changed. It is still unusual to get a job without a face-to-face encounter with your boss-to-be. Interviews are used by 75 per cent of companies for every category of staff they employ, according to an Industrial Relations Services (IRS) survey published in September. The same proportion of firms believe that, of all the selection tools available, interviews have the most influence on their appointment decisions.

But these days you cannot rely just on your skills as an interviewee to get the job you want. There is a good chance that you will have to start proving yourself well before you reach the interview room.

A recent analysis of recruitment methods by the Institute of Personnel and Development found that 61 per cent of firms also used aptitude tests, 43 per cent sent out personality questionnaires and 30 per cent evaluated potential staff at assessment centres. Professional and managerial staff are especially likely to be put through a wide range of selection techniques before they reach the final interview with the employer.

'By the time you've reached this stage, you are 90 per cent there in terms of an acceptance by the employer that you can do the job,' says Bill Robbins, director of the senior executive centre at Drake Beam Morin.

'Although you may be tested further on the skills and experience the company thinks are especially important, the interview is likely to focus more on your motivation for the job and how well you will fit into the organisation and its culture.'

Selection panels are now putting increasing effort into probing candidates' inner values to see whether they match those of the company. Your values could even be assessed by psychological tests conducted during the interview itself.

A test devised by occupational psychology consultancy Criterion Partnership requires candidates to select, rank and then discuss cards containing value-reflecting headings or statements such as 'money and status', 'opportunity to make independent decisions' and 'I need approval in work'.

Criterion has also developed an interview exercise that assesses candidates by asking them to discuss what they believe to have been the causes of positive or negative past work experiences. Someone who is inclined to blame themselves for negative events may be judged not to have sufficient emotional stamina to take on a job dealing with customer complaints, for example.

In today's job marketplace, you can expect the interview to be a 'structured' event – each candidate will be asked the same predetermined questions – rather than a process guided by whatever questions happen to float into the minds of the panel. (This standardisation aims to provide a better basis for comparing candidates and reducing bias on the grounds of race or gender.) The IRS survey found that nine out of ten interviews are now structured, compared with seven out of ten two years ago.

An increasing number of interviews are also 'situational'. This means that candidates are asked questions such as 'What would you do if...?', an approach that lets them provide practical examples of how they would tackle particular situations, whether or not they have had any direct experience of them.

Despite their increasing rigour, interviews are generally becoming a lot less formal. Candidates and interviewers are now much more likely to sit on sofas than face each other across a large mahogany table. Fran Minogue of recruitment company Norman Broadbent believes that selection panels 'aim to relax people so they can open up and do as much talking as possible.' This new informality also reflects the decreasing importance attached to hierarchy within organisations.

The biggest change in the style of interviews will be noticed by senior staff with skills currently in short supply in the labour market. 'At this level, interviews are increasingly a conversation between equals,' suggests Bill Robbins. 'That's a big change.'

Yet despite all efforts to bring the interview process up-to-date, employers frequently make the wrong choice. Although the interview remains the centrepiece of organisations' selection procedures, it is in fact a highly unreliable predictor of a candidate's suitability. When Oxford Psychologists Press examined all the evidence, they found that interviewing came third from bottom in a list of eight methods of selection. Only astrology and graphology scored worse.

But you would be best advised not to point this out to a potential employer – at least not until you have definitely been offered the job.

Grammar

1 Write one word in each gap. The exercise begins with an example (0).

Testing … testing … testing

Is the nation's obsession with examining (0) ...*its*...... pupils placing a continuous burden of toil and stress on teachers, parents and children?

At Clapham Manor primary school in south London on Thursday, 24 children, all 10 or 11 years old, sit in silence completing, along with (1) .... estimated 599,976 children in classrooms around the country, a key stage 2 English writing test.

Some fidget, some look around the room, but most (2) .... diligently. They have to deliver one piece of writing from four choices.

Their teacher has read through the paper with them. They have had 15 minutes (3) .... plan and 45 minutes to write. They are in their normal classroom, but some parts of their walls have (4) .... to be covered – aides-to-learning like "explanation" words.

When the exam finishes there is no heavy sighing, (5) .... hint of tears. They just sit while their teacher gathers their papers, and wait (6) .... the next thing, which happens to be *The Guardian* asking them (7) .... it went. Four thought it was hard. Fourteen thought it was easy. Twelve (8) .... nervous before. Sixteen enjoyed it. Four thought their parents were worried about how they would (9) ....

"You don't have to look for things to write – it's just your imagination," said Ali.

"We have done (10) .... many practice tests before this that it was easy," said Rachel.

Speaking

1 Work with a partner. Allow each other one minute to talk without interruption on one of the following subjects:

- what I have particularly enjoyed during my CAE course
- what I shall always remember about the people in this class
- the unit that I enjoyed most from this book.

2 Now discuss with the class as a whole what your plans and hopes are for the next few months, for keeping up your English and for your life in general.

Grammar folder

Unit 1

Conditionals

Conditional sentences are often considered to be one of four main types:

- Zero conditional is used to talk about common states or events.
  if / when + present simple + present simple
  If she knows you well, she is more talkative.
  When we see each other in the street, we say hello.

- First conditional is used to talk about possible future states or events.
  if / when + present simple / continuous + *will / be going to*
  If you go away to study, you'll meet a lot of new people.
  I'm going to start without him if he doesn't come soon.

- Second conditional is used to talk about unlikely or imaginary states or events in the present or future.
  if + past simple / continuous + *would / could / should / might*
  If she spoke Spanish, she could apply for the job in Madrid.
  If they had the money, they would leave their jobs and travel the world.
  With *be*, the second conditional uses *were* instead of *was* in formal contexts.
  If I were / was good at languages, I'd learn Japanese.

- Third conditional is used to talk about imaginary states or events in the past.
  if + past perfect + *would / could / should / might* + *have* + past participle
  If we had studied other cultures at school, we might have been more confident about travelling.
  If you had arrived in Japan three months ago, you would have seen the cherry blossom.

Mixed conditionals

Different conditional forms are sometimes mixed, particularly second and third conditionals.

- A third conditional cause is sometimes linked to a second conditional result to show the imaginary present result of an imaginary past event or situation.
  If my parents had never met, I wouldn't be here now!

- A second conditional cause is sometimes linked to a third conditional result to show how an ongoing situation produced an effect in the past.
  If I knew anything about computers, I would have applied for a website design job.

Other conditionals

There are a number of other conditional sentences formed with different patterns of tenses to the four main types described above. Some common examples of alternative conditional structures are:

- *if / when* + present simple + imperative
  This is used to make suggestions or to give advice or instructions.
  If you need a translator, please let me know.
  Get off the train when you get to the third station.

- *if / when* + present simple / present perfect + *can / could / would / should / might*
  This is often used to make suggestions or offer advice.
  She could give Martin the message if she sees him later.
  If you've studied English, you should try to speak it.

Notice that when the *if* clause is first in the sentence, it is followed by a comma. There is no comma when the main clause comes first.

- We can use *will* after *if* when we talk about the result of something in the main clause, or in polite requests.
  Post the parcel at the main post office if it will get there quicker.
  If you will just wait a moment, I'll tell Mr Jackson you're here.

- To make the request more polite, we can use *would*.
  If you would take a seat for a moment, I'll let Mr Jackson know you're here.

- We can leave out *if* and put *should* at the beginning of the clause, particularly in formal or literary English.
  Should you wish to extend your stay, please inform reception.

- We can use *was / were not for* or *had not been for* to say that one situation is dependent on another situation or person.
  If it hadn't been for the tour guide, we would never have seen those carvings in the caves.

- We can use *if* + *was / were* + *to* + infinitive to talk about imaginary future situations.
  If the technology were to become available, we would be able to travel across the world in just a couple of hours.

Unit 2

Prepositions and adverbs

- A preposition is a word that expresses the relation between the word(s) before it and the preposition's object which follows it. The object of a preposition is a noun or noun group. Prepositions in their most basic use indicate direction and position.
  Jane's moving to the Isle of Skye. (direction)
  Write the address on this envelope. (position)

- Many prepositions can also be adverbs and are used without an object.
  He went in. (*in* is an adverb)
  He went in the house. (*in* is a preposition)

- An adverb is a word that modifies or qualifies a clause. There are different types of adverbs, including adverbs of place, manner, time, frequency and duration.
  There's a good hotel nearby. (place)
  She writes entertainingly. (manner)
  My parents write to me regularly. (frequency)

Words which can be commonly used as both adverbs and prepositions include:

about   above   below   down   in   near   off   outside   up

A good dictionary will tell you if a word is a preposition or an adverb.

Unit 3

Wish and *if only*

Wish and *if only* are used to express wishes and regrets.

- *Wish* / *if only* + past simple is used to express a wish or regret about a general state that exists in the present, or a usual or regular event or habit.
  He wishes he was a photographer instead of an actor.
  If only we had longer holidays.
  If only driving to work didn't take so long.

- *Wish* / *if only* + *would* is also used to express a wish or regret about a usual or regular event or habit. We use *would* when the person or thing doing the action could change their behaviour if they chose to. It is often used to complain about someone's behaviour.
  If only the children would be quiet.
  I wish you would look for a job.

- *Wish* / *if only* + past perfect is used to express a wish or regret about the past by saying how we would like the past to be different.
  I wish I had trained as a doctor instead of as a teacher.
  If only she had thought more about her career while she was still at school.

- *Wish* + infinitive is used in very formal language to mean *want* + infinitive. It can be used to talk about the past, present or future.
  Napoleon wished to keep his battle plans a secret until the very last moment.
  Please be quiet. The Director wishes to say a few words.
  I'm sure she'll wish to thank you for your gift.

- Note that when people talk about their wishes for the future, it is unusual to use the verb *wish*; the verb *hope* is usually used.
  I hope you enjoy your stay in our town.
  She hopes to get a job in television.

It's time

There are several different structures that can be used with *it's time*. The meanings are very similar:

- *It's time* + infinitive
  It's time to go home now.

- *It's time for* + object + infinitive
  It's time for us to go home now.

- *It's time* + subject + past simple (a little more formal)
  It's time we went home now.

- *It's time* + subject + past continuous (more colloquial)
  It's time we were going home now.

- To say that something should have been done already, *about time* and *high time* can be used.
  It's about time we went home.
  It's high time we went home.

Would rather / would sooner

Would rather and *would sooner* are used to express a preference for one situation or event over another. They mean the same as *prefer to* + infinitive.

- *Would rather* / *would sooner* + infinitive is used to express a preference about a general situation or event, or about a possible future situation or event.
  I'd sooner work days than nights.
  I'd rather / I'd sooner travel the world than go to university.

- *Would rather* / *would sooner* + subject + present simple / past simple is used to express a preference for another person (or thing) to do or not do something generally or in the future. The use of the past simple expresses the preference a little more tentatively or politely than the present simple.
  I would rather she works than does nothing.
  He'd sooner you didn't tell anyone about the interview yet.

- In formal contexts the subjunctive is used. Instead of the present simple we use the infinitive without *to*; past subjunctive is the same as past simple except for *be*, where the past subjunctive always uses *were*.
  I'd rather he go now.
  I'd sooner she were happy in her work.

- *Would rather* / *would sooner* + *have* + past participle is used to express a preference for one situation or outcome in the past over another.
  When he was young, he'd rather have been a photographer than an actor. (But he is / was an actor.)

- *Would rather* / *would sooner* + subject + past perfect is used to express a wish or preference that actions or events in the past were different, and it is often used to talk about another person's actions.
  I'd rather you had asked me before you borrowed the car yesterday.
  I'd rather it hadn't rained all through the holiday.

Unit 4

Modals: *may, might, can, could*

Modal verbs give an indication of a speaker's attitude and of the relationship between the speaker and the person spoken to. Modals can indicate degrees of certainty, uncertainty, formality, informality, tentativeness, respect and politeness.

Ability

- *Can* expresses ability in the present; *could* expresses general ability in the past.
  He's lucky he can remember facts very easily.
  When I was a child I could speak Welsh but now I've forgotten it completely.

- To talk about an achievement or something that was done with difficulty, we do not use *could*. We can use *was / were able to*, *managed to* + infinitive or *succeeded in* + verb + *-ing*.
  She managed to / was able to memorise all the words before the test.
  On holiday, they succeeded in holding a conversation with a vocabulary of just 50 words.

- We can also use *was / were able to*, *managed to* + infinitive or *succeeded in* + verb + *-ing* to express that someone was successful in doing something on one occasion.
  Were you able to get his autograph after the concert?
  We managed to find my mobile phone by ringing my own number.
  After queuing for an hour, we succeeded in getting tickets for the show.

Permission

- *Can* is often used to express permission and *cannot / can't* is often used to express prohibition in the present and in general time. *Could* and *couldn't* are used to express permission and prohibition in the past.
  You can leave whenever you want. (permission)
  In the UK, children cannot leave school until they are 16. (prohibition)
  In the 1950s, children in the UK could leave school at 14. (permission)
  In the 1950s in the UK, young adults couldn't vote until they were 21. (prohibition)

- *May* is sometimes used to express permission and prohibition in the present. It is more formal and polite than *can*.
  Members may not wear jeans or T-shirts at formal ceremonies.

Requests, suggestions and polite orders

- *Can* and *could* are both used to make offers and requests and to give polite orders and suggestions. *Can* is informal; *could* is neutral.
  Can / Could I help you with that? (offer)
  Can / Could you test me on these words? (request)
  You can / could check the recipe and find the ingredients while I wash up. (polite order / suggestion)

- *Might* is sometimes used to request permission very politely but is usually used only in highly formal situations.
  Might I be allowed to give an opinion on this matter?
  Might I suggest that we take a vote on this proposal?

Possibility and probability

- *May, might* and *could* are used to speculate about the possibility of events and situations in the present and future. *Might* indicates a lower probability or more uncertainty than *may* and *could*. In the negative, *could not / couldn't* indicates almost total certainty, much greater than *may not* or *might not / mightn't*. (In modern English *mayn't* is extremely unusual and should not be used.)
  They could decide to take the train. (possible)
  She may get here on time if she catches the early train. (possible)
  She might get here on time if she catches the later train. (less probable)
  She couldn't arrive before 10, it's impossible. (certain)

- *May, might* and *could* + *have* + past participle are used to speculate about events and situations in the past.
  They're late. They may have been held up in the rush hour traffic.
  I left a message at their hotel but they might not have got it yet.
  They couldn't have met by coincidence in London; it's too big.

- *May, might* and *could* + *have* + past participle are used to talk about possibilities in the past that we know didn't actually happen. The context has to be examined to decide whether the structure has this meaning or whether it expresses speculation about something that perhaps did actually happen as described above.
  Didn't you use a map? You might have got lost. (But you didn't.)
  She was very intelligent and could have gone to university. (But she didn't.)

- *Cannot / can't* is used to express negative certainty about the present based on evidence.
  This bill can't be right. We've only had two coffees!

- *Cannot / can't* + *have* + past participle is used to express negative certainty about the past based on evidence.
  This doesn't taste like pizza. She can't have followed the recipe.

- *Can* and *could* are used to talk about theoretical possibility. *Could* indicates less confidence than *can*.
  The school can take 1,000 pupils and it usually does.
  The school could take 1,000 pupils but it would be difficult in terms of space.

- *May, might* and *could* + *be* + verb + *-ing* are used to speculate about events and situations in the immediate present and in the future.
  Where's Sam? He might be studying in his room.
  Fiona could be managing her own company a year from now.

Unit 5
Relative clauses

Defining relative clauses

- Defining relative clauses give essential information so that we can identify who or what is being talked about. The relative clause follows immediately after the noun referring to the person(s) or thing(s) we are talking about.
  The woman who showed the most determination got the job.

- We do not put commas at the beginning and end of a defining relative clause.

- We can sometimes omit the relative pronoun. The relative pronoun must be used when it is the subject of the following verb.
  She showed me photos of the gorillas (which / that) she had studied.
  She showed me photos of the gorillas which / that lived nearby. (The relative pronoun must be used here because it is the subject of *lived*.)
  The letter (which / that) you received in September explains our position.
  The letter which / that arrived in September explains our position. (The relative pronoun must be used here because it is the subject of *arrived*.)

Non-defining relative clauses

- Non-defining relative clauses give non-essential, extra information about something or someone.
  Dian Fossey, who was born in the USA, made a major contribution to the study of primates.

- We use a comma before and immediately after the clause.

- We cannot omit the relative pronoun in non-defining relative clauses.

Relative pronouns

Many relative clauses are introduced by a relative pronoun.

- *Which* and *that* refer to things but *that* is not used in non-defining relative clauses.
  The study that she published last month is remarkable.
  Her most recent study, which she's just published, is her best yet.

- *Who* refers to people.
  Dian, who has specialised in primates, has spent a lot of time in Africa.

- *Whom* refers to people if they are the object of the clause. It is very formal and not commonly used in modern English.
  Professor West, whom I worked with recently, has won the Nobel prize.

- *Whose* can be used with things or people and expresses possession or belonging.
  She is a scientist whose work is world famous.
  The book, whose focus is African primates, is very influential.

- *When* refers to time.
  She described the moment when she first saw a wild gorilla.

- *Where* refers to place.
  She spent many years in Africa, where she observed gorillas in the wild.

Prepositions in relative clauses

- In neutral English, and sometimes in modern formal English, prepositions can be placed at the end of the sentence. In formal English, putting prepositions at the end of the sentence is sometimes considered bad style. Formal sentences are often constructed to place the preposition earlier in the sentence.

  That was the story which the film was based on.
  That was the story on which the film was based.

- When the preposition is placed earlier in the sentence, *that* cannot be used.
  That's the research that/which she received the award for.
  That is the research for which she received the award.

- When the preposition is placed earlier in the sentence, *whom* must be used as the relative pronoun when the object is a person.
  She spoke to a professor that / who / whom she is friendly with.
  She spoke to a professor with whom she is friendly.

Unit 6
Phrasal verbs

- Phrasal verbs are made up of more than one part. They are verbs with prepositional or adverbial particles. Some common examples are:

  put off   look up to   take in   do up   break out   get out of   turn down

- The meaning of a phrasal verb is often not obvious from the meaning of its components and so it is probably best to learn them as individual items.
  make off with = steal something and carry it away quickly

- There are many phrasal verbs in English and they are most frequently, though not exclusively, used in spoken English and in more informal writing. There is often a single word with the same meaning which is preferred in more formal writing.
  The football match has been put off until next week.
  The football match has been postponed until next week.
  The price of petrol has gone up three times already this year.
  The price of petrol has increased three times already this year.

- Many phrasal verbs have more than one meaning.
  He asked her to stop singing as it was putting him off. (distract)
  The football match has been put off until next week. (postpone)
  Don't be put off if you can't do it straight away. (cause someone to change their mind about doing something)
  Would you put off the light before you leave? (switch off)

Word order restrictions vary for different phrasal verbs.

- Some verbs can have their object before or after the particle.
  We did our bathroom up last year.
  We did up our bathroom last year.

- If the object is a pronoun, it must go between the two parts of the verb.
  We did it up by ourselves.

- Other verbs can only take an object after the particle. With such verbs the pronoun also follows the second part of the verb.
  She has fallen for the boy who lives next door. Fortunately, he has also fallen for her.

There is more information about the grammar of phrasal verbs in the grammar folder for Unit 23.

Unit 7
Cause and effect

Cause and effect can be expressed in a number of different ways.

- Verbs and verb phrases
  The following verbs all introduce **effect** (= consequences or results):

  lie behind   bring about   generate   give rise to   lead to   produce   result in

  Summer clubs for school students in the UK have led to a decrease in the crime rate.
  A poor diet will result in health problems.

  The following verbs all introduce **cause**:

  arise from   be based on   come from   stem from

  Her attitude stems from her background.
  The success of the company is based on the employees' hard work and enthusiasm.

- Conjunctions and adverbs
  The following conjunctions and adverbs show **relationships between cause and effect**:

  because   consequently   so   therefore

  She got to the top in her career because she spoke to all the right people.
  He is ambitious, so he doesn't mind staying late at work most evenings.

- Prepositions
  The following prepositions all introduce **cause**:

  because of   due to   for   owing to

  Rosie got the job because of her pleasant manner.
  Owing to the storms, all trains have been cancelled.
  I couldn't sleep for worrying.

- Nouns and noun phrases
  The following nouns refer to **cause and effect**:

  aim   basis   consequence   explanation   motive
  outcome   purpose   reason   result

  The aim of the programme was to give students work experience.
  His laziness is the reason why he is not as successful as he could be.

Unit 8
Modals: *must, should, ought to, shall, will, would*

Must

- *Must* can be used to express obligation. *Mustn't* expresses prohibition. The past form of *must* used to express obligation is *had to* and the negative is *wasn't / weren't allowed to*.
  You must do exactly what the exam questions ask you to do.
  You mustn't talk during the exam.
  We had to write two compositions in last week's exam.
  We weren't allowed to take any books into the exam.

- *Must* can also be used to make deductions from evidence and expresses certainty. The past form of *must* for deduction is *must + have + past participle*. We use *must be going to + infinitive* to make deductions about the future. The negative of *must* for this meaning is *can't* (see Unit 4).
  That must be John coming up the steps – I recognise his footsteps!
  The train is late – the heavy snow must have caused delays.
  They bought lots of paint – they must be going to decorate.

- *Must* and *mustn't* are used to give strong advice.
  You must stop smoking.
  You mustn't give up hope.

- *Must* and *mustn't* are used to make recommendations.
  You must see Spielberg's new film – it's brilliant!
  You mustn't miss it.

- *Must* and *mustn't* are used to talk about strong necessity.
  We must have oxygen to survive.

Ought to and *should*

- *Ought to* and *should* are used to say that something seems likely because it is logical or normal.
  It's 6 o'clock. He ought to / should be home soon.

- *Ought to* and *should* can be used to give advice or suggest that something would be a good idea.
  You ought to / should tell her how you feel.
  Someone ought to / should open a café here because there isn't one for miles.

- *Ought to* and *should* are used to talk about duty and express weak obligation.
  People ought to / should wait in the queue and not push in.

- *Ought to* and *should* are used to criticise actions or attitudes.
  People ought to / should show more respect for old people.

- *Ought to* and *should* are used to talk about the importance of doing something.
  The manager suggested that we ought to / should leave the restaurant as quickly as possible.
  We ought to / should get back before the sun goes down.

- *Ought to* and *should* are used to talk about necessity.
  Sports clothes should be light and allow you to move easily.

- The negative forms are *ought not to* or *oughtn't to* and *should not* or *shouldn't*.
  You oughtn't to / shouldn't be late on your first day at work.

- The past forms are *ought to / should + have + past participle*.
  You ought to have / should have told us you were coming.

Will and *would*

- *Will* and *would* are used to make polite invitations and requests. *Would* is more polite.
  Will / Would you sit here, please?

- *Will* and *won't* are used to describe habits and characteristic behaviour in the present and in general. If *will* is stressed, it indicates the speaker's irritation with or negative opinion of the habit.
  He will / he'll watch TV all evening. Sometimes he won't talk for hours.
  *He **will** play golf every weekend, instead of helping me in the garden.*

- *Would* and *wouldn't* are used to talk about past habits and characteristics. If *would* is stressed, it indicates the speaker's irritation with or negative opinion of the habit.
  Every evening she would / she'd sit in the garden reading her newspaper. She wouldn't stop until she'd read every page.
  *He **would** insist on smoking. It killed him in the end, of course.*

- *Will* is used to express demands, insist that something happens in the future or express determination.
  You will do as I say immediately!
  I will / I'll go where I want and don't try to stop me!

There is more information about other uses of *will* and *would* in the grammar folders for Unit 1 (conditionals) and Unit 10 (future forms).

Unit 9
Participle clauses

The table below shows the different participle forms for the verb *wash*.

Participle	
Present active	*washing*
Present passive	*being washed*
Perfect active	*having washed*
Perfect passive	*having been washed*

- Participle clauses with a present participle can be used adjectivally.
  Look at that man sitting in the corner. (= who is sitting in the corner)
  Who is the girl being interviewed by the journalist? (= who is being interviewed)

- All participle clauses can be used adverbially.
  Feeling exhausted after the flight, I went to bed as soon as I got to the hotel. (= Because I felt exhausted …)
  Washed by hand, this jersey will keep its shape for years. (= If it is washed by hand …)

- Perfect participle clauses are often adverbial clauses showing when or why something happened.
  Having made your decision, it is not possible to change your mind. (= When you have made …)
  Having spent happy holidays in Spain as a child, she was keen to return there with her own family. (= Because she had spent …)

- The subject of the participle clause is usually the same as that of the main clause. However, it is possible to have participle clauses with a different subject.
  There being no money left, we had to start making our way home. (= Because there was no money left …)
  It being too late to get a bus, we took a taxi. (= Because it was too late …)

- When the participle clause describes a situation, a different subject is often introduced with the word *with*.
  I was beginning to get a headache with the children all talking at the same time.
  With it / It being Sunday in New Zealand, we couldn't find any shops open.

Unit 10

Future forms

The future in English can be expressed in many different ways.

Will

- *Will* is used to talk about a future action or event at the point of decision.
  I'll come to the cinema with you tonight, I think.

- *Will* is used to make predictions about the future.
  You will meet a tall, dark stranger.

- *Will* is used to make promises.
  I'll buy you a car for your birthday.

Going to

- *Going to* is used to talk about intentions. Sometimes it is used to talk about plans and arrangements based on intentions (but the present continuous is more commonly used for talking about arrangements).
  We're going to visit our friends in New Zealand next winter.

- *Going to* is also used to talk about future events and actions based on present evidence, especially when we can see that the event is imminent.
  The way Brazil are playing at the moment, they're going to win the match.
  Watch out! We're going to hit that tree!

Present continuous

- The present continuous is used to talk about plans and arrangements for the future. A time reference often makes the future meaning clear.
  What are you doing tonight?
  We're meeting early tomorrow morning.

Present simple

- The present simple is used to talk about timetables and schedules.
  Our train leaves at 6.30 tomorrow morning.

- The present simple is used with future reference in subordinate clauses after time conjunctions such as *when, before, until, as soon as.*
  We'll reply when we hear from you.
  I hope you'll write to us as soon as you get home.

Be + infinitive

- *Be* + infinitive is formal. It is used in rules or instructions, or to talk about official plans. It is particularly common in news reports.
  Staff are not to use company telephones for personal calls.
  The Prime Minister is to visit South America next month.

Future continuous

- The future continuous focuses on an action or event in progress at a specific time in the future.
  This time next week I'll be lying on a beach in the sun.

Future perfect

- The future perfect looks forward to a future time and then looks back from that point.
  By the end of next year we'll have finished the project.

Future in the past: *was / were going to / would* + verb

- These forms are used to look back to a past time and talk about the future as it was at that past time.
  By the time I left school I knew I was going to / would become a doctor.

There is more information on first and second conditionals in the grammar folder for Unit 1.

Unit 11

Direct and reported speech

Grammatical changes

Some features of grammar in direct speech must be changed in reported speech.

- When we report what someone said, we tend to change the verb tense, which is called 'backshift'. Personal pronouns, demonstratives and other references to the 'here and now' may also need to be changed.
  'I've seen a bank clerk wearing a nose ring.'
  She said that she'd seen a bank clerk wearing a nose ring.
  'I'll be arriving at your house at 10 am tomorrow.'
  She said that she would be arriving at my house at 10 am the next day.

- Most modal verbs do not usually change, but *can* changes to *could* and *will* changes to *would*.
  'You must dress professionally at all times.'
  He told us we must dress professionally at all times.
  'You should have a dress code.'
  She suggested that we should have a dress code.
  'I can pay cash.'
  He said he could pay cash.
  'I'll pay by credit card.'
  He said he'd pay by credit card.

- When something is reported that is a general truth, or if the situation hasn't changed yet, there is often no tense change.
  She said that darker coloured clothes generally look smarter.
  My neighbour's 4-year-old told me she wants to be a dress designer when she grows up.

- In reported questions, the subject usually comes before the verb and the auxiliaries *do*, *does* and *did* are only used in negative reported questions. *Yes / No* questions are reported with *if* or *whether*. Question marks are not used in reported questions.
  'Which suit do you prefer?'
  She asked (me) which suit I preferred.
  'Why don't you like shopping?'
  He asked (me) why I didn't like shopping.
  'Could you help me choose some new shoes?'
  She asked (me) if / whether I could help her choose some new shoes.

Verbs used to report speech

We can use a wide variety of verbs to introduce reported speech. Different verbs are followed by different structures. The list below shows some common verbs and their dependent patterns. Note that *that* may be omitted after most of the common reporting verbs.

- *advise + to +* infinitive
  She advised us to check the contract carefully.

- *agree + that* (optional) */ + to +* infinitive
  He agreed (that) our money would be refunded.
  He agreed to refund our money.

- *ask + if/whether / + to +* infinitive
  We asked if we could have more training.
  We asked to have more training.

- *complain + that*
  We complained that the service was very slow.

- *deny + that* (optional) */ + -ing*
  She denied (that) she had taken the credit card.
  She denied taking the credit card.

- *insist + that* (optional) */ + on + -ing*
  He insisted (that) we stay at his house.
  He insisted on our staying at his house.

- *invite + to +* infinitive
  She invited us to visit any time.

- *offer + to +* infinitive
  They have offered to help.

- *promise + that* (optional) */ + to +* infinitive
  The management has promised (that) training will be provided.
  The management has promised to provide training.

- *recommend + that* (optional) */ + -ing*
  I recommend (that) you book well in advance.
  I recommend booking well in advance.

- *regret + that* (optional) */ + -ing*
  He regrets (that) he won't be able to attend the ceremony.
  He regrets not being able to attend the ceremony.

- *say + that* (optional)
  The manager said (that) we should arrange an appointment.

- *suggest + that* (optional) */ + -ing*
  She suggested (that) I buy the black jeans.
  She suggested (that) I should buy the black jeans.
  She suggested buying the black jeans.

- *tell + that* (optional) */ + to +* infinitive
  His sister told him (that) he should get a job.
  His sister told him to get a job.

- *threaten + that* (optional) */ + to +* infinitive
  The bank manager threatened (that) she would take away my credit card.
  The bank manager threatened to take away my credit card.

- *warn + that* (optional) */ + to +* infinitive */ about + -ing*
  She warned me (that) credit was expensive.
  She warned me not to use credit.
  She warned me about using credit.

Unit 12

Past tenses and the present perfect

Past time can be expressed in many different ways in English. Some examples of the different forms used to refer to the past are described below.

Past simple

- The past simple is used to talk about a completed action, event or situation at a particular time or over a particular time in the past.
  The train left at 8.30 am.
  We lived in London until I got a job in Oxford.

- The past simple is used to talk about repeated actions in the past.
  He read a chapter of the book every night before going to sleep.
  We went to the beach at weekends in the summer.

Past continuous

The past continuous cannot be used with stative verbs (*be, know, love*, etc.), which describe a state rather than an action. With stative verbs the past simple is used.

- The past continuous is used to talk about a situation or action in progress around a point in time in the past.
  I was living in London when Kennedy was assassinated.
  What were you doing at 9 on Tuesday evening?

- The past continuous is used to talk about a situation or action in progress that is interrupted by another event.
  While I was thinking about the problem I suddenly had the most amazing idea.
  The plane was coming in to land when it was struck by lightning.

- The past continuous is used to emphasise that two situations or events were happening simultaneously.
  While I was trying to phone her, she was trying to phone me!
  I was putting the toys away and the children were getting them back out again.

- The past continuous is used with *always* and *forever* to talk about repeated actions or behaviour.
  They were forever asking for favours, but they never did anything for anyone else.
  She was always offering to babysit so that my husband and I could go out.

Present perfect simple

- The present perfect simple is used to talk about past events or situations in a time period that extends from the past up to the present. It is often used to talk about experience. The specific time is unknown or unimportant and we cannot use words which mark the specific moment when the event happened (e.g. *yesterday, last year*).
  That shop has had three new managers and it's still losing money.
  I've been to Russia. – When did you go? – I went last June.

- It is also used to say how many times something has happened in that period.
  They've lived at three different addresses since June.

- The present perfect simple is used to talk about an event in the past that has a result in the present. In this use the focus is on the effect or importance of the past event at the present moment. The event is often, but not always, in the recent past. The specific time is unknown or unimportant and, again, we cannot use words which mark specific points in time like *yesterday* or *last year*.
  Cancel the skiing trip – I've broken my leg.
  Has he finished that report yet?

- The present perfect simple is used to talk about the duration of an event or situation which started in the past and extends up to the present. The specific starting point or the length of the period is given.
  How long have you worked here? – I've been here for two months.
  I've played the piano since I was four.

Present perfect continuous

The present perfect continuous cannot be used with stative verbs (*be, know, love*, etc.), which describe a state rather than an action. With stative verbs the present perfect simple is used.

- The present perfect continuous is used to talk about past events which continue up to the present or up to a time in the recent past.
  I've been watching this film on TV but I'm going to turn it off if something doesn't happen soon.
  She's been helping me with the housework but now she's got bored with it.

- The present perfect continuous is used to talk about repeated past events in a time period that extends up to the present.
  The car has been breaking down a lot recently.
  He's been seeing a new girlfriend most evenings.

- The present perfect continuous is used to talk about an event, action or behaviour in the recent past that has a result in the present. The action may be finished or unfinished. In this use, the focus is on the present evidence for the past event. The specific time is unknown or unimportant and we cannot use words which mark specific points in time.
  It's been raining. (The rain has stopped but the streets are wet.)
  You look exhausted. Have you been working hard? – Yes, but I've almost finished.

- The present perfect continuous is used to talk about the duration of an event or situation which started in the past and extends up to the present. The specific starting point or the length of the period is given.
  Has she been writing her novel for a long time?
  She's been working on it for about six years.

Past perfect simple

- The past perfect simple can be used in similar ways to the present perfect simple, but instead of referring to actions or events up to the present, it refers to actions or events before a particular time (or before another event or action at a particular time) in the past.
  I'd only just sat down at my desk and my boss was asking me where the letters were. (one event happening before another)
  Before I was 18, I hadn't been outside my home town. (experience)
  When I got home, I realised I had left my key at the office so I couldn't get into my flat. (result)
  I'd lived in the house since I was a child and was sorry to leave. (duration)

- Unlike the present perfect, the past perfect can refer to specific times in the past.
  We already felt like old friends even though we had only met that morning.
  He asked me when exactly I had first heard about the problem.

Past perfect continuous

The past perfect continuous cannot be used with stative verbs (*be, know, love*, etc.), which describe a state rather than an action. With stative verbs the past perfect simple is used.

- The past perfect continuous can be used in similar ways to the present perfect continuous, but instead of referring to actions or events up to the present, it refers to actions or events up to a particular time (or up to another event or action at a particular time) in the past.
  The government had been watching the situation closely and were considering whether to intervene. (continuous action)
  She'd been helping at a charity soup kitchen on and off for a few months. (repeated action)
  From the piles of books I knew she'd been working on her thesis again, and I could hear her typing frantically at the keyboard in the next room. (evidence)
  They had been planning their expedition for months before I joined their team. (duration)

- The past perfect continuous can be used in other similar ways to the present perfect continuous, but instead of referring to actions or events up to a recent past, it refers to actions or events up to just before a particular time (or just before another event or action at a particular time) in the past.
  The students had been protesting about the cuts all day, but when I arrived that evening everything was quiet. (continuous action)
  He'd been drinking. I could smell it on his breath. (evidence)

- Unlike the present perfect continuous, the past perfect continuous can refer to specific times in the past.
  At breakfast I wondered why I felt so tired, then I remembered that at 2 am I'd been listening to my neighbours arguing again.

Unit 13

-*ing* forms

With verbs

The -*ing* form occurs in various grammatical patterns and is used to perform different grammatical functions.

- The -*ing* form can be the subject of a verb or the object of a verb.
  Travelling broadens the mind. (subject)
  I dislike travelling by ship. (object)

- Common verbs which are followed by an -*ing* form include:

  admit   avoid   begin*   consider   delay   deny
  dislike   enjoy   forget**   hate*   imagine   intend*
  like*   love*   mind   miss   practise   prefer*
  remember**   resent   risk   start*   stop**
  suggest   try**

  I considered living in Ireland for a while.
  I don't remember telling anyone.

Verbs marked * can also be followed by an infinitive with no change in meaning. Verbs marked ** can also be followed by an infinitive, but the meaning is different. (For example *He tried to do it a different way* means he attempted it, but we don't know if he did it. *He tried doing it a different way* means he actually tested a different method, but we don't know if the new method was any better or worse.)

- Verbs which are followed by the -*ing* form can also be followed by the passive -*ing* form, which is *being* + past participle.
  She enjoys being looked after.

- The verbs *need, want* and *require* can be followed by -*ing*, but this has a passive meaning.
  The machine needs / wants / requires servicing. (The machine needs to be serviced.)

After prepositions

- The -*ing* form can be the object of a preposition. The -*ing* form (rather than the infinitive) always follows a preposition.
  He isn't interested in listening to stories.
  They apologised for being late.
  He never tires of listening to Mozart.
  You should spend more time on renovating the house.

After common phrases

The -*ing* form follows some common phrases.

- *it's (not) worth*
  It's worth getting a book about the country before you go.

- *as well as*
  I play the guitar as well as playing the saxophone.

- *it's no good / use*
  It's no use crying; it won't change anything.

- *there's no use / point in*
  There's no point in waiting because he's not coming.

- *instead of*
  Let's take the car instead of walking in the rain.

- *can't help*
  I can't help laughing whenever I see that film.

- *to be / get / become used to*
  After a few years of travelling by tube, I've got used to people ignoring each other.

After determiners

- The -*ing* form can be used after determiners in formal English to show the possessive.
  Does my listening to the radio bother you?

Unit 14

The passive

When to use the passive

- We use the passive when the action is more important than the person or thing doing the action (the agent).
- We often use the passive when the agent is unknown.
- The passive is often used in more formal situations, such as lectures, academic writing and news reports.

How to form the passive

- The passive is usually formed by moving the object to the front of the sentence. Because of this, usually only transitive verbs can become passives; transitive verbs are verbs which have an object. We cannot say *It has been happened* because *happen* is intransitive.

- However, some intransitive phrasal verbs can also be passives.
  He woke up because of the noise. (active)
  He was woken up by the noise. (passive)

- Passives use the appropriate form of the verb *to be* and the past participle of the main verb. The appropriate form of the verb *to be* is the form that you would use for the verb in the equivalent active sentence. For example:
  Someone is stealing it. – It is being stolen. (present continuous)
  Someone has stolen it. – It has been stolen. (present perfect)
  Someone stole it. – It was stolen. (past simple)
  Someone was stealing it. – It was being stolen. (past continuous)
  Someone had stolen it. – It had been stolen. (past perfect simple)
  Someone will steal it. – It will be stolen. (future simple)

- When a verb has two objects, either object can be the subject of a passive clause. The object that is more important to the message of the sentence is generally the subject.
  Active: *Jill gave her brother the money.*
  Passive: *Her brother was given the money.* / *The money was given to her brother.*

- We can use a passive construction + *by* + agent, when the agent is important to the message.
  Her portrait was painted by Picasso.
  She's been awarded a medal by the Queen.

- The passive with modals is formed with the modal + *be* + past participle. The past form is modal + *have been* + past participle.
  She might be interviewed on TV tonight.
  She should have been interviewed long before now.

The passive used for reporting information

We can use the passive form of reporting verbs to give ideas or opinions without saying exactly where the ideas come from.

- Verbs typically used in the passive for this purpose include:

  assume   believe   claim   consider   feel   hope   report   say   think

- We can use *it* + passive (*that*) + active clause, where *it* is the impersonal pronoun that does not refer to a real subject (like in *It's raining.*).
  It is said (that) most computer users are women.
  It is thought (that) most computer users surf the net.

- We can use passive + *to* + infinitive.
  Most computer users are said to be women.
  Most computer users are thought to surf the net.

- We can use *there* + passive + *to* + infinitive (usually *be*).
  There is reported to be an increasing threat to our ecosystem.
  There are believed to be more than 600 species of trees per hectare in tropical rain forests.

- We can use passive + perfect infinitive, which indicates that the event has already occurred.
  The president is known to have been involved in the incident.
  There is thought to have been a cover-up by her staff.

There is more information about the passive -*ing* form in the grammar folder for Unit 13.

To have / get something done

- subject + *have* / *get* + object + past participle. We use this construction to say that the subject arranges for something to be done by someone else.
  I'm going to get / have my hair cut.
  She's going to get / have her portrait painted.

- The same construction is used to say that something is done to a person or thing belonging to the subject of *have* / *get*.
  I had my passport stolen on holiday.
  I left my bag open and got my passport stolen.

Although both structures can be used in the above examples, there are some differences in meaning when using *have* / *get something done*.

- We use *have something done* to imply that the subject of the sentence is not responsible for or has no control over what happens.
  I had my passport stolen while I was away.
  She had her wisdom teeth taken out last year.
  However, *get* can also be used in sentences like these in informal spoken English. We also tend to use *have* to focus on the result of an action (rather than the action itself).
  I'll have the report finished by tomorrow morning.

- We use *get something done* to imply that the subject of the sentence causes something to happen (perhaps accidentally) or they are to blame for it.
  I'll get the letters sent out to you first class.
  I got my hand trapped in the door of the car.

Won't have

- *Won't have* + object + present participle / past participle. This can be used to say that we will not allow someone to do something, or something to happen.
  I won't have you watching TV all day.
  She won't have her holiday ruined by them.

Want it done

- *Want* + object + past participle. This can be used to say that we would like someone to do something or we would like something to happen.
  I want the report finished by next Monday.
  Put your car in my garage. We don't want it damaged in the street.

Unit 15
The infinitive

The infinitive in English is the base form of the verb. It is called the full infinitive when *to* is used before the verb and the bare infinitive when there is no *to*.

  I want to watch the film tonight. (full infinitive with *to*)
  Let me see the newspaper. (bare infinitive without *to*)

The full infinitive is used:

- after certain verbs. Common examples include:

  afford   agree   appear   ask   choose   expect
  help   hope   intend   prefer   pretend   promise
  seem   want

  I asked to see the head teacher.
  We expect to arrive by eight.

- after impersonal *it* + *be* + adjective where the adjective describes the event that follows.
  It was good to see her again.
  It's always interesting to hear your views on life.

- after verbs which follow the pattern verb + someone + *to do* something. Common examples include:

  allow   ask   beg   encouraged   force
  persuade   teach

  My mother persuaded me to buy a computer.

- after the verbs above when we use them in the passive.
  He was allowed to choose for himself.

- after *be* with the meaning of a formal instruction or information about the future.
  You are to report here at 8 tomorrow morning.

- to express purpose.
  She's saving her money to go on holiday.

The bare infinitive is used:

- after verbs which follow the pattern verb + someone + *do* something. Common examples include:

  have   let   make

  I'll have the waiter bring us more water.
  His father lets him play football.

- after modal auxiliary verbs (but remember that some modals contain *to* in themselves: *have to do*, *ought to do* and *need to do*).
  We might go to Italy on holiday this year.
  We should get some brochures.

Unit 16

Articles and determiners

There are many different rules about the use of articles and determiners in English. Here are some of the points which cause difficulty for advanced learners of English.

- No article is used before uncountable and plural nouns when used in a general sense.
  I like music.
  She's interested in animals and wants to be a vet.

- When there is a following phrase or clause specifying exactly what is being talked about, the definite article is required before uncountable and plural nouns.
  I like the music they play at the jazz club in town.
  Are the animals in the rainforest safe in their environment?

- *A* or *an* is used the first time a singular countable noun is mentioned but after this *the* is used since the reader or listener is clear about what is being referred to.
  A bird was trapped in the room and Anna called for her brother to help her free the poor creature.

- Singular countable nouns must always have an article or some other determiner (like *each*, *my*, *this*) except for a few fixed expressions like *by car*, *in hospital*, etc.

- *The* is not used with the names of most countries. It is, however, used with plural names or names of countries which contain a common noun.
  The Philippines (plural), *The United Kingdom* (kingdom = common noun), *The United States* (plural and state = common noun)
  (Note that these nouns behave like singular nouns with verbs: *The United States is a huge country.*)

- *The* is used with playing instruments but no article is used with playing games.
  Mary's hobby is playing the guitar and mine is playing chess.

- *The* can often be used before *car, train, bus, plane, ferry* or *boat* when talking about the use of different types of transport in general, even when the mode of transport has not previously been referred to. *A* is also used.
  Are you going to take the train / a train or the bus / a bus to London tomorrow?

- Parts of the body are usually preceded by a possessive pronoun rather than an article when they are talked about in the context of their relation to a specific body or bodies. When parts of the body are talked about in general, *the* is normally used.
  Sally has sprained her ankle.
  The liver is the largest organ in the body.

- The word *own* must be preceded by a possessive pronoun rather than *the* or *a*.
  When did you first get your own car?

- When we talk about the units in which commodities are generally bought or sold, we often use *by* + *the*. When we talk about price, we usually use *a /an*.
  Her parents used to buy coal by the ton.
  Those chocolates are nearly $100 a kilo.

- If we miss ou t *a* before *few* and *little*, the meaning is changed to mean *not many / not much*.
  She had a few friends. (some)
  She had few friends. (less than you would expect)

- We use *a /an* when describing someone or something in a way that applies to others.
  Kim is an interesting character. (There are other interesting characters in the world.)

- *Each* and *every* precede singular nouns.
  Every girl has her own locker and each class has its own cloakroom.

Unit 17

Language of persuasion

Listed below are some of the structures that can be useful for persuading people to do things. There are many other different expressions which could be added to each set. However, the lists provide an indication of the variety of language that is available. While language used for persuasion is very sensitive to register and context, there is overlap between the lists. Some more informal phrases may be used in formal situations and vice versa. Tone of voice, for example, can also help to make something more or less formal.

- Formal writing (e.g. discursive essay, business letter)
  It goes without saying that …
  One of the most successful ways of … is ….
  Most experts in the field agree that …
  It cannot be denied that …
  There is every reason to believe that …
  The advantages of … strongly outweigh the disadvantages.
  My opinion is borne out by research.
  The point I am making can be effectively illustrated by an example.
  There are three main reasons why I hold this view.

- Formal speech (e.g. at a business meeting)
  But surely the best course of action would be to …
  Surely the most sensible thing would be to …
  I really think it would be a pity if we didn't …
  But surely it's in our own interests to …
  How can I persuade you to …
  Can't I persuade you to …
  Couldn't you be persuaded to …
  Are you quite sure you won't reconsider?
  Are you quite sure you've taken everything into account?
  I think you might regret it later if you didn't …

- Informal speech (e.g. to a friend)
  Come on!
  Go on!
  Don't be like that!
  Please!
  Go for it!
  Can't you just …
  Won't you …, please.
  Please let me …
  Why don't you …
  Do …
  It won't (hurt / take long / cost much)!
  Do it for my sake!
  Not even for me?
  Just this once!
  You're not going to let me down, are you?

- Neutral speech
  I really think you should …
  Are you really sure you can't …
  Surely you could …
  You'd do well to …
  You'd be well advised to …
  Think it over, at least.
  Give it some thought, please.
  How can I convince you?

Unit 18

Cleft sentences and other ways of emphasising

Cleft sentences create emphasis by using a relative clause.

- Cleft sentences often use *the thing / something* or *the person / someone*, etc. For more emphasis, *one thing / person*, etc. is used.
  The thing (that) I like about him is his honesty.
  One person (who) I can't understand is the Prime Minister.

- We can use *the only* or *all* to emphasise that we're excluding everything else.
  The only thing that interests me is your happiness.
  All (that) I want is your happiness.

- *The thing that* is often replaced with *what* (making a nominal relative clause).
  What I really liked was the climate.
  The climate was what I really liked.

- When we want to talk about actions in the main clause of cleft sentences, we use a *be* + infinitive clause.
  What we often do on cold, dark winter nights is light a big fire.

- Cleft sentences are often formed with impersonal *it + be*.
  It was you that created this problem, not me.

- Cleft sentences can be used to emphasise the subject or the object of a sentence.
  My brother cut down the apple tree.
  It was my brother who cut down the apple tree. (not someone else)
  It was the apple tree that my brother cut down. (not another tree)

In addition to cleft structures, other ways of emphasising include the following:

- use of *so* and *such*
  He's such a nice man!

- use of exaggerated lexis
  We're starving!

- use of intensifying adverb
  She's absolutely wonderful.

- use of simile
  You're as cold as ice!

- use of *on earth*, after a question word
  Why on earth did you say that?

- use of inversion (exchanging the position of the subject and verb) after a negative adverbial
  Under no circumstances would he agree to that.

- use of inversion after a restricting adverbial
  Little did she guess what would happen next.

- Auxiliary verbs in spoken English are not usually stressed (except for modal auxiliaries), and are usually contracted, e.g. *I am* becomes *I'm*. If we stress them, it adds emphasis to the sentence. This emphasis is used in various ways, e.g. to show determination, to convince someone or to contradict someone.
  *I **will** finish this race, or I'll die trying.*
  *I **am** going to tell him. I promise.*
  *I don't think she's coming. – She **is** coming. I know for a fact.*

- In present and past simple forms, *do* and *did* are used as stressed auxiliaries before the main verb to give emphasis.
  I do enjoy a good detective novel!
  You did get permission for this, didn't you?

There is more information about inversions in the grammar folder for Unit 19.

Unit 19
Emphasising

For emphasis, certain adverbs and adverbial phrases can be put at the beginning of a sentence or clause with an inversion of the following verb; the position of the subject and verb is the same as in question forms. These structures are often used in literary or formal contexts. The adverbials are referred to as *broad negatives* and have negative or restricting meanings.

Forms of inversion

- When the verb is used in a form with an auxiliary, the structure is adverbial + auxiliary + subject + main verb.
  Hardly had I started speaking when he interrupted me.

- When the verb is used in a form with more than one auxiliary, the structure is adverbial + first auxiliary + subject + other auxiliaries + main verb.
  Never have I been introduced to so many people in a single night.

- With present / past simple, the structure is adverbial + *do* / *did* + subject + main verb.
  Never did he consider he might be discovered.

- With the simple form of *be*, the main verb is placed before the subject.
  Rarely was he at home.

Common examples of adverbials used in these structures are listed below:

- *hardly*
  Hardly had we set foot outside when it began to rain.

- *little*
  Little did I ever imagine that I would one day be working here myself.

- *never*
  Never have I seen anything more remarkable.

- *no sooner*
  No sooner had she walked in the room than everyone fell silent.

- *not only … but also*
  Not only did he cook dinner for everyone but he also tidied the kitchen after everyone had gone home.

- *on no account*
  On no account am I going to tell him what I think of him.

- *seldom*
  Seldom have I encountered such rudeness!

- *under no circumstances*
  Under no circumstances could we ever agree to such an arrangement.

There are other adverbials which are followed by different patterns of inversion from those listed above. These include:

- *so … that*
  The structure is *so* + adjective + *be* + subject + *that*.
  So alarmed was he that he fell from his horse.

- *only after / not until*
  Only after and *not until* introduce a clause. Consequently, the inversion comes after the whole *only after* or *not until* clause.
  Only after this project is completed could we contemplate taking on something new.
  Not until you convince me that you are committed will I give you my agreement.

Unit 20
Hypothesising

Listed below are some of the structures that can be useful for signalling a hypothesis. There are many other expressions which could be added to each set, but the lists provide an indication of the variety of language that is available. While language used for hypothesising is sensitive to register and context, there is overlap between the lists. Some more informal phrases may be used in formal situations and vice versa. Tone of voice, for example, can also help to make something more or less formal.

- Formal writing and formal speech
  On the assumption (that) *oily fish is good for the heart, you should start eating it at least once a week.*
  Provided (that) *you are careful, your health problems should not recur.*
  Allowing for the fact (that) *eating a lot of fruit and vegetables is known to be healthy, what else might there be about these people's lifestyle that could explain their longevity?*
  Given that *he has been a heavy smoker since he was a teenager, it is not surprising that he is having respiratory problems now.*
  If we were to *go back to medieval times, we would probably be rather shocked at the level of hygiene we found.*
  Were we to *go more deeply into this subject, we should probably come to the conclusion that people in the past became immune to many of the germs that would have a devastating effect on the pampered modern body.*
  Had we *access to the documents that we now know were destroyed in the fire a hundred years ago, we could be much better informed about how things really were at that time.*

- Formal speech
  If I may speculate for a moment, *any new government would seem unlikely to put much more money into the health service, whatever their election promises.*
  Speculating for a moment, *I would like to consider what might happen if we encouraged garlic as part of everyone's everyday diet.*
  Let us take a hypothetical case: *two twins are separated at birth and are brought up in two very different homes, one in which a healthy and varied diet is the norm and the other in which the child is fed almost exclusively on junk food.*
  Let us imagine / consider / suppose / assume that *this house once belonged to a rich merchant, his wife and their four young children.*
  Let us imagine / consider *what life must have been like for women in the past.*

- Neutral speech and informal writing
  If we had more examples of women's writing from that period, we would be much more able to comment with confidence on how things really were for them then.
  I wonder whether people were basically more or less stressed in past times.
  Suppose you had the opportunity to go back to any period in the past, when would you choose?
  What if we could be transported back to Ancient Greece? Wouldn't it be wonderful!
  Just imagine having the opportunity to listen to Socrates or Plato!
  If only we could know more about how ordinary people felt in the past!

Unit 21
Range of grammatical structures

- Making grammatical choices is more than simply a matter of choosing between correct and incorrect structures; you also choose from a range of structures, all of which are correct. In written English especially, too much repetition should be avoided for the sake of style, and variety is important in holding a reader's (or listener's) attention. In an exam situation, variety also allows the examiner to appreciate the breadth of knowledge the student has, but structures must be used in appropriate contexts and without errors.

- The intended meaning is the starting point of any communication. Before we can phrase our ideas, we must have a clear idea of the meaning we wish to express. Only then can we select a grammatical form that is appropriate to convey that meaning. Consider particular features of the situation you have in mind that may require the use of a particular form. For example, does it involve a relationship in time between two events, and, if so, should a perfect form be used? Or is it an event still in progress at that point, calling for the use of a continuous form? Is there some sort of cause and effect relationship that could be described using a participle clause? Using appropriate vocabulary is essential, of course, but the choice of suitable grammatical forms is equally important.

- Bear in mind that in addition to meaning, aspects of register such as formality also need to be considered when putting an idea into words. Other features, like emphasis, may be important too.

- When a grammatical form has been selected, it is then necessary to pay close attention to how the form is constructed so as to avoid inaccuracies. It is here that small details, such as correct auxiliary verbs or choice of *-ing* forms versus infinitive, become important as they may change the apparent meaning entirely in unintended ways.

Unit 22
Linking devices

- We use **because** to indicate the cause of an event or situation. It is used to link two clauses together within a single sentence. We need a comma between the clauses only if the sentence begins with *because*, not when *because* is in the second clause. In informal English, we often use *Because* to start an answer to a preceding question.
  Many animals sleep through winter because the temperature and light levels are so low.
  Because the temperature and light levels are so low, many animals sleep through winter.

- Where the cause is a noun or noun phrase, we use **because of**.
  Many animals sleep through winter because of the low temperature and light levels.
  Because of the low temperature and light levels, many animals sleep through winter.

- We use **however** to indicate that one fact or idea contrasts with another, which is usually in the preceding sentence(s). As a linking device, *however* must have punctuation before and after it. *However* tends to be less common in neutral English, where sentences with *but* are more commonly used.
  Some people feel low in energy when the light levels fall. However, it is believed that low light levels make people more creative. / It is believed, however, that low light levels make people more creative.

- We use **on the one hand** and **on the other hand** together to contrast or compare two facts or ideas. They are usually used in different sentences and can be several sentences apart. Used in this way, they must have punctuation before and after. Occasionally, they occur together in the same sentence with a conjunction.
  On the one hand, tanned skin can look very attractive. On the other hand, tanned skin tends to age faster.
  On the one hand, tanned skin can look very attractive, but on the other hand, it tends to age faster.

- We use **on the other hand** on its own to contrast or compare a fact or idea with something that was said previously.
  There would be lots of advantages to living somewhere that was hot all year round. On the other hand, I think I'd miss watching the seasons change.

- We use **contrary to** to indicate that a fact or an idea contrasts with another which is untrue. *Contrary to* is followed by a noun or noun phrase. It is often used in fixed expressions like *contrary to common belief / opinion …*
  Contrary to what is commonly thought, the world already produces enough food for everyone.
  The world, contrary to what is commonly thought, already produces enough food for everyone.

- We use **whereas** to indicate that a fact or idea contrasts with another in the same sentence. We often use it to talk about small differences between things that are quite similar. *Whereas* can come at the beginning of a sentence, and a comma is needed between the clauses if this is the case.
  Whereas the hole in the ozone layer is largely the result of CFCs, global warming is caused mainly by carbon dioxide.
  Global warming is caused mainly by carbon dioxide whereas the hole in the ozone layer is largely the result of CFCs.

- We use **indeed**, followed by a comma, to introduce information that reinforces or extends a point just made. It is highly formal.
  Sunshine can be harmful to health. Indeed, it can be fatal.

- We use **in conclusion** to indicate the beginning of the final point or summary of what is being said.
  In conclusion, it can be said that unless the population as a whole pays more attention to atmospheric pollution, our grandchildren may face a very uncertain future.

- We use **on the whole** to indicate that we are speaking generally without taking account of unusual cases.
  On the whole, industry is trying to bring carbon emissions under control.

- We use **therefore** to indicate that something follows logically from what has been said, or to introduce a result of it.
  The climatic problem is immense. Therefore, we should encourage all countries to cooperate on this issue. / We should therefore encourage all countries to cooperate on this issue.

- We use **given this** to indicate that if we accept something is true, then what we are about to say follows logically from it.
  We know that overexposure to sunlight can cause skin cancer. Given this, the government should promote the use of sun creams.

- We use **despite** or **in spite of** to indicate that something is not influenced or prevented by something else. *Despite* or *in spite of* is followed by a noun phrase or *-ing* form.
  Despite warnings about global warming, we are not doing enough to reduce pollution.
  In spite of it being so cold, they walked further and crossed the frozen lake.
  Despite or *in spite of* cannot be followed by a finite verb (so we cannot say *Despite we have warnings about global warming, we are not doing enough to reduce pollution* or *In spite of we were so cold, we walked further and crossed the frozen lake*). However, *despite* or *in spite of* can be followed by a clause with a finite verb after *the fact that*.
  Despite the fact that we have all the information at our fingertips, we do not seem to listen to the warnings about global warming.
  In spite of the fact that they were so cold, they walked further and crossed the frozen lake.

- We use **in comparison** in formal language to examine the difference between two things.
  Britain has a moderate climate. In comparison, Poland experiences more extreme temperatures.

- We use **although** and **though** to indicate that there is an unexpected contrast between what happens in the main clause and what happens in the adverbial clause.
  Although / Though most people traditionally live along the coast, the kindest climate is not to be found in the coastal regions.
  Though is often less formal. *Though* (but not *although*) is also used as an adverb to indicate that the information in a clause contrasts with the information in a previous sentence.
  I like going there on holiday. I wouldn't like to live there, though.

Unit 23
Phrasal verbs

There are different types of phrasal verbs which are used in different ways. It is always useful to consult a good dictionary to check their meaning and structure.

Verb + adverb

- Some of these phrasal verbs have no object.
  The school is gearing up for sports day.
  If you go ahead, I'll see you later in the café.
  I'll be there at 8 unless something crops up.
  The truth hasn't sunk in yet.

- Some of these phrasal verbs need an object. If the object is a noun, it can be placed before or after the adverb. If the object is a pronoun, it must be placed before the adverb. Verbs of this type in the unit are:

  carry out   jot down   make out   sift out   take out

  We need to sift out the good ones.
  We need to sift the good ones out.
  We need to sift them out.

- Some of these phrasal verbs have a very limited set of objects or are expressions. The noun comes after the adverb, and we do not use pronouns with them.
  You must pluck up courage and face the situation.
  We might get the contract, but I don't hold out much hope.

Verb + preposition

- These phrasal verbs need an object, which is always placed after the preposition.
  I could look at that picture for hours.

Verb + adverb + preposition

- Some of these phrasal verbs need an object, which is always placed after the preposition.
  I must get on with some work.
  You should always stick up for your friends.

- Some of these phrasal verbs need two objects. The first one is always placed after the verb and the other after the preposition.
  He didn't want to come, but I talked him into it.

There is more information about phrasal verbs in the grammar folder for Unit 6.

Unit 24
Linking devices

- We can use *as* to begin a subordinate clause to indicate that an event or situation happens or exists at the same time as another. In this use *as* is a conjunction joining two clauses in the same sentence. A comma is needed if the subordinate clause comes before the main clause.
  I saw my friends waving to me as I finished the marathon.
  As I finished the marathon, I saw my friends waving to me.

- We use *by then* to say that something happens before that point in time.
  I arrived late. By then, everyone had left and the place was deserted.

- We can begin subordinate clauses with *provided* to say that something is conditional. A comma is needed if the subordinate clause comes before the main clause.
  Provided (that) it doesn't rain, the Fun Run should be a good day out.
  The Fun Run should be a good day out, provided (that) it doesn't rain.

- We use *result in* + noun to express effect.
  The rain may result in the race being cancelled.

- We can use *so* as a conjunction to talk about the consequence of an event, and as an adverb to indicate a conclusion or realisation that is a consequence of previous events or information.
  I saw you so I know you were there. (conjunction)
  There's Lucy! So she did come! (adverb)

- We use *what is more* (*what's more* is informal) to add emphasis to a point which supports or extends a previous statement.
  She finished in record time. What's more, she didn't seem tired.

- We can use *to cap it all* to express that something is the final event in a sequence that is already becoming difficult to endure. It can begin a sentence or occur in the middle of one. It is an informal idiom.
  It was crowded, I couldn't see the runners, there were no hot dog vans about and, to cap it all, it started raining.

Unit 25

Complex sentences and adverbial clauses

Complex sentences have at least two clauses: a main clause and at least one subordinate clause. Adverbial clauses are subordinate clauses which give information about the main clause, such as time, place, manner, reason, condition, concession, etc.

- Adverbial clauses of time are usually placed just after the main clause. They can be placed before the main clause, followed by a comma. They use conjunctions including:

  after   as   as soon as   before   every time
  since   until   when   while

  We used to eat baskets of strawberries every time we visited the farm in summer.
  Every time we visited the farm in summer, we used to eat baskets of strawberries.

- Adverbial clauses of place tell us where somethng happens.
  You can park your car where I usually put mine.
  Wherever he goes, he makes friends with people.

- Adverbial clauses of manner tell us how something happens. They are often participle clauses with *by* or *from*.
  He made his living by / from painting pictures of the rich and famous.

- Adverbial clauses of reason tell us why something happens. If they come before the main clause, they are followed by a comma. They often use *because* but they can also use the conjunctions *as*, *for* and *since* (with the same meaning as *because*).
  She moved to the coast as she was told her health would benefit from the sea air.

- We use adverbial clauses of condition to talk about possible situations and their consequences. When placed before the main clause, they are followed by a comma. These clauses usually use *if* or *unless*.
  If you look at the website, you will find all the information you need.
  You won't find the information unless you check the website.

- We use adverbial clauses of concession to talk about information that contrasts with information in the main clause, or seems surprising in some way in relation to the main clause. These use conjunctions including *though*, *although* and *even though* (which is stronger). When placed before the main clause, they are followed by a comma.
  Although we felt we were being too ambitious, we all agreed to get the report finished by Friday.

Unit 26

Like, alike, as, so and *such*

Like, alike and *as*

- We use subject + verb + *like* + noun to talk about similarity. It can be used for emphasis, and is often used in idioms.
  She sounds just like her father, in fact she reminds me of him in many ways. (similarity)
  He eats like someone who hasn't seen food for a year. (emphasis)
  Dennis drinks like a fish. (idiom)

- We can use *alike* as an adjective meaning similar or identical.
  The twins are very alike in character as well as appearance.

- We use subject + verb + *as if* / *as though* + clause to give a description, or offer a possible explanation of something. It can also be used for emphasis. (In informal spoken English, we can use *like* instead of *as if* / *as though*.)
  He always talks to you as if / as though he were addressing a whole lecture theatre. (description / emphasis)
  Her essay looked as if / as though it had been written in a hurry. (description / possible explanation)

- We use *as* + adjective + *as* to make comparisons, but this structure can be used for emphasis, and is often used in common idioms.
  Our house is as old as theirs. (comparison)
  They've got a bath as big as a swimming pool. (emphasis)
  The room was as cold as ice. (idiom)

- We can use *as* in different types of adverbial clauses, e.g. time, place, manner, but *like* is only used in clauses of manner. In clauses of manner, *as* is more formal.
  As (she is) the head of the department, Ann has her own assistant. (reason)
  As Ann arrived, I was typing a letter. (time)
  I always organise the meetings as / like Ann does. (manner)

So and *such*

- We use *so* and *such* for emphasis. *So* is followed by an adjective or adjectival phrase (e.g. adverb + adjective). *Such* is followed by a noun or noun phrase (e.g. article + adjective + noun).
  The book was so good.
  It was such a good book.
  It was so good a book. (this is less common)

- The structures above can be followed by *that* to show the result.
  The book was so good that I couldn't put it down.
  It was such a good book that I couldn't put it down.
  It was so absorbing a book that I couldn't put it down.

Unit 27

Emphasising

Cleft sentences and other ways of emphasising are also covered in Unit 18. Unit 19 looks at forms of inversion which are often used for emphatic effect and Unit 26 covers *so* and *such*, which also have a role to play in emphasis.

- *What* is often used at the beginning of exclamations.
  What a pity!
  What nonsense!
  What a fool I was!

- We can use *what* + the part of the sentence that normally follows the subject + verb.
  The ambassador has a remarkably informed view of world affairs.
  What a remarkably informed view of world affairs the ambassador has!
  What is often followed by an adjective, sometimes with an adverb to modify the adjective. Even without an adjective or adverb, the structure still indicates something unusual about the noun, either good or bad.
  What a view of world affairs the ambassador has!

- *How* is often used at the beginning of exclamations.
  How lovely!
  How mean you are!
  How sweetly she sings!
  How he's aged!
  How cool is that!

- We can use a comparative structure for emphasis. The noun phrase used for comparison usually contains a negative and is placed at the beginning of the sentence. Sometimes set expressions are used, e.g. *nowhere on earth, nothing in the world.*
  No resort in Europe has a better beach than this.
  Nobody I know has as many holidays as she does.

- We can create emphasis by strengthening adjectives with adverbs.
  We've got bargains at unbelievably low prices.
  I hear the Taj Mahal is astoundingly beautiful.

- 'Fronting' means placing the information we want to emphasise at the front of the sentence.
  The best time to visit Paris is in spring, in my opinion.
  Spring is the best time to visit Paris, in my opinion.
  In my opinion, the best time to visit Paris is in spring.

Unit 28

Adverbials expressing opinion

There is a type of adverbial that is used to indicate the attitude of the speaker (or writer) to the entire event or situation described in the sentence as a whole. These are sometimes called sentence adverbs. Like certain other adverbials, this type can be placed in many positions in the sentence. The more common positions are:

- at the beginning of the sentence, usually separated by a comma:
  Evidently, he hadn't read the book or he would have understood what I was saying.

- before the main verb (except for the verb *be*. We place the adverbial after *be*):
  They've apparently decided to buy a house in Scotland.
  The east coast of Scotland is surprisingly warm in summer.

- at the end of the sentence, especially in spoken English:
  We arrived late, but the film started late, fortunately.

Some common adverbs which can be used to indicate the attitude of the speaker include:

apparently   astonishingly   curiously   evidently
indisputably   inevitably   interestingly   predictably
regrettably   surprisingly   unbelievably   understandably
undoubtedly   unexpectedly

Unit 29

Gerunds and infinitives

Gerunds and infinitives are dealt with separately in the grammar folders for Units 13 and 15. The following notes deal in more detail with those verbs which can be followed by both the gerund and the infinitive. These fall into three groups:

Verbs which can be followed by the gerund or the infinitive with no change in meaning.

- The choice is purely a matter of the user's stylistic preference. Such verbs include:

  begin   can't bear   continue   hate   like   love
  prefer   start

  She began unpacking her case as soon as she arrived.
  She began to unpack her case as soon as she arrived.

- Note that the *-ing* form is not used after *would like / would love / would hate / would prefer.*
  I like / love / hate / prefer eating / to eat in Chinese restaurants.
  I'd like / love / hate / prefer to eat in a Chinese restaurant tonight.

Verbs which can be followed by either the gerund or the infinitive depending on whether there is a person after the verb.

- Where there is a person after the verb, these verbs are followed by *to* + infinitive. Where there is no person after the verb, these verbs are followed the gerund. Such verbs include:

  advise   allow   forbid   permit

  The rules didn't allow dancing. The rules didn't allow us to dance.
  He advised taking a vacation. He advised us to take a vacation.

Verbs which can be followed by either the gerund or the infinitive but the choice affects the meaning of the sentence.

- Such verbs include:

  forget go on mean regret remember stop try

- We use *forget*, *remember*, and *regret* + *to* + infinitive when we think about the action first and then do it (or don't do it). When these verbs are followed by the gerund, it means we think about the action afterwards. Note that *regret* is very formal when followed by infinitive + *to* and is usually used with verbs such as *inform* or *notify* to give information.
  I don't remember meeting her before, but she assures me that we met last year.
  I must remember to ask for her telephone number.
  I regretted missing the party.
  We regret to inform you that your contract with this company will not be renewed.

- We use *go on* + gerund to indicate that the same action or situation continues. *Go on* + *to* + infinitive introduces a new action or situation.
  The manager went on talking for nearly an hour.
  My teacher at high school went on to become a university lecturer.

- Followed by a gerund, *mean* is the same as *involve*. With *to* + infinitive it is the same as *intend*.
  If I want to pass the exam it will mean working hard.
  I mean to work hard and pass the exam.

- *Stop* followed by a gerund means *cease*. If *stop* is followed by *to* + infinitive, it means that some action that has not been mentioned has been stopped for the purpose of doing another action.
  We stopped (driving) to look at the scenery.

- Followed by *to* + infinitive, *try* means the same as *attempt*. Followed by a gerund, *try* means to experiment with something.
  I tried to contact him by phone but there was no answer. (I attempted to contact him but was unsuccessful.)
  I went to his house and tried knocking on his window, but there was still no answer. (I knocked on his window but it didn't help.)

Unit 30

Using a range of structures

As described in Unit 21, it is important to use a range of grammatical structures. Here are some further examples for the four functions discussed in Unit 30.

Advice

- conditionals
  If you didn't buy so many new clothes, you could save lots of money.
- modals
  You should / could spend less on luxuries.
- inversion
  Were I in your position, I think I'd try to find an evening job.
- present simple
  Taking it in turn to cook simple meals for friends is a cheap way of spending an evening.

Reminiscing

- *used to*
  I used to spend hours looking for shells on the beach.
- *would*
  I would build huge sand castles that were bigger than I was.
- past simple
  I once built a raft from old driftwood and some rope that I found.
- present perfect
  I've always loved going to the seaside.

Telling a story

- past simple
  Marlena looked up at the clouds moving quickly across the sky and felt a sense of envy.
- past continuous
  The Monday morning bus queue was waiting idly for its dreary future to arrive.
- past perfect
  She had often thought about escaping to a new life where nobody knew anything about her.
- inversion
  Never before had she felt this way.

Hypothesising

- conditionals
  If humans hadn't evolved to become the dominant species on the planet, the world would be a very different place.
- *wish*
  I wish we could go back and save from extinction all those species that we have wiped from the face of the earth.
- indirect questions
  I wonder how many new species might have appeared in the absence of humans.
- inversion
  Had evolution followed a different course, who knows what might have happened!

Self-study folder

The following pages contain all of the answers to exercises, sample answers for writing tasks, the tapescripts, and additional notes and vocabulary. *The Map of Objective CAE Student's Book* on pages 4–7 gives full details of the language and exam skills covered in each unit. *The Content of the CAE Examination* on pages 8–9 provides information about the exam, with links to the relevant Exam folder.

Unit 1

pages 10–13

Speaking and Reading

1

The pictures show famous monuments in different countries. Name the country for each monument.

> **Answers**
> a The Blue Mosque, Istanbul, Turkey
> b The Great Wall of China
> c The Eiffel Tower, Paris, France
> d The White House, Washington DC, USA
> e Christ the Redeemer statue on Corcovado, Rio de Janeiro, Brazil

2

> **Answers**
> a Cambridge, UK   b Sydney, Australia   c Cape Town, South Africa   d Cairo, Egypt   e Buenos Aires, Argentina

How to find the answers:

Text a
The *River Cam* and the *university* with *medieval* buildings are features that identify Cambridge.

Text b
The Opera House – one of the world's most famous is in Sydney; *Harbour Bridge* and the *Manly ferry* – these are all features of Sydney.

Text c
Southern hemisphere and *Table Mountain* tell us it must be Cape Town.

Text d
Islamic country, the Nile and *Pyramids* tell us this is Cairo.

Text e
Carlos Gardel is a famous tango dancer and Argentina is famous for the tango.

Useful vocabulary
extract a
amid *prep.* in the middle of
setting *n.* location
linger *v.* stay, remain

extract b
plumes of spray small drops of water in the air in the shape of a feather

extract c
moorland *n.* open hill countryside covered with rough grass and other short plants

extract d
sprawls *v.* (to sprawl) covers a large area

extract e
stacked *v.* (to stack) piled, heaped
gridlock *n.* roads blocked by traffic

3

> **Answers**
> 1 b   2 c   3 a   4 c   5 b   6 a

4

Question **a** may lead you to discuss whether English has become a means of communication between people who do not speak each other's languages. In this case English is a *lingua franca*.

Question **b** prompts you to think about whether people need to speak more languages now than before, or if in fact computer translators will make that unnecessary.

Question **c** is designed to raise the issue of register and culture. We probably speak in a more formal way to older people if we do not know them very well. Question **d** asks you to think about which types of questions may be taboo in different cultures, for example, in Britain we generally avoid directly asking how much a person earns or how old a woman is once she is over a 'certain age'.

Conditionals

The Grammar folder in the back of the Student's book provides explanations and further examples of the grammatical areas covered in the units (page 190).

1

This exercise helps you to check what you already know about conditional forms.

Type	Tense – *if* clause	Tense – main clause	Use
zero	present simple/ continuous *do/does; is/are doing*	present simple/ continuous	to talk about common states or events
first	present simple/ continuous *do/does; is/are doing*	*will* *to be going to* present simple/ continuous	to talk about possible states or events
second	past simple/ continuous *did/was doing*	*would* + infinitive without *to*	to talk about a situation which is hypothetical or very unlikely to happen
third	past perfect simple/continuous *had done/had been doing*	*would have* + past participle *would have done*	to talk about the past and say that now it is impossible to do anything about it

2

This exercise provides sentences which introduce some of the more advanced forms of conditionals.

Answers
a If you experience any difficulties, I'll be available to help you.
b If it hadn't been for Jane's intervention, the meeting would have gone on far too long.
c I'll turn on the air conditioning if it makes you feel more comfortable.
d If you take your seats, ladies and gentlemen, the concert will begin.

3

Answers
1 otherwise 2 Given 3 If so 4 unless 5 Provided

Reading

2

Answers
a Many British people tend to try to avoid potential personal conflict by backing off and allowing the other person a way out without causing embarrassment. On the other hand, confrontation is acceptable on large public occasions.
b letting off steam
c in response to an offer to avoid conflict

Vocabulary

1

Suggested answers
to offer a way out   to express their true feelings
the immediate linguistic consequence
taking a middle route   engaging in open conflict
make errors   unfamiliar environment

2

Suggested answers
a ring b give, grant, ask c mild d genuine, heartfelt, sincere, warmest e realise f bear, cause, endure, feel, inflict, kill, soothe, stand, suffer

Listening

Go through the information in the Exam spot. The first task is slightly different from the real exam as here there are only seven options. (The real exam has eight options to choose from.)

1

Look at the pictures and speculate about where these places might be and what it would be like to visit them.

Go through the instructions. Listen to the recording and match the speakers to the pictures. In the exam you have to do both tasks as you listen to the text twice.

Answers
1 C 2 E 3 B 4 A 5 D

2

Answers
1 E 2 C 3 F 4 A 5 G

The underlined parts of the tapescript confirm the answers.

Speaker 1: We went to some incredible places, a place which has the most famous mosque in the whole of North Africa. We went in and then some boys came and, well, they wanted to show us around. Well, we were a bit dubious but they did anyway. After that, they asked us to come to a carpet museum, and they said, really, you have to see that, it's wonderful, there are old Tunisian carpets. So we decided to go with them. <u>And guess what! The museum turned out to be a carpet shop, owned by the father of one of the boys. And of course, he wanted to sell us a carpet</u> (E). We actually didn't want to buy one because we didn't have enough space in our backpacks, but finally he managed to persuade us to buy one. So my friend, yeah, she bought one.

To thank us for that, the boys guided us around the town and we ended up going down these <u>really narrow alleyways, and we had no idea where we were because this whole city was like a maze</u> (picture C). Then we came to a house and we realised it was the house of one of the boys and we were invited in by his family and <u>we had tea, coffee, nice biscuits, and it was a really, really good experience</u> (E).

Speaker 2: My story is actually a bit bizarre. I was going to Florida and first we took <u>a plane</u> (picture E) to New York and then to Florida and during the trip from New York to Florida I felt that I had to go to the bathroom. And in front of me there was a girl, she was about, perhaps twenty-five, very good-looking, who went into the bathroom, but she didn't lock the door, it was still on the er, … it wasn't completely locked. And I thought that maybe I should knock on the door and tell her that her door wasn't completely closed, but I didn't. And I also had a funny feeling that this wouldn't turn out well. And I was right because about thirty seconds later the door flew open <u>and there she was on the loo, and she gave out a loud shriek</u> (C) and me and the rest of the queue just stood there in disbelief, totally in shock.

Speaker 3: Four years ago I went to <u>Indonesia</u> with my parents and my sister, which was, of course, a very beautiful holiday. First, we went to Sumatra and er, there we met a man who wanted to show us his village. So we went off with him. <u>The village was very small</u>, perhaps five hundred inhabitants, maybe less. And it was very special because the people there had never seen tourists before. So they acted like, yeah, they treated us like very special people, which we aren't, of course. <u>They were a bit shy at first but then somehow we managed to communicate, and what I realised is that people, good people, are the same perhaps the world over</u> (F).

Speaker 4: Well, with a few friends from my rowing club, we went on a weekend in the middle of winter in Holland. When we got there we couldn't even get out on the water, it was way too cold and we were in <u>this big, er, shed</u> (picture A), the size of a football pitch. There was no heating, the water was coming through the roof. The whole time it was windy and terrible. We went there by bike and it was about three hours, I think. And we just, you know, went on automatic pilot and went on and on and on. And in this shed we couldn't get warm and people <u>started getting really irritable and we started fighting over stupid, stupid things, for example, who has to cook dinner, who has to do the dishes, and we were really nasty to each other</u> (A). And we had to sleep all together in one corner otherwise we'd freeze to death. There were about twenty-five of us all huddled together, <u>trying to sleep and hating each other</u> (A).

Speaker 5: Whenever people talk about <u>dolphins</u>, they always say they're very intelligent creatures but I never really grasped the idea of how intelligent they are until this summer when I went to Zanzibar, which is a little island off Africa. And one of the things I did there was actually <u>swimming with dolphins</u>. When you go there, there are a few locals and <u>you go on a boat</u> (picture D) with them, <u>and even before you've seen anything their enjoyment really rubs off on you. They're laughing all the time and when they find some dolphins, they're really proud of themselves because they've found some dolphins and they know that you're really going to love it</u> (D). What you have to do then is, you have to jump in the water, when the boat stops you jump in the water, and if you're lucky, the dolphins come straight at you, and then they dive really deep in the water so you can't see them any more. They hide themselves and then they come back. And when you see the look in their eyes, you see they're just making fun of you! And for me that's proof of how smart dolphins really are.

Exam folder 1

Paper 3 Part 1
pages 14–15

There is a full description of the exam on page 14. Paper 3 has 6 parts and you have 1 hour 30 minutes to complete the paper.

1
The test focus is vocabulary in Paper 3 Part 1. The general area *vocabulary* can be subdivided into categories such as phrasal verbs and the exam tests a range of different vocabulary areas.

If you have a dictionary of collocations and a dictionary of phrasal verbs, it would be useful to use them at this point.

Expressions: the expression here is *to catch sight of*.

Collocations: bakery products *go stale*, fruit, vegetables and meat *go rotten*, milk *goes sour* and butter *goes rancid*.

Phrasal verbs
put up means *erect*
lay up is usually used in the passive and means *to be forced to stay in bed* usually with an illness, e.g. *She's been laid up in bed with 'flu for a week.*
get up means *to get out of bed*
set up means *to establish a company or business.*

Linking words
Although and *despite* are both contrastive linking devices but *despite* does not fit the sentence. It would have to be: *He decided to go despite the fact that his family begged him not to/despite his family begging him not to.*

Useful vocabulary

to skim *v.* to move just above the surface or to read something quickly to understand the main points
to graze *v.* to break the surface of the skin
to rub *v.* to press repeatedly against something in a circular or up and down movement
to scrub *v.* to rub something hard in order to clean it

Go through the task *Aunt Margaret's kitchen* following all the steps in the Advice box.

Answers
1 A stale *(collocates with cigarette smoke)*
2 B stacked *(means put in an ordered pile)*
3 D built-in *(means fixed to the wall/floor)*
4 B crockery *(the collective word for cups, plates, bowls etc.)*
5 B pulled *(to pull a door to means to close it)*
6 C fond *(to be fond of means to like)*
7 D bulk *(to buy in bulk means to buy in large quantities)*
8 A slice *(a cake can be cut into slices or pieces)*
9 C home *(this collocates with at home)*
10 D scattering *(letting them fall in many different directions – collocates with crumbs)*
11 D scrubbed *(traditionally wooden tables are scrubbed clean)*
12 B set *(set out here means put in place)*

Unit 2

pages 16–19

Writing

1

Answers
to give information about finishing exams
to thank a friend for a present
to give information about a holiday

2

Answers
a This letter does not give an exact address. The writer wants to draw attention to the fact that she is on holiday in Scotland rather than give the traditional house number, street and town. In many informal letters, English people will just write the name of their town as a short form of the address. The date in this letter is written as *Midsummer* rather than the traditional day, date and year. It is common to leave out the year in informal letters.
b beginnings: *Dear Sarah, Hello Sarah,* endings: *See you, Love and kisses, Lots of love, All the best*

c resembles spoken English, e.g. *Anyway, what I really wanted to say was …*
   informal vocabulary, e.g. *nightie* instead of *nightdress*
   slang, e.g. *swipe* instead of *steal/take*
d use of dash to indicate a pause
   brackets to denote an aside
   exclamation marks and rhetorical questions to engage the reader
e yes
f She wrote *PS* (postscript) followed by the information she had forgotten.
g Paragraph 1 I've gone from the stress of exams to the quiet of a holiday in a remote place.
   Paragraph 2 Thank you for the present/T-shirt.
   Paragraph 3 I'm going to explore other parts of the island tomorrow.

Prepositions and adverbs

Grammar folder page 190

2

Answers
a on the phone   b married to   c (from) sleeping
d from / for   e on my way, at home
f suffer from, in the summer   g in a rut
h for next to nothing   i throughout the country
j on time   k to the pub, under age   l as a teacher
m on duty

3

Make sure that you read the whole text first before you start to fill in the gaps. This technique will stand you in good stead for the exam.

Answers
1 to   2 in/for   3 in   4 about   5 to   6 off   7 up
8 at   9 of   10 until/to   11 in   12 from   13 among/in
14 aside/away/down   15 with   16 of

4

Answers
a It was difficult to read the handwriting, so *bladder* was confused with *ladder*.
b They usually reacted strongly *(indignant uproar)*. The mother accepted that she would have to read out the long letter to everyone *(sigh of resignation – unfurled the twenty odd pages)*.

Vocabulary

Answers
a foot   b last   c power   d round   e answer   f ran

Listening

2

Answers Question	Main idea	Extra information
Rebecca		
Where are you from in England?	Nottingham	in the East Midlands
Have you studied any foreign languages?	French and German at school	a little bit of Italian in Italy
Amanda		
Where are you from in England?	Bath	near Bristol
Have you studied any foreign languages?	Spanish	very difficult so gave up

Further details can be found in the tapescript.

3

Answers Topic	Main idea	Extra information
Rebecca		
hobbies	wants to do self defence and dancing	wants new hobbies – only reading and music now
future hopes and dreams	be rich; have a donkey sanctuary; another degree, travel	when she's sixty on a Greek island; in History then Masters degree
living or working abroad permanently	yes	for a few years, somewhere sunny, warm and relaxed
earliest memories of school	Maths problem	couldn't watch TV with other students; went home; was told off by everyone
Amanda		
hobbies	theatre; pictures; dancing	not much time for hobbies; thrillers/suspense; Middle Eastern dancing and yoga; didn't like yoga
future hopes and dreams	be happy	further studies, PhD when older
living or working abroad permanently	yes	end days in foreign country – different work ethos
earliest memories of school	school report	opened it instead of parents, was hit by teacher

The underlined parts of the tapescript confirm the answers.

Part One

Examiner: First of all, we'd like to know a little bit about you. So Rebecca, where are you from in England?

Rebecca: I'm from <u>Nottingham, in the East Midlands</u>.

Examiner: Mm. And where are you from, Amanda?

Amanda: I'm originally from <u>Bath, near Bristol</u>.

Examiner: And have you studied any foreign languages, Amanda?

Amanda: For a while I studied <u>Spanish but I found it very difficult and gave up</u>.

Examiner: Rebecca?

Rebecca: I did <u>French and German at school</u> and then I <u>learnt a little bit of Italian when I went to work in Italy. So for a couple of weeks we had a crash course in Italian.</u> That's about it.

Part Two

Examiner: Now, I'd like you to ask each other something about your interests and leisure activities. So ask each other questions. Rebecca, could you start please?

Rebecca: Er, do you have any hobbies, Amanda?

Amanda: Mm. My hobby is <u>going to the theatre and going to the pictures. I know it's not much of a hobby but I don't really have a lot of time for hobbies.</u>

Rebecca: Er, what are your favourite films?

Amanda: What kind of films do I like best?

Rebecca: Yeah.

Amanda: I like thrillers, suspense. That's my favourite.

Rebecca: Oh, I don't like those. I'm no good with those. I get too scared. I don't watch any of it because I have my hands over my eyes.

Amanda: So what are your favourite hobbies, Rebecca?

Rebecca: <u>I want to take up self defence. I'm starting new hobbies because I haven't really got any at the moment apart from reading and music but I'm going to take up self defence and dancing classes, something like that.</u>

Amanda: I've done a sort of Middle Eastern dancing. <u>It's like an Egyptian belly dancing but it's not Egyptian, it's a kind of, um, country form where your hips actually go down instead of upwards. And you're dressed in lots of clothes, you're not showing any stomach or anything. So, yeah, I did that for a little while but I get fed up with things really, get bored and move on. I did yoga and that annoyed me. It used to make me anxious.</u>

Rebecca: Did it? Yoga made you anxious?

Amanda: Yeah, because you have to go and relax all your body and then ... you go right from your toes, up your body and then you go down it and relax it again and I used to think, Oh my God, I've got to relax it all again and it made me anxious.

Examiner: Right. Ask each other about things you hope to achieve in the future. Rebecca, what would you like to achieve in the future?

Rebecca: Er, I want to be rich. I've got a little dream, and this won't be until I'm sixty and I don't know what I'm going to do until I'm sixty, but when I'm sixty, I'm going to have a donkey sanctuary.

Amanda: She wants to be Brigitte Bardot!

Rebecca: I'm going to live on a Greek island and wear the same dress and the same straw hat every day and wander around on the craggy stones, in the heat and under the olive trees with my donkeys and my goats.

Amanda: That sounds lovely.

Rebecca: Oh, I really fancy that. What about you?

Amanda: I want to be happy. I want ... I don't know really. I think I just want to be happy more than anything else. I mean ideally, I'd like to carry on with further studies. I wouldn't mind doing my PhD. I'd like to do that. But I just haven't got time.

Rebecca: Mmm.

Amanda: But I will. I'll be a wacky old lady in jeans and blue rinse hair and do my PhD aged seventy or eighty.

Rebecca: I'd like to do another degree because I did English and I'd like to do one in History and then do a Masters degree from that rather than a Masters in English. History is more interesting to me at the moment. And I want to travel.

Examiner: How would you feel about living or working abroad permanently?

Amanda: Absolutely love to.

Rebecca: Yeah, I'd like to, definitely for a few years. That's one of my ambitions.

Amanda: I'd like to end my days in a foreign country. I think in England we like, work all the time, and really people, especially in Mediterranean countries, people work to live and we live to work and we need to get back to that same kind of ethos that they have.

Rebecca: It would just be nice to live somewhere where it's always sunny and warm and more relaxed. As you say, you can get like stressed out if you're at work, but then when you've finished work, you know, you've got a good few hours of sunlight left and you can go to the beach.

Amanda: Unless you went to Iceland of course!

Rebecca: I wouldn't do that though. I'd move to a hot country.

Examiner: And then what are your earliest memories of school?

Amanda: My earliest memory of school is when I was in the infants, I was about four or five. I went to a very strict school and every term you got a report to take home. And I remember the teacher saying, whatever you do you must not open this report, it must go home to your parents. And well, you know, I just thought that's a cue to open it. So I remember opening up the report and then she hit me, whacked me, hard with a ruler.

Rebecca: Really?

Amanda: Yeah, I really hated her. That's one of my earliest memories.

Rebecca: My earliest memory is in infant school again. And I was doing this Maths problem and I really couldn't work it out. And everyone else had gone off to watch this TV programme that we were allowed to watch once a week. And the teacher said, you've got to stay here and finish this. And I thought, right then. I got up and I walked home. It was a good mile back to my house. And I got there and my mum was, what are you doing here? And at the school they had everyone looking round the school grounds for me and the headmaster was looking in the street for me.

Amanda: Did you get told off?

Rebecca: Yeah, absolutely, by everyone ...

Writing folder 1

Informal letters
pages 20–21

1

> **Answers**
> a a friend writing to a friend – giving news about holiday plans – promising to tell him/her about the holiday when he/she returns
> b a friend writing to a friend – saying thank you for a present
> c a friend writing to a friend – regretting the fact that the friend could not go to a party as he/she was ill – giving news about who was at the party and hoping the friend will get better soon

4

> **Suggested answers**
>
> **Greetings**
> referring to last letter:
> *It was wonderful to read all your latest news ...*
> *Thanks for giving me all the latest gossip ...*
> *I couldn't believe it when I read that ...*
>
> referring to time since last letter:
> *It's ages since I last heard from you. What have you been up to?*
> *Thanks for getting back to me so quickly about ...*
> *I thought it must be about time I dropped you a line ...*
>
> apologising for delay in replying:
> *I'm really sorry I've taken so long to get back to you but ...*
> *I know you haven't heard from me for ages. Sorry! But I've been ...*
> *Sorry for not writing sooner but ...*
>
> thanking for last letter:
> *Thanks for writing and telling me all about your plans for the summer holidays.*
> *Thanks for updating me with all the latest news – I'd been wondering what happened to ...*
> *It was great to get your letter – thanks – Do you think ...*

Thanking

for a present:
I really can't thank you enough for the book, it's just what I wanted.
Thanks a million for the scarf; it'll go with my ...
The perfume is just perfect; thank you so much.

for a party:
Thanks for the party, it was great. I met such a lot of new and interesting people!
Thanks for putting on such a brilliant party, it was the best ...
The party was just wonderful, you went to such trouble to ...

for an invitation:
It's really kind of you to invite me to the wedding and I'd love to come.
Thanks for the invitation. I'll be there!
Yes, I'll be able to make dinner on Wed. Many thanks for the invitation.

Refusing an invitation
Thank you so much for the invitation but I'm afraid ...
It's very kind of you to invite me to the housewarming but I'll be on holiday then.
Sorry I won't be able to make the party; I'm staying with friends in Paris that weekend.

Congratulating
Well done!
Congratulations on passing your driving test!
I knew you could do it!

Giving your opinion
I reckon ...
If you ask me ...
What I think is ...

Giving advice
Well, you could always ...
Have you tried ...ing
If I were you, I'd ...

Unit 3

pages 22–25

Reading

1

Sample questions
What are your beauty secrets? What are the advantages and disadvantages of modelling as a career? How long have you been a model? What would you like to do when you stop modelling?

3

Answers
a her family upbringing
   the fact that she comes from Denmark
b She just went in, did the job and then left.
c She went to Paris while the fashion show was on so she met people in the fashion business.
d photography
e She has worked with many great photographers and some of their experience has rubbed off on her. She also knows what it feels like to be photographed.
f She has her own magazine and the idea was that she should be the creative director but she just wants to write and take some of the photographs.
g Men are intimidated by female models until they start talking to them.

Useful vocabulary
glitziest *adj.* (*glitzy* = showy, fashionable, intending to attract attention)
to have your feet on the ground to be practical, level-headed
grounded *adj.* having a solid, secure background
no baggage no beliefs and feelings which influence how we think and behave – often negative
you soak it all in you absorb/learn from it
branched out started to do something different
to come across as to seem to be

Listening

1
Suggested skeletons in the cupboard could be:
• several lovers
• drugs/alcohol
• crime
• problems in childhood.

2

Answers
school life, a person who helped him, fans, his working relationship with a director, his marriage, his daughter

3 and 4

Answers
a a person in the public eye is written about in newspapers and seen on TV
b a person who hurts or frightens others
c an unkind remark made intentionally to annoy and upset someone
d situation where things go wrong and it feels as if nothing can be done to prevent it
e became aware of a person's feelings and situation

f playing the role of bad people who harm others or break the law
g a nervous/anxious person
h it can become very unpleasant
i unable to stop thinking about something
j I wanted all the public attention for myself
k it's a secret

The underlined parts of the tapescript confirm the answers and the vocabulary is in bold.

Interviewer: With me today in the studio is David Burns, who freely admits that he has had a troubled past. And when I read through this potted biography; a difficult childhood, married to a fellow soap opera star, a relationship with a famous actress, an 11-year-old daughter from a subsequent relationship … all I can say, David, is that your life has been a roller coaster. It's no wonder you're constantly **in the public eye.** Do you think it all started in your teenage years?

David: <u>I think it all stemmed from when I was at school. When I was about 14 I was picked on by a</u> **bully.** <u>One day he went too far with a</u> **taunt** <u>about my mother. I snapped; I really laid into him.</u>

Interviewer: What happened?

David: <u>Oh, there was a big fuss at school and I was branded a troublemaker.</u> My mum began to think she couldn't cope with me. Things were going from bad to worse.

Interviewer: And how did you get out of that **downward spiral**?

David: I was lucky. <u>A drama teacher we had really</u> **tuned into me.** She said I could choose to go whichever direction I wanted. I could continue playing truant, getting into trouble or I could make something of myself. She said I had talent. Was I prepared to ignore that for a life of trouble and misery?

Interviewer: I wonder if directors see that tough upbringing because the irony is that you've specialised in **playing villains** …

David: I've always been **an edgy person.** I can bring that out if the part demands it. I've got a dark side. People say they can see an element of that in my eyes.

Interviewer: And how does that affect your fan mail? Does it mean that people think they don't like you as a person as well as the parts you play?

David: Er, I get a very mixed reception. <u>There are fans that write very complimentary letters, saying I'm good-looking and that sort of thing, but then there are those who seem to become obsessed and</u> **it can turn nasty.**

Interviewer: What do you mean?

David: Well, for example, <u>a fan became</u> **obsessed**, <u>sort of jealous, and she caused me a lot of problems. She didn't like anyone in the TV series getting near me. She'd send 50 letters every week and pictures from the show with</u> <u>everyone cut out except me.</u> Then she wrote to another cast member saying she knew I had a daughter. That's when I went to my producer who contacted the police and social services got involved.

Interviewer: Tell us about your experience in *Joseph and The Amazing Technicolor Dreamcoat* …

David: I played the lead role. I did it for two years – and then I got sacked. <u>The director saw I was getting a lot of attention. I think it was thought I was</u> **hogging the limelight.** It may have been internal politics, but I wasn't even given the chance to give my final performance.

Interviewer: And tell us about your marriage to your fellow soap opera star Julia Watts …

David: <u>Looking back, I don't think we were destined to grow old together.</u> We just didn't know it at the time. But she's a great actress. She could be in the soap for another 20 years. She's brilliant in it. We've each said things in the press which I'm sure we both regret. I was offered a fortune to tell my story, but I'm not interested. But when she was in another TV series which did quite well, she couldn't give an interview without having a go at me.

Interviewer: And what about your daughter, Sarah?

David: <u>She's 11 and she's very beautiful and assured.</u> Her mother, Carol, was a model. We separated a couple of years ago, <u>but we've always put Sarah first. She lives with Carol and I see her every other weekend.</u>

Interviewer: Will you ever marry again?

David: Yeah, I hope so. I'm in a relationship with someone who's not in show business. But **my lips are sealed** on that. All I'll say is that I do believe in marriage.

Wish and *if only*

Grammar folder page 191

1

Answers
a had started   b had/had had
c would come/came/had come
d to inform   e to be disclosed   f were/was
g would brighten up/had brightened up
h wouldn't ask/didn't ask/hadn't asked   i had known

It's time, would rather/sooner

1

This exercise establishes which structures are possible after *It's time* and *would rather/sooner*.

Answers
It's time + **a** and **e**
I'd rather/sooner + **b** and **e**
c and **d** are not correct with either structure

2

> **Answers**
> **1** had/would have **2** read **3** woke
> **4** had been born **5** to do

Vocabulary

1

> **Answers**
> **a** 4 **b** 1 **c** 6 **d** 2 **e** 3 **f** 5

Meanings

Definitions taken from *Cambridge International Dictionary of English*, 1995.

a **take the biscuit** – (look up *biscuit*) (infml) If you say *something* or *someone (really) takes the biscuit*, you mean that someone has done something that you find particularly annoying or surprising

b **test the water(s)** – (look up *test*) is to find out what people's opinions of something are before you ask them to do something or try and sell them something

c **deliver the goods** – (look up *goods*) also, *come up with the goods*, means to produce what is wanted

d **call the shots** – (look up *call*) also, *call the tune*, someone who *calls the shots* is in the position of being able to make the decisions which will influence a situation

e **bridge the gap** – (look up *bridge*) to bring together/make it seem as if two things are not so different

f **see the light** – (look up *see*) to understand something which you didn't understand before

2

> **Answers**
> **1** test the water **2** delivered the goods
> **3** called the shots **4** saw the light

4

> **Answers**
> **1** c **2** e **3** a **4** d **5** b

Definitions:

a **to be over the hill** – (look up *hill*) Someone who is *over the hill* is considered too old, esp. to do a particular job

b **to be on the spot** – (look up *spot*) to be at a place where an event is happening or has just happened

c **to be in the running** – (look up *running*) to still have a reasonable chance

d **to be up to the mark** – (look up *mark*) to be as good as the usual standard

e **to be in on the action** – (look up *action*) to be at the place where something important or interesting is happening

f **to be under the weather** – (look up *weather*) to feel ill

Exam folder 2

Paper 3 Part 2
pages 26–27

1

> **Answers**
> **a** preposition   of
> **b** reflexive pronoun   herself
> **c** linking device   whereas/while
> **d** determiner   every
> **e** verb   need
> **f** relative pronoun   which/that
> **g** linking device   whether/if
> **h** possessive pronoun   its
> **i** part of phrasal verb out
> **j** linking device   Although/Though

6

> **Answers**
> **1** which   pronoun
> **2** as   linking device
> **3** its   possessive pronoun
> **4** turns   part of phrasal verb
> **5** thus/so/therefore linking device
> **6** When/Once   linking device
> **7** something   pronoun
> **8** whether   linking device
> **9** can/may   modal verb
> **10** into   preposition
> **11** from   preposition
> **12** Also/Moreover/   linking device
>   Furthermore
> **13** this/our   determiner
> **14** without   preposition
> **15** let/allow   verb

Unit 4

pages 28–31

Listening 1

2

Do the exercises as you listen.

Gently lean your head to one side. Breathe in. Rest for three seconds and then breathe out. Repeat to the other side.

Lift your arms up from your sides to above your head and hold for three seconds. Breathe in. Place your arms behind your head and breathe out. Repeat twice.

Bend your foot upwards, spread your toes and hold for three seconds. Point your foot downwards, clenching your toes and hold for three seconds. Repeat twice.

3

> **Answer**
> The imperative is used in the example. This could also be expressed using a polite request.

Speaking

1

> **Answers**
> 1 e 2 b 3 g 4 c 5 a 6 d 7 f

Reading

2

> **Useful vocabulary**
> **a alert** *adj.* on the lookout, lively
> **b merely** *adv.* just, only
> **e engage** *v.* use, involve
> **aid** *v.* help
> **f rhymes** *n.* words that have the same sound at the end
> **acronym** *n.* an abbreviation formed by the initial letters of words

4

> **Useful vocabulary**
> **syllable** *n.* unit of pronunciation said without interruption
> **tedious** *adj.* boring
> **eliminated** *v.* got rid of
> **get by** *v.* manage
> **cues** *n.* signals, hints
> **recall** *v.* remember
> **spin-off** *n.* indirect benefit
> **core** *adj.* central, important
> **albeit** *conj.* even though

Modals: *may, might, can, could*

Grammar folder page 191

1

> **Answers**
> **a** ability **b** offer **c** negative certainty **d** request
> **e** order **f** theoretical possibility **g** permission

2

> **Answers**
> **1a** The use of *could* suggests a general ability; the person could always get into the house by the back door.
> **1b** The use of *was able to* suggests that the person is referring to one specific achievement/occasion.

2a She may get here ...	*may* is used for possibility
2b May I use ...	*May* is used for asking for permission (formal)
3a She might get here ...	*might* is used for possibility (smaller possibility than *may*)
3b Might I make a suggestion?	*Might* is used for asking tentatively for permission (formal)

Listening 2

1

> **Answers**
> **1** *Phoning the cinema*
> **a** press 1
> **b** press 2
> **2** *Phoning an airline*
> **a** press 2
> **b** press 4
> **c** bring your flight details and some form of identification with a photograph on it
> **3** *Phoning a telephone and Internet provider*
> **a** call 0800 952 43 43 or visit the website at www.askstl.com
> **b** press 2 to speak to the fault management centre
> **c** press 5 to speak to Telesales

The underlined parts of the tapescript confirm the answers.

1 Thank you for calling MovieMax Booking Information Service. Please press the star key on your telephone twice now. If you wish to book for *Cast Away*, please press 1 now, otherwise stay on the line for all other films. If at any time during the call you make a mistake and want to change the previous selection, press the star key. If you wish to book for *Cast Away*, press 1. If you wish to book for any other film and know the details, press 2. If you'd like information, press 3.

2 Thank you for calling PanAir, Europe's low fares airline now available for easy booking on *PanAir.com*. If you are using a Touch-Tone phone, please select one of the four following options. For timetable information, please press 1. If you wish to make a booking, press 2. For general enquiries, press 3. Or to book a last-minute promotional offer, press 4. If you are not using a Touch-Tone phone, please hold the line and a PanAir agent will be with you shortly. Please note that PanAir is now a ticketless airline. In order to check in all you need are your flight details and a form of photo ID. A receipt will be sent to you but it is not necessary for check-in. Thank you for calling PanAir.

3 Hi, thanks for calling STL. Please listen carefully to the following options which are designed to help us assist you with your call. If your call is regarding information for our exciting new Internet service, STL World, which is available through your PC or even through your TV, please call our exclusive hotline number on 0800 952 43

43, that's 0800 952 43 43. Alternatively, visit our website at _www.askstl.com_. If you would like to make a payment by credit or debit card, please press 1 on your telephone key pad. If you need to report a fault on your service, including the Internet, please press 2 to speak to our fault management centre. If you have an enquiry about an existing account and would like to speak to a representative, please press 3. If you would like to change the channels you currently subscribe to, please press 4 to leave your account details. If you are not an existing customer and would like information about the services we offer, please press 5 to speak to Telesales. For all other enquiries, please hold while we transfer you to a customer service representative.

Vocabulary

1

Answers			
dis-	_il-_	_im-_	_in-_
disappear	illogical	immature	inaccessible
discontinue	illiterate	imprison	insensitive
distrust		impolite	inconclusive
		immaterial	
_ir-_	_non-_	_mis-_	_un-_
irresistible	non-iron	mislead	unbelievable
irregular	non-smoker	mistrust	untimely
			unexpected

2

Answers
a _im-_ before words beginning with _m_ and _p_
b _il-_ before words beginning with _l_
c _ir-_ before words beginning with _r_

3

Answers			
-able	_-ation_	_-ency_	_-ful_
photocopiable	emancipation	emergency	deceitful
countable	dramatisation	frequency	careful
employable	recommendation	tendency	respectful
arguable			
recommendable			
respectable			
reliable			
_-ly_	_-less_	_-ment_	_-ness_
timely	countless	judg(e)ment	rudeness
rudely	timeless	employment	calmness
frequently	speechless	argument	
calmly	careless		
	pointless		

Writing folder 2

Essays
pages 32–33

1 and 2

Answers		
Stage of essay	**Content**	**Purpose**
Introduction	General statement Definition(s) – optional Scope of essay	1 To introduce the reader to the topic ✓
		2 To explain what is understood by some key words/concepts
		3 To tell the reader what you intend to cover in this essay ✓
Body	Arguments Evidence	4 To express important ideas ✓
		5 To support ideas with examples ✓
Conclusions	Summary Relate the argument to a more general world view	6 To remind the reader of the key ideas ✓
		7 To underline the writer's point of view ✓

3

Answers
while, On the one hand, In addition, for example, On the other hand, and the like, because, and, In my opinion, Moreover
Most of the linkers are formal; _and the like, and_ and _because_ are less formal.
On the one/other hand, In addition, for example, In my opinion and _Moreover_ are followed by a comma.

4

Example answer		
• Who is the reader? my teacher		
• Style? Formal		
• Length? 250 words		
Stage of essay	**Content**	**Purpose**
Introduction	– More people are studying English	1 To introduce the reader to the topic
	– English, Spanish, Chinese as world language?	2 To tell the reader what you intend to cover in this essay
	– Discuss ways in which it will be easier	
	– Examine what we may lose	

Body	For one language	3 To express
	Everyone learns at young age – easy (eg bilingual children) Travel: easier to make arrangements, get help, get info, meet people Study: easier to follow any course, anywhere (but not always poss – visas etc.) Better job prospects Might lose: Cultural identity Thrill of travel	important ideas 4 To support ideas with examples
Conclusion	Many activities will be easier but keep cultural identity/traditions	5 To remind the reader of the key ideas 6 To underline my point of view

Unit 5

pages 34–37

Speaking

2

Answers
a to express sympathy for a person's ill health
b to apologise for an awkward situation
c to remind someone about an unpaid invoice
d to offer someone employment
e to introduce a colleague
f to request information

3

Answers
a 2 b 6 c 1 d 4 e 7 f 3 g 5

4

These salutations are used in British English, but there are other forms, mainly American English, e.g. *Yours truly*.

Answers
Dear Ms Ryan ------------------------ *Yours sincerely*
Dear Sir/Madam ---------------------- *Yours faithfully*

Reading

1

The notes in brackets confirm the answers.

Answers
1 f Start from the End (*decide what the results of ...*)
2 c Get to the Point Early (*the heading is a paraphrase of this heading*)
3 e Put Yourself in Your Reader's Place (*how would you respond?*)
4 g Say it Plainly (*write as you talk, naturally*)
5 h Use Active Verbs (*the paragraph gives examples of how the active voice is more appropriate*)
6 d Never Write in Anger (*Emotion will evaporate .... handle problems in an upbeat manner*)
7 b End with an Action Step (*this heading summarises the paragraph*)
8 a Be Professional (*this paragraph describes a professional presentation of your letter*)

Writing

Examples of formal letters:

Type of letter	From	To
a letter asking for information	student client	university/college travel agency bank
a letter making a booking	a holiday a course theatre seats	hotel travel agency theatre
a letter of complaint	guest holiday-maker student customer	travel agency school/college company (faulty product)
a letter of application	job applicant student	company college

This is not a comprehensive list of all formal letter types; add to it with your own suggestions.

1

Answers
up-to-date knowledge on travel options, excellent organisational skills, IT literate, good communication skills, self-motivation, organisation, ability to work to deadlines, good numeracy

Vocabulary

The connotation of words changes with time and fashion, e.g. *wicked* now retains its original meaning *evil* but it has the meaning *very good* in youth culture.

> *Connotation* is a feeling or idea that is suggested by a particular word although it is not necessarily part of the word's meaning.

1

The mini-biography on Dian Fossey gives useful background information about her.

Answers
a false b true c false d false e false

2

Answers

Positive	Negative	Neutral
mansion	shack	house
praise	judgment	evaluation
state-of-the-art	new-fangled	modern
	nosy	inquisitive
courageous	foolhardy	
innocent	gullible	naive

3

Answers
1 sound 2 steely 3 solitude 4 detailed
5 keen 6 intriguing

Relative clauses

Grammar folder page 192

1

Answers
a defining relative clause
b non-defining relative clause

2

Answers
a This sentence means that *all* government officials wanted to convert gorilla habitats to farmland.
b This sentence means that only *some* government officials wanted to convert gorilla habitats to farmland.

5

Answers
a Dian lived in a hut which had no electricity. (no alternative)
b The film of the story of her life made an impact ~~that~~ many people will never forget.
c The story ~~which~~ she told in the film made Dian Fossey a household name.
d The clothes ~~that~~ she wore in the jungle were old and worn.
e The place where she grew up has a different sort of beauty. (no alternative)
f The place ~~that~~ she grew up in is known to few, even in the USA.
g The people who made the film about Dian immediately realised the remarkable effect ~~that~~ her story has on whoever sees it.
h She had an inspirational quality which defies analysis. (no alternative)
i Her animals were often the only 'people' ~~that~~ she talked to for days on end.
j Dian had an intimate relationship with the land, which to a large extent determined the way ~~that~~ she lived.

6

Answers
a This is the area of research on which he is working.
b Here are some new statistics in which you will be interested.
c Is this the advertisement for the job for which you are applying?
d Is this the experiment about which you were reading?
e Is this the person with whom you have entered into correspondence?
f She received a reply from the editor to whom she sent her paper.
g Social Sciences is the category into which his work falls.
h The college has cancelled the conference for which you wanted to enrol.

Listening

3

Check that the whole sentence is grammatical and makes sense.

Answers
a a camera crew b calm c sixth d petrol
e sponsors f boat g at university

The underlined parts of the tapescript confirm the answers.

Interviewer: The darkness refuses to lift over the racetrack and the rain is beating against the windows of the motorhome. A tiny white race suit is hanging in the corner but the young man sat back on the sofa is not ready for it yet as he rubs his eyes and comes to terms with the fact that he could still be snuggled up in bed instead of putting himself on display yet again at such an unearthly hour. James, how did you get yourself into this business?

James: Well, it's all down to Frank Weston. He took a calculated risk with me when I was completely unknown. And then, as you know, it was a rapid change for me as I suddenly became famous.

Interviewer: How has your family coped with your fame and I suppose their fame too?

James: Well the fame thing doesn't bother me, most people don't disturb me when they see me eating in a restaurant or something like that but I think my mum finds it a bit unsettling, you know, having to deal with a <u>camera crew</u> every time she comes out of the house. And in fact, my sisters now, they don't come down to the track to see me race, they watch me on TV at home.

Interviewer: Your father has shown great faith in you, hasn't he?

James: Well, I think both of us have had many doubts at times about my talent but he reckons it's being <u>calm</u> which makes the difference between champions and the rest. He's amazing too; he's become really hardened to the constant attention. And he's the one who has to watch from the sidelines. I think that must be a lot worse than doing the race.

Interviewer: Yes, you had a scary moment in Australia, didn't you?

James: Yeah, I'd qualified twenty-first and in the race got up to <u>sixth</u> position before my car gave out. It was real scary. You've only got split seconds to make life and death decisions. In an instant I knew something had gone wrong with the car and then you've got to get off the track and out of the way of the other drivers as fast as you can.

Interviewer: And you did it. But from an early age you proved that you've got what it takes.

James: Oh, I don't know. When I left school as a teenager it was just hard work. I went from track to track around Europe. And, yeah, I suppose when I had to live in Italy and Belgium on my own it was a bit tough, but my dad was a great support. There were loads of funny times then too. I remember once my father had to borrow money for <u>petrol</u> so that I could get home for a race in Scotland. And that's only a couple of years ago.

Interviewer: Things are very different now; you've got <u>sponsors</u> queuing up to take you on and make you a millionaire.

James: And I've already got more money than I'd ever dreamed of. And I'm trying to be sensible with the money but I must admit to one or two indulgences.

Interviewer: Yes, I've heard about the Ferrari in the garage and the BMW sports car. What's next on the list?

James: You make me sound irresponsible and I suppose to many people I must seem that way. But it's strange what money and fame can do to you. I mean it just seems normal to me now to have all those things and, in fact, next on my shopping list is a <u>boat</u>. I'd love that, to have it somewhere hot.

Interviewer: Does this mean that you have nothing or little in common with your old school friends now?

James: When I go back home I still meet up with my old mates but lots of them have moved on too, they're at <u>university</u> in different places so I only get to see them when they have holidays and they're back at home too. I suppose at our age people are moving around a lot and doing different things. I don't think my situation is any different. It's just that I've changed jobs. But when we meet up we still talk about the same things.

Interviewer: He might just be a lad with his mates but on Sunday he will be the new young star of Formula One, driving in front of five hundred million TV viewers.

Units 1–5 Revision

pages 38–39

Grammar

1

Answers
1 could say   2 hadn't come / wasn't / weren't
3 go / we went   4 could have come / had come / were
5 grew   6 had come / were

2

Answers
1 D   2 B   3 C   4 A   5 D   6 A
7 C   8 B   9 C   10 D   11 C   12 D

Vocabulary

1

Suggested answers
a sit, take, pass, fail   b enter   c forces, laws, wonders
d clear, creative, great, lateral, logical, muddled, original
e accumulate, amass, have, honour, pay off

2

> **Answers**
> **a** misled **b** shatterproof **c** popularity **d** boyhood
> **e** underdone **f** reclaim **g** heartless

3

> **Answers**
> Words with negative connotations: simplistic shack
>   gorge/gobble aggressive criticism
> Words with positive connotations: a challenge
>   inexpensive inquisitive childlike innocent

5

> **Answers**
> **1** in/for **2** with **3** across/onto **4** from **5** on
> **6** to **7** into **8** with **9** in **10** at **11** on
> **12** to/of **13** at/from **14** in **15** for/in

Unit 6

pages 40–43

Listening

1

> **Answers**
> **a** Her boyfriend had decided he had got tired of her and
>   wanted to end their relationship.
> **b** She dialled an automatic recorded message from his
>   phone while he was away for a month and then left the
>   phone off the hook.
> **c** It is a matter of opinion whether it was effective or not,
>   but it must have been satisfying in that it would have
>   resulted in an enormous phone bill for her ex-boyfriend.

The underlined parts of the tapescript confirm the answers.

Oh, talking of revenge, I read about a great one once. There
was this girl, <u>she'd been dumped by her boyfriend</u>, 'cos he'd
decided he'd gone off her and he told her to move her things
out of his flat before he got back from a business trip. I think
he was going to the States for a month or something. Anyway,
she moves her stuff out straightaway but before she leaves, she
picks up the phone and dials the speaking clock. <u>Then she
leaves the phone off the hook while the clock goes on
speaking the time to an empty flat.</u> 'At the third stroke, it'll be
ten twenty-five and thirty seconds …' So the boyfriend finds
it when he returns four weeks later. <u>You can imagine what the
bill was like after a solid month of phone calls.</u> Even at local
rates, it'd be huge! That must have been <u>really satisfying</u> for
the dumped girl!

2

> **Answers**
> **1** For: Andy
>   From Name: Eddie
>   Number: 245908
>   Message:
>   Does history project have to be handwritten or can it be
>   typed? Please ring back before 7 (has to go out then).
>
> **2** For: Michael Removals
>   From Name: Robert Smith
>   Number: 0207 562 4957
>   Message:
>   Recommended by Richard Johnstone.
>   Wants to know charges and availability to move a few
>   things on 22nd or 21st. Is moving beds, chests of
>   drawers, fridge, washing machine, etc. out of house
>   (moving about one mile). Also could you plumb in
>   washing machine for him?
>
> **3** For: Nicky
>   From Name: Leila
>   Number: not given
>   Message:
>   Just wants a gossip. (Jo's resigned – wants to tell you
>   why!)
>
> **4** For: Nicola Smith
>   From Name: Paolo
>   Number: 0802 334 567 (mobile)
>   Message:
>   Your seminar next Tuesday to start at 11 and finish 3.30
>   (with lunch in middle) rather than 2–5. Group really on
>   the ball, need loads of stretching activities. Best if doing
>   things rather than listening. Nice but hard work. Ring
>   with any queries.
>
> **5** For: Michael
>   From Name: John
>   Number: not given
>   Message:
>   Bob's stag party tonight meeting in *Red Lion* NOT *Slug
>   and Lettuce*.
>
> **6** For: Andy
>   From Name: Alex
>   Number: not given
>   Message:
>   Has new PlayStation game. Do you want to go round
>   this evening at 7 and play it?

The underlined parts of the tapescript confirm the answers.

Speaker 1: Hi, this is a message for <u>Andy</u>. I wanted to know about our homework. <u>The history project</u>. <u>Can we word process it</u> or has it got to be handwritten? I hope we are allowed to type it! Please could you ring me back? Oh, this is <u>Eddie</u>, by the way, I don't think I said. In case you've lost my number, it's <u>245908</u>. I've got to <u>go out at 7-ish</u>, so I hope you get back before then. Bye.

Speaker 2: Hello, is that <u>Michael Removals</u>? Richard Johnstone gave me your number and suggested I contact you. I was wondering if you could <u>move some stuff for me on the 22nd, or the 21st if you don't work on Saturdays</u>. It's not a lot of stuff, <u>just some beds and chests of drawers and bits and pieces</u> into a house I'm going to rent out and it's only moving <u>about a mile</u>. Oh yes, and there's a <u>fridge</u> and a <u>washing machine</u> too. Would you be able to <u>plumb those in for me as well</u>? Could you get back to me and <u>let me know your charges and availability</u>? My name is <u>Robert Smith</u> and I'm on <u>0207 562 4957</u>.

Speaker 3: Hi, <u>Nicky</u>. It's <u>Leila, just ringing for a bit of a gossip</u>. Nothing important but there's some news you might be interested to hear. <u>Jo's decided to resign</u>. And wait till I <u>tell you why</u>! There'll soon be nobody left there at all! Anyhow, <u>give me a ring when you get back</u> and I'll fill you in on all the gory details. Bye.

Speaker 4: This is a message for <u>Nicola Smith</u>. It's <u>Paolo</u> calling about <u>the seminar you're doing for us next Tuesday</u>. Could you <u>get here for 11 rather than 2</u> and then <u>we'll finish at 3.30 not 5</u>. So you'll still be doing <u>three hours</u> but it'll be <u>broken up by lunch</u>. And I'd better warn you that the <u>group are really on the ball</u>. So <u>come prepared with loads of stuff</u> to keep them going. <u>They like doing things rather than just listening</u> so make sure you come with plenty of stretching activities. They're very <u>nice but pretty hard work</u>. So don't say you haven't been warned. Ring me back if you've got any queries. It's probably easiest to catch me on my mobile – that's 0802 334 567.

Speaker 5: Hi, <u>Michael</u>? This is <u>John</u>, I've been trying to catch you all day but your machine's been on all the time and I don't really like talking to these things. Seems like I've got no choice now as I won't be near a phone for the next hour or so. Er, <u>we're meeting for Bob's stag party in the *Red Lion* tonight not the *Slug and Lettuce*</u>. Er hope you'll get this in time. If you haven't turned up by 8.15, I'll try ringing the *Slug*. Cheers.

Speaker 6: <u>Andy</u>? This is <u>Alex</u>. I've got this brilliant <u>new PlayStation game</u>. I only got it today and I'm already on level 6. Do you want to <u>come round and try it later on</u> this evening? Dad says I've got to get my homework done first but that should only take ten minutes. <u>Come at 7</u> if you can. Bye.

Phrasal verbs

Grammar folder page 193

At CAE level you should be feeling more confident about using phrasal verbs. When you learn a new one write it down in an example sentence, as this will help you to learn it in a typical context.

1

> **Answers**
> 1 Please could you *ring* me *back*?
>   I've got to *go out* at 7-ish,
>   so I hope you *get back* before then.
> 2 into a house I'm going to *rent out*
>   Would you be able to *plumb* those *in* for me as well?
>   Could you *get back* to me
> 3 when you *get back*
>   I'll *fill* you *in* on all the gory details
> 4 it'll be *broken up* by lunch
>   *Ring* me *back* if you've got any queries.
> 5 If you haven't *turned up* by 8.15
> 6 Do you want to *come round*

2

> **Answers**
> **a** out **b** through **c** up **d** through **e** on
> **f** over/on **g** up **h** off **i** off, up

3

> **Answers**
> **b** 1 **c** 6 **d** 7 **e** 4 **f** 10 **g** 9 **h** 3 **i** 8 **j** 5

Vocabulary

1

> **Answers**
>
> | have | do | make |
> |---|---|---|
> | a baby | the cooking | a cake |
> | a go | someone a favour | a mistake |
> | a party | your best | a phone call |
> | dinner | the housework | an effort |
> | fun | your homework | an excuse |
> | | | dinner |
>
> | take | both *have* and *take* |
> |---|---|
> | a photo | a bath |
> | hold of | a chance |
> | part | a nap |
> | someone seriously | a phone call |
> | someone's word for it | a shower |

2

> **Answers**
> **a** do **b** make **c** has/takes **d** make
> **e** take **f** have **g** do

Speaking 2

Schwa is the name given to the most common vowel in the English language i.e. the vowel used in the second syllable of ˈlʌn.dən or the third syllable of ˈɛl.ɪ.fənt. Schwa is never stressed.

Reading along with a native speaker on a tape is a very good way to improve your English pronunciation as it helps you to use a natural rhythm and intonation. It is impossible to keep up if you give too much importance to unstressed vowels, so make sure that you do not stress any of the schwa vowels.

1

> **Answers**
> Oh, talking of revenge, I read about a great one once. There was this girl, she'd been dumped by her boyfriend, cos he'd decided he'd gone off her and he told her to move her things out of his flat before he got back from a business trip. I think he was going to the States for a month or something. Anyway, she moves her stuff out straightaway but before she leaves, she picks up the phone and dials the speaking clock. Then she leaves the phone off the hook while the clock goes on speaking the time to an empty flat. 'At the third stroke, it'll be ten twenty-five and thirty seconds …' So the boyfriend finds it when he returns four weeks later. You can imagine what the bill was like after a solid month of phone calls. Even at local rates, it'd be huge! That must have been really satisfying for the dumped girl!

Reading and Speaking

1

> **Answers**
> **a** Because the writer is writing on a train and is working with a very small keyboard. Both of these factors make it difficult for him to press the correct keys.
> **b** I am writing this on the train. I am writing this, not just on the train, but on my telephone on the train. My telephone is simultaneously picking up my email and I have just ordered a book from the Cambridge University Library, via their website. All on my telephone! Isn't technology wonderful?
> **c** The writer tells us that he has a phone with Internet connection and that he has a Macintosh Powerbook G3 computer. He thinks both are wonderful and clearly finds it very exciting that they can do what they do.

> **d** Telephone communications have changed a great deal in the writer's lifetime. He can remember when homes typically had at most one phone. This was fixed and certainly could not be moved from room to room. To be able to make a call from another room involved a time-consuming and complex process of adding cables and drilling holes. Now you can literally make calls from almost anywhere using a tiny personal phone.
> **e** The capitals draw attention to the fact that it was something special, something that people would talk about in tones of awe.
> **f** All the different ways that we now have of communicating may actually add to the stress that people feel.
> **g** The point of the story about President Carter is that it is very unusual for people to stop and think before speaking. Many people speak but have nothing really to say.

2

You could write answers to these questions. Here are some possible answers, but there are many other points that you might prefer to focus on.

a   These aspects of modern communications technology might make people feel more harassed – you can never be out of contact with your work (or your family); people expect instant answers to their communications; the fact that people use mobile phones in public places can be stressful; you become dependent on technology, so if it breaks down you feel lost.

b   'Information overload syndrome' is when people feel depressed or disturbed because there is so much information available for them to get to grips with and they feel they cannot cope. Most people have probably felt this when they look up something on a search engine on the Internet and are provided with dozens of possibilities.

c   These means of communication can be seen to have the disadvantage of never allowing you to have a break from work or other commitments. Although this is wonderful in an emergency, it does mean that some people can never 'switch off'.

d   People often talk about the weather during long-distance phone calls or in chat rooms or they use the Internet to play games.

e   The most popular topics in Britain are probably sport, television programmes, work, the news, the weather, transport problems, relationships, family, holidays etc. Of course, what people talk about depends very much on their own personality and interests as well as on whom they are talking to.

f   Men probably talk a lot more about sport, whereas women talk more about relationships and family. Women perhaps talk more to establish relationships with the people they are talking to and they are probably more open about their feelings and more prepared to expose their own weaknesses. Men possibly talk more to solve problems or to show their own strong qualities.

g The basic topics of interest have probably not changed very much although, of course, television programmes could not have been talked about 100 years ago. Perhaps people used to talk more about the most popular stories in magazines. 100 years ago people's lives were also, possibly, more focused on their own local area as much less information would have been available to them.

h It has improved the quality of life, in that it has made education and entertainment more accessible to people wherever they are and whatever their circumstances, but it has also made life more complex as more choices inevitably bring more conflicts.

Exam folder 3

Paper 3 Part 3
pages 44–45

1

Answers
1 (adverb) viciously   2 (adjective) courteous
3 (noun) team   4 (verb – past tense) ordered
5 (noun) union   6 (adjective) unruly
7 (verb – past participle) saved   8 (noun – plural) pupils

2

Answers
Verbs	Adjectives	Nouns
unwrap	unsafe	disappearance
de-ice	disloyal	insecurity
misspell	insane	unease
untie	uncomfortable	discomfort
disentangle	non-European	immobility
misunderstand	irresponsible	imbalance

4

Answers
1 inspection   2 violence   3 leadership   4 outrageous
5 uncontrollable/uncontrolled   6 later   7 properly
8 councillors   9 successful   10 unsatisfactory
11 remarkably

5

Answers
1 happily   2 skilled   3 recognition   4 unfamiliar
5 injury   6 dislodged   7 safety   8 discharged
9 convulsions   10 psychological   11 limitations/limits
12 marriage   13 fortunately

Unit 7

pages 46–49

Reading

1

Answers
a 10,000 young people aged 12 to 25
b the legacy of the prosperous 80s, the changing nature of work, the targeting of youth culture, a new work ethic
c Big business needs the kind of young people who are now preferring to set up businesses of their own.
d The words refer to the key factors affecting young people's attitudes to work today.

2

Answers
1 for   2 whom   3 making   4 what   5 everything
6 were   7 their   8 own   9 in   10 being   11 to
12 best   13 such   14 in   15 else   16 are   17 up
18 at   19 which   20 would

3

Answers
a False. Reasons include a desire for financial independence, to be valued and challenged but not just to get rich.
b True, although it was investigating attitudes not only to work but also to the family and to other aspects of life.
c False. The economy was strong (*buoyant*) and people were encouraged to take risks.
d True.
e False. Many large companies have targeted young people, specifically trying to attract them to buy their products.
f True.
g True.
h False. The article says that established businesses need young people on their staff in order to survive and so should be doing more to attract them.

Vocabulary

1

Answers
1 setting   2 drives   3 strike   4 decline
5 stage   6 industry

2

Answers
1 legacy   2 buoyant   3 eroded   4 targeting
5 buckling down   6 reap

Cause and effect

Grammar folder page 193

It could be useful to try to use the expressions in the box to write sentences about yourself and other people you know to explain why you or they behaved in particular ways. Use a dictionary to help you.

1

> **Answers**
> the reason for   reasons why   had a profound influence on
> resulted in   be a consequence of   stems from
> have its roots in

2

> **Answers**
> 1 to   2 towards   3 on   4 about   5 as
> 6 of   7 As   8 why

3

> **Answers**
> motive, grounds for, so, accordingly, explanation, objective,
> outcome, thanks to

How did I become an actor? Well at school when I was about sixteen or seventeen I was in quite a few plays and once my godfather who was a television director came to one of these plays just to see what was going on, not in any professional sense. There wasn't any other sort of motive. He just really came to see me work as his godson. And we, we did the play and afterwards he and I were sitting having a chat and he thought maybe having seen my work there was, had I ever thought of going into the theatre as a profession? He thought there were grounds there for a possible career move. So I wrote to the drama schools and, I don't know, filled in all the forms and did everything that was asked of me and accordingly I was called up to London for an audition and I was late. They wanted an explanation of course – the trains had held me up – but anyway, I got there, I did my audition and waited to hear what was going to happen. The audition's quite interesting. You have a couple of pieces to do and then they give you a scene. They want to know, as an actor, if you can tell what the objective is in the scene, whether you think the outcome of the scene can go one way or another. They're quite interesting moments, they're improvised. And that was that, and then after about two or three months I heard from the drama school and I'd got in. So it was thanks to my godfather really that I'd managed to go to drama school and I did a two-year course and here we are, I'm speaking to you.

Writing

2a and b

> **Answers**
> **a**
> **Introduction to the work experience programme**
> • ten students did work experience
> • in supermarket doing range of types of job
> **Usefulness of the programme**
> • learnt about life behind scenes of supermarket including learning to respect people who work there
> • learnt a bit about complex international operation of supermarket
> • learnt about importance of being able to deal with people of very different types
> • gained confidence
> **Drawbacks to the programme**
> • felt exploited at times
> • do not ever want to work in supermarket again
> • would have preferred experience in possible future area of work
> **Conclusion**
> • programme in general a very good thing
> • would prefer to have opportunities to do different types of jobs
> **b**
> The headings are appropriate and useful in that they state clearly what each paragraph includes. The report is clear and unambiguous and uses headings to inform and guide the reader. The report therefore follows a fairly standard pattern.
> **c**
> *Firstly, Secondly, Thirdly, Finally* – listing points
> *Moreover* – adding a point
> *For example* – giving an example
> *In conclusion* – drawing a conclusion
> *However* – making a point that contrasts in some way with what has gone before
> **d**
> The suggested headings may be very different from each other but you should generally write four or five headings. The first heading will be an introductory one of some kind and the last one a conclusion. The headings in the middle will vary more.

Speaking 2

If you are working alone you will not be able to do the survey presented in these exercises. Instead, after thinking about the questions 1, 2 and 3, add at least eight other features which might attract people to jobs in the list provided in 4. If you already have a job, write a paragraph about your own work and which features it has. If you are not yet in work, write a paragraph about the job from the list in 1 which you think enjoys most of these features and the one which has fewest of them.

Listening

Speaker 1: When I was at school I decided I definitely wanted a career and I thought of what I could do that involved working with other people. I'd had various Saturday jobs working as a hairdresser and it was only until I got an apprenticeship that I really thought this is what I want to do with my career. I love the work because you meet different people every day. You can be creative which is important to me. I suppose if there are any downsides it's that some of the times you can get other people's hair on your clothes and that can take some picking off. But on the whole it's something I really love doing.

Speaker 2: Well this job found me really. A friend recommended me and so I did a job for somebody and it seemed to work out quite well. I never fancied doing a run-of-the-mill job, sort of nine to five sort of thing, and I quite like the secrecy of the job, I think really. You do have to do some boring office work but the best bit's out on the street. I'm quite a private man by nature so it sort of suits me and detective work, well it's laborious at times but quite rewarding too.

Speaker 3: Well, initially I wanted to be an actress and then I realised that wasn't going to happen so I've always been keen on fitness and I used to go to a judo class every week, then got more and more interested and sort of went three or four times a week, and it was my teacher there that sort of suggested to me why didn't I become a stunt woman? So he introduced me to somebody and I've been on sets ever since really. There's a lot of travel which sometimes gets me down but I do get to meet the famous people which is great and I travel the world, which is something I've always really wanted to do, so I've involved everything that I really love – travelling and fitness, and meeting famous people – so I really enjoy my work.

Speaker 4: Well, I sort of got into it by accident really. I needed a bit of extra money in the summer holidays and I've always liked the, you know, the outdoors and getting out in the mornings and all that sort of thing so I just decided to give it a try and keep on going. It was reasonably lucrative, you know, it's not a great sort of one for money but you do get cash which is the one thing I like in this job. You know, it goes straight in your hand and I like the exercise, you know, it is, it's quite sort of strenuous work and you know, you get out in the mornings, have a bit of a scrub around and the nice thing is the satisfaction, is people's faces, looking at people's faces afterwards when they realise they can actually see outside again.

Speaker 5: Well, at school I'd always been really interested in fitness. I was actually a gym champion when I was young and then I decided what to do when I grew up and yeah, it was, it was a really good choice in the end because what I really like is helping other people to get fit and to actually bring the best out of them. I can advise them what to do and what not to do, what's best for their muscles and yeah, it's really worthwhile. I suppose the thing I don't like about it is that it's sometimes a bit insecure, like I did have a job actually in a health club once but I didn't like that so much so now I'm just freelance and I suppose it's a bit insecure but on the whole, I really like it.

Speaker 6: Well, first of all I did an English degree and then I didn't know what to do really after that, and I wanted to sort of get out and, you know, do a job where you sort of meet a lot of people and so I fell into this job really. It's great, you know, because the hours are sort of very long but, you know, you get to sort of meet a lot of interesting people and, you know, the things I really like about it is that you know you're always breaking a story so whatever you get involved in is, you know, is really sort of quite interesting and it's quite sort of cutting-edge, you know. And I mean, I suppose the thing I don't like about it is that people always say that journalists are sort of, you know, the scum of the earth sort of thing but, you know, I don't agree really. I think we do a very worthwhile job. I think that, you know, if someone stands up, sort of sticks their head, you know, above the parapet and that, it sort of – and they're famous, then, you know, it's in the public's interest to sort of find out as much as possible about them, you know, and that's what I do.

Speaker 7: I think it was clear to my family what I was going to be when I grew up from quite an early age. I'm the eldest of five and my brothers and sisters always came to me for advice, and in the end actually my mum used to come to me for advice, or she'd like to talk things over or as a family we liked to try and find out why things happened as they did and that sort of thing, so at school we didn't really study psychology as a subject on its own but as part of biology we did look at the way people work and why they do what they do. It was a long training but something that's absolutely worthwhile. My belief and commitment in human beings, I suppose, is what made me become a psychologist. I suppose if there's anything that I find disappointing, at the same time it has to be a benefit, and that's that if I've had a chat with someone or I've helped someone, I can't necessarily see the changes in them in their everyday lives so I suppose I just have to look very closely when they come and see me next time. But it really is the best job in the world to me.

Speaker 8: Yes, I was an only child, no brothers and sisters. My mother left my father when I was about seven years old so every holiday from school I used to be with my father. I used to follow him everywhere and his job was a sports commentator for motor racing, Formula One, and so he travelled all over the world following the races and I went with him. I suppose it was inevitable in a way that I was going to follow him into that. He, a couple of times he actually gave me the microphone when I was a little boy to – and I spoke and it went out on television. I met all the famous drivers and the smell of the pit lane and the noise from the cars and everything was, was a very powerful thing that led me into, into this profession. Now, now I don't like it. I feel under pressure, I don't see enough of my own family. I'm travelling all over the world. I have two children and as soon as I can, as soon as my children are old enough – they're at school – I'll pack it in. I'll retire, I'll, you know, go past the chequered flag because I've had enough.

Writing folder 3

Formal letters
pages 50–51

1

Answers
a F (I: not your name, only your address) **b** F **c** F,I
d F,I **e** I **f** I **g** F

2

Answers
a apologise, delay, replying
b should, grateful, could, further
c acknowledge, receipt
d enclose, self, addressed
e would, appreciate, response
f forward, hearing, earliest, convenience

3

Answers
a ✔ **b** ✗ **c** ✗ **d** ✔ **e** ? **f** ✔

5

A
Dear Sir or Madam

Last Saturday my husband and I returned from a fortnight's holiday in your new holiday village. Unfortunately, our holiday did not live up to the claims made by you.

We had a number of problems. The advert stated that the self-catering chalets would accommodate six people. The chalet was far too small for us, however, it could surely sleep six if two of the people were babies. We had no choice but to book a room for my parents in a nearby hotel. The 'on-site restaurants' of the advert were also disappointing. There was in fact only one of them and it was more of a 'snack bar' than a restaurant.

Although we spent two weeks at the holiday village, two of the excursions did not take place. We were not able to have excursions either to the mountains or to the historic castles of the region. As one of our main reasons for choosing the village was the opportunity it would give us to visit the castles, we were very upset when we learnt that this trip would not be running this year. We had little choice but to hire a car to make the visit independently. This, although extremely enjoyable, was an unexpected expense.

In view of the fact that your advertisement misled us with regard to both the accommodation and the excursions we feel that you should provide compensation for both the disappointment we all experienced and the extra expense caused.

Yours faithfully

B
Dear Sir

I am very concerned that your readers may be left with the wrong impression of Grandton, the town that was so strongly criticised in an article in your newspaper last week.

It is quite unjust to claim that there is nothing of historic or architectural interest in the town. Our 1000-year-old cathedral is considered by many to be one of the most beautiful cathedrals this country has to offer and the design of its roof is unique. The town has a number of fascinating museums which are visited by increasing numbers of tourists each year. The fact that many of these tourists return for a second visit the following year surely proves that Grandton is an interesting and enjoyable place to visit.

As for the comment dismissing all the restaurants in our town, I can only presume that the writer of the article did not visit any of them. We have an excellent range of restaurants to match every pocket. The most famous one, The Three Boatmen in the Market Square, attracts people from all over the country to sample its justly renowned seafood.

I would urge your readers to come and see Grandton for themselves and not be put off by someone who, unlike any other visitors I have ever come across, was not able to appreciate the beauty and interest of our delightful town.

Yours faithfully

Unit 8

pages 52–55

Speaking 1

1

Answers
1 wristwatch (1904)   2 electric dishwasher (1914)
3 sliced bread (1928)   4 pop-up toaster (1937)
5 biro (1945)   6 video recorder (1956)
7 can with ring-pull (1962)   8 personal stereo (1979)
9 computer mouse (1984)   10 MP3 player (1997)

Vocabulary

1

Answers
a
courting	having a romantic relationship
contours	shape
suction pad	piece of rubber that fixes itself to a smooth surface using suction
treadmill	wide wheel turned by people climbing on steps around its edge (used in the past to provide power for machines or as punishment)
mop	stick with material on one end for washing floors
pivotable	can be moved about a fixed point

b
mini-	small (e.g. *minicab, mini-series, Mini Disc*)

c
-able	can or able to be (e.g. *disposable, regrettable, comparable*)
-less	without (e.g. *hopeless, thoughtless, careless*)

d
common	separate
flexible	inflexible, rigid
inner	outer
drives	halts, stops
mess up	keep tidy
stowed	unfolded

2

Answers
Positive	Negative
absorbing	grotesque
breathtaking	hackneyed
brilliant	hideous
delightful	ill-conceived
enchanting	impractical
engrossing	monstrous
ingenious	pointless
inspired	repulsive
ravishing	ridiculous
stunning	trivial

3

Answers
a breathtaking b ridiculous c ingenious d hackneyed
e stunning f repulsive g ill-conceived, delightful

Listening

1 and 2

Answers
Speaker 1: car (bike also mentioned)
Speaker 2: washing machine, hair dryer
Speaker 3: contact lenses (microwave also mentioned)
Speaker 4: Swiss army knife (pepper mill also mentioned)

	Positive adjectives	Negative adjectives
Speaker 1	brilliant, great	impractical, ridiculous, pointless
Speaker 2	good, eco-friendly, inspired, ingenious, great, breathtaking	repulsive, trivial
Speaker 3	indispensable, brilliant, extraordinary, inspired	vain, ugly, hideous
Speaker 4	brilliant, wonderful	terrible, grotesque, impractical, fastidious, pointless

Speaker 1: Well, I'm sorry to say it living in London but I couldn't do without my car. I love having my car. I mean it's, it's tiny, it's a soft top, it's completely impractical for most journeys but I love it and driving round in the country, well, it's just brilliant. I have a great time in it. I also, I couldn't do without my bike which is somehow a better idea around London. I can use it a lot more and I can get round all the traffic jams because it's just ridiculous in a car. You just spend your time hanging around waiting all the time. It's pointless.

Speaker 2: Well, I've got a little baby and one thing I really couldn't do without is my washing machine, especially – I know it sounds really repulsive – but we actually wash our nappies. It's, it's really good and that might sound trivial but not these days because, I don't know, it's so eco-friendly to have washable nappies and it's an inspired design, our washing machine, because it's got lots of features like the half-load button for example and yeah, it's very ingenious the way it can do that. And another thing I really couldn't do without is my hair dryer. Oh I love my hair dryer! It's really great. I think that's another piece of breathtaking design because it's really great the way that you can have a cold shot at the end of the dry so it doesn't make your hair too hot really. Yeah, those are the things I really couldn't do without.

Speaker 3: Well, my contact lenses are indispensable to me. They are, apart from being a brilliant invention, they – without them I couldn't see. I'm too vain to wear glasses so I really do need them. I mean, I think they're an absolutely extraordinary and inspired invention. But the other thing that I couldn't possibly live without is my microwave and to have that, I mean as ugly and hideous as it is in the corner, is an absolute boon to my life and being able to heat things up at the last minute and cold cups of coffee suddenly become wonderfully hot, so I'm – yes, without those two, with those two things I'm fine. Without them, I'm lost.

Speaker 4: Two things that I can't live without? Let me think. One of them goes everywhere with me, is a pepper mill for black pepper. I do a lot of travelling and I always – a terrible old piece of stuff, I mean it's, it's quite grotesque. It's not a normal wooden black pepper mill. It's got, it's made out of, almost looks like a small tree. It's quite impractical, I can't pack it anywhere and when you turn the top not much pepper comes out but I've had it for so long now, it automatically finds its way into my case when I, when I go away. My other thing that I have everywhere, and it sounds a bit, a bit fastidious, is my Swiss army knife. I think it's a brilliant piece of engineering really. There are several things on there that are quite pointless. I'm never going to get a stone out of a horse's hoof and there's a little swirly piece of metal with a funny nodule on the end. I don't know what that's for. It's a wonderful piece of engineering, though, and I take it everywhere with me and I couldn't live without it. I really don't think I could.

Modals: *must, should, ought to, shall, will, would*

Grammar folder page 194

Many learners of English make much less use of modals than native English speakers do. Try to use them in your speaking and writing as this will help the examiners to appreciate that your English skills are really at an advanced level.

1

> **Answers**
> **a** ought to   **b** should   **c** must   **d** must have
> **e** should have   **f** must   **g** shouldn't have
> **h** should   **i** would   **j** will   **k** must, shall

2

> **Answers**
> **a** obligation   **b** requesting   **c** advice   **d** deduction
> **e** advice   **f** offering   **g** deduction   **h** past habit
> **i** requesting   **j** advice

3

> **Answers**
> **a** must   **b** should / ought to   **c** should have, must have
> **d** would   **e** mustn't   **f** should / ought to   **g** Will
> **h** shouldn't have

Speaking 2

When you are watching a TV drama or film in English, pay attention to the exclamations that people use. Note down any other ones that you hear together with the function that they have in the context in which you hear them.

1

> **Answers**
> Expressing agreement: a, e, i
> Expressing admiration: b, g
> Expressing surprise or disbelief: c, h, k, l, n
> Expressing sympathy: d, f, j, m

2

> **Suggested answers**
> **a** Brilliant!   **b** Poor you!   **c** How extraordinary!
> **d** Oh dear!   **e** Fantastic!   **f** Surely not!   **g** Me too!
> **h** What a shame!

3

Suggested answers are in brackets.

1 The safety pin was invented in 1849. (Surely not!)

2 I've got dreadful toothache! (Poor you!)

3 When Mrs Lincoln, the wife of President Lincoln, had her photograph taken after her husband had been assassinated, the photograph included a ghostly image of the President. (How extraordinary!)

4 You have been selected to advise the Prime Minister on the problems of education in this country. (You must be joking!)

5 My grandfather, my mother, my sister and I were all born on the same date – the 6th of June! (What a coincidence!)

6 There are 400 billion stars in the Milky Way. (That's incredible!)

7 From 13th June 1948 to 1st June 1949, one person in Los Angeles hiccuped 160 million times! 60,000 suggestions for cures were received before he eventually stopped. (You must be joking!)

8 King Gustav II of Sweden thought that coffee was poisonous. He once sentenced a man to death by ordering him to drink coffee every day. The condemned man in fact lived to be very old! (How amazing!)

9 The first alarm clock was invented by Leonardo da Vinci. It woke the sleeper by gently rubbing the soles of his feet. (Fantastic!)

10 The common housefly may be the biggest threat to human health. It carries 30 different diseases which can be passed to humans. (Surely not!)

Exam folder 4

Paper 3 Part 4
pages 56–57

2

Answers			
1	mean	15	flat
2	figures	16	put on
3	Put on	17	bar
4	flat	18	figures
5	put on	19	mean
6	bar	20	put on
7	Mean	21	bar
8	bar	22	flat
9	flat	23	figures
10	mean	24	bar
11	bar	25	put on
12	flat	26	flat
13	figures	27	figures
14	mean	28	put on

4

Suggested answers	
(Other examples may also be found.)	
a	palm, hands, sets, common
b	strip, pad, top
c	belt, drives, collar, panel
d	wearing, head, support, frame
e	wear, seat, down

5

Answers				
a bank	b score	c stick	d beat	e eye

Unit 9

pages 58–61

Speaking 1

Even if you do not think it is likely that you may use English to study another subject, remember that the number of courses which are available online is growing very rapidly. A high proportion of these courses are available mainly in English and so it is increasingly likely that people may use English for study purposes even without going to an English-speaking country.

Reading

Answers
a 1 sociolinguistics 2 history 3 economics
4 law 5 psychology
b 1 e 2 b 3 d 4 a 5 c
c Suggested answers
1 The observation of language change
2 Changes in eighteenth century Russian life
3 Consumerism prevails
4 Minority in law
5 Experiments in extra-sensory perception

2

Answers
a a firm no b before c previously d behind
e spare money f stage where nothing more is needed
g reaches h previously i permission j get
k the other way round l make a difference between

3

Here are some of the key chunks from the texts.
Text 1 – recent work in (sociolinguistics), has raised (once again) a (long-standing) question, the answer to that question following the example of, all that you can possibly hope to
Text 2 – as a (further) symbol of, an important symbolic change, as it were
Text 3 – the immediate crisis (of 1968) soon passed, dismissed it as a (fantasy), did their bit to
Text 4 – fixes the age of majority, holding office as
Text 5 – experiments have shown that, this is by no means necessary, be taken as evidence of

Vocabulary

1

Suggested answers

Verb	Noun	Adjective
occur	occurrence	occurring
found	founder	founding
–	consequence	consequent, consequential
oblige	obligation	obligatory
disappear	disappearance	disappearing
glamorise	glamour	glamorous
authorise	authority	authoritative, authorised
vary	variety	various
presume	presumption	presumptive
perceive	perception	perceptive perceptible

2

Suggested answers
a It is obligatory for (all) pupils to wear school uniform.
b There is a wide / large / great variety of animals which are indigenous to Australia.
c Burglaries are an everyday occurrence in this part of town.
d The mountaineer is presumed to have died in the blizzard.
e Giving up work to bring up a child and the consequent loss of income is difficult for many women.
f How do people in your country perceive the role of the United Nations?
g Cambridge University Press was founded in 1534.
h Modern films tend to glamorise violence.

Participle clauses

Grammar folder page 194

2

Answers
a Because they hoped to gain a speedy victory, the army invaded.
b They killed many people who were living in the border areas.
c Because it was a Sunday, most of the shops were shut.
d Charles I was generally considered a weak king and was eventually beheaded.
e Because he had previously learnt their language, Picton was able to communicate with the tribe.
f When you have measured the wood carefully, cut it as indicated.

3

Answers
a Walking round the exhibition, I caught sight of an old school friend at the far end of the gallery.
b Having made so many mistakes in her homework, Marti had to do it all over again.
c Being only a child, she can't fully understand what is happening.
d Not knowing anyone / Knowing no one in the town to spend the evening with, Jack decided to have an early night.
e Considering all the inequalities of life before the revolution, it is surprising that a revolution did not happen sooner.
f Having climbed to the top of the church tower, be sure to walk right round, admiring the view from each of the four sides.
g We set off at midnight, hoping to avoid the rest of the holiday traffic heading for the coast. OR Setting off at midnight, we hoped to avoid the rest of the holiday traffic heading for the coast.
h Seeing me, he stood up, knocking his glass to the floor.

Speaking 2

1 **A:** Did you go to the cinema last night?
  B: No, but I went to the <u>theatre</u>.
2 **A:** Did you go by bike to the theatre last night?
  B: No, <u>Marco</u> was using my bike last night.
3 **A:** Did you go to the theatre by bus last night?
  B: No, I went to the theatre by <u>taxi</u> last night.
4 **A:** Did you go home by taxi last night?
  B: No, I went home by taxi <u>two</u> nights ago.
5 **A:** Anne's wearing a lovely green dress.
  B: It's a green <u>blouse</u> and <u>skirt</u>, actually.
6 **A:** Did you have a good time at the party last night?
  B: Yes, we had a <u>brilliant</u> time.
7 **A:** Are you hungry yet?
  B: I'm not <u>hungry</u>, I'm <u>starving</u>.

8 A: Are you hungry yet?
   B: <u>I'm</u> not hungry but <u>Tina</u> is.
9 A: Are you tired?
   B: Yes, I'm <u>exhausted</u>!
10 A: Are you feeling a bit cold?
   B: Yes, I'm <u>freezing</u>!

Writing folder 4

Reports and proposals
pages 62–63

1

> **Suggested answers**
> a
> **Types of reports:**
> scientific report, e.g. of experiment
> business report, e.g. of progress made over last year
> sports report, e.g. of football match played
> school report, e.g. of child's progress over a term or year
> shareholders' annual report, e.g. of company's
>   performance over the year
> product report, e.g. weighing up the good and bad
>   features of different products of the same type
> **Types of proposals:**
> academic proposal, e.g. about research with a view to
>   getting some money or a place at university
> work proposal, e.g. with a view to introducing some
>   innovation at the workplace
> social proposal, e.g. a plan for change that aims to
>   persuade readers of the desirability of such changes
> c
> It will probably have some or all of the following:
> factual title
> clear statement of aims at beginning
> facts presented unambiguously
> clearly drawn conclusions at the end
> headings used frequently to help clarify
> d
> An article aims to be interesting and lively as well as clear,
>   whereas the main aim of a report is to be unambiguous
>   and straightforward.
> An article may be more personal in style and approach.
> The title of an article aims to be eye-catching rather
>   than factual.

2

> **Sample answers**
> **Possible proposal for task 2A**
>
> (Note that this suggested answer is about the length of
> the pieces of writing you have to do in Paper 2 of CAE.)
>
> I should like to apply for the Alice Lumsden Travel Grant
> for next year.
>
> My aim is to use the money to travel to New Zealand to work
> for a year in a hotel. I have already been offered a job and
> accommodation once I arrive and so should be self-supporting
> while I am there. However, I need to pay for my own fare and I
> would not be able to do this without the grant.
>
> <u>Benefits for my studies</u>
> Spending a year in an English-speaking country would be
> extremely helpful for my study of the language. I can read
> and write reasonably well, but I know that my speaking
> and listening skills can be greatly improved. I am sure that
> the best way for me to make progress in these areas is to
> immerse myself in an English-speaking environment.
>
> As I am also planning to make my career in the tourist
> industry, the experience of working in a hotel should
> prove an invaluable one.
>
> <u>Benefits for college</u>
> I hope that the college might also gain from my stay in
> New Zealand. We already have a number of sporting and
> cultural links with colleges there and I would be happy to
> do anything I could while I was there to support and
> develop those links further.
>
> I would also like to send back a fortnightly report in English
> about my experiences which might be of interest and use
> to students considering a similar placement next year.
>
> I hope very much that you will give my request serious
> consideration and should be happy to discuss it further
> with you at any time convenient to you.
>
> **Possible proposal for task 2C**
> **Physical Fitness and Our Class**
> <u>Aims</u>
> Roberto Perez and I decided to investigate the amount of
> physical activity done by the members of this class. We
> suspected that most of the people in this class were
> spending much less time on physical fitness activities
> than they used to do five years ago and that this might be
> one of the reasons why many of them feel overtired and
> rather stressed.
>
> <u>Survey</u>
> We asked the twenty members of the class the following
> questions:
> • How much time do you spend on physical fitness
>   activities each week?
> • What sports and other physical activities do you do
>   every week?
> • Do you do more or less physical activity now, than you
>   did five years ago? To what extent?

- To what extent do you feel more or less stressed now than you did five years ago?
- Would you like to spend more time on physical activities than you do? Why (not)?

We then analysed the responses by age, sex and marital status.

Results

We found that 90 per cent of students in the class do less physical activity than they used to, and less than they would like to do. The most popular activities are walking, jogging, swimming, cycling and dancing, but some students also named football, tennis, golf, yoga, skiing, go-karting and judo as activities that they do occasionally. Most of the students in the class said that they did between 2 and 5 hours of sport or other physical fitness activities per week. Two students do between 5 and 10 hours and 4 do less than two hours.

When asked why they did not spend more time on physical activities, most blamed the lack of provision in this area. The nearest sports centre or gym is over 20 miles away. Moreover, membership is very expensive which makes it a problem for students.

Conclusions

There is a clear correlation between age, sex and marital status and the amount of time spent on physical activity. Younger single males are most likely to do more sport than females, especially than those females who are slightly older and who are married.

There also appears to be a correlation between lack of physical activity and stress. Although all but one of the students in our class claimed to feel more stressed now than they did five years ago, the four people who devote least time to keeping fit are those who complained of considerably increased stress levels.

Unit 10

pages 64–67

Speaking 1

A speech can be any kind of formal or semi-formal public speaking. It can be political, of course, but people also make speeches at weddings, when colleagues leave work, after a formal dinner, etc.

This speech was delivered by Martin Luther King, a black American clergyman and civil rights campaigner, on the steps at the Lincoln Memorial in Washington D.C. on August 28, 1963, as the climax of a civil rights march on Washington. He was advocating a non-violent approach to his campaigners but was himself assassinated five years later.

Reading

These exercises aim to check that you understand the basic gist of the speech. Do not worry too much about details at this point. We shall look at more specific aspects of the language used in the speech in later exercises.

1

Listening

1

Go back to Mississippi, go back to Alabama, go back to South Carolina, go back to Georgia, go back to Louisiana, go back to the slums and ghettos of our northern cities, knowing that somehow this situation can and will be changed. Let us not wallow in the valley of despair.

I say to you today, my friends, so even though we face the difficulties of today and tomorrow, I still have a dream. It is a dream deeply rooted in the American dream.

I have a dream that one day this nation will rise up and live out the true meaning of its creed: 'We hold these truths to be self-evident: that all men are created equal.'

I have a dream that one day on the red hills of Georgia the sons of former slaves and the sons of former slave owners will be able to sit down together at the table of brotherhood.

I have a dream that one day even the state of Mississippi, a state sweltering with the heat of injustice, sweltering with the heat of oppression, will be transformed into an oasis of freedom and justice.

I have a dream that my four little children will one day live in a nation where they will not be judged by the color of their skin but by the content of their character. I have a dream today.

You can find examples of some of the other listed techniques in the first part of the speech in Reading 1:
- drawing attention to the location where the speech is taking place (*a great American, in whose symbolic shadow we stand*)
- alliteration (*dark and desolate*)
- appealing to the audience's senses (*seared in the flames, a joyous daybreak to end the long night of captivity, cooling off*)

2

> **Answers**
>
> 1 a   2 d   3 b   4 e   5 c

3

> **Answers**
>
> You may come up with other suggestions that you find acceptable but some of the main techniques used in these speeches are indicated here in brackets after the relevant places in the tapescripts.
>
> **Speaker 1:** I've known Johnny since our first day at school when we were five (*presenting interesting or surprising facts*). We were two scared little boys sitting at the same table hoping that we were going to enjoy this strangely exciting new world (*appealing to the audience's emotions*). Now Johnny is beginning another new stage of his life. In some ways it may be rather like starting school again (*making analogies or comparisons*). Especially, of course, as Megan, his beautiful bride (*appealing to the audience's senses*), is a teacher herself. Johnny as teacher's pet! None of the staff at Morley Primary School would ever have expected that of him (*humour*)!
>
> **Speaker 2:** You may not believe it of an old man like me but it seems no time at all (*exaggeration*) to me since I had a 'shining morning face', as Shakespeare so aptly put it (*quoting famous lines*), a face that was amazingly once as young and eager as those of yours that I see before me now. I too was dreaming of a life beyond the inevitably restricted confines of these walls (*making analogies or comparisons*), I promised your headmaster that I would not be either too sentimental or too long-winded. I guess I'd better change track before I fail on the sentimental count, but I promise to do my best to be brief. I hear your sighs of relief from the back of the room, cooling me nicely on this sweltering day (*humour, appealing to the audience's senses*)!
>
> **Speaker 3:** Maria, you are a beautiful baby (*appealing to the audience's senses*). May you grow up to bring your own parents as much joy as they have brought their own parents in so many different ways and most recently, possibly best of all, by producing you! A quick check on the Internet showed me that you share your birthday with the philosopher, Jean-Paul Sartre and the actress, Jane Russell (*presenting interesting or surprising facts*). Brains and beauty. Like mother, like daughter (*appealing to the audience's emotions, mixing short and long sentences*)!
>
> **Speaker 4:** This next slide (*using visual aids*) shows the narrow pathway down to Petra, the 'rose-red city half as old as time' (*quoting famous lines*). We were there on one of the hottest days of the whole trip (*appealing to the audience's senses*) but who could not be impressed by the glorious red-sandstone buildings of this city, reputedly the oldest city in the world? (*asking rhetorical questions*) Once known as Palmyra, it grew to importance because of its location enabling it to control the trade routes of the ancient world (*presenting interesting or surprising facts*).

> **Speaker 5:** Well, Fiona. You've been working here (*drawing attention to the location where the speech is taking place*) for longer than any of us, including the boss and we're all going to miss you very much. We've clubbed together to get you this little token of our appreciation for all the good – and occasionally not so good – times we've shared together (*appealing to the audience's emotions*). We hope that whenever you make yourself some coffee you'll think of us and the thousands of coffees we've shared over the years. Remember us all as you drink your favourite cappuccino – with plenty of chocolate, of course (*appealing to the audience's senses*). But I'd like everyone now to raise a glass of something a bit stronger than coffee (*humour*) to wish you, Fiona, all the very best for a long, happy and healthy retirement.

Speaker 1: I've known Johnny since our first day at school when we were five. We were two scared little boys sitting at the same table hoping that we were going to enjoy this strangely exciting new world. Now Johnny is beginning another new stage of his life. In some ways it may be rather like starting school again! Especially, of course, as Megan, his beautiful bride, is a teacher herself. Johnny as teacher's pet! None of the staff at Morley Primary School would ever have expected that of him!

Speaker 2: You may not believe it of an old man like me but it seems no time at all to me since I had a 'shining morning face', as Shakespeare so aptly put it, a face that was amazingly once as young and eager as those of yours that I see before me now. I too was dreaming of a life beyond the inevitably restricted confines of these walls. I promised your headmaster that I would not be either too sentimental or too long-winded. I guess I'd better change track before I fail on the sentimental count, but I promise to do my best to be brief. I hear your sighs of relief from the back of the room, cooling me nicely on this sweltering day!

Speaker 3: Maria, you are a beautiful baby. May you grow up to bring your own parents as much joy as they have brought their own parents in so many different ways and most recently, possibly best of all, by producing you! A quick check on the Internet showed me that you share your birthday with the philosopher, Jean-Paul Sartre and the actress, Jane Russell. Brains and beauty. Like mother, like daughter!

Speaker 4: This next slide shows the narrow pathway down to Petra, the 'rose-red city half as old as time'. We were there on one of the hottest days of the whole trip but who could not be impressed by the glorious red-sandstone buildings of this city, reputedly the oldest city in the world? Once known as Palmyra, it grew to importance because of its location enabling it to control the trade routes of the ancient world.

Speaker 5: Well, Fiona. You've been working here for longer than any of us, including the boss and we're all going to miss you very much. We've clubbed together to get you this little token of our appreciation for all the good – and occasionally not so good – times we've shared together. We hope that whenever you make yourself some coffee you'll think of us and the thousands of coffees we've shared over the years. Remember us all as you drink your favourite cappuccino – with plenty of chocolate, of course. But I'd like everyone now to raise a glass of something a bit stronger than coffee to wish you, Fiona, all the very best for a long, happy and healthy retirement.

Vocabulary

1

> **Answers**
> a punishment b light, punishment c light
> d economics e heat f economics
> g natural environment, light
> h natural environment, heat i natural environment

2

> **Answers**
> a *will foot the bill* (will pay)
> b *went up in smoke* (vanished)
> c *am tied up* (am busy)
> d *feeling all at sea* (not knowing what you should do)
> e *shedding light on* (clarifying)
> f *light dawned* (she realised)
> g *common ground* (points that could be agreed on)
> h *was pilloried* (was strongly criticised)
> i *in debt* (very grateful)
> j *put its money where its mouth is* (be prepared to spend money as well as to talk)
> k *will get your fingers burnt* (will get into trouble)

Future forms

Grammar folder page 195

The choice of which future form to use can be one of the most difficult ones. Although your meaning will probably still be clear if you make the wrong choice, your use of language will not sound totally natural. The most common mistake made by advanced learners is to not use the present continuous for future plans. The best way to talk about plans is to say, for example: *What are you doing this evening / at the weekend / next summer? I'm going to the theatre next Tuesday / We're spending next July in Spain.*

1

> **Answers**
> a 5 b 1 c 6 d 4,6 e 8 f 9 g 7 h 3 i 10 j 2

2

> **Answers**
> a I'm going b get c we'll be lying d he'd leave
> e to get f leaves / is leaving g are, are going to spend
> h gets, she's going to study i will have set foot

Speaking 2

If you are working alone why not write an essay on one of the topics presented here? Write a proposal in which you try to persuade the local authorities in your area to make some changes that you feel are necessary with regard to one of these issues:
- the environment
- leisure facilities
- local transport.

These three topics have been chosen as they are all topics that often feature in CAE Paper 2.

Units 6–10 Revision

pages 68–69

Reading

2

> **Answers**
> Correct paragraph order – C, E, F, B, D, A, G

3

> **Answers**
> a fair b draw c hit d set e bear f bar

4

> **Answers**
> 1 alphabetical 2 obsessive 3 coverage 4 addiction
> 5 extension 6 editor 7 expensive 8 pride 9 latest
> 10 survival

Unit 11

pages 70–73

Reading

2

Read the base text first. Then read paragraphs A–G and fit them into the gaps 1–6.

Answers
1 C 2 F 3 A 4 G 5 D 6 E

Notes to confirm the answers:

1C The paragraph is an introduction to the system and what it can do.

2F The use of *M&S* means paragraph F must come somewhere later than the second paragraph of the base text, which refers to *Marks and Spencer* (the full name) and then *M&S*. F explains how M&S will trial the new technology.

3A *they* in paragraph A refers to *shoppers* in the previous paragraph and it explains how the portable device works.

4G Paragraph G explains how the customer will get scanned and acts as a link to the next paragraph which explains what customers do once they have been scanned.

5D *That card* refers back to *a smart card* in the previous paragraph.

6E By reading the final paragraph, we can see that paragraph E introduces the idea of the device being embarrassing and the final paragraph is the solution to that potential problem.

Vocabulary

1

Answers
1 browsing 2 tailored 3 sleeveless 4 pencil
5 aubergine 6 wear 7 slim 8 suede 9 fake
10 look

Listening

2

Think about the following questions:
In which jobs is appearance important?
What do you think *dress-down Friday* is?
What is *body jewellery*?
Why might some people object to a dress code?

3

Answers
a reception b a tie and a dark suit c accountants
d dress-down Friday e smart-casual
f (a) training day(s) g a nose ring h civil liberties
i Human Resources

The underlined parts of the tapescript confirm the answers.

Now, it's been brought to my attention that certain members of staff have been flouting the dress code. So I want to make it crystal clear to everyone just exactly what's expected in terms of attire. Those of you who work in reception must be, how shall I put it, business-like at all times. You are the first person visitors see when they enter the building. Whether they then go on to the Managing Director or the canteen is irrelevant. You create the first impression of the company; and as we all know, first and last impressions count. Now, for men that means a tie and a dark suit – accepted business practice. For women, a suit, er, that can be a trouser suit, or a smart dress or skirt and jacket. It goes without saying that hair and so on needs to be neat and tidy.

The accountants. You never know when a client may come in to see you. You may think you're not in the public relations business but in a way, you are. And I know most of the time people make appointments but there are odd occasions when someone just happens to be in the area and decides to come in. In this case you are the embodiment of your profession. This is a firm with a good reputation. Clients expect their accountant to reflect this, not only in their work but also in the way they present themselves. Don't forget, in many people's eyes sloppy clothes means sloppy work, and I must say, I tend to agree.

The only possible exception to this is the so-called dress-down Friday. This new idea. And of course that only applies if you have no appointments with clients in your diary. Now, this doesn't mean that you can turn up wearing whatever you like. It's got to be 'smart-casual'. That's what it says here. And that still means a tie, but you can wear smart jeans and a jacket or even a sweater.

Now, something's come to my attention that I'm not at all happy about and that is training days. It seems as though some of you have got the idea into your head that when you're on a training day that means you can dress like a student. It does not. You're still a representative of this company. When you go out to management college, you are judged there too. I've heard remarks about a certain man who turned up wearing a nose ring. This is not acceptable; it's all in the company's dress code, which you've all had a copy of. What I want to emphasise is that it's a matter of professional pride, the way you dress.

I know some people start murmuring about civil liberties and all that, but I'm sorry, as I see it, we're all here to do a job of work. We are employees of a company and as such we have to toe the line and not only in what we do and how we do our job, but also the way we dress.

If anyone feels particularly aggrieved by any of this, all I can suggest is that you take it up with the Human Resources department. Go up to the fifth floor, you know, next to the UK department. But really, I hope I won't have to refer to this again and I expect to see a dramatic improvement in personal presentation.

Direct and reported speech

Grammar folder page 196

1

The aim here is to extend your range of reporting verbs and to point out that we do not always change the verb tense.

> **Answers**
> a exactly what was/is expected in terms of attire.
> b those of us who work/worked in reception must/had to be businesslike at all times.
> c us that in many people's eyes sloppy clothes meant/means sloppy work.
> d she was/is not at all happy about the way some people dressed/dress for training days.
> e it seemed/seems as though some of us had/have got the idea into our head that when we were/are on a training day we could/can dress like a student.
> f who had turned up to a management college wearing a nose ring.
> g it was/is a matter of professional pride, the way we dress.
> h we had/have to toe the line.
> i if anyone felt/feels particularly aggrieved by any of that/this, all she could suggest was/is that we take/took it up with the Human Resources department.
> j she wouldn't have to refer to this/that again.

3

> **Answers**
> a 2   b 1,4   c 2,4   d 3   e 2,3   f 2   g 1,3   h 1,4
> i 1   j 3   k 3   l 4   m 2   n 1

4

> **Answers**
> a buying   b another style to us   c promised myself
> d that she would refund   e to be   f her name was
> g I was   h recommended   i that you pay
> j to help me   k the Isa Hotel to you

Speaking 2

Go through the the Exam spot about Part 2 of the Speaking test. You will be able to find examples of Part 2 tasks in Practice Test Books and the CAE Handbook.

1

Comparing means looking for similarities whereas *contrasting* means looking for differences. Using appropriate linking devices helps you structure your response to Part 2 of the Speaking test.

> **Suggested Answers**
> | **Comparing** | **Contrasting** |
> |---|---|
> | is similar to the other picture in/in that ... | however |
> | shows the same kind of ... | although |
> | like the second picture, ... | on the one hand |
> | is much the same as | on the other hand |
> | | while |

2

All these plans are good. It may depend on the pictures and the task as to which one is most suitable.

3

> **Answers**
> a C   b but, and, then, in contrast   c 2   d 3

The underlined parts of the tapescript confirm the answers.

Examiner: In this part of the test, I'm going to give each of you the chance to talk for about a minute and to comment briefly after your partner has spoken. First, you will each have the same set of pictures to look at. They show people wearing different types of clothes.

Angela, it's your turn first. I'd like you to compare and contrast these pictures, saying what the clothes might tell us about the wearer. Don't forget, you have about a minute for this, all right? So, Angela, would you start please?

Angela: I, I'd like to talk about pictures a and b <u>as they are both pictures of men but they are wearing very different clothes</u>. In picture a, we can see a man wearing a pin-striped suit and in fact the stripe is quite prominent; it's not a subtle sort of stripe that the typical businessman wears. <u>And</u> there's another interesting thing about the suit; it's got pink lining – <u>that's quite flamboyant</u>. <u>Then</u> this man is wearing a tie – pale pink with dots of a deeper pink. Again, that's outrageous, some might say.

This leads me to think that perhaps he's not a businessman who works in a bank or insurance company but perhaps he's something to do with the arts or in advertising. It's got to be a profession which allows him to express his slightly extrovert personality.

<u>In contrast</u>, in picture b there's a man wearing casual clothes. He's wearing some sort of brown top with a zip and then over that he's got another blue jacket which is undone. It looks as if it's made of that fleece material. He's got a scarf tucked into his top. His trousers have got large pockets on the sides of the legs – quite fashionable, I think. I'm not absolutely sure but perhaps they might be made of corduroy. And then he's wearing walking boots.

Looking at this picture, I would say this man is enjoying some time at the weekend, out in the country – he's a man who loves being out in nature and he's quite a free thinker. I can't imagine him working in a bank either – look at his hair. <u>He could be a teacher.</u>

Examiner: Thank you. Now, Luciano, which picture shows the clothes that you would be most comfortable wearing?

Luciano: Oh, definitely picture b. I feel much better when I'm wearing casual clothes and I would certainly never wear a suit like that!

Examiner: Thank you.

Exam folder 5

Paper 3 Part 5
pages 74–75

1

Answers
1 The essay *made a great impression on* me.
2 Sarah *insisted on speaking (only)* English with the visitors.
3 There was a *sharp increase in* the price of petrol last month.
4 I *caught sight of* the postman for a minute as he passed my window.

2

Answers
1 The phrasal verb is *to hand something down to someone* – *to* is missing.
  The secret recipe *is handed down to* each new generation
2 The given word is in the past tense and cannot be changed.
  The present *came as a complete surprise* to me.
3 The spelling of *emotion* is wrong.
  The child's mother *was overcome with emotion* when he was found.
4 The idiom for *to help someone* is *to give someone a hand*.
  Could you possibly *give me a hand* with this suitcase?

3

Answers
1 c   2 e   3 b   4 f   5 a   6 d

4

Answers
1 in   2 of   3 from   4 in   5 with   6 in

5

Answers
1 If we don't get the 8 am train, *it will mean* missing lunch.
2 Italian football players are *said to earn the highest* salaries.
3 The tour operator *apologised for not* emailing the details earlier.
4 Your accountant *should have given you* better advice.

6

Answers
1 A medical certificate *wasn't required for* my USA visa.
2 The island *is rich in* natural resources.
3 Gina *does nothing but* complain.
4 The candidate *gave honest answers to* the questions.
5 If the tennis court *hadn't been so wet*, the match wouldn't have been cancelled.
6 I'd *be on your side* even if you weren't my friend.
7 He *flatly refused to* help me.
8 Could you get some fruit *on your way* home?

Unit 12

pages 76–79

Speaking 1

In a nutshell means to express something in a brief way. We often use the fuller phrase *to put something in a nutshell*.

Reading 1

1

Suggested answers
a He had been advised to travel from New York to Petrograd via Vladivostok as this way would be safer.
b As the station restaurant was crowded, they were sharing a table at dinner time.
c He was tall and very fat and he did not look after his clothes.
  He was well-educated, he spoke English well and he could discuss literature.
d He says he is a journalist, but it is inferred that he wants to keep his real profession secret. He could be a secret agent, a criminal, an undercover police officer or a politician.

2

Answers
a stout   b paunch   c sallow   d shabby
e tiresome   f dissimulation

Useful vocabulary
idle *adj.* lazy
crown *n.* the top of a person's head
marked *adj.* noticeable
frankness *n.* honesty/openness

Listening 1

2

> **Answers**
> **a** He drank vodka, he was talkative, he was of noble birth, a lawyer by profession. He had been in trouble with the 'authorities' so he had had to be abroad a lot. He had been doing business in Vladivostok. He would be in Moscow in a week. He was a widower.
> **b** She was Swiss, and spoke English, German, French and Italian perfectly and good Russian. She had taught languages at one of the best schools in Petrograd.
> **c** The narrator seems to have found it unusual that the Russian told him so much about himself unasked. He felt the Russian's question about whether he was married was a little too personal. The narrator was wondering, while the Russian was telling his story, whether he would have time to eat before his train left. The narrator found it laughable that anyone could love the Russian to distraction as he found him very ugly.

The underlined parts of the tapescript confirm the answers.

By this time we had persuaded the waiter to bring us some cabbage soup, and my acquaintance pulled a small bottle of vodka from his pocket which he invited me to share. I do not know whether it was the <u>vodka or the natural loquaciousness</u> of his race that made him communicative, but presently he told me, <u>unasked</u>, a good deal about himself. <u>He was of noble birth, it appeared, a lawyer by profession, and a radical. Some trouble with the authorities</u> had made it necessary for him to be much abroad, but now he was on his way home. <u>Business had detained him at Vladivostok, but he expected to start for Moscow in a week</u> and if I went there, he would be charmed to see me.

'Are you married?' he asked me.

<u>I did not see what business it was of his</u>, but I told him that I was. He sighed a little.

'<u>I am a widower</u>,' he said. '<u>My wife was a Swiss</u>, a native of Geneva. She was a very <u>cultured woman. She spoke English, German and Italian perfectly. French, of course, was her native tongue. Her Russian was much above the average for a foreigner. She had scarcely the trace of an accent.</u>'

He called a waiter who was passing with a tray full of dishes and asked him, I suppose – for then I knew hardly any Russian – how much longer we were going to wait for the next course. The waiter, with a rapid but presumably reassuring exclamation, hurried on, and my friend sighed.

'Since the revolution the waiting in restaurants has become abominable.'

He lighted his twentieth cigarette and I, looking at my watch, <u>wondered whether I should get a square meal before it was time for me to start.</u>

'My wife was a very remarkable woman,' he continued. '<u>She taught languages at one of the best schools for the daughters of noblemen in Petrograd.</u> For a good many

years we lived together on perfectly friendly terms. She was, however, of a jealous temperament and unfortunately she loved me to distraction.'

<u>It was difficult for me to keep a straight face. He was one of the ugliest men I had ever seen.</u> There is sometimes a certain charm in the rubicund and jovial fat, but this saturnine obesity was repulsive.

3

The significant words are *jealous* and *unfortunately*. They may imply that the Russian had to do something drastic about his wife's jealousy.

> Useful vocabulary
> **loquaciousness** *n.* talkativeness
> **abominable** *adj.* awful/unpleasant
> **a square meal** *n.* a good/decent/satisfying meal
> **to keep a straight face** – not to laugh
> **rubicund** *adj.* having a red face (literary)
> **jovial** *adj.* friendly, good-humoured
> **saturnine** *adj.* serious/unfriendly (literary)
> **repulsive** *adj.* unpleasant/disgusting

Reading 2

> **Answers**
> **a** She was quite old, not attractive and she said unpleasant things.
> **b** It was stormy. She threw out a coat of his that he loved. He found her boring. They had rows which he tried to ignore as he tried to lead his own life. He accepted the way she was as much as possible. He wondered whether she loved or hated him.
> **c** The dream could be a kind of omen.
> **d** This question is open to interpretation but you may suspect that the Russian will kill his wife as in her dream.

> Useful vocabulary
> **complexion** *n.* the natural appearance of the skin, especially on the face
> **merely** *adj.* only
> **equitable** *adj.* even/balanced
> **acrimonious** *adj.* bitter/angry
> **balusters** *n.* balustrade = railing to prevent people from falling over the edge of stairs

Listening 2

> **Answers**
> **a** The Russian began to think about the dream too. He realised his wife thought he hated her and could be capable of murdering her. When he walked up the stairs it was impossible not to imagine the scene his wife had described in her dream and think about how easy it would be.

b No. He had wished to be free of her, that she might leave him or die a natural death, but not that he could murder her.

c For a short time she became less bitter and more tolerant.

d The second dream was the same as the first.

e Perhaps because the memory of the situation was so vivid. Perhaps because he had murdered his wife.

f She fell over the baluster and was found dead at the bottom of the stairs by a lodger.

g He seemed nervous, he had a malicious, cunning look and his eyes sparkled.

h Did the Russian murder her or was it an accident? We do not know for sure but this is the narrator's suspicion or nagging doubt.

The underlined parts of the tapescript confirm the answers.

'She was much shaken. I did my best to soothe her. But next morning, and for two or three days after, she referred to the subject again and, notwithstanding my laughter, I saw that it dwelt in her mind. <u>I could not help thinking of it either, for this dream showed me something that I had never suspected. She thought I hated her, she thought I would gladly be rid of her, she knew of course that she was insufferable, and at some time or other the idea had evidently occurred to her that I was capable of murdering her.</u> The thoughts of men are incalculable and ideas enter our minds that we should be ashamed to confess. <u>Sometimes I had wished she might run away with a lover, sometimes that a painless and sudden death might give me my freedom, but never had the idea come to me that I might deliberately rid myself of an intolerable burden.</u>

'The dream made an extraordinary impression upon both of us. <u>It frightened my wife, and she became for a while a little less bitter and more tolerant.</u> But when I walked up the stairs to our apartment it was impossible for me not to look over the balusters and reflect how easy it would be to do what she had dreamt. The balusters were dangerously low. A quick gesture and the thing was done. It was hard to put the thought out of my mind. Then some months later my wife awakened me one night. I was very tired and I was exasperated. She was white and trembling. <u>She had had the dream again.</u> She burst into tears and asked me if I hated her. I swore by all the saints of the Russian calendar that I loved her. At last she went to sleep again. It was more than I could do. I lay awake. I seemed to see her falling down the well of the stairs, and I heard a shriek and the thud as she struck the stone floor. I could not help shivering.'

The Russian stopped and beads of sweat stood on his forehead. He had told the story well and fluently so that I had listened with attention. There was still some vodka in the bottle, he poured it out and swallowed it at a gulp.

'And how did your wife eventually die?' I asked after a pause.

He took out a dirty handkerchief and wiped his forehead.

'By an extraordinary coincidence <u>she was found late one night at the bottom of the stairs with her neck broken.</u>'

'Who found her?'

'<u>She was found by one of the lodgers</u> who came in shortly after the catastrophe.'

'And where were you?'

I cannot describe the look he gave me of malicious cunning. His little black eyes sparkled.

'I was spending the evening with a friend of mine. I did not come in till an hour later.'

At that moment the waiter brought us the dish of meat that we had ordered, and the Russian fell upon it with good appetite. He shovelled the food into his mouth in enormous mouthfuls.

I was taken aback. Had he really been telling me in this hardly veiled manner that he had murdered his wife? That obese and sluggish man did not look like a murderer, I could not believe that he would have had the courage. Or was he making a sardonic joke at my expense?

In a few minutes it was time for me to go and catch my train. I left him and have not seen him since. But I have never been able to make up my mind whether he was serious or jesting.

Useful vocabulary

notwithstanding *adv.* despite

dwelt *v.* (to dwell) lived, stayed

burden *n.* difficulty duty/responsibility

exasperated *adj.* very angry/annoyed

shriek *n.* to give out a short loud cry

thud *n.* the sound of something heavy hitting a hard surface

at a gulp *adj.* in one swallow

malicious *adj.* wishing to harm others

cunning *adj.* clever at planning something to get what you want

shovelled the food ate quickly

I was taken aback I was shocked

sluggish *adj.* slow moving without energy

sardonic *adj.* showing a lack of respect in a humorous but unkind way

jesting joking

Past tenses and the present perfect

Grammar folder page 196

1

> **Answers**
> called   was passing   asked   knew   were going to wait   hurried   sighed

2

> **Answers**
> **a** I had read many other stories by this author before I read *The Dream*.
> **b** correct
> **c** The short story was made into a TV drama last year.

d The author owned an interesting collection of antiquarian books.
e correct
f correct
g correct
h In the story the villain almost got away with it but the body was discovered.
i correct
j correct
k The first page of the book seemed very boring, that's why I didn't read it.
l He had been writing for magazines for years before he was discovered by Hollywood.
m It's the first time I've written a story.
n correct
o Are you sure the Russian committed the murder? I thought it was the lodger.

Vocabulary

1

> **Answers**
> a small wooden table
> an exciting, extensive new menu
> a beautiful red silk dress
> a shabby black suit
> a huge sallow face

2

> **Possible answers**
> a light airy modern sitting room
> an old-fashioned panelled library
> a dirty industrial town
> a lovely peaceful park in spring

Speaking 2

1

> **Answers**
>
> | **walked** /t/ | **loved** /d/ | **started** /ɪd/ |
> | --- | --- | --- |
> | chanced | engaged | instructed |
> | passed | obliged | landed |
> | | dined | crowded |
> | | shared | |
> | | entertained | |
> | | buried | |

3

> **Answers**
> **a** /t/ **b** /d/ **c** /ɪd/

4

> **Answers**
>
> | /t/ | /d/ | /ɪd/ |
> | --- | --- | --- |
> | asked | called | invited |
> | helped | discovered | needed |
> | jumped | enjoyed | rented |
> | looked | lived | visited |
> | missed | rained | |
> | reached | saved | |
> | worked | travelled | |

Writing folder 5

Reviews

pages 80–81

2

> **Answers**
> **Facts about the film**
> sequel to *Mission: Impossible* (directed by Brian de Palma), directed by John Woo, mammoth hit in the US, hero is Ethan Hunt (played by Tom Cruise), has to cut holiday short to save Australia and the world from a lethal virus that has fallen into the hands of villains, they ask £37 million to surrender their half of the virus
>
> **Phrases that convey the writer's opinion**
> a story line that makes sense, klunky, goofy, despite its faults it's quite an engaging film, not nearly as good as the original, it isn't a dud, it's a little unclear, it's a great relief when the tangled threads of the plot finally coalesce
>
> **Things included to interest and entertain**
> has holes big enough to drive the entire United States Marine Corps through, there are seven of us globally (i.e. intelligent self-respecting critics), (the way the plot is described in the third and fourth paragraphs), it's almost a shame that Woo had to even bother with a plot

6

> **Answers**
> **a** 2, 4 **b** 5, 12 **c** 3, 8 **d** 7, 9 **e** 1, 6 **f** 10, 11

Unit 13

pages 82–85

Speaking 1

1

The meaning of *leaf through* in the title of the unit is: You leaf through a book or a magazine by turning the pages quickly and reading only a little of it, e.g. *The passengers were leafing through magazines in the airport shop.*

Reading

1

2

Listening

1

The underlined parts of the tapescript confirm the answers for exercise 2.

On April 10th, 1912, the pride of the White Star Line, the *Titanic*, embarked on her maiden voyage from Southampton, via Cherbourg and Queenstown to New York. As was the case with the majority of west-bound liners, Queenstown was scheduled as the last port of call before crossing the Atlantic. One of the last family rituals, performed in the house of the family, was the American wake, which grew out of the tradition of waking or watching the dead. The emigrants were unlikely to return home and so were 'dead' to those who were left behind. For the elderly in particular, parting was a painful experience. The wake was the last opportunity for family and friends to be joined with their loved ones before they departed on their journey.

The railway came to Queenstown in 1862, providing emigrants with a convenient means of travelling to the emigration port. The fond goodbyes usually culminated at the railway station, where tearful partings were sometimes eased by the excitement of setting out on a new adventure to a new land. Passengers on the *Titanic* were no doubt looking forward to travelling on the brand new luxury liner.

Over the previous fifty years, Queenstown had become established as the most important emigration port of the southern part of Ireland. In ten years over one thousand emigrants left Queenstown every week over the busy spring and summer months. Most were bound for North America in search of a better life.

A total of 123 passengers embarked at Queenstown on April 11th. Three travelled first class, seven in second class, while the remainder were berthed in third class or steerage accommodation. With steamships plying the Atlantic on a regular basis, Queenstown was a bustling place in 1912. To satisfy American immigration regulations, intending passengers had to pass a medical check. Trachoma, a disease of the eyes, was of particular importance and was sufficient to deny an emigrant the right to travel. Waiting for the ship to arrive, passengers would sometimes be entertained with music. For some, the last chance to buy some trinket as a reminder of home had to be resisted; money had to be prudently managed. Emigrants at Queenstown sometimes could not board a liner because it had its full complement of passengers and then they had to wait until the next ship arrived in port. The pride of the White Star Line arrived at Roche's point, the outer anchorage of Cork harbour, at 11.30 am. Meanwhile, the intending passengers went to the White Star Line quay to board the paddle steamer tenders, *Ireland* and *America*, which would ferry them to the liner. After boarding the tenders, they proceeded to the deep-water quay located beside the railway station to load mail bags from the train. The two tenders then travelled out to the *Titanic* along with a number of smaller vessels carrying vendors who hoped to sell local specialities such as lace and souvenirs to the wealthy passengers on board.

At 1.30 pm an exchange of whistle indicated that the tenders' business was complete and the *Titanic* weighed anchor to the strains of *Eirin's Lament* and *The Nation Once Again*. A total of 1,308 passengers were on board when *Titanic* left Queenstown together with 989 crew, making a total of 2,297 people. Shortly before midnight on the 14th April 1912, *Titanic* struck an iceberg and sank with the loss of over 1,500 lives. Of the 123 passengers who boarded at Queenstown, only 44 survived.

Useful vocabulary

1 **embark** *vb.* to go on to a ship e.g. We embarked at Liverpool for New York.

2 **maiden** *adj.* of or about the first of its type e.g. The Titanic sank on her maiden voyage.

3 A **port of call** *n.* a place where you stop for a short time, esp. on a journey. When you arrive in the city, your first port of call should be the tourist office.

4 **berth** *n.* a bed in a boat, train, etc., or a place for a ship or boat to stay in a port, e.g. She booked a berth on the train from London to Aberdeen.
   berth *v.* e.g. The ship berthed (= was tied up at the port) at Sydney and so we spent a day touring the city.

5 **ply** *vb.* to work at (esp. a job involving selling things), to sell, or (esp. of a taxi driver) to drive around or wait in a regular place looking for passengers. Fishermen in small boats ply their trade (= regularly work at their job) up and down the coast.

6 **anchorage** *n.* The bay is well-known as a safe anchorage (= place to anchor).

7 **quay** *n.* a long structure, usually built of stone, where boats can be tied up and load and unload their goods

8 **paddle steamer** *n.* large boat that uses steam and a paddle wheel to move through the water.

9 **tender** *n.* a vehicle used for transporting water, wood or coal, esp. one which is pulled behind a railway engine or used by the fire service, or a small boat used for transporting people or goods between a larger boat and the coast.

10 **vessel** *n.* formal, a large boat or ship
    a cargo/fishing/patrol/sailing/supply vessel
    At the height of his shipping career, he owned about 60 oceangoing vessels.

11 **weigh anchor** – When you *weigh anchor*, you pull up the anchor and sail away.

12 **board** *n.* e.g. As soon as I was *on board* (= on the boat, train or aircraft), I began to have second thoughts about leaving.

2

Answers
a an/the American wake   **b** railway   **c** over 1,000
d medical check   **e** lace and souvenirs   **f** 2,297

-*ing* forms

Grammar folder page 198

Further examples of the -*ing* form: to be used to doing something, to avoid doing something, eating is one of life's pleasures.

1

Answers
a 3   **b** 5   **c** 6   **d** 1   **e** 4   **f** 5 and 7   **g** 2 and 5

2

Answers
2 e   **3** c   **4** f   **5** d   **6** b
-*ing* forms: **b** tending, encouraging   **c** travelling
d taking, making   **e** setting out   **f** feeling

3

Answers
a correct
b Since he started his new job, he's got used to *getting* up very early.
c *Having* time to spend talking with friends is very important.
d I'm looking forward to *seeing* you soon.
e correct
f It's no use *telling* me now that you can't finish the report. You should have told me last week.
g What I miss is not *being* able to have lunch with all my family every Sunday.
h correct
i I'm fed up with not *having* all the facilities I need to do the job properly.
j correct

Speaking 2

Further examples of inserting /j/ or /w/ in linking:

/j/	/w/
we‿are	to‿it
I‿am	through‿Italy
see‿it	are you‿interested?

1

Answers
a Type 1   **b** Type 2: insert /j/   **c** Type 2: insert /w/
d Type 1   **e** Type 2: insert /j/ between *we are* and *quay at*

2

Exam folder 6

Paper 1 Part 1

pages 86–87

1

Answers
1 There was something in the stance or movement of the accompanist and the woman that strongly suggested that they were about to kiss.
2 A musical event, because the word *accompanist* suggests a musician accompanying a singer.

2

Answers
1 D 2 A

3

Answers
3 C 4 A

4

Answers
3 Alastair Marriott, whose new work *Kiss* was created for her, understands that it is in her expansiveness that Bussell's dance is at its most appealing. Her limbs have a gorgeous plush, her legs especially seem to unfold in a swelling *legato*, her back melts at the very touch of air – Bussell is big, her dance is big and Marriott has offered her choreography which is undoubtedly big in gesture.
4 Yet somehow it seems to be at odds with the conceit (and the length) of the work which is inspired by the quiet and intimate love of the sculptor Auguste Rodin and his muse Camille Claudel:

5

Answers
5 C 6 A

Unit 14

pages 88–91

Listening and Reading

Useful vocabulary
sermon *n.* a talk given by a vicar/priest
eulogy *n.* a talk given when someone has died or stopped working
summing up *n.* given by a judge towards the end of a trial
official statement *n.* this usually comes from the government about something which must happen or the government's comment on something

Answers
1 c 2 d 3 b 4 a

The underlined parts of the tapescript confirm the answers.

Speaker 1: Now we have, <u>over the last four days</u>, heard that the goods were taken from the warehouse on the night of February 14th. <u>The theft</u> was discovered by Mr White when he arrived on the morning of February 15th. There is overwhelming <u>forensic evidence</u> which <u>puts Geoff Warren in the frame</u>. His <u>fingerprints</u> were found on the window along with fibres from his jacket. Later, <u>police officers</u> found some of the goods at his home address in Germaine Street.

Speaker 2: <u>It was announced by the Prime Minister this morning that the General Election will be held on May 3rd.</u> The election campaign is to start with immediate effect with the three main parties having air time on both TV and radio over the coming weeks.

Speaker 3: Jill Davies <u>will be remembered</u> both as devoted mother and wife and also for her work at St Thomas's hospital where she worked as a paediatrician for many years. She will remain in the hearts of all those who knew her even though <u>her body may have departed this world</u>. Her pioneering work with neo-natal babies at the hospital has meant that many more families have had the joy of taking home their newborn. The procedures she introduced are now an established part of hospital life.

Speaker 4: We can see in our communities many who are in need and the <u>parable of the Good Samaritan</u> teaches us that we should not pass by those in need. Those who, for whatever reason, cross our path in our daily life, and are less fortunate than ourselves, should be shown true compassion. Even the smallest gesture, such as listening for an extra few minutes to someone who has a problem, can make all the difference.

2

> **Answers**
> a 2   b 5   c 4   d 3   e 1

Listening

1

> **Answers**
> 1 a or b   2 b   3 b   4 c

2

> **Answers**
> a 6,000   b 9,000, 1.3 million   c 1.5 million years
> d 300,000   e gestures   f primitive, basic, natural
> g tools, at night (time)

The underlined parts of the tapescript confirm the answers.

In this lecture on the evolutionary factors of language, I'm going to begin by looking at early language in humans. Writing began about 6,000 years ago, so it is fair to say that speech preceded that, although estimates of when humans began to speak range from 9,000 years ago to 1.3 million years ago. Primitive tools have been found that date back to 1.5 million years BC – the tools show that our ancestors had at least low level spatial thinking. Later tools, about 300,000 years old, are more advanced, revealing that cognition was on a level that was similar or equal to modern intelligence – tools had been planned in three dimensions, allowing for abstract thought – the cognitive capacity for language was present.

Krantz (1980) argues that language emerged 50,000 years ago because then the fossil records show that significant changes took place. Tools became more sophisticated and specialised, projectiles appeared along with fire and there was a large spread and expansion of the population. According to Krantz, the cause may have been to do with the emergence of full language and a new cognitive competence in humans.

Presumably, initially, people used gestures to communicate, then gestures with vocal communication. Both provided an evolutionary push towards a higher level of cognition, fuelled by a need to communicate effectively and the frustration at not being able to do so. Pettito and Marentette (1991) examined deaf infants, and found that they start to babble, and then because there is no auditory feedback they stop. Deaf children use manual babbling (an early form of sign language equivalent to the vocalisations of hearing infants) but this manual babbling stage starts earlier than in hearing children and ends sooner. Pettito and Marentette suggest that manual language is therefore more primitive, basic and natural than spoken language, a clue that the first languages were iconic, not spoken.

The emergence of tool use with spoken language is particularly interesting. Possibly, hands were needed to manipulate tools, and humans found it difficult to communicate with sign language and use tools at the same time. Vocal communication, if possible, would allow the hands to do other things. Also, a vocal language would allow humans to communicate at night time, and without having to look at each other.

Reading

1

> **Answers**
> 1 B   2 C   3 A

> Useful vocabulary
> **constraint** *n.* something which controls or limits
> **fall into place** – logically acceptable
> **upright** *adj.* vertical
> **to slant** *v.* to lean in a diagonal position
> **interlaced** *adj.* joined
> **hindered** *v.* (to hinder) limited
> **appendage** *n.* something which exists as a smaller and less important part of something larger
> **choke** *v.* not to be able to breathe because the throat is blocked
> **lifespan** *n.* the length of time a person lives

The passive

Grammar folder page 198

1

The passive is formed with *to be* + past participle. There is a fuller explanation in the Grammar folder.

2

> **Answers**
> 1 e   2 h   3 b   4 i   5 g   6 d   7 c   8 a   9 f

To have/get something done

2

a *to get something done* often has a reflexive meaning, to talk about things we do to ourselves. It is less often used to talk about longer, more deliberate, planned actions where to *have something done* would be more suitable.

b *won't* in this sentence means *will not allow*.

c *want something done* is used to say that *we would like someone to do something* or *we would like something to happen*.

Vocabulary

1

> **Answers**
> 1 overlooked 2 underpractised 3 introductory
> 4 reference 5 excellent 6 scientific 7 relatively
> 8 memorable

Writing folder 6

Information sheets
pages 92–93

2

> **Answers**
> jargon, very formal language, long sentences

3

This activity together with activity 4 guides you through the preparation and planning for writing a contribution to an information sheet.

> **Suggested answers**
> **A** tourists; a contribution to the brochure; what can be done on a countryside holiday, kinds of accommodation, weather conditions
> **B** visitors to your company; a brief history of the company; main activities, plans for the future, any other points that you think are important
> **C** a London museum; items of great interest from your country; a contribution to the guide; history of the items, their importance within and outside your country

4

> **Suggested answers**
> Key parts of the question: Your town, visitors, Tourist Board, activities or visits for the young people and older people, balance of fun activities and more intellectual activities for the different age ranges
> Content: Examples of country activities, e.g. sports, parks, walks, wildlife parks, historical places to visit
> Style: welcoming, using lots of adjectives to describe places. Informal or neutral language would be suitable.
> Headings:
> **Country activities/places**
> Possible subheading: What to do in the countryside or (name of region)
> **Information about accommodation**
> Possible subheading: Where to stay
> **Information about the weather**
> Possible subheading: Weather reminder (this will depend on the place and its local climatic conditions)

Unit 15

pages 94–97

Speaking 1

1

> **Answers**
> a 1 b 3 c 4 d 2

Reading

2

> **Answers**
> 1 B 2 D 3 C 4 A 5 C

Speaking 2

1

In the article, Jonathan's opinions are:
- I think children want to feel proud of their parents because it makes them feel secure in a Darwinian sense.
- I have inherited from my father a strong sense of the importance of doing the right thing.
- I believe strongly in proper bedtimes, that chores have to be done and that certain times of the day … are reserved for adults.
- But I want to make my children into the sort of children I want them to be.
- We live in a liberal age when people feel they should take a back seat in making moral decisions.
- I don't believe in reasoning with my children.
- I can't stand all those Saturday morning programmes that are …
- I think it's the parents' job to preserve childhood as long as possible …
- Today's parents can often be very lazy.
- I am strict about homework and achievement. Our children will work hard until they finish university and I think they will thank me for the rest of their lives.
- I don't like the attitudes in football.

Go through the Exam spot. It is important that you work well with your partner in Part 3 of the CAE Speaking test. You will be expected to contribute fully to the task and to develop the interaction. You should also be sensitive to turn-taking and neither dominate nor give only minimal responses.

2

Make notes of the different phrases you can use in the Speaking test, for example:

Inviting opinions	Giving an opinion
What do you think?	I think …
Do you agree?	As far as I know
And you?	Well, in my opinion
What about you?	I've heard …

Justifying an opinion	Summarising
because	So, if we summarise …
so	So, what shall we decide/say?
since	Right, so you think … and I think …
	So, shall we agree to disagree?
	So, if I've understood correctly, …

Answers
1 A appropriate   B inappropriate
2 A inappropriate   B appropriate
3 A appropriate   B inappropriate
4 A inappropriate   B appropriate

4

See 2 above for phrases for giving opinions and supporting them. You may also need phrases for agreeing or disagreeing:

Agreeing
- That's a good point.
- I'm sure you're right.
- Absolutely!
- That's exactly what I think too.
- That's true.
- I hadn't thought of that.
- Exactly!

Disagreeing
- Well, I'm not so sure about that.
- Yes, but what about …?
- I'm not sure that I really agree with that because …
- Well, I see what you mean, but don't you think that …
- Yes, but isn't it true that …
- You have a point there but …
- I'm sorry but I can't agree.

The infinitive

Grammar folder page 199

1

Answers
Infinitive with *to*: decide to, want to, used to, be going to, know how to, allow (children) to, have to, would like to, need to, persuade (people) to, ask to, try to, be prepared to

Infinitive without *to*: should live (up to), make (them) feel, might call, will agree, let (them) watch

2

Answers
a I don't want *you to* think I'm doing this as a punishment.
b correct
c I must *go* home before I miss the last bus.
d In my opinion parents should not let their daughters *wear* make-up until they are over 16.
e correct
f correct
g correct
h It was fantastic *to see* so many young people enter the competition.
i correct

Listening

2

Answers
1 H   2 E   3 B   4 C   5 G

3

Answers
1 F   2 G   3 C   4 D   5 A

The underlined parts of the tapescript confirms the answers.

Speaker 1: Well, this is already my favourite series of the year. They're slices of TV heaven. I watched *I Love the Seventies* and enjoyed it thoroughly but as a thirty something who was on the brink of those troubled teenage years at the start of the eighties, this new series was always going to bring back the best and the worst memories! I admit to having a sort of emotional vested interest in this period but when it's executed as well as this, I feel absolutely no shame!

Speaker 2: Well, the only thing I can compare this with really is the equally brilliant *Predators*, which was a fascinating and amazing nature documentary. I guess what makes these prehistoric times really come to life is the use of computer imagery, it's just so impressive. And added to that, there's a kind of tongue-in-cheek commentary, it just makes it one of the most enjoyable evenings I've had for a long while.

Speaker 3: Mm, I sat down to watch this period piece with great interest. Now, yeah, I basically approve of employing composers to write new music, but the Tudor period boasts some of England's greatest composers and finest music, so why couldn't some of it have found its way into this programme? After all, we know what music was performed at the great state occasions described in the narrative and yeah, there are plenty of performers who could have done it justice.

Speaker 4: Yeah, it was, it was great to see that this programme was coming back on TV, I mean it's been off our screens for far too long, but what has happened to the format? I mean the programme seemed to be more about the presenter than anything else. The recipes looked delicious but why on earth can't we have normal shots of him preparing the dishes? There seemed to be something obscuring every shot, completely distracting the viewer from what was going on. If it wasn't a vase of tulips, it was a bowl of lemons or, more often than not, some floaty greenery.

Speaker 5: Well, what an absolute delight and a perfect presenter, and no, I am not the presenter's grandmother, just your average music addict who, well, I want to tell as many people as possible about this lovely late-night programme. And for anyone who finds music an endless adventure, full of familiar delights and new experiences, this programme is without gush, without formality, without advertising, well, it's the one for us!

Units 11–15 Revision

pages 98–99

Reading

> **Answers**
> a He says he has left a present inside which he wanted his wife to take to Ellen.
> b She is frantic as she does not want to be late.
> c The main clue as to their relationship is in the part about the combs. Mrs Foster criticises her husband and he reacts angrily. We can imagine that she has to be a dutiful wife, letting him get his own way.
> d The use of direct speech and short sentences adds to the sense of urgency.

> Useful vocabulary
> **rug** *n.* a small carpet
> **to unbutton** *v.* to undo a coat or jacket
> **Confound it!** – an expression of annoyance

Grammar

> **Answers**
> 1 to be   2 to fetch   3 lying   4 to remain
> 5 to say   6 flocking   7 to find   8 to stand up to
> 9 to secure   10 complaining

Vocabulary

Remember that you must watch out for negative prefixes.

> **Answers**
> 1 possibly   2 foolishness   3 misery   4 unnecessarily
> 5 timing   6 purposely (or purposefully)   7 unhappy

Unit 16

pages 100–103

Reading

1

> **Answers**
>
> | Text | What is being reviewed | Critic's opinion |
> |------|------------------------|------------------|
> | A | hotel | favourable |
> | B | novel | favourable |
> | C | computer game | favourable |
> | D | music album | neutral |
> | E | website | favourable |

2

> **Answers**
> 1 a false (he stumbled on it, i.e. he found it by chance)
>   b true
>   c the answer is not given in the extract
> 2 a true
>   b false (it is a romance that reads more like a thriller)
>   c true
> 3 a true
>   b false (they have pea-sized brains, i.e. are stupid)
>   c the answer is not given in the extract
> 4 a true
>   b the answer is not given in the extract
>   c false
> 5 a true
>   b the answer is not given in the extract
>   c true

3

> **Answers**
>
> | Text | Words identifying the topic | Positive words and expressions | Negative words and expressions |
> |------|------------------------------|-------------------------------|--------------------------------|
> | B | Howard examines – subtle romance – reads more like a thriller – parallels with the author's own life | the trap is gently laid – we sit back transfixed – subtle – added piquancy – prepare to be seduced | callous con man – predator and prey – to watch the kill (NB These are describing aspects of the story rather than being negative opinions of the novel.) |
> | C | veteran gamers – arcade classic – proceed across the screen – platforms – iMac | hours of light-hearted entertainment | won't stretch your iMac to the limits (slightly but not very negative in tone) |

D	rock's gothic underworld – noise-mongering – quiet piano balladry – songs – record	finest (positive opinion of the previous record) – maintain the contemplative style	morose noise-mongering (negative opinion of pre-1997 records) – takes half a pace backwards towards his anguished past
E	Speechtips.com – was still under construction	sweat no more – concise guide – in easy steps – common-sense advice should be compulsory reading	unfortunately

Speaking 2

1

> **Answers**
> **a** don't **b** giving **c** well **d** right **e** words
> **f** matter **g** convinced **h** whole, take

3

You are often asked to write a review in CAE Paper 2 and so, even if you are working through this book on your own, it will be useful for you to plan and write a review yourself. Choose any subject that interests you and write a review that draws attention to both the strengths and the weaknesses of what you are reviewing as this will allow you to demonstrate a wide range of language.

Articles and determiners

Grammar folder page 200

The specific problems that students have with articles and determiners in English depend to a certain extent on their first language. Read the notes on articles and determiners in the Grammar folders. Mark any sections that you feel are particularly difficult for you. Try to bear these points in mind when you are writing and speaking in English.

1

> **Answers**
> **Review A**
> **a** It is the name of a hotel and these usually take a definite article – *The Holiday Inn*, *The Ritz*, *The Red Lion*, etc.
> **b** It is the first time the loch has been mentioned.
> **c** It is talking in general rather than about a specific group, in which case *the Americans* or *some Americans* might be used.

> **Review B**
> **a** It is asking a general question about any intelligent woman and any con man. The same idea could be expressed by using the words in the plural: *Have you ever wondered how intelligent women could fall for callous con men?*
> **b** The process of a con man tricking a woman.
> **c** Because it is referring to the specific author of the novel that is being reviewed.
> **Review C**
> **a** Because possessive adjectives are usually used when referring to parts of our bodies in English, e.g. *I've hurt my leg*, not *I've hurt the leg*.
> **b** Because it is referring to a specific, named game.
> **Review D**
> **a** Because the phrase 'quiet piano balladry' is modified by a following expression, 'of 1997's *The Boatman's Call*'.
> **b** Because these refer to unique aspects of our environment.
> **Review E**
> **a** *Few* without *a* would suggest that the objective is to say as little as possible, which clearly does not make sense in the context.
> **b** *The* is used in the first two sets of brackets because it is referring to a specific situation whereas *notes* and *memory* are being considered more generally.

2

> **Answers**
> **a** Life is hard! (No article used in general statements.)
> **b** The life of the poor in a country with no welfare state is very hard. (The article is used in general statements where the noun has a post-modifying phrase.)
> **c** My brother is a biochemist in London. (The indefinite article is used when saying what people's jobs are.)
> **d** Jack broke his leg skiing. (A possessive adjective is usually used before parts of the body.)
> **e** He's only 18 but he already has his own business. (A possessive adjective is usually used before *own*.)
> **f** Maria's on a business trip to the People's Republic of China. (*The* is not used with most countries but it is used with plural names for countries or with places whose name contains a common noun like *Republic* or *Federation* or *Kingdom*.)
> **g** Do they sell fruit in the USA by the kilo or the pound? (*The* is used in measuring expressions with *by*.)
> **h** Since they built the tunnel, fewer people are using the ferry. (*The* is often used with means of transport to refer to the type of transport being used, rather than a specific bus, car or boat, e.g. *I take the bus to work*.)

Listening

3

Man: Did you see that film, *Billy Elliott*? Did you like that?

Woman: I did, I really – I loved the little boy in it, I thought he was great, yeah.

Man: Did you? Were you convinced by his dancing, did you …

Woman: I wondered whether he was a trained dancer.

Man: Yeah, I can tell you he isn't, because I worked with him.

Woman: Oh, really, did you? Was he nice?

Man: He was lovely, he's a lovely young kid, yeah.

Woman: I'll tell you what I didn't really like, I thought that Julie Walters was a bit unconvincing, actually.

Man: Oh, did you?

Woman: Yeah.

Man: Isn't that funny! I mean I have reservations about some of the things. I couldn't believe that his, his dad – I don't know if you remember the scene where they suddenly fall back laughing off the, they're on a fence or a wall somewhere.

Woman: That stile or a wall, yeah.

Man: And suddenly they all, it's all loving happy families and until then he's been bashing around the house.

Woman: It's a bit over-romanticised.

Man: Yeah.

Woman: I'll tell you what I did really like, though, was *Moulin Rouge*. Have you seen that?

Man: Did you? Yeah, I was blown away by the first ten minutes, the first quarter of an hour. It just, it's so in your face and brash and brave and – I just needed a couple of breathing spaces in it afterwards because I just, it just seemed unrelenting, do you know what I mean?

Woman: Yes, I know what you mean.

Man: Just pow pow pow!

Woman: I thought Nicole Kidman's singing was a bit dodgy sometimes.

Man: Yeah. I thought they both did remarkably well. I, I mean, you know …

Woman: I heard that Ewan McGregor really went for it with the singing. He just absolutely – had a great time.

Man: I can believe that because it just looked fantastic. I mean he's, I think Baz Luhrmann is an amazing director.

Woman: So do I – the audience …

Man: He always does something different.

Woman: Visuals are stunning I always think.

Man: Yes, it's wonderfully brave, I just think it's a brilliant film.

Vocabulary

1

2

Exam folder 7

Paper 1 Part 2
pages 104–105

2

Unit 17

pages 106–109

Speaking 1

1

There are no right and wrong answers to this question. The point of the task is simply to help you imagine why people of different types might be attracted by the different advertisements. Thinking in detail about what to apply for and why will help you to prepare a realistic proposal.

Reading

1

> **Possible answers**
> The sorts of things that would give your application a better chance of success are:
> - finding out as much as you can about what sort of information the people awarding the grant require
> - deciding exactly where you want to go and why
> - finding out about what exactly your expenses would be
> - finding reasons for your travel that have a strong educational or social value
> - planning a clear, well-organised proposal.

2

> There are no absolute right and wrong answers here although the first six in the list are almost certain to be relevant in any situation and the last one, which emphasises reading the directions or instructions, is also important in any circumstances.

Listening

1

> **Possible answers**
> d Useful techniques might be:
> - to persuade them of the social value of what you would like them to do
> - to offer to do something for them in return
> - to flatter them
> - to encourage feelings of guilt if they don't do it
> - to show them that what you are proposing is less dangerous / expensive etc. than they imagine.

2

Answers

	What speaker wants others to do	How speaker tries to persuade them
1	mother wants toddler to eat his vegetables	encourages, plays games, eats some too, praises
2	schoolboy wants friend to play truant from school in order to watch a football match	reassures that they won't be found out, taunts by calling him a coward, exhibits great confidence in own plans
3	boss wants workers to do some overtime	explains why it's necessary, shows sympathy with how workers must be feeling, threatens
4	girl wants friend to lend her a special dress to wear to a party	promises to be careful, explains why she wants it so much, praises the dress, promises to do various favours for friend in return
5	sales person is trying to sell a fitted kitchen	uses very positive language about the offer, emphasises throughout what a bargain it is, says it will all be very easy for the customer
6	teenager wants to persuade mother to let her stay out late	reminds mum that there is no school next day, uses moral blackmail, tries to reassure mum, says all friends are going to be allowed, reminds mum how good she's been
7	wife wants to persuade husband that they should move to a house in the country	emphasises benefits to children, says husband could use commuting time productively and so would be freer when home
8	sales assistant in clothes shop wants to persuade woman to buy a dress	flatters, goes into detail about why the dress is good for the specific customer, points out how versatile it is

Speaker 1: Now look, fish fingers and peas and carrots and broccoli. Oh, you like broccoli, don't you? Let me just put that on the fork. There, you have that. Go on, open your mouth. That's a good boy. You chew, that's it. And now a carrot. There you go, in it goes. You take that carrot, that's a good boy. Can I have some, can mummy have some? Oh, that's lovely, thank you. Now you have some, go on. You have that spoon. One for you, one for me. Good boy.

Speaker 2: Hey, Rog, it's Jim, hey, how are you doing? Listen, tomorrow afternoon, you know we're playing QPR? Yeah yeah, well it kicks off at 3, you up for it? Yeah? No, don't worry, don't worry. No, he won't, he won't, they won't know. They'll never know, I mean it's PE tomorrow afternoon. They're never going to know. There's forty of us all in white shorts. How are they going to know there's two of them missing, you know what I mean? Now come on, yeah, come on. No, don't be such a coward. Yeah, yeah, 3 o'clock, yeah, we'll bunk off around lunch time and then we'll go down and come back. It'll be all over by, what, half-five? We'll be back, yeah, it'll be brilliant.

Speaker 3: Now, I think you all know why we've had to meet today. I've got the monthly figures back from head office and for the third month running, sales are down and we all know the margins are getting tighter so we've got to try and get a march on the competition. I'm going to have to ask some of you to put in more overtime. No, no, I know, I know that's not going to be very popular and there's not going to be a great deal of money in it for people but we really have to get ahead of the opposition here, OK? I mean if you don't want to do it, maybe you'd be better off finding a job with them.

Speaker 4: Oh, go on, oh, look. I don't want that, I don't want the red one. I actually just want to borrow the blue one. Oh, it's beautiful, go on, you know it suits me, please! I wouldn't ask unless it was for this party. I mean I've been, I just think he's going to be there and I'd just like to look nice and that dress is the most beautiful thing I've ever seen. Look, I won't spill anything on it, I promise, I – I won't even drink anything all night. I won't eat anything either. There'll be no crumbs, nothing, I promise. Look, I'll wash up for a month or take your bike in. I'll do all your washing. Oh, please let me?

Speaker 5: Good morning, I wonder if I could just take a few seconds of your time just to tell you about a special offer we're doing at the moment. We're in your area and we're doing free quotations on brand new kitchen units. Now these units are made to measure, they're marvellous, they're handmade by our craftsmen up in Yorkshire. Therefore it's very much cheaper making them directly from our workshop than going to the shops and also you don't have to pay at all for anything this year so basically we'll install the kitchen for you and you don't have to pay anything till next year. Now that's a fantastic offer, I'm sure you'll agree.

Speaker 6: Oh, go on, mum, please let me stay out. Look, all the others are going to be there and there's no school the next day. Oh, go on, please let me! Do you remember you said that if I started doing better in French you'd let me stay out? Well, I got good marks, didn't I? Oh, go on, mum. And I'll get a taxi home and I'll pay for it. Look, everyone else is going to be there, please let me go, oh, go on, mum. I know you want me to be happy, don't you?

Speaker 7: Look darling, I know you love the city but, well, we don't often go out and use it, do we? So I was thinking perhaps if we moved to the country? I mean we'd get more for our money out there. Think of the children. They could actually walk to school, mm? Not take that horrible tube. I do hate them using the tube. It'd be cheaper, wouldn't it? And well, the air is much much cleaner and therefore much more relaxing. They could play. Wouldn't all the time have to be on their backs worrying. And think of you, you wouldn't have to drive into work. You could get the train and do some work on the train so therefore you can play with the children in the evening. Oh, think about it, please?

Speaker 8: Yeah, the mirror's right over here, yeah. Oh, it really looks lovely. Yeah, oh, it's gorgeous on you though, you've got such a lovely figure. What size is that one? Oh, it's a size ten, yeah well there you are, you see. I can only get into size twelve/fourteen. You are lucky. Well, I'll tell you what, though. That dress really looks nice because the way it's cut over your hips, you see if you just turn round there, look, look in the mirror there. It's ever so nice. And the colour's good on you as well because, like, green, green really goes with red hair. Yeah, oh, I think it's really nice, yeah. You could do with getting that one and it's quite good because you can use that dress for all sorts of things, couldn't you? You could go to parties in it and wear it out anywhere really.

Language of persuasion

Grammar folder page 201

1

Answers
1 a   2 b   3 a   4 a   5 a   6 b   7 b

Vocabulary

1

Answers
1 grant   2 terms   3 stick   4 sense   5 current

Speaking 2

If you are working alone, write a dialogue in which two people are planning a holiday together; one person has chosen one of the holidays in the photos and the other person has chosen a different one. They are each trying to persuade the other to come on the holiday they have chosen. Your dialogue should consider some of the aspects of the holiday in the box in **a** as well as anything else that you feel is relevant.

Writing folder 7

Set texts
pages 110–111

4

Possible answers
• most interesting character
• key moment in the plot
• relationship between two main characters and how this develops during the story
• the way the writer interests the reader in reading more
• the importance of the place where the story is set
• the importance of the period when the story is set
• the significance of the title of the story
• whether the story makes / would make a good film
• whether the story resonates with anything in the students' own lives
• anything unsuccessful about the story
• how appropriate the story is for someone learning English

5

Suggested answers
Article: is written for a large audience, about whom the writer knows little beyond the fact that they read a magazine of a particular type; benefits from a title and an opening sentence that will intrigue readers and encourage them to read on; aim is to interest

Report: is mainly concerned with facts; has to be clearly organised and expressed; headings may be a useful way of guiding both the reader and writer through the text; it is often necessary to finish with a recommendation and if so the reasons for the recommendation should be clearly and unambiguously stated; aim is to inform

Review: the reader wants to get a general impression of what is being reviewed but does not want a detailed description of the plot; aim is to help the reader decide whether to read the book / watch the film for themselves

Essay: written for a teacher and so is likely to be in a neutral to formal style; should be clearly structured and logically argued; aim is to impress in terms of both content and style

Unit 18

pages 112–115

Reading

1

Answers
a He is at a party.
b He is telling a lot of lies, pretending that he hears people, pretending that he knows people and so on.
c Perhaps because he wants to make the other person feel good or because he wants to make himself look good.

2

Answer
He mentions lying about b, c and f. With g, he pretends to like a joke that he didn't hear rather than pretending to like a joke that he didn't find amusing.

3–6

Answers
3 a The writer can't hear what 'Mr ... er ... er' is saying to him.
  b The writer is misled by the homophones, *reign* and *rain*.
4 no

5 He comes to the conclusion that it is sometimes a good idea not to be too honest. The reason is that being pointlessly honest can lead to long, tedious conversations which are of no interest to anyone and may be embarrassing for both participants.
6 a 3 b 2 c 1

7

Although you may never have done any of the things listed by the writer, it would be an unusual person indeed who has never told any of the 'social untruths' mentioned in the article.

Vocabulary

1

There are a great many good collocations and chunks in this text, as in most pieces of English speech or writing. Here are some of the ones you might have chosen:
– *catch the name of*
– *statistics show that*
– *apart from one or two obvious exceptions*
– *have always been interested in*
– *to be common knowledge*
– *hopelessly mixed up*
– *sustain the fiction that*
– *make a joke*
– *in short*
– *we're getting on wonderfully*
– *have no conceivable purpose*
– *on second thoughts*

2

Answers
a 8 b 3 c 6 d 11 e 1 f 7 g 12 h 4
i 9 j 10 k 5 l 2

3

Answers
a catch your name   b hopelessly mixed up
c on second thoughts   d home town
e a year's free supply   f are twisting my arm
g with one or two obvious exceptions
h no conceivable purpose   i field of research

Cleft sentences and other ways of emphasising

Grammar folder page 201

2

Tapescript and answers
1 I do believe what you're saying. (Emphasis given to auxiliary verb *do*.)
2 He's such a nice man and has been so kind to us. (Use of *so* and *such*.)

3 I'm boiling! (Use of exaggerated lexis.)
4 He's intensely jealous of his sister. (Use of intensifying adverb.)
5 That joke is as old as the hills! (Use of simile.)
6 Little did he imagine what was going to happen next. (Use of inversion after a restricting adverbial.)
7 Never was so much owed by so many to so few! (Use of inversion after a negative adverbial.)
8 What on earth is that man doing? (Use of *on earth*, only used after a question word.)
9 I really like this exercise very much indeed! (Use of intensifying adverbials such as *really*, etc.)

3

Answers
a Jake *does* admire her work.
b I *do* love you.
c Mary *did* do her very best.
d I *did* use to be able to dive quite well.
e They *have* agreed to help us.

5

Answers
a No, I *am* right.
b I *did* give you the right information.
c I *do* help you with the housework.
d He *didn't* cheat.
e I *shall/will* be able to!
f I *haven't* forgotten it!
g Yes, she *is* going this year.

Listening

2
1 What have you enjoyed most about studying English?
2 What interesting things have you done recently?
3 How would you feel about living abroad permanently?
4 What kind of parties do you enjoy?
5 What are your plans for the future?
6 Have you always lived in the same place?
7 What would you say has been the most memorable event in your life so far?
8 How would you describe your best friend?

Answers
Better answers are given by:
1 woman **2** man **3** woman **4** man
5 man **6** woman **7** man **8** woman

The underlined text confirms the answers.

Examiner: What have you enjoyed most about studying English?

Man: Well, actually I found it quite hard. I think first of all the pronunciation of many words is very very different in English, something to do with the spelling maybe. There are very many words, so it's difficult to learn them all and the main thing I think is the verbs, I'm used to putting at the end of a sentence, not at the beginning or the middle so that's difficult.

Woman: I've really enjoyed now that I can speak English so much better going to see films and understanding exactly what is going on. I also like being able to find my way around, understanding street signs and of course listening to English pop songs and knowing what they are singing about. And I also really enjoy English people. They are very friendly and of great interest to me.

Examiner: What interesting things have you done recently?

Man: Well, funnily enough last Saturday I went to a football match in England which I've never been to before and that was a great experience, very very exciting and it's good to be amongst so many people. I enjoyed that very very much.

Woman: I have been shopping in a supermarket. I have taken a bus around town, I have visited some friends and also read a book.

Examiner: How would you feel about living abroad permanently?

Woman: Oh, that's something I would really like to do. I think you get a very interesting sense of yourself when you live abroad and you can meet very interesting people.

Man: I have a friend who, a school friend, who went to live in France for a few months and he said that for the first two months it was very good, very exciting but after that he said that he started to miss his friends and his family, and he wanted to get home and it wasn't so good after that.

Examiner: What kind of parties do you enjoy?

Woman: Well, I don't really enjoy going to parties at all.

Man: For me it depends what kind of mood I'm in. Often I like going to parties where you can dance a lot and there's loud music playing and other times I like going to parties where you can talk to people and get to know them, get to meet them and I think most of all I like going to parties that last a long time, you know? They go on all over the weekend maybe, or – not just one evening.

Examiner: What are your plans for the future?

Man: Well my course here lasts another three and a half months and as soon as that finishes, I'm going to stay with a family and get a job I hope, earn a little bit of money and travel around England because I haven't seen much of England, and then after another four months I am going back home to see my family and go back to my studies there.

Woman: Well, I don't know really. I haven't made any definite plans at the moment.

Examiner: Have you always lived in the same place?

Man: Oh, no, no, I've lived in a lot of different places.

Woman: Yes, I've <u>always lived in just one place</u> and for me I really enjoy this. It's a <u>great sense of community life</u> and I've known people in my village who have <u>known me all my life</u> and <u>I've known them for as long as I can remember</u>. <u>Whenever I go out, I meet someone that I know</u>. For example, all my friends from school still live in the same village and I, it's something I really really like.

Examiner: What would you say has been the most memorable event in your life so far?

Man: Er, I think probably when I was eighteen I was given my <u>birthday present</u> which was a <u>weekend course</u> in how to, <u>how to jump with a parachute</u>. And a few weeks later I went up in a plane and <u>I actually jumped out of the plane</u> with the parachute, and that was something I will remember for ever, for sure.

Woman: I think my earliest ever memory was when I first started going to nursery. I remember the first day and I had to say goodbye to my mother and I was very upset but as soon as I went inside, there were so many things to look at and play with. It was, you know, something I can remember very clearly.

Examiner: How would you describe your best friend?

Woman: My best friend is Silke and <u>she has a brilliant sense of humour</u>. She is also a <u>very good gymnast</u>. She is <u>eighteen years old</u> and she has <u>short brown hair</u> and I have <u>known her since we were very young</u> and she is <u>very intelligent</u> as well.

Man: Gerhard is my best friend. I've known him a long time from school, from early school and he's, he's good, you know.

5

What people talk about when they meet for the first time will vary a bit from one culture to another but in Britain or the USA it is likely to be:

- the weather
- work
- transport
- families
- sport
- the news
- holidays

6

First man: Oh, Jason, can I introduce Sophie? This is Sophie, she works in our Cologne office. Sophie, this is Jason.

Sophie: Hi, Jason.

First man: Jason's the manager of our – sorry. He's the manager of the branch in New York.

Sophie: Yeah, pleased to meet you.

Jason: And you. You're in Cologne, right?

Sophie: Yeah, that's right, yeah.

Jason: Yeah, did we meet before because I was in Cologne a couple of years ago? I don't think we met then, did we?

Sophie: No, I don't think so. I can't remember your face but I've only worked for the company for a couple of months you see, so …

Jason: Oh, right, OK, so who did you work for before?

Sophie: Oh, well I was with Smith & Goldberg in Philadelphia.

Jason: Oh, really, in Philly? Excellent! I know it well, I grew up there actually.

Sophie: Oh, really?

First man: I spent a year at graduate school there. Great place, isn't it, great place?

Jason: Yeah, yeah, it's great.

Sophie: Amazing coincidence. Absolutely yeah, oh I loved my time there. I'd have been really happy to stay actually but …

First man: Did you have to come back?

Sophie: Yeah, well the thing is my husband's German so …

Jason: Oh, right.

Sophie: Yeah, we wanted to come home and then we'd be closer to the family because when our little boy was born, we thought it would be nice for him, you know.

First man: How many children have you got?

Sophie: Well, now we've got a little boy, Adam, and we've got a girl as well called Maisie. Little girl, yeah, she's just two.

First man: Have you got children, Jason? I can't remember.

Jason: No, no, I don't have any kids right now but you know – never too late! So you know, of course I have to get a wife first but – you know, that could be arranged, I guess!

Answers

1 b **2** b

Answers

Second man: name is Jason, manager of branch in New York, was in Cologne a couple of years ago, grew up in Philadelphia, unmarried, no children

Woman: name is Sophie, works in Cologne office, has only worked for company for a couple of months, worked previously for Smith and Goldberg in Philadelphia, loved Philadelphia, husband is German, wanted to be closer to home when first child, son called Adam, was born. Also has little girl called Maisie.

Exam folder 8

Paper 1 Parts 1, 3 and 4
pages 116–117

1

Answers

1 B **2** B

2

Answers

a 1 **b** 3 **c** 2 **d** 3,5 **e** 4 **f** 1 **g** 5 **h** 3 **i** 2,5 **j** 2

Unit 19

pages 118–121

Reading

1

If you are working alone, write as many sentences as you can describing each of the pictures. Try to write at least five sentences about each picture.

2

> **Answers**
> a 1 b 3 c 2

3

> **Answers**
> a 1 b 3 c 2

5

> **Answers**
> **Text 1**
> a Younger, single, highly educated people who earn more money.
> b Again, younger, single, highly educated people who earn more money.
> c People of all social groups.
> **Text 2**
> d They were both interested in the idea of preserving food by freezing it.
> e Bacon died and was not able to carry his experiment through.
> f Because the process of freezing prevents food from going off and it can be done so quickly that ice crystals do not form and thus spoil the cellular structure of the foodstuff.
> **Text 3**
> g Margaret is younger than her sister and looks less thoughtful and more instinctive.
> h That life is short perhaps, and childhood quickly passes.
> i This will depend on personal opinion but there are both happy elements (carefree scene, father's pride in his daughters) and sad elements (the fragility of life, the rapid passing of happy moments) in the painting.

Vocabulary

1

> **Answers**
> 1 noun 2 adverb 3 adjective (comparative)
> 4 noun 5 noun 6 adjective

2

> **Answers**
> 1 Painter 2 faintly 3 deeper 4 childhood
> 5 precision 6 attentive

3

> **Answers**
> a adverb: scientifically b noun: breadth
> c adjective: inconclusive d adjective: leisurely
> e verb: clarify f adjective: argumentative
> g noun: helping h adjective: unhygienic
> i adjective: invigorating j verb: defrost

Emphasising

Grammar folder page 202

Emphasising what you say by using inversion after a negative or restricting adverbial can be a good way to show that you have mastered more advanced structures in English. However, you have to be careful that you use them in an appropriate way. When you are reading and listening to English, try to be aware of when these structures are used. This should help you to get a feel for when it is appropriate to use them.

2

> **Answers**
> a Never in my whole life have I tasted anything so awful!
> b Under no circumstances are credit cards accepted.
> c Not until much later did we find out about his research.
> d Only when we arrived back at the lab did we realise what had happened.
> e Not only did we lose our passports but also all our money.
> f Hardly had we got there when the fire alarm went off.
> g Little does he know what's in store for him.
> h Only after her death did I learn her secret.

Listening

Speaker 1: I think my favourite photograph is the one I've got on my kitchen wall at home. It's – you've probably seen it, it's quite a common one. It's, it's a black and white photograph taken from, I'm going to guess something like the 1930s, and it's a few workers in New York high up, building a skyscraper or something, and they're taking a lunch break and they're all sitting on, on a girder or whatever it is and they've got their packed lunches and they're way way high up, and when I first saw this picture I, I couldn't look at it originally because, well I don't have a great head for heights and so it just made me feel a bit funny about the whole thing because you can see, in the background you can see Central Park and the rest of Manhattan. And it's quite eerie but it's also extraordinary that they don't have any kind of safety gear on, and if you look at the left of the picture, there's, there's two guys, one of them is offering the other one a light for his, for his cigarette and every time I look at it, I keep imagining he's going to pull his hand forward as the guy reaches to try and light his cigarette and fall off. Maybe that just says something about me. But it's just, it's just such an evocative picture. It just makes me think of what conditions must have been like, the work conditions and there's something quite romantic about it, I suppose. We live in a sort of sanitised age and that kind of thing wouldn't happen any more but it's just, it's just a wonderful picture and they all look tired but just so contented so high up above the ground. It's quite extraordinary.

Speaker 2: The picture that actually comes to mind is something that I bought about a year and a half ago from Spitalfield Market. It was just staring at me. You know when you're sort of looking around and every time you turn round you keep seeing this picture. Didn't really have any money on me, shouldn't have been spending but I just fell in love with it. It's a huge black and white print in charcoal on Japanese very textured paper. It's very sort of feely-touchy, you want to sort of get hold of it, picture of a bull. At the time I was going out with a Taurean so it seemed very right to go and buy it. I've just got it over my fireplace and it just seems to watch me wherever I am in the room. It's got a beautiful thick black frame as well. It's really an armful of a picture, it's huge but I absolutely love it. I just really like the, the naive quality of the picture. It's very sort of childlike the way it's been drawn, as I as a child would obviously draw the face of a bull, and also having met the artist – she'd only done a couple of them – it was nice to meet the person who'd actually drawn the picture. It's just very special to me. Some people love it, some people hate it but I'm really glad I made that impulse buy and got it.

4

If you are working alone, prepare your talk and then record it if possible. Listen to it again a week or two later and try to be as objective as you can about it.

How interesting is the content?
How good is the delivery?
How effective is the use of language?

Writing folder 8

Articles
pages 122–123

1

Suggested answers		
	Article	**Report**
Who it is usually written for	a wide audience who you don't know and who will only read it if it catches their interest	a boss or some other person in authority
What its aims usually are	to interest, entertain or inform the readers	to inform
Any special characteristics of its layout	will usually have an eye-catching title and subheadings	informative title and subheadings; may use bullet points or numbered points in order to make its structure even clearer
Any special characteristics of its register	may be any register – it depends on the readership of the magazine or newspaper	unmarked or formal
Any other special characteristics of its style	the writer will try to be interesting, amusing or original, in order to catch and hold the readers' interest and attention	must be absolutely clear and unambiguous in what it says; usually has clear introduction presenting what it is going to say and usually comes to some distinct conclusion at the end

2

Answers
a report (topic, phrases like *In conclusion*, fairly formal, very clear language)
b article (topic, rather literary vocabulary like *balmy, chugged*)
c article (informal style, e.g. *never in a million years*, use of suspense)
d report (topic, formal vocabulary, e.g. *ascertain*)
e article (topic, rather informal style)

Unit 20

pages 124–127

Reading

1

> **Answers**
> 1 D 2 C 3 A 4 B 5 E

2

> **Answers**
> Text A   **a** outstanding   **b** witty   **c** a masterpiece
> Text B   **a** plot   **b** bug
> Text C   **a** bully   **b** chin up
> Text D   **a** enhance   **b** bust
> Text E   **a** shaping   **b** distracted

4

The story which actually won the competition – *Like Mother, Like Son* – probably won because you can sense powerful feelings coming through the words. First, the lonely unhappiness of the young boy at boarding school and the lack of sympathy from his mother. Then, the depression of an old lady put into a home and the unfeeling response of her son. You feel that the son had nursed his feelings of bitterness throughout his whole life and is now enjoying his revenge on his mother. There is also a satisfying parallelism between the two letters.

You may, of course, be able to think of reasons why you would have chosen a different story as the winner.

Vocabulary

Are there any idioms like these in your own language based on parts of the body? It may help you to learn these if there are any similar idioms in your own language.

1

> **Answers**
> **a** 4 (finger)   **b** 8 (toes)   **c** 3 (heart)   **d** 2 (hand)
> **e** 7 (ears)   **f** 1 (head)   **g** 6 (feet)   **h** 5 (eye)

2

> **Answers**
> **a** 5   **b** 7   **c** 4   **d** 1   **e** 8   **f** 2   **g** 3   **h** 6

3

> **Answers**
> 1 fell head over heels in love   2 to give her a hand
> 3 has her head in the clouds   4 has set her heart
> 5 keeps her on her toes   6 was all ears
> 7 bite his tongue   8 was down in the mouth
> 9 is breaking my heart   10 racked my brains
> 11 put his mind at rest
> 12 to keep my fingers crossed

Hypothesising

Grammar folder page 202

1

Speaker 1: It's great to see you again. It's a pity we haven't kept in touch with any of the other classmates, isn't it? Do you think we're the only ones who ended up as teachers?

Speaker 2: Maybe. I often wonder whether Bill managed to get a job in politics, don't you?

Speaker 1: Well, I do know that he stood as a candidate in the last election but didn't get in.

Speaker 2: Perhaps he will this time round. Just imagine having a friend in parliament!

Speaker 1: Mm. Suppose he became a minister one day!

Speaker 2: Yes, if only he was Minister of Education! We could write to him asking him to put up teachers' salaries!

Speaker 1: Or what if he were Prime Minister! That'd be even better. I'd love to see the inside of Number 10. Yeah, perhaps we should try and get back in touch with him just in case!

> **Answers**
> These expressions are all the ones in the first group. All the expressions in box A are used. These are the ones which are most likely to be used when hypothesising in relatively informal situations.

2

> **Answers**
> **1a** If we were to appoint a new deputy head, that would allow me to spend a lot more time in the classroom.
> **1b** Were we to appoint a new deputy head, that would allow me to spend a lot more time in the classroom.
> **2a** If I had more time in the classroom, it would give me more of a finger on the pulse of school life.
> **2b** Had I more time in the classroom, it would give me more of a finger on the pulse of school life.
> **3a** Let us imagine how a deputy would use his or her time.
> **3b** Let us consider how a deputy would use his or her time.
> **4a** Let us suppose that a deputy would take over a lot of the day-to-day running of the school.
> **4b** Let us assume that a deputy would take over a lot of the day-to-day running of the school.

3

> **Answers**
> The speaker is arguing that class sizes at primary school should be no larger than 20 pupils. The points are:
> - it will become easier to attract good quality teachers
> - pupils will enjoy school more and there will be fewer discipline problems
> - children will learn more quickly which will benefit society
> - if enough teachers can be found, the policy can be implemented within five years
> - building budgets for schools will have to be increased
> - the fact that the birth rate has fallen will make it easier to implement the policy than it might otherwise have been.

I am proposing that class sizes at primary school be reduced to a maximum of twenty pupils.

If I may speculate for a moment, I believe that it will be much easier to attract good quality graduates into the teaching profession if they're guaranteed an environment in which they can truly teach each individual child.

Speculating further for a moment, children will enjoy school far more and there will be fewer problems of alienation and truancy among young people.

Let us take a hypothetical case: a rather shy child starts school at four and a half. He is in a class with 36 other children. The teacher never seems to notice when he has trouble understanding the lesson and he gets into the habit of not bothering about being able to keep up with the work. He often soon learns that the one way to get attention is to be disruptive.

On the assumption that children learn more, faster and with greater enjoyment if they are in smaller groups with more individual attention, I have every reason to suppose that the implementation of this proposal would have far-reaching benefits for the future of our society.

Provided that we are able to find enough appropriately talented and suitably qualified primary school teachers, I think that there is no reason why the proposal should not be implemented throughout the country within the next five years. Allowing for the fact that more classrooms will be required if class sizes are to be reduced, we shall have to increase schools' building budgets for the next couple of years. Given that the birth rate has fallen over recent years, it should be more straightforward to implement this proposal now than it would have been ten years ago.

Listening

2

> **Answers**
> 1 a (How Success Can Go to One's Head)
> 2 b (A Moment in Venice)
> 3 c (August When the Statue in Her Garden Gives Her Most Pleasure)

Speaker 1: An Aboriginal spent years carving and shaping pieces of wood, missiles to bring down the birds that flew above.
Finally, one day his perfected Bu-Mrang turned in the air and winged its way back to him, silent and swift, straight towards the head.
'Yaroo!' he exclaimed. 'I've just invented the ...'

Speaker 2: They collided in St Mark's Square.
As they apologised in their different languages, he sensed that something had passed between them.
His heart had been touched.
In that moment something magical had occurred.
He watched her vanish among the gathering of people and pigeons.
She had stolen his wallet.

Speaker 3: In the summer of the rain and batik skies, he came by moonlight once again and stood outside, barefoot and soaking wet, the rain dripping opals down his ivory cheeks. Only in August would he come and the marble stand, whereupon he stood, would remain empty for one blissful night.

Units 16–20 Revision

pages 128–129

Writing

> **Answers**
> 1 Now, be honest! Most of us, in the course of our working day, tell the odd little fib.
> 2 We may pretend we've nearly finished something when we've barely started it or say
> 3 someone is in a meeting when they don't want to take the call. But it's very easy for
> 4 white lies to turn into something more serious and the assumption that little
> 5 porkies are a necessary part of a secretary's role is a dangerous one. 'Most
> 6 secretaries and PAs are used to telling white lies for the boss,' says Ros Taylor,
> 7 business psychologist and author of *The Key to the Boardroom*. 'If he asks you to
> 8 do something that is slightly more dishonest, the easy thing is to assume that it's
> 9 OK, that he wouldn't ask you to do something illegal. Unfortunately, that isn't always
> 10 the case.' Last month, a PA to a chief executive who was being tried for fraud
> 11 admitted in court that she had faked documents to smooth the passage of a huge
> 12 deal. She argued that lying was standard practice in the city and that she was
> 13 simply trying to protect her boss. But must secretaries sign up to a culture of
> 14 dishonesty? What happens if you want to tell the truth? 'I've done things that I know

15 are dishonest,' says Kate Matheson, PA to the director of a large property company.

16 'It's easy to feign ignorance. I've shredded things that, deep down, I know should be

17 kept, and been asked to change figures on documents that, if I really thought

18 about it, I'd know shouldn't be changed, but my boss is top dog in a huge

19 organisation and I'm not about to say no to him. I've always assumed that since I'm

20 doing what I'm asked, it couldn't get me into trouble.'

21 This is a common misconception. The fact is that any untruth, even a seemingly

22 harmless white lie, can lead to trouble, and the best policy is to try to avoid

23 dishonesty from the start. 'Because I've done the odd thing that is a bit

24 questionable in the past, it's even more difficult to say no now,' says Kate Matheson.

25 'My boss can say, "Oh well, you did it last time!" What can I say to that?'

Grammar

Answers
1 not 2 what 3 one 4 to 5 the 6 (a)round
7 only 8 most 9 was 10 at 11 long 12 a

Reading

Answers
1 B 2 G 3 A 4 E 5 F 6 D

Unit 21

pages 130–133

Speaking

1

a The photos show a beach holiday, perhaps a package holiday; a mobile home and backpacking.

b Suggestions: people who are very busy and have little time to plan a tailor-made holiday, people who do not want to be alone/isolated on holiday, people who like the security of a tour operator in the resort.

c Advantages: freedom, go off the beaten track, meet locals
Disadvantages: often have to 'rough it', don't stay in luxurious hotels, can be lonely.

Listening

1

Words which could be associated with the pictures include:
Picture a: ice cream, hot, sightseeing, monuments
Picture b: current, river, banks, deep, wet
Picture c: lost, phrase book, language, locals, pronunciation

2

Answers
a 1a 2e 3g 4b 5c 6d 7f
b 1a 2g 3c 4f 5e 6d 7b
c 1a 2d 3g 4f 5c 6b 7e

3

Answers
1 you know 2 not a good idea 3 But 4 So anyway
5 er 6 Why? 7 why did we have to run?

Interviewer: So you were travelling by train into Italy, were you?

Alan: Yes, yes, it was me and the rest of the family, and we were supposed to be getting eventually to Calabria, way down in the south. And it was a very nice train journey really, through France and then across the Alps. I think it was early morning we arrived in Turin. And it was just supposed to be a short stop and then the train would continue on further south. I mean, I was in one of these wagon-lit sleeping cars. So the train stopped and there was lots of activity, and people got off, and I went back to sleep again, and I thought, well, I'll wake up again a bit later and have my breakfast. And then I woke up again and realised nothing had happened. We were still, sort of stuck at this platform in Turin main station. And I was actually, I was in one compartment, a male, a male only compartment, and my wife and children were in the other compartment. And I realised there was nobody else in my compartment, everybody had gone, I was all on my own. So I walked down the corridor and then found the rest of my family, also totally bewildered. But luckily, this was a wagon-lit thing so there was an attendant at the end, who spoke good English. So the last people left in the carriage, more or less now, we were, there was a few other, other bewildered international travellers, so we asked the wagon-lit attendant and he said, 'Oh, there's a strike. Er, there's a strike of station masters. Nobody else, just station masters have gone on strike.' So all the trains, with one or two odd exceptions, were stuck in the place they'd stopped, that's where we were going to stay until the station masters …

Interviewer: So had everyone else got off?

Alan: So all the Italians had got off, the local people had got off because there's no point in going any further, and us long-distance travellers then had to decide what to do. There were rumoured to be one or two local stopping trains running and so a lot of people just jumped on those going goodness knows where, somewhere south. And we thought, well, we've a wagon-lit carriage to ourselves, it's bound to start running again some time, and you know, we've got the services of our personal attendant, and it's Turin. So we thought we'll just stay here and see what happens. I mean, in fact, for those few of us who stayed on the train, it was quite nice because they gave us free vouchers to go out to lunch. And eventually they said, 'Oh this train will run again in the evening.' So we had a day in Turin. So we walked around, had an ice cream. It was a Sunday and we went down around the river and had a lovely free lunch. Came back in the evening to discover the strike had now finished and this huge long train finally rolled out of Turin station with about twenty passengers altogether.

Simone: So, well, er, basically, we went to Australia for our honeymoon, and we spent three months travelling around Australia, and went all the way round on the bus. On one particular day we were up in the north of Queensland, in this particular place where the rainforest meets the ocean, stuff like that. Anyway, we had about two hours until our coach left to go back south again. And my husband said, 'Oh er, let's go for a walk.' So OK, fine. So we decided to follow the road and then down this path. Anyway, it was lovely, and we lay on this beach, and the beach was fantastic. There was nobody there. The ocean was, you know, fantastic, blue colour and we were lying there thinking, oh, you know, this is the life. And then we looked at our watches and realised actually we were going to miss our bus. So we thought, OK, this is what we're going to do. We're going to take a short cut. Instead of going back to the road and back round to the other side of this hill, we'd just walk over the hill. Simple. So we walked over this hill and then we were sort of confronted with this problem that we had er, this what was, in effect, a river that cut off our side of the beach from the other, which is where our hotel was. So we thought, well, we don't want to walk through the ocean 'cos at that time of the year you've got these er, box jellyfish which are really dangerous so you can't walk in the water. Well, we thought, if we walk in the river, then we'll be safe, you see. So we start walking through this river and you know, I'm thinking, it's only going to go up to my knees so it'll be OK. We get to the middle and it's up to our waist. And you know, I'm thinking this was not a good idea, you know. But we'll walk nice and slowly, we'll get to the other side and we'll just have to sit in wet, wet clothes for about twelve hours while we're travelling south on the bus. So anyway, what happened was, er, we got about half way through and suddenly my husband goes, 'Quick! Run!' And I said, 'Why?' And he said, 'Just run, just run.' So we start running and the water is literally in waves over our head and you know, we get to the other side, and I'm standing there with water dripping off my hair and everything is drenched at this point, and I'm going, er, 'And why did we have to run?' And he goes, 'Well, I just had a really bad feeling.' And I start, you know, you idiot, er, anyway, we just start walking, and I'm going, 'I'm never going to listen to you again, and look at me, and I'm going to have to sit on a bus now for twelve hours and I'm going to be really uncomfortable, and blah, blah'. And we get down there, probably about a hundred yards, and there's this big sign, which you can only see the back of from where we've come. And as we walk round this sign, there's this big billboard, and on the billboard it's got written, 'Crocodile Infested River. Do NOT cross!' So Bill just kind of looked at me, and I just looked at him, and I went, 'OK'. And we didn't say anything else, we just walked to the bus.

Mick: Well, this is about something very embarrassing that happened to me about ten years ago. And ten years ago I'd been living in Greece for three years and instead of coming directly back to England from Greece, I thought, well, I'll, I'll come back and take a year and go slowly through all the countries of Europe and er, do it that way. So the first place I was going to visit after Greece was going to be Yugoslavia, and I didn't speak a word of Serbo-Croat, so I thought well, I need a phrase book of some sort. And the only one I could find was in a little shop in the village where I was living in Greece and that was, there was this Greek into Serbo-Croat and well, it was really cheap, and I never thought at the time that that would be a problem. And er, all the way through Greece I kept practising and practising all these phrases. When I finally got into what was then Yugoslavia, er, every time I said something, people would start laughing at me or looking at me really strange and I thought, well, it's the pronunciation, obviously. So after a few weeks of sort of trying different phrases in different ways and different pronunciation, finally I met someone who spoke English there, and they pointed out that I was saying absolutely ridiculous things. And when we looked at the phrase book, the, one page was in Greek and the next, the facing page was, in Serbo-Croat. But when the book had been put together, they got the wrong pages. So I was going round saying, 'Good morning', but what I was actually saying was, 'Can I see the menu, please?' And things like that. So it was no surprise that people were looking at me as if I was completely mad.

4

A filler is a word we use when we need a bit of extra time to think about what we want to say, e.g. *Well, um, er.*

Answers
1 filler 2 feeling 3 linking device 4 linking device
5 filler 6 direct speech 7 direct speech

5

People use fillers to gain time to think, to modify what they are going to say and to remember. The following table provides more examples of fillers, linking devices, attitude words and direct speech.

	Alan	Simone	Mick
Linking devices	and, so, also, and then, but, because	so, and, and then, instead of, anyway, because (cos)	and, instead of, so, when … But
Fillers	er, yes, I mean, well, sort of, more or less now, you know	so, well, er, basically, OK, you know, sort of, what was in effect, you see	well, er
Words that show feeling or attitude	luckily, eventually, bewildered	fine, simple	embarrassing obviously, finally, as if I was completely mad
Direct speech	Oh, there's a strike. Oh, this train will run again in the evening.	Let's go for a walk. Quick! Run! Why? Just run. And why did we have to run? I just had a really bad feeling. You idiot. I'm never going to … blah, blah. OK.	Can I see the menu, please?

Reading

1

Answers
1 C 2 B 3 A

Think back over the listening and the two reading extracts. The differences between descriptive/narrative writing and descriptive/narrative speaking are:

Descriptive/narrative writing	Descriptive/narrative speaking
Vocabulary: a wider range; less repetition. More attention paid to style/stylistic devices, e.g. imagery, similes, inversion. Grammar: more controlled; a greater range of structures. More complex use of subordinate clauses	More informal or dramatic vocabulary. Grammar less controlled; some restarting of sentences/redirection of sentences. Use of incomplete sentences

Vocabulary

1

These words are onomatopoeic; say the sentences and repeat the underlined words to see if you can hear their meaning.

Answers
1 c 2 f 3 a 4 e 5 d 6 g 7 b

2

Answers
1 adjective 2 noun 3 adjective 4 verb 5 adverb
6 noun 7 adjective 8 noun

3

Answers
aesthetic: adjective   fairy tale: noun   freedom: noun
gorgeous: adjective   gravitate: verb   ocean: noun
riot: noun/verb   rowing: adjective/present participle
visually: adverb.

4

Answers
1 gorgeous 2 freedom 3 rowing 4 gravitate
5 visually 6 riot 7 aesthetic 8 fairy tale

Range of grammatical structures

Grammar folder page 203

1

Answers
was brought up, didn't really have, was like, we had, used to go, used to sit, I find, gravitate, I've realised, unless I can see …, I don't feel, I've been to, I think, we went, hanging, had, I'd never been, we splurged out, it was, I love staying, when I travel.

Answers
1 told / had told 2 was going to happen / would happen
3 was cycling / had been cycling
4 arranged / had arranged 5 lay 6 needed 7 set
8 saw 9 was sitting 10 looking 11 turned
12 smiled 13 rendered 14 thinking 15 came

3

Sample answer
The thirteen-hour flight had been filled with eager anticipation: the first visit for three excited Europeans to South America. Having read an impressive array of guide books, we were ready to live this experience to the full and nothing was going to stop us! We arrived in Buenos Aires in the middle of the night and caught tantalising glimpses of the city as the taxi raced us to our hotel. The following morning we were anxious to immerse ourselves as quickly as possible in the wonderful atmosphere of the city.

Exam folder 9

Paper 2 Parts 1 and 2
pages 134–135

1

Answers
a two
b one
c two
d 1 hour 30 minutes
e 400–480
f yes
g newspaper/magazine articles, contributions to longer pieces, formal and informal letters, reports, reviews, proposals, competition entries, information sheets, essays
h Part 1 assessment focus: content, effective organisation of input, appropriacy to the intended audience and accuracy
i Part 2 assessment focus: content, range, style/register with attention to how successfully the candidate has produced the text type required

Go through the Advice box for this paper.

Sample answer
Learning English can be fun – and here's how

If you have ever wondered about learning English or perhaps even started classes and then given up, you will be interested to hear about the modern approach to language teaching and learning. While it has to be admitted that a sound grounding in the grammar and a good range of vocabulary are essential, if you want to be a good communicator in a language, the way language is introduced and then practised has to be motivating and relevant for today's learners.

English clubs can offer a stimulating environment in which to brush up your English and it can be much more than just language training; it can be a social event in its own right.

For example, at Tops English Club you will find a fascinating programme of events ranging from film nights followed by discussion to an evening sampling English regional food. Music evenings frequently attract new members and there are competitions with attractive prizes, for instance, if you have ever fancied yourself as a film director or producer, you could enter for the Club's film festival.

English clubs enable their members to enjoy what they normally enjoy but all in an English-speaking atmosphere. In fact, you enjoy yourself so much you often forget you're speaking English. You also make lots of new friends with the same international outlook on life. If you have been put off by stories of learning English as being dull and boring, think again and look at what your nearest club has to offer. You may well be pleasantly surprised.

Unit 22

pages 136–139
Reading

2

This exercise helps you develop the language to respond to charts/graphs/diagrams, etc. In a graph we have the vertical-Y axis and the horizontal-X axis. *Axis* is the singular form and *axes* the plural form.

Answer
The vertical Y-axis shows by how many degrees the temperature varied from the norm (what was usual or expected), and the horizontal X-axis represents time (1850–2000).
This graph shows that global temperatures have been increasing since 1850.

3

> **Answers**
> **a** A mixture – there are facts about what scientists have discovered and predictions about the future which are educated guesses.
> **b** Three: the IPCC, Dr Wainwright and Mark Gibson.
> **c** **IPCC**
>   debate about how high the rise in temperature will be
>   discovery that Earth is less able to absorb carbon dioxide
>   predictions about what a 4°C increase would mean
>   **Dr Wainwright**
>   feedbacks in global carbon cycle and what that means
>   humans to blame for increase in temperature
>   **Mark Gibson**
>   4°C rise not inevitable
>   ways to mitigate predicted rise in temperature

4

> **Answers**
>
> | IPCC | is more likely | QS |
> | --- | --- | --- |
> | | have discovered | S |
> | | it would wipe out | QS |
> | | would be displaced | QS |
> | | is likely | QS |
> | **Dr Wainwright** | could mean | NSS |
> | | there is little room for doubt | QS |
> | **Mark Gibson** | is not inevitable | S |
> | | If ... we could cut | QS |

> Useful vocabulary
> **drought** *n.* continuous dry weather
> **dire** *adj.* extremely serious
> **concede** *v.* admit
> **wipe out** *v.* destroy completely
> **gloomy** *adj.* depressing, disheartening

Vocabulary

1

> **Answers**
> **a** 7 **b** 8 **c** 6 **d** 1 **e** 2 **f** 3 **g** 5 **h** 9 **i** 4

2

> **Answers**
> **1** force nine gale **2** torrential rain **3** ice cap
> **4** high tide(s) **5** sea defences **6** below freezing

Linking devices

Grammar folder page 203

Further examples of sentences which give examples of different linking devices:

Britain has a temperate climate. By way of contrast, Hong Kong has a tropical climate.
In comparison with Mexico, Sweden experiences colder temperatures.
Many people believe that the whole of the African continent is hot and dry. On the contrary, there is a huge variety of climatic conditions throughout the continent.
Although some areas of sAustralia are desert, many others produce lush tropical jungle.
While Siberia experiences some of the coldest temperatures imaginable, other parts of Russia enjoy a sub-tropical climate.
The west of Britain has quite heavy rainfall whereas the east receives comparatively little rain.

1

> **Answers**
> **1** On the other hand **2** However **3** whereas
> **4** contrary to **5** Indeed **6** because

2

> **Answers**
> increase   rise   fluctuation   decrease
> decline   reduction   fall   drop

3

> **Answers**
> **a** In conclusion, we can say that the world's temperature has risen significantly over the last couple of decades.
> **b** On the whole it may be said that / It may be said that, on the whole, we are experiencing more extreme weather conditions.
> **c** Therefore it can be concluded / It can therefore be concluded / It can be concluded, therefore, that scientists are following all climate changes with increased interest.
> **d** Given this, it may be deduced that unless countries reduce carbon emissions, the climate is under threat.

Listening

1

> **Answers**
> Tim: floods, global warming, greenhouse gas emissions, sea level, storms
> Wendy: El Niño, floods, droughts, global warming, storms

2

The underlined parts of the tapescript confirm the answers.

Tim: Some people say, good, it's great if the world's warming up. We'll have better holidays. But if they stopped to think for a second, they'd realise it's serious. I mean, if it gets warmer, it stands to reason <u>that more water will evaporate from the oceans and surely that means more storms</u> somewhere else. There's evidence that there are more storms, hurricanes and so on and that they're more intense. Now that more accurate records are kept we can see that <u>global warming</u> is a fact.

Another aspect of global warming is how this will affect the <u>sea level</u>; it'll definitely rise. I read something recently which suggested that the sea might rise by as much as half a metre over this century, you know, because as the ice melts, the oceans expand. Imagine what <u>effect that'll have on low-lying areas</u> around the world.

Another thing that gets me is that we know all this and yet we're not reducing our <u>greenhouse gas emissions</u> anything like fast enough to stop the effects of climate change. We might be able to slow it down a bit but I think that's all.

Wendy: I know it seems as if there are more cases of extreme weather, like <u>floods</u> and droughts, but I wonder if it's only that we hear about them more than before because of the news on TV and the fact that now it's easier to communicate world events to everyone and very quickly. Surely there's always been severe weather. <u>Storms</u> are a natural phenomenon, after all.

OK, I admit there is evidence of global warming, but is there evidence to show that that's what's causing severe weather? Wouldn't we have had these hurricanes and so on anyway? I mean nobody even really knows how storms form and the path they'll take. You see, what it is, is that the consequences are much greater these days. The world is more densely populated so in terms of the effect on population and financial loss the results are more devastating. But perhaps we should study the data more rather than the hype.

Everybody's heard of <u>El Niño</u> and La Niña and I must admit that that must be showing something, but from what I hear, the jury's still out on whether it's global warming that's exacerbating events.

3

> **Sample sentences**
> Tim believes there is evidence that storms are becoming more intense whereas Wendy thinks it may just be that we read more about them these days.
>
> Both Tim and Wendy believe that there is such a phenomenon as global warming but their views on how this affects the world's climate differ.

Writing folder 9

Descriptive writing
pages 140–141

1

> **Answers**
> A There will be description of schools and their facilities now and in 50 years' time.
> B There will be description of the instruments and performers and the audiences' reactions.
> C There will probably be less description in this task and more advice and recommendations.
> D There will be some description of the offices now and possibly in the future.

3

> **Answers**
> a two music events, review, music website, compare and contrast, the instruments and singers, the ability of the performers, the audiences' reactions, which event you enjoyed more and why,
> c people interested in music
> d lively and entertaining
> e instruments: guitar (bass, rhythm, electric, classical), drums, keyboard, synthesiser, violin, cello, double bass, French horn, trumpet, clarinet, flute, fiddle, mouth organ, etc.
> performers: jazz, rave, pop, classical, etc.
> audiences: age (young people, early twenties, middle-aged, older people), size (packed-out hall, half-full club), reactions (a standing ovation, a cool response, slow to warm up, appreciative), etc.
> f Introduction: the occasions when you went to two events
> Second paragraph: the two different bands, their instruments and singers
> Third paragraph: the ability of each band
> Fourth paragraph: the audiences' reactions
> Conclusion: which event you preferred and why

Unit 23

pages 142–145

Speaking 1

1

> **Key**
> If you have mainly As, people might see you as a doormat; unless you are more assertive when complaining, people might wipe their feet on you.
> If you have mainly Bs, it might help if you learn to relax before you complain.
> If you have mainly Cs, you have a sensible approach to complaining and should get what you want.

Reading

3

> **Answers**
> 1 D 2 H 3 F 4 A 5 G 6 C

> Useful vocabulary
> **spouting hot air** – saying a lot of things in a very angry way.

Phrasal verbs

Grammar folder page 204

2

> **Answers**
> a correct
> b I looked through the guarantee but I couldn't find out how long it was valid for.
> c correct
> d correct
> e We don't hold out much hope, but we are still trying to get compensation.
> f Trying to get a satisfactory answer to my queries took up the whole morning.
> g correct
> h I didn't really want to spend so much on a TV, but Frank talked me into buying it.

3

> **Answers**
> 1 plucked up   2 get on with   3 make out
> 4 stick up for 5 put across   6 sink in
> 7 took to   8 has turned out / turns out

Listening

2

> **Answers**
> 1 C 2 B 3 A 4 A 5 B 6 C

The underlined parts of the tapescript confirm the answers.

One of the most important situations in our professional life is when we feel we have to ask for a pay rise. It can be awkward but if you aren't assertive and say what's on your mind, it may lead to you feeling undervalued and having a negative attitude to your work and workplace.

A positive attitude, forward planning and perfect timing are the keys to getting a pay rise. You may be asking for a number of reasons, ranging from a bigger workload or the increased cost of living to the fact that you've found out that a colleague is getting more than you. But these arguments will be secondary to your worth to the company.

Start by taking an objective look at your career. Are you good at your job? Are you punctual and reliable? Do people know who you are, and for the right reasons? Are you worth more than you're getting paid? If so, how much?

Are there any problems that you need to address? If so, make the changes subtly, over a period of time. Bosses are not stupid, and sudden bouts of punctuality just prior to a pay negotiation will seem like the worst type of creeping.

When planning your negotiation, don't base it on your gripes. Even if you think your future in the company doesn't look too rosy, bear in mind the 'what's in it for me?' factor. You may want extra money for all those things that are on your want list, for a holiday or a car, but your boss will be more convinced by an argument based on your quality of work and dedication.

To strengthen your viewpoint, plan for potential objections. If your boss is going to resist, what points is he or she likely to bring up? You could raise some first, along with arguments in your defence. For example, the sort of line you could take is, 'I know most pay rises are linked to set grades in this company, but I believe that my job has changed sufficiently to make this an exceptional case.'

Bartering can be embarrassing, but you will need to feel and sound confident. Remember that negotiations are a normal part of business life. Never pluck a sum out of the air. Know exactly what you will ask for and what you will settle for.

The timing of your communication can be crucial. Keep an eye on the finances and politics of the company to avoid any periods of lay offs or profit dips. If your boss can be moody, get an appointment for his or her most mellow time of the day. Never approach the subject casually. An on the hoof approach will make your boss twitchy.

There's always the chance that you won't get what you ask for. This is often the point at which reasonable demands and negotiations can turn into conflict. Never issue ultimatums, and don't say you'll resign if you don't mean it. Boost your confidence and your argument by having a backup plan (that is, what you'll do if you don't get the pay rise you want). Plan for the future by staying positive, asking when you could next apply and what can be done in the meantime to help your case.

Writing

1

Exam folder 10

Paper 4 Part 2
pages 146–147

1

3–5

This is an example of the productive task – sentence completion. In the exam there are eight questions in Part 2.

The underlined parts of the tapescript confirm the answers.

When youth culture emerged in the early 1950s, jeans were a marvellous symbol, along with the explosion of music, films and the whole advent of this thing of youth culture, jeans were adopted as the dress of <u>rebellion</u>. They were frowned upon by your parents if you wore them when you went out. That was considered inappropriate because they were seen as <u>work pants</u>. However, this censorial attitude of parents only resulted in jeans being adopted by youth gradually throughout the world.

And they were saleable across international boundaries because they have fantastic qualities, just as a product in themselves, I mean, they are what I would call an <u>organic</u> product, the more you wear them the better they get; although they're very egalitarian, they just fit you.

And on top of all that you lay upon this, this idea of youthfulness, you put that together with these functional qualities and a symbol of the opening up of America.

Remember, you know, culture in the 50s was all coming from the United States, rock and roll started in America, that's where its <u>roots</u> were, that's where the roots of jeans are.

Some people wonder if jeans have had their day now that that terribly exciting stage is long over. Well, there are those who still wear the classic jeans today but perhaps much more importantly the mass of provincial youth also wear jeans but very different jeans, especially in Europe. They tend to wear imports from <u>Asia</u>, cheaper ones, and they use them not as a symbol of non-conformity but of peer-group conformity. So young men will wear their straight-legged black jeans out to the disco and if you're not wearing that, you're not one of them. So there's diversification of the use of jeans. You've got the clubber, who goes for the <u>brand names</u> but not the classics, and black rather than blue because young men differentiate between everyday wear, that's blue jeans. And then when they go out, they're actually dressing up in these black jeans, smart black jeans, shoes and a shirt.

Some people have suggested that young people are going off jeans because the establishment are wearing them, we've seen <u>presidents</u> wearing them and there is a degree of currency in that but it's how you wear them. You can wear them in a very different way to somebody else. Certain brands have that ability, like the Mini car; it can be driven by pop stars or little old grannies. Certain brands get beyond something that's only worn by one group after a period of time and jeans are certainly in there. So now it's the brand you wear, how you wear them, do you wear them loose or tight, washed out, with a crease down them? The codes become smaller and smaller. And you can still rebel in jeans. If you were to go to a very smart function and you wore jeans with the knees ripped, that would be a symbol of rebellion. And all this means jeans are here to stay, at least for the foreseeable future.

Unit 24

pages 148–151

Listening

2

Answers			
	Where	**Who**	**Topic**
Item 1	Australia	International aid group Oxfam The Aborigines	The rights of Aborigines
Item 2	Sydney, Australia	A lone athlete The President	The end of the Paralympics

3

Examples of labour laws are the minimum age at which children can start work, the maximum number of hours worked, safety and hygiene regulations, the minimum wage, etc.

4

Answers
a No
b employing children and not paying workers the minimum wage
c Workers are working illegally and therefore don't want to complain or they are so desperate for the work that they think it's better to have any job rather than no job at all.
d She is sewing clothes in a factory.
e Her boss said he would report her to the authorities and say she had lied about her age.
f No

The underlined parts of the tapescript confirm the answers.

1 *The News Today.* News twenty-four hours a day. It's fifteen hours GMT. You're listening to *The News Today.* Hello and welcome. Next, a bulletin of world news, followed in five minutes by *News from Around the World.* This week Richard James provides a glimpse of life in North Korea, Mark Holder reviews an album of South American love songs, Michael Martin visits Western Nepal, John Duncan meets the Chileans who live under the ozone hole in South America and Marion Southgate brings us a story of mermaids and diamonds from Angola. That's all in our edition of *News from Around the World* in about five minutes. Later, it'll be

politics from Westminster here in London: an analysis of current events in British government. That's all to come in the next hour. But first, here's a bulletin of the latest world news.

2 A report by the international aid group Oxfam is investigating Australia's role in protecting the basic rights of its native people, the Aborigines. The report identifies what it calls alarming gaps between the rights and access to services of indigenous people and those available to other Australians. It says there could also be cases of structural discrimination in the country's laws and regulations and calls for an investigation into constitutional change.

The eleventh Paralympic Games in Sydney, Australia, have ended with a spectacular carnival show and party. A lone athlete made his way to the centre of the arena. His arrival was the cue for a massive pyrotechnic display that raced around the stadium. Then followed displays from circus performers and dancers, huge inflatable animals. The President declared the games the best ever.

3 Working under cover, I have discovered that many companies throughout the world are flouting the child labour laws and minimum-wage laws. And you can't pin this down to one particular part of the world or say that it only happens in big cities as opposed to country areas. I have witnessed with my own eyes child labour in cities in so-called developed nations and workers being paid well below the legal requirements in every type of work you can imagine, from agriculture to clothes factories. Unfortunately it's very difficult to get workers to complain and the reasons are numerous, from they're working illegally and therefore don't want to complain or they're so desperate for the work that they think it's better to have any job rather than no job at all. And unscrupulous employers are cashing in on this.

This overcrowded, noisy factory is in a city in Europe where outside people are eating pepper steaks in posh restaurants, driving fast cars and earning a fortune. In here it's a different picture; it's like something from another age, rows and rows of women sewing clothes in a factory down a back alley just off a fashionable shopping street. This is what you call sweatshop labour; people working unimaginable hours, for half the minimum wage. I talked to a girl here, let's call her Janine, she's 14 and instead of going to school, she comes here to work to earn money so that she can help out with the finances at home. At first she'd intended to do it for just a couple of weeks during the holiday, but when she suggested that she might leave, her boss told her that if she left, he'd report her and tell the authorities that she'd lied to him about her age. And of course, the more school she missed, the harder it was to go back. A vicious circle.

Vocabulary

1

> **Answers**
> **a** read **b** weigh **c** guest **d** mail
> **e** whole **f** miner **g** jeans

2

> **Answers**
> **a** one **b** meat **c** cell **d** sew **e** stares **f** blew
> **g** sale **h** wear **i** waist **j** threw

Reading

2

To binge means to eat in an uncontrolled way.

> **Answers**
> **a** **True** they are a victim of their genes
> **b** **False** it also raises the possibility of deigning a drug ... this means the drug is not yet available
> **c** **False** using mice which have differences in their ability to taste sweet foods. Both teams used two different types of mice.
> **d** **True** ... in the gene called T1R3 ... It contains information which produces a protein called the sweet taste receptor.
> **e** **False** the results did not provide chocoholics with an excuse to give up dieting
> **f** **True** We have produced this gene through evolution because sweet foods in nature are not poisonous and also give us energy. We all need to have some sugar in our diet.
> **g** **False** ... using this discovery to develop artificial sweeteners ...

> **Useful vocabulary**
> **chocoholic** *n.* a person who loves chocolate so much they are 'addicted' to it
> **craving** *n.* a strong and uncontrollable desire for something
> **a sweet tooth** a liking for sweet foods
> **initiates a cascade of events** starts a lot of events happening one after the other
> **sought** *v.* (from *to seek*) to intend/try (in other contexts, *to look for*)

Linking devices

Grammar folder page 204

1

> **Answers**
> **1** as **2** because **3** Then **4** So **5** Despite **6** even
> **7** but **8** And what's more **9** To cap it all **10** By then

> **Useful vocabulary**
> **to take something in one's stride** to deal with something calmly (the phrase in the headline has a double appeal as *stride* means a long step when walking or running)
> **to jostle** *v.* to knock or push against someone in order to move past them when you are in a crowd
> **to be awash with** to be covered with
> **plucky** *adj.* brave
> **haze** *n.* usually means a thin fog but here it means that things were unclear because of the pain
> **flagging** *v. (participle)* becoming tired
> **to tingle** *v.* to have a feeling as if a lot of sharp pins or needles are being put quickly and lightly into your body
> **to unravel** *v.* to understand (in this context)
> **to be encased** *v.* covered or enclosed

Writing folder 10

Formal writing
pages 152–153

1

Give us a ring soon is informal English, probably spoken and used to someone the speaker knows well. *We look forward to hearing from you at your earliest convenience* is formal English, almost certainly written and probably written to someone the speaker does not know well.

2

It is impossible to be absolutely precise about the ordering of these, but they are likely to be in roughly the following order (where 1 is the least formal and 9 the most formal).

> **Suggested answers**
> • proposal to a benefactor on how you would spend the money he might give you
> • report for your boss
> • contribution to a tourist guidebook
> • letter of complaint to a newspaper
> • leaflet for a local sports club
> • competition entry for an international magazine
> • review for an English Club newsletter
> • article for a student magazine
> • letter to a pen friend

3

> **Answers**
> • It is not usually appropriate to use verb contractions in formal writing.
> • Try to avoid phrasal verbs in formal writing although sometimes there is no alternative or the alternative would sound too stilted to be appropriate.

- Avoid slang or colloquial expressions in formal writing – if they are included, it will be done for some special effect.
- Layout is more fixed in formal contexts.
- Structure is always important, but because you are more likely to be writing formally to someone whom you do not know and with whom you do not have so much shared knowledge, clarity of structure is particularly important.
- Again this is important in all kinds of writing but may perhaps be particularly so in formal writing (as one means of clarifying structure).

4

Suggested answers
a It was somewhat difficult to collect as much data as we had originally hoped.
b The men tended to express views that were slightly more conservative than those of the women.
c A number of our respondents raised some important concerns.
d Interviewees' responses depended on their age, gender, occupation and educational background.
e I would now like to discuss further several important aspects of the survey.

5

Suggested answers
a lovely, fascinating   b stimulating, talented
c sumptuous, spectacular   d varied
e glamorous, impressive

6

Answers
a 1 Firstly   2 Secondly   3 Moreover   4 Finally
b 1 Although   2 So   3 However   4 Consequently
c 1 then   2 Firstly   3 when   4 Gradually   5 After that
   6 especially   7 because   8 Finally

7

Sample answer

Proposal for improvements to college facilities

The following proposal outlines how the students' academic and living facilities might be improved. It is felt that both these areas are important for students to be able to make the best of their time at this college.

Academic facilities
Firstly, the provision of more computers in the library would be a significant improvement, as this would allow students to do research on the Internet without having to wait so long for the use of a computer and moreover, it would

enable students to type up their assignments more easily. In addition, more self-access language courses should be made available, so that students can do basic language training in a variety of languages. In a global economy, it is essential that future employees are equipped with at least three languages.

Accommodation
It is suggested that the residence be refurbished in order to bring the accommodation up to today's standards. That would include putting en-suite bathrooms into the bedrooms which do not have this facility. Moreover, the kitchens could be updated by providing microwave ovens. The lounges should be refurbished in order to provide a lighter and more modern atmosphere.

Conclusion
It is believed that the suggestions above would make a huge difference to student life in the college. It is also believed that it is important to address both areas because if a student is content with his social life and accommodation, he will better be able to concentrate on his studies.

Unit 25

pages 154–157

Reading

4 and 5
Formal words or phrases are underlined and the informal paraphrase is given in italics afterwards.

Suggested answers
(Formal words or phrases are underlined and the informal paraphrase is given in italics afterwards.)

We can learn a great deal *a lot* about behaviour by simply *just* observing the actions of others *what other people do*. However, *But* everyday observations are not always made carefully or systematically. Most people do not attempt *try* to control or eliminate *get rid of* factors that might influence the events they are observing. As a consequence, *So* erroneous conclusions are often drawn *we often come to the wrong conclusions*. Consider, *Think about*, for example, the classic case of Clever Hans. Hans was a horse that was said by his owner, a German mathematics teacher, to have amazing talents. Hans could count, do simple addition and subtraction (even involving fractions), read German, answer simple questions ('What is the lady holding in her hands?'), give the date, and tell the time. Hans answered questions by tapping with his forefoot or by pointing with his nose at different alternatives shown to him. His owner considered *thought* Hans to be *was* truly intelligent and denied using *said he didn't use* any tricks to guide his horse's behaviour. And, in fact, Clever Hans was clever even when the questioner was someone other than *wasn't* his owner.

Newspapers <u>carried accounts</u> *published stories* of Hans's performance, and hundreds of people came to <u>view</u> *see* this amazing horse. In 1904, a scientific commission was <u>established</u> *set up* <u>with the goal of discovering</u> *to discover* the basis for Hans's abilities. The scientists found that Hans was no longer clever if either of two circumstances existed. First, Hans did not know the answers to questions if the questioner also did not know the answers. Second, Hans was not very clever if he could not see his questioner. A slight bending forward by the questioner would start Hans tapping, and any movement upward or backward would <u>cause</u> *make* Hans <u>to stop</u> *stop* tapping. The commission <u>demonstrated</u> *showed/proved* that questioners were unintentionally <u>cueing</u> *prompting* Hans in this way.

This famous <u>account</u> *story* of Clever Hans <u>illustrates the fact</u> *shows* that scientific observation (unlike casual observation) is systematic and controlled. <u>Indeed</u> *In fact*, it has been suggested that control is the <u>essential ingredient of</u> *the most important thing in* science, distinguishing it from non-scientific procedures (Boring, 1954; Marx, 1963). In the case of Clever Hans, investigators exercised control by <u>manipulating</u> *changing*, one at a time, conditions such as whether the questioner knew the answer to the question asked and whether Hans could see the questioner. By exercising control, taking care to investigate the effect of various factors one by one, a scientist <u>seeks to gain</u> *tries to get* a clearer picture of the factors that actually produce a phenomenon.

6

> **Suggested answers**
> 1 from somebody in the English Group   2 have to go to
> 3 be a good chance   4 other   5 is/will be   6 sent
> 7 give out

Complex sentences and adverbial clauses

Grammar folder page 205

1

> **Suggested answers**
> a he could answer any question he was asked.
> b someone other than his owner asked the questions.
> c he could not see the questioner.
> d carefully observing what happened.
> e many people were suspicious of his owner and his act.
> f Hans could see him.

Listening

2

> **Answers**
> 1 what information you need to find out
> 2 they are done under time pressure
> 3 inexperienced researchers are often impatient
> 4 decide on the type of questionnaire to be used

> 5 yourself
> 6 items prepared by other researchers
> 7 write a first draft of the questionnaire
> 8 format
> 9 effective wording of questions
> 10 re-examining and rewriting
> 11 people who know about the topic / experts
> 12 eliminate bias
> 13 pretest
> 14 typical of people who will answer the real questionnaire
> 15 ambiguous
> 16 offensive
> 17 interviewers
> 18 edit the questionnaire

The underlined parts of the tapescript confirm the answers.

It's important to realise that the results of any survey are useless if the questionnaire was poorly constructed. Although there's no substitute for experience when it comes to preparing a good questionnaire, there are a few basic principles. I'm going to describe six basic steps in preparing a questionnaire.

The first step in questionnaire construction, deciding <u>what information you need</u> to find out, should actually be the first step in planning the survey as a whole. This decision, of course, determines the type of questions to be included in the questionnaire. It's important to project the likely results of the survey if the proposed questionnaire is used and then decide whether these findings will answer the questions the study is intended to address. Surveys are frequently done under considerable <u>time pressure</u>, and <u>inexperienced researchers</u> are especially prone to impatience. Just remember that a poorly conceived questionnaire takes just as much time and effort to administer and analyse as a well-conceived one. The difference is that a well-constructed questionnaire leads to interpretable results. The best we can say for a poorly designed instrument is that it's a good way to learn how important careful deliberation is in the planning stages.

The next step is to decide on the <u>type of questionnaire</u> to be used. For example, will it be <u>self-administered</u> or will trained interviewers be using it? This decision is determined primarily by the survey method you have selected. For instance, for a telephone survey, trained interviewers will be needed. In designing the questionnaire, also consider using <u>items which have been prepared by other researchers</u>. There is no reason to develop your own instrument if a reliable and valid one already exists. Besides, if you use items from a questionnaire which has already been used, you can compare your results directly with those of earlier studies.

If you decide that no available instrument suits your needs, you'll have to take the third step and <u>write a first draft</u> of your questionnaire. You should consider the format <u>and ordering of questions as well as the effective wording of questions</u>.

The fourth step, <u>re-examining and rewriting</u>, is essential. Questions that appear objective and unambiguous to you may strike others as slanted and ambiguous. It's really helpful to have your questionnaire reviewed by experts, both those who have knowledge of survey research methods and those <u>with expertise in the area of your study</u>. For example, if you're doing a survey of students' attitudes towards the campus food service, it would be advisable to have your questionnaire reviewed by the campus food service director. When you're dealing with a controversial topic, ask representatives of both sides of the issue to screen your questions for possible <u>bias</u>.

By far the most crucial step in the development of a sound questionnaire is step five, the <u>pretest</u>. A pretest involves actually administering the questionnaire to a small sample of respondents under conditions as much as possible like those to be used in the final administration of the survey. Pretest respondents must also be <u>typical of those to be included in the final sample</u>; it makes little sense to pretest a survey of nursing home residents by administering the questionnaire to college students. There is one way, however, in which a pretest does differ from the final administration of the survey. Respondents should be interviewed at length regarding their reactions to individual questions and to the questions as a whole. This provides information about potentially <u>ambiguous</u> or <u>offensive</u> items.

The pretest should also serve as a dress rehearsal for <u>interviewers</u>, who should be closely supervised during this stage to ensure that they understand and adhere to the proper procedures for administering the questionnaire. If major changes have to be made as a result of problems arising during the pretest, a second pretest may be needed to determine whether these changes solved the problems. After pretesting is completed, the final step is to <u>edit the questionnaire</u> and specify the procedures to be followed in its final draft.

Units 21–25 Revision

pages 158–159

Grammar

1

Suggested answers				
Listing	Concession and contrast	Cause	Result	Summing up
first and foremost F last but not least N one, two three N	despite/in spite of N/F however N/F but N/I yet F	because N as N/F since N/F (participles) e.g. Realising	therefore F consequently N/F as a result N/F thus F	in conclusion F to conclude F to sum up F to summarise F/N in brief N/F

first(ly), second(ly) N above all N	although N even though N much as F all the same I even so N nevertheless F	on account of N/F owing to F because of I/N	and so I so that I/N so ... that N enough and too (for someone) to + infinitive I/N	altogether I/N overall I/N then I

2

Answers
Whilst concession   *also* listing   *As* cause   *then* result

Reading

Useful vocabulary for 1 and 2
maverick *n.* a person who thinks and acts in an independent way, often behaving differently from the expected or usual way **to rock the boat** do or say something which will upset people **complacent** *adj.* feeling a calm satisfaction with your own abilities so that you do not try harder **constraints** *n.* limits **to ponder** *v.* think carefully about something **to be an advocate of something** to speak in support of something **to nurture** *v.* to take care of / protect **to grapple** *v.* to struggle/fight with **to paper over the cracks** – to hide weaknesses or problems

3

Answers
1 diplomat   **2** challenger   **3** innovator   **4** challenger **5** innovator, diplomat   **6** judge   **7** expert   **8** expert **9** judge, diplomat

Vocabulary

Answers
a drive   **b** path   **c** team   **d** test   **e** gap   **f** ease

Unit 26

pages 160–163

Speaking

1b

The phrases could be used in many different ways but here are some possibilities. (You will hear the phrases used also in the listening text which follows.)

This area is internationally recognised as one of the best places for scuba diving anywhere in the world.
The outdoor restaurant in the picture is one of the best places to eat in the town.
It offers a complete range of local specialities.
There are spectacular views from the hotel windows.
If you are in search of the ultimate adventure, you can do a number of extreme sports here.
The area is clearly perfect for all kinds of water sports.
The hotels on the island offer all kinds of luxurious facilities.
You can enjoy a sumptuous lunch at the restaurant in the picture.
There are guided tours round interesting historic sights for those who prefer the cultural experience.
For those who like luxury there are a number of first-class hotels.
Scuba diving gives you the chance to see the diverse marine life of the region close-up.
Spending a holiday here offers you a once-in-a-lifetime experience.

Listening

1

> **Answers**
> the Grand Canyon   the Northern Lights
> the Great Barrier Reef   Mount Everest
> the Harbour at Rio de Janeiro   Victoria Falls
> Paricutin in Mexico

The underlined parts of the tapescript confirm the answers.

Located on the northern tip of Australia's East Coast, the tropical city of Cairns is internationally recognised as the gateway to the Great Barrier Reef, one of the seven natural wonders of the world. The city is home to 100,000 people and also boasts the fifth busiest international airport in Australia with many carriers flying directly into Cairns from countries around the world. Cairns is a tropical city with many outdoor restaurants and cafés and great shopping for all tastes, as well as offering a complete range of accommodation options from budget right through to five-star.

Great Adventures cruises have been running trips to the Great Barrier Reef for more than 100 years and, as a result, are recognised as an industry leader. Great Adventures offer daycruises to Green Island, a beautiful 6,000-year-old coral bay. It is perfect for lazing on white coral sands, swimming or snorkelling on the surrounding coral reef or relaxing around the luxurious day-visitor facilities – all just 45 minutes crossing from Cairns. A full range of options on the island include introductory scuba diving, certified scuba diving and guided snorkel tours, as well as a crocodile farm, parasailing and private beach hire.

For those wanting the ultimate reef adventure, cruise from Cairns to the luxury of Great Adventures multi-level pontoon on the Outer Reef. The pontoon features undercover seating and tables where you can enjoy a sumptuous buffet lunch. There's also a sundeck, full bar facilities, an underwater observatory, a semi-submersible coral viewing tour and a swimming enclosure for children. You'll be able to snorkel or dive among the reef's spectacular coral gardens and diverse marine life. A once-in-a-lifetime experience!

3

> **Answers**
> a false: it is in north-east Australia
> b false: it is the gateway to the Barrier Reef but not actually on it
> c false: it is the fifth busiest international airport in Australia
> d true
> e false: it is 6,000 years old
> f false: it takes 45 minutes by boat
> g false: it is not all under water
> h false: *a once-in-a-lifetime experience* means that it is a very special experience, not that you are only allowed to go there once

4

> **Answers**
> busy airport   tropical city   many outdoor restaurants and cafés   great shopping   range of accommodation   trips to the Great Barrier Reef   day cruises to Green Island   lazing on white coral sands   swimming   snorkelling on the surrounding coral reef   relaxing around the luxurious day visitor facilities   scuba diving   guided snorkel tours   crocodile farm   parasailing   private beach hire   multi-level pontoon on the Outer Reef with undercover seating and tables for lunch, a sundeck, bar facilities, an underwater observatory, a semi-submersible coral viewing tour, a swimming enclosure for children

Reading

2

Answers
Travelled by: car (Landcruiser)
Driver's aim: to keep the car off the ground as much as possible
How Tashi felt about the journey: he seemed to enjoy it
Difficult aspects of the journey: very bumpy
Good aspects of the journey: good visibility and not much other traffic
Scenery: mountains and river
What could be seen on the river: coracles (small boats)
Boats made of: yak skins, a wooden frame, yak hair and yak butter

5

Answers
1 C 2 D 3 D 4 A

Vocabulary

1

Answers
a 6 b 2 c 4 d 5 e 1 f 9 g 7 h 8 i 10 j 3

2

Answers
a off the beaten track b hit the road
c picture-postcard d black spot
e no room to swing a cat

3

Answers
a picture-postcard, stone's throw from (the beach usually), home from home. These emphasise the attractive aspects of places.
b black spot, tourist trap, no room to swing a cat. These emphasise the unattractive aspects of places.

Like, alike, as, so and *such*

Grammar folder page 205

5

Answers
a Oxford and Cambridge are alike in some ways.
b We saw such amazing scenery in the Himalayas.
c It was so far to the campsite.
d Our holiday cottage looked just like the one allocated to our friends.
e She looks as if she has just returned from a tropical holiday.

Writing

1

Answers
From the informal chatty letter
It's a great hotel with loads of character. The bedrooms get a bit chilly at night and the uncarpeted corridors can be noisy but it's worth putting up with a few minor inconveniences as it has so much atmosphere in other ways. The food is fantastic and you can stuff yourself at breakfast so you don't need to eat again till the evening.

From the brochure
The hotel has a magnificent location overlooking the broad spread of the gulf and most of the bedrooms enjoy sea views. Each room has its own luxuriously-appointed en suite bathroom and is individually decorated with many original finishing touches. The superb restaurant offers a wide range of delicious dishes to suit all tastes.

3

Sample answer
I'm having a wonderful time here in the Canaries. The hotel is fantastic – really elegant and luxurious. I could certainly get used to this kind of life – it's just a pity I could never afford it every year.
Love
Simone

4

Sample answer
Cashel House
Little Lane
Abbotsford
Tel 01253 297635
4-star hotel in 10 acres of grounds. 32 bedrooms. 13 garden suites. Seafood a speciality in the restaurant. Snack lunches sold in the bar. Equestrian centre adjacent to hotel offering guided pony treks. Tennis, sea-fishing, golf all available in the vicinity.

5

Sample answer
Dear Sir/Madam

Last week I returned from a week's holiday with my family in your hotel. Although we enjoyed our stay on the whole, we were disappointed that several claims made in your advertisement turned out not to bear much relation to reality.

Firstly, your advert claims that there is 24-hour room service, but when our flight was delayed and we arrived at 2.30 am we were told that it was impossible to have anything to eat at that time.

Secondly, the advert assures potential visitors that the hotel caters for every creature comfort. Yet on a number of occasions our shower would only provide us with cold water. Surely constant warm water is not too much to expect from a hotel that promotes the luxury of its facilities?

Thirdly, the hotel professes to pride itself on its 'quiet elegance'. Yet the room we had was actually quite noisy. We could hear every word spoken by the people in the room next to us. This was quite disturbing as they woke up very early and made it impossible for us to sleep late.

We feel that we deserve some financial compensation as we booked your hotel because of the claims made in your advert and were extremely disappointed when they turned out to be false.

We look forward to hearing from you.

Yours faithfully

Exam folder 11

Paper 4 Parts 1, 3 and 4
pages 164–165

3 and 4

Answers					
1 D	2 B	3 A	4 D	5 C	6 A

Interviewer: With me in the studio today is Julia Crawley, who runs a management consultancy which deals with women in business. Now Julia, if the majority of companies were run by women, what difference do you think it would make? I mean, what did you bring to the company you started?

Julia: Many people had warned me of the difficulties of being a female manager – to begin with, getting people to take you seriously. Male friends of mine, in similar management roles always seemed to be worried about how long a woman would stay with a company and whether family commitments would mean she was less loyal than a male manager. I remember when I started as a manager it was natural for me, and I think it is for most women, to want to work with others, to see what they could contribute, and I told them what I was bringing to the table.

Interviewer: Mm. It is important that everyone realises they are important in a company, that every individual is as important as any other, isn't it?

Julia: One of the first female management gurus, Jennifer Alderton, put forward as her 'articles of faith' respect for all staff. She introduced me to the concept of power with rather than power over. Usually when power is discussed, it's taken to mean having power over someone else, getting that person to do what you want him to do, either through actual physical means or through persuasion.

Interviewer: And what do you see as being some of the drawbacks of the traditional male-run business?

Julia: Well, we've had hundreds of years of command control, maybe more, and it kind of works, although days can be lost as disputes are debated and in the meantime, machines are standing idle. And it's a very uncomfortable sort of organisation to work in, isn't it? I think now that people want more from their job; they don't want to be treated as an easily replaceable machine.

Interviewer: Mm. What other concepts that you value might we find in a female-run business?

Julia: Well, it would seek out differences. Say you'd been doing a particular procedure the same way for years and then someone challenged that. By positively encouraging criticism, you'd open up far more creativity and as a result the company would go forward at a faster pace. It's usually the people who have hands-on experience of systems that can see shortcuts.

Interviewer: And at the same time recognising that it's crucial for people to have a balance between their work and home life.

Julia: Yes, this is an issue which has been widely discussed in many countries and there have been some high-profile men and women who have given up highly-paid, highly-responsible jobs because of the demand it was making on their time to spend more quality time with friends and family. The fact that these people were in the public eye has moved the debate on no end. I think where we need to go with this now is helping other countries where it is less acceptable for people to say, 'It's 6 o'clock so I'm off now' to realise that good workers are alert workers who've enjoyed their free time and have slept well.

Interviewer: Is this where you're going to channel your efforts from now on?

Julia: It's tempting, because I can see that with better communication skills the work place can become a far more attractive place to spend time. However, I'm getting involved in a scheme which backs small businesses which are struggling to get off the ground due to lack of cash. There are some great ideas out there with a demand for the product; but for a small company they've already invested all they had in setting up and getting a working prototype. So that's what appeals to me at the moment.

Interviewer: Well, good luck with that, Julia, and thank you for talking to us today

5

Answers
1 D   2 B   3 C   4 G   5 H

6

Answers
1 B   2 C   3 F   4 G   5 A

Speaker 1: It's funny how we became friends, I mean that doesn't usually happen with clients, but Sarah's so outgoing. We got on like a house on fire. We chatted away while I was trimming, colouring or whatever it was and then she started bringing her daughter in too and we'd put the world to rights as I cut. And then one day she said she was having a barbecue and would I like to come along. Not many who come to the salon would do that. And since then we've become good buddies.

Speaker 2: At first I thought she was a bit bossy, but after a while I realised that it's just her way of getting things done with the minimum amount of fuss and I must say she's great to share an office with. We work like demons while we're working and then usually take our breaks together. Last year we started going to the gym together after work on Wednesdays. She approaches exercise in the same way as work.

Speaker 3: She's been such a help. I mean more and more we rely on parents getting involved and helping out with social events. Sarah's a great organiser. I know if I hand over something to her, it'll be done in a jiffy, before you've had time to blink. Her daughter's the same. We wanted to have a sports day to help raise money for some new equipment that we need for the music department. I just mentioned it to Sarah and the next thing I knew there was a list of activities and who would supervise them on my desk. I wish she worked with me full time!

Speaker 4: Gosh, it seems like forever. She's really changed though. You'd never believe it but she used to be quite shy. She'd never answer questions unless directly asked. But she was a bit of a swot, always did her homework on time. In year eight she won some prize or other for literature I think. I knew then that she had been quietly developing into a very clever girl. Even though I moved away when I got married, we've kept in touch.

Speaker 5: We met while we were both doing push-ups. I'd been going to the gym for ages but could only really do about ten push-ups. She immediately wanted to better my pathetic effort and I must admit it made me work harder too. I'd say she rises to the challenge. I've seen it as she goes round. If she sees another woman can do such and such a thing, she wants to do more. Mind you, I suppose that's how she got where she is.

Unit 27

pages 166–169

Reading and Listening

1

Answer
picture c

2

Answers
a We learn that the girl is about 15 and that she is very self-possessed/confident.
b Because he has some kind of nervous problem and needs a rest.
c Because his sister met these people about four years ago and has given him a letter of introduction to them – she thinks he needs to meet people in the country.
d No, he isn't. He seems to have little desire to meet new people.
e We learn that it has French windows (windows that are also doors) and that these are open to a lawn. It also seems to have a slightly masculine rather than feminine atmosphere to it.

4

Answers
a false – there were three men
b true
c false – the bodies were never found but it was presumed they had drowned in a bog
d true
e false – it was a white raincoat
f true

"Out through that window, three years ago to a day, her husband and her two young brothers went off for their day's shooting. They never came back. In crossing the moor to their favourite snipe-shooting ground they were all three engulfed in a treacherous piece of bog. It had been that dreadful wet summer, you know, and places that were safe in other years gave way suddenly without warning. Their bodies were never recovered. That was the dreadful part of it." Here the child's voice lost its self-possessed note and became falteringly human. "Poor aunt always thinks that they will come back someday, they and the little brown spaniel that was lost with them, and walk in at that window just as they used to do. That is why the window is kept open every evening till it is quite dusk. Poor dear aunt, she has often told me how they went out, her husband with his white waterproof coat over his arm, and Ronnie, her youngest brother, singing 'Bertie, why do you bound?' as he always did to tease her, because she said it got on her nerves. Do you know, sometimes on still, quiet evenings like this, I almost get a creepy feeling that they will all walk in through that window –"

6

"Here they are at last!" she cried. "Just in time for tea, and don't they look as if they were muddy up to the eyes!"

Framton shivered slightly and turned towards the niece with a look intended to convey sympathetic comprehension. The child was staring out through the open window with a dazed horror in her eyes. In a chill shock of nameless fear Framton swung round in his seat and looked in the same direction.

In the deepening twilight three figures were walking across the lawn towards the window, they all carried guns under their arms, and one of them was additionally burdened with a white coat hung over his shoulders. A tired brown spaniel kept close at their heels. Noiselessly they neared the house, and then a hoarse young voice chanted out of the dusk: "I said, Bertie, why do you bound?"

Framton grabbed wildly at his stick and hat; the hall door, the gravel drive, and the front gate were dimly noted stages in his headlong retreat. A cyclist coming along the road had to run into the hedge to avoid imminent collision.

"Here we are, my dear," said the bearer of the white mackintosh, coming in through the window, "fairly muddy, but most of it's dry. Who was that who bolted out as we came up?"

"A most extraordinary man, a Mr. Nuttel," said Mrs. Sappleton; "could only talk about his illnesses, and dashed off without a word of goodbye or apology when you arrived. One would think he had seen a ghost."

"I expect it was the spaniel," said the niece calmly; "he told me he had a horror of dogs. He was once hunted into a cemetery somewhere on the banks of the Ganges by a pack of pariah dogs, and had to spend the night in a newly dug grave with the creatures snarling and grinning and foaming just above him. Enough to make anyone lose their nerve."

Romance at short notice was her speciality.

Vocabulary

1

> **Answers**
> a undergoing
> b soul
> c far
> d place
> e appearance
> f make
> g paid
> h laboured
> i heels
> j word
> k ghost
> l notice

2

> **Answers**
> a laugh, sigh, smile
> b chatted, droned, harped
> c avert, escape, prevent
> d a long time, his salary, most of his income
> e confidence, head, mind

Emphasising

Grammar folder page 206

1

> **Answers**
> *Romance at impressively short notice was her speciality.* (Use of intensifying adverb.)
> *No one was better at romance at short notice than she was.* (Negative or restricting adverbial put at beginning of sentence followed by inversion.)
> *Romance at short notice was her most particular speciality.* (Fronting.)
> *What she did best was romance at short notice.* (Cleft sentence.)
> *What a talent she had for romance at short notice!* (Exclamation.)
> *Romance at short notice was such a speciality of hers!* (Use of *such/so*.)
> *Never could she be bettered as far as romance at short notice was concerned.* (Inversion after negative adverbial.)

2

> **Suggested answers**
> a How unreliable are the conclusions that we draw about people from their appearance.
>   Very unreliable are the conclusions that we draw about people from their appearance.
>   Few are the conclusions that we can reliably draw about people from their appearance.
> b What surprising behaviour from the girl!
>   Surprising indeed was the girl's behaviour!
>   Never in my life have I been so surprised as by the girl's behaviour.
> c How shocked I was by what she said next!
>   Very shocking were her next words!
>   Rarely have I heard such shocking words.

Writing

3

> **Sample answer**
> What Joe did was astonishing because he had always been determined to succeed as a lawyer. When we were at school and university together I was the one who spent most of my free time on the football field, the tennis court or the dance floor. Only rarely could I persuade Joe

to join me. His books and his ultimate goal were far more attractive than sports trophies or pretty girls. His tall dark good looks and his warm smile would have won him most of the girls at the disco but he insisted that romance could wait until he had got the job of his dreams.

His efforts were certainly rewarded with success. He left school with top grades and graduated with first class honours while I barely scraped a pass. He sailed into a job in the top law firm in our town. 'I'm so happy' he told me at the end of his first week's work. 'Now I feel that all that hard work and missing out on the good times you were having was worth it'.

That is why I couldn't believe it when Joe rang me six months later to tell me that he was quitting his job and was going hitch-hiking round the world for a year 'to get my head together'. We met up at a little café in town and over a cracked mug of coffee he told me that he'd fallen in love with a woman he'd met through a case at work. She'd been accused of fraud and he'd got her off. Now they were going to travel the world together.

I felt as if I'd been winded. Sensible, reliable Joe had a side to his personality that I had never dreamt existed.

Writing folder 11

Informal writing
pages 170–171

1

> **Answer**
> I've known Ted <u>for donkey's years</u> – in fact, ever since we were <u>kids</u> at school together – and <u>he's</u> a <u>really nice guy,</u> <u>one of the best.</u> I'd give him the job <u>like a shot</u> if I were <u>in</u> <u>your boat (excuse the pun!).</u> <u>Don't be put off</u> by the fact that he can sometimes seem <u>a bit bossy</u> – that's just because he's such a well-organised <u>bloke</u> himself, he <u>can't</u> <u>stand it</u> when other people are slow to <u>get their act</u> <u>together.</u> <u>He's got loads of</u> experience of working with other people and he can be relied on to <u>get things going.</u> <u>Go for it</u> and give him the job – you <u>won't</u> regret it.

2

> **Suggested answer**
> <u>I have</u> known Ted <u>for a long time</u> – in fact, ever since we were <u>children</u> at school together – and <u>he is</u> a <u>very warm-</u> <u>hearted, responsible person.</u> <u>I would</u> give him the job <u>immediately</u> if I were <u>in your position.</u> <u>You should disregard</u> the fact that he can sometimes seem <u>rather assertive</u> – <u>that is</u> just because <u>he is</u> such a well-organised <u>person</u> himself, he <u>can find it difficult</u> when other people are slow to <u>organise themselves.</u> <u>He has a great deal of</u> experience of working with other people and he can be relied on to <u>be</u> <u>motivated.</u> <u>I would recommend that you take the decision</u> <u>to</u> give him the job – you <u>will not</u> regret it.

3

> **Answers**
> The informal words are marked I and the formal ones are marked F.
> **a** It's <u>daft</u> (I) to <u>alight</u> (F) from a bus while it is moving.
> **b** Jack lives in a flat <u>adjacent</u> (F) to the local <u>chippie</u> (I).
> **c** Julia always wears very <u>snazzy</u> (I) <u>apparel</u> (F).
> **d** John's life was <u>torn asunder</u> (F) by the death of his <u>missus</u> (I).
> **e** When talking to the <u>fuzz</u> (I), it <u>behoves you</u> (F) to be polite.
> **f** Jenny's birthday <u>bash</u> (I) <u>ceased</u> (F) at midnight.
> **g** The <u>deceased</u> (F) man left all his <u>clobber</u> (I) to his nephew.
> **h** You must give the office a <u>bell</u> (I) if you intend to make any change of <u>domicile</u> (F).
> **i** Lawrence <u>dwelt</u> (F) in a remote village in Tibet for <u>yonks</u> (I).
> **j** Richard is an <u>erstwhile</u> (F) <u>mate</u> (I) of my husband's.
>
> **Formal versions**
> **a** It is imprudent to alight from a bus while it is moving.
> **b** Jack lives in a flat adjacent to the local takeaway restaurant.
> **c** Julia always wears very stylish apparel.
> **d** John's life was torn asunder by the death of his wife.
> **e** When talking to the constabulary, it behoves you to be polite.
> **f** Jenny's birthday celebrations ceased at midnight.
> **g** The deceased man left all his worldly goods to his nephew.
> **h** You must telephone the office if you intend to change your domicile.
> **i** Lawrence dwelt in a remote village in Tibet for many years.
> **j** Richard is an erstwhile friend of my husband's.
>
> **Informal versions**
> **a** It's daft to get off a bus while it is moving.
> **b** Jack lives in a flat right next to the local chippie.
> **c** Julia always wears very snazzy gear.
> **d** John's life was ripped apart by the death of his missus.
> **e** When talking to the fuzz, it's a good idea to be polite.
> **f** Jenny's birthday bash stopped at midnight.
> **g** The dead man left all his clobber to his nephew.
> **h** You must give the office a bell if you intend to change your address.
> **i** Lawrence hung out in a remote village in Tibet for yonks.
> **j** Richard is an ex-mate of my husband's.

4

> **Answers**
> **a** 7　**b** 5　**c** 15　**d** 18　**e** 11　**f** 17　**g** 3　**h** 1　**i** 2　**j** 10
> **k** 12　**l** 4　**m** 16　**n** 9　**o** 6　**p** 14　**q** 13　**r** 8　**s** 19

5

> **Answers**
> **a** oodles　**b** bubbly　**c** chuck　**d** chomp　**e** mega
> **f** higgledy-piggledy　**g** beasties　**h** broke　**i** slog

6

> **Answers**
> You'll never guess   drop by   hit the town   reckon
> into   have a bite   fancy   mo   prezzie   crash   chocs
> bottle   wild about   brave it

Unit 28

pages 172–175

Speaking

1

> **Answers**
> a carry-on luggage   b the carousel   c to board
> d the hold   e the check-in   f overhead bin

Reading

1

> **Answers**
> a noisy children on planes
>   excessive carry-on luggage
>   luggage going missing on planes
>   poor compensation for lost luggage
> b The article suggests that noisy children could be seated
>   with their parents behind a screen at the back of the
>   plane. It also suggests – though not seriously, of course
>   – that children could be put in the hold!
>   To solve the problem of excessive carry-on luggage, it
>   suggests that airlines should be stricter about sticking
>   to regulations concerning the permitted size and
>   weight of hand luggage.
>   Nothing is suggested directly for dealing with the
>   problem of luggage going astray.
>   To solve the problem of inadequate compensation, it
>   suggests that at least triple frequent-flier air miles should
>   be awarded for distances travelled by one's luggage.

2

> **Answers**
> a A quotation may say something in a memorable way,
>   perhaps because it is succinct, well-expressed or amusing.
>   Using a quotation allows the writer to make a strong first
>   impression at the beginning of a piece of writing.
> b *Negative externality* is not a phrase in common usage but
>   it is explained in the text. It means doing something that is
>   nice for one person but causes problems for others.
> c *Outrage*, i.e. extreme anger or fury.
> d *Lug* gives the idea of carrying something that is heavy and
>   awkward to move. *Take* does not have these connotations
>   and so is a much less appropriate word to use.

e *Luggage* is personified (spoken about as if it were human)
  in the sentence *You took a flight from London to Tokyo;
  your luggage and your smart clothes decided to hop on to
  one to Los Angeles.*
f *Paltry* means ridiculously small.
g Wal-Mart sells cheap clothes whereas clothes at Armani
  are very expensive. Although it is not possible to work out
  which is the expensive company and which is the cheaper
  one, it should be clear from the context that the prices at
  the two kinds of shops are very different.
h It is inserted to make it clear that the writer is deliberately
  referring to the traveller with a lot of hand luggage as *a
  man* and is not merely using *his* as a generic pronoun to
  stand for either *his* or *her*. The writer is pointing out that it
  is usually men who have heavy hand luggage.
i These two sentences make the point that if you *fight the
  flab*, i.e. go on a diet and lose weight, you will be able to
  take more luggage on board as hand luggage. The last
  sentence reminds the reader of the opening quotation of
  the article where Jean Kerr linked diets and planes.

Vocabulary

1

Suggested answers Words from the text	Meaning	Other words from same root (in typical phrase)
agree	have the same opinion	to disagree with someone; an amicable agreement; a(n) (dis)agreeable person; the agreed outcome
undeterred	not discouraged	a nuclear deterrent; an effective deterrent; to deter an attack
excessive	too much	excess baggage; to exceed the speed limit; excessively violent; excesses of behaviour
concede	admit reluctantly	to make no concessions; concessionary tickets; concessive clause
forcibly	using strength or power	force of will; forced laughter; a forceful character; a force to be reckoned with; forces in physics
frequent	happening often	frequently absent; word frequency; to frequent a place (note stress on verb is on the second syllable, not the first as in the adjective)
compen-sation	payment for loss or damage	to compensate for bad weather; compensatory benefits
correlation	connection	to correlate statistically; smoking and heart disease are correlated

2

> **Answers**
> **a** stressful **b** disagreeable **c** deterrent
> **d** exceeding **e** concession **f** enforce
> **g** frequency **h** correlation **i** compensation

Adverbials expressing opinion

Grammar folder page 206

1

> **Answers**
> **a** The writer seems to be in favour of putting children
> behind screens at the back of the plane and thinks it is
> a pity that this idea has not been taken up by airlines.
> **b** The writer thinks it is correct of the airlines to be strict
> about the weight and size of what is permitted as
> hand luggage.
> **c** The writer understands why people want to carry their
> luggage on board as it is often necessary to wait for a
> long time to retrieve luggage from the hold and
> sometimes you wait in vain for your cases.

2

> **Answers**
> **a** fortunately **b** apparently, evidently
> **c** indisputably, undoubtedly **d** inevitably, predictably
> **e** surprisingly, unbelievably **f** ironically

3

> **Answers**
> **a** Fortunately **b** inevitably
> **c** Predictably **d** apparently

Listening

2

> **Answers**
> **Flying**
> Advantages: Fast; comfortable; you get well treated;
> minimal carrying of luggage.
> Disadvantages: Cost; long waits at airports; luggage can
> get lost.
> **Rail travel**
> Advantages: See the countryside as you travel through
> it; more flexibility to travel when you
> want; more relaxing; suitable for shorter
> journeys.
> Disadvantages: Not always reliable.
> **Cycling**
> Advantages: Freedom to go where you want, stop
> where you want; healthy; exhilarating.
> Disadvantages: Not so good if it's cold and windy or very
> wet; you have to be fit.

Interviewer: This article says that your personality is revealed by the kind of transport that you like best. What's your favourite means of transport, Jack?

Jack: <u>Oh, well</u> there's no doubt about that, flying. Flying is my number one choice. It's <u>undoubtedly</u> the fastest of any option available. It's <u>generally speaking</u> the most comfortable if you're prepared to pay a little money and you get treated very well. Your luggage gets taken care of. You just hand it all in. It's all sorted for you. I think it's a wonderful –

Stephen: <u>Sorry</u>, you say your luggage gets taken care of for you? I think one of the biggest disadvantages in air travel is the way your luggage can disappear and get sent off all over the world, don't you? Have you not found that?

Interviewer: I agree with that, <u>yes</u>.

Jack: <u>Um, well</u> not in my experience but you know, if that occasionally happens, <u>well</u>, it's going to happen anywhere isn't it?

Stephen: Occasionally! It's almost a predictable thing now, I think, with air travel.

Katie: I think you're very fortunate if you don't get your bag missing. <u>I mean</u> the other thing that I find amazing that you didn't mention was the predictably long waits. <u>I mean</u> you can be stood there, looking at the board, waiting for your flight and you could have been on holiday already –

Stephen: If you've got a family with you it's an unbelievably long time. It's horrendous. Do you not find that?

Jack: No, I'm a fan, <u>I'm afraid</u>. I couldn't live without it.

Katie: <u>Alright then</u>.

Interviewer: What about you, Katie?

Katie: <u>Well</u>, I'm a great one for rail travel. I've got a railcard and it gets me everywhere I want to go. <u>You know</u>, I get the opportunity to see the countryside which is something I love because I was brought up in the country and you get to see such a different sort of terrain and I feel very fortunate. I think it's really flexible. I can ring up, I can change my ticket at the last minute, I can get to all sorts of places and I can just sit back and relax. I love it.

Stephen: Do you trust it? <u>I mean</u> is it a reliable form of transport?

Katie: <u>OK, well</u> –

Stephen: It's not is it?

Katie: <u>In short</u>, not always, no.

Jack: And it's slow, isn't it? <u>I mean</u> it's – you can't say it's quicker than flying, can you?

Katie: No, but you'd hardly want to fly from Birmingham to Barnsley, would you? <u>I mean</u> it's <u>like</u> – <u>you know</u>, it's just something that, that you do really. It's enjoyable.

Stephen: <u>Well, I don't know</u>, it's not for me.

Interviewer: <u>And</u> what's your view on this, Stephen?

Stephen: <u>Oh</u>, I'm a passionate believer in exercise. I'm very keen on fitness, outdoor life. I cycle everywhere, long distance cycling. That's my way of getting round and I like it very much. I can set off when I want, I can do what I want. It's healthy, it's exhilarating, choose exactly where I want to go, see the things I want to see, stop when I want to stop and start when I want to start.

Katie: You must be unbelievably fit to do that.

Stephen: <u>Well</u> thank you very much, I am. I am pretty fit. But –

Jack: When do you eat? <u>I mean</u> –

Stephen: When you stop, <u>you know</u> I stop at <u>like</u> a little pub or –

Jack: <u>But then</u> you have to stop, don't you? <u>I mean</u> you don't really get anywhere.

Stephen: Sorry?

Katie: I was just going to say how cold you'd get. You'd have to stop and eat quite often to keep warm.

Stephen: <u>What</u>, just to keep warm?

Jack: And wet. <u>Certainly</u> if you're cycling here. <u>I mean</u> –

Katie: <u>Yeah, and</u> hills as well. I think just sit back and relax.

Stephen: Really? I'd love to see you two on a bicycle.

Katie: A tandem?

Jack: <u>Oh alright then</u>.

3

> **Answers**
> The discourse markers are underlined in the tapescript. Their functions include: to introduce a new topic; to allow the speaker time to think; to organise an argument; to convey an opinion; to reformulate what has already been said; and to suggest agreement or disagreement.

Speaking 2

1

> **Answers**
> 1 as I was saying   2 I know   3 so   4 then   5 stupidly
> 6 you mean   7 just my luck   8 I suppose   9 certainly

Exam folder 12

Paper 5
pages 176–177

2

There are many different things that you can say when describing these cartoons, of course, but the first one is poking fun at the indirectness of English and how polite formulae are very long and complicated. It is not enough to get the message across, it has to be done in what is considered the correct way for it to have the desired response, even if the person in the picture might have drowned by the time he finished saying help in the polite way! In the second picture it is humorously pointed out that it is not enough to know how to ask questions in English, you also have to be able to understand the response. This is, of course, a problem for foreigners working with a phrase book in any country where they do not know the language.

3

It is hard to imagine how a chess set would be of use in language learning as it is so largely played in silence but you should be able to think of ways in which all the other pictures illustrate something that might have a place in a self access centre.

Unit 29

pages 178–181

Listening

1

Thinking in advance about what a speaker might say can help you to start thinking along the right lines.

2

> **Answers**
> 1 • System based on tests makes children hate school and learning.
> • Schools should be freer – pupils should study what and when they want.
> • Portfolios of work and references from teachers are better than tests.
> • Testing creates too much pressure – children are stressed.
> **Arguments against**
> • Children need boundaries, discipline.
> • Good to ask them to show what they can do under pressure.
> 2 • Summer holidays are too long – children forget what they've learnt.
> • Short terms and short school days make life very difficult for working parents.
> • Extra time at school could be used for music, sport, drama.
> **Arguments against**
> • Children already spend a lot of time at school.
> • They need unstructured leisure time.
> • Separation of worktime and playtime is a good thing.
> 3 • Expensive private schools take the best teachers and students.
> • Not fair for some children to get a worse education because their parents have less money.
> • Free education would mean equal opportunity for all.

1

First man: My feeling really is that children at school are just disciplined too much these days. I mean, I just think that basing an education, an education system on tests and then punishing children if they don't do very well in them or they don't do what's expected, it's just a sure way to make most pupils hate school and hate learning, and just not want to participate at all. I think it would be so much better if schools were just kind of freer places where pupils could study what they wanted to and when they wanted to. And instead of all these tests all the time, why don't students – it would be so much better if they were just simply able to show future employers or universities or whatever portfolios of their own work and together with personal references from their teachers.

Second man: I don't know, sounds like a logistical nightmare to me, doesn't it? I mean –

Woman: I mean, children, they do need boundaries, they do need some sort of discipline, don't they? They need to be told what and, you know, where they can go, what they can do. If they don't, they just go mad. They go wild. And it helps them, I think.

First man: But there's so much pressure on them, I just think, from all these tests all the time.

Second man: Isn't that good, though? I mean, just putting them under, I agree we don't want too much pressure but isn't it good that actually they have to try and show what they can do under pressure situations?

First man: I think it's good if you respond well to the pressure but if you don't then, you know, so many kids are just, are so stressed. I mean you get four and five year olds who, or seven year olds, this first seven-year-old test, who are apparently, you know, stressed because they've got to do their SATs tests at seven.

Second man: But if it's all portfolios of work, it'll end up being, you know, a lot of the parents' work, won't it?

Woman: Yeah.

First man: Well, yeah that's true.

2

Woman: Well, I actually believe that term time is too short. The summer holidays just seem to go on for an eternity and during that time, the kids, they forget everything they've learnt from school. I just, I do actually think they need a longer time in class. The days are just, they're just far too short and with me having, you know, to work and having to get back for half past three, half past four, whichever child it is, I just can't cope with that time. I think it would do the kids really – I think they'd benefit if they could stay longer at school. It doesn't have to be work but if they just stayed there and, you know, I don't know, did music or sport, drama – I mean Phoebe loves doing drama – it would just be, well it would help me and I think they'd benefit, don't you think?

First man: Well, I mean frankly I don't. I think it depends, again it depends on the child and I think kids actually spend a lot of time at school and it means that they don't get any time at home and they don't get any time to kind of just sit around and –

Woman: Well, they've got all weekend.

First man: Yeah, but that's not very long. I mean, a lot of these kids, you know, if they're young children, to be at school from kind of nine in the morning until six at night when their parents who work come and pick them up, that's a hell of a long time to be at school.

Second man: And I think it's good that the kids learn, you know, when is worktime and when is playtime and once they've separated those, I think that's that's a good thing, isn't it?

Woman: No, I think you can combine the two and I think they can learn a lot from the other children. If they're always at home with their parents or their siblings, I just think it's really good they're working, you know, different classes, different ethnic communities all the time. I don't know. I just really feel that they'd benefit a lot more than being at home and being in a routine. Which we do have to have, a routine.

First man: But with more classes as well, I mean I do think schools are asking more and more of kids and actually it can be quite stressful for them.

3

First man: One thing that does make me angry about all this, though, is how much education costs. I mean the bottom line is I think education should be free for everybody because the, you know, a lot of poorer people in society just don't have that money. They don't have that money to send their kids to the better schools and what happens then is that the comprehensive schools are not as good because the private schools take all, they take the best teachers, they take the best students. I really believe very strongly that education should be free for everybody and you have a level playing field.

Second man: Well, it's great in theory but I always think that in the end if people have the money and they want to spend it on their children's education, then they should be allowed to.

Woman: Absolutely, and also if, you know, for those people that can afford private education, that releases more money for the state, for the state schools, doesn't it?

First man: Well, does it? Does the money get back there? Do you really think that goes back down to the ground roots? I don't think it does.

Reading

2

> **Answers**
> **a** head of Dulwich College Preparatory School in London
> **b** School should be fun and should not be dominated by exams. Children should be sheltered from exam pressures while they are young.
> **c** The writer of the article clearly doesn't agree with him, though children and many parents probably would!

3

> **Answers**
> Positive words: rousing, nurtured, rounded, cushion, sheltering
> Negative words: burnout, hothouse flower children, wilt, scream, sin, showered, blasphemy, boot camp, misguided, cosseting, smothering
>
> What the words suggest:
> rousing — that the speech made people feel vigorous and inspired
> nurtured — that something is lovingly cared for
> rounded — (of an education) well-balanced and not too narrowly academic
> cushion — protect from accidents or problems
> sheltering — protecting from difficulties
> burnout — when someone has pushed themselves so hard that they have no energy or enthusiasm left
> hothouse flower children — pushed to achieve too much at too early an age for their own good
> wilt — die from lack of water or nourishment
> scream — call out loudly (it suggests that the headlines are large and eye-catching)
> sin — evil, against the will of God (this word has strong religious associations)
> showered — given a lot of something without having to make any effort
> blasphemy — terrible thing to say (like cursing a religious person)
> boot camp — a tough place where army cadets train
> misguided — having the wrong ideas
> cosseting — treating too softly
> smothering — over-protecting

Vocabulary

1

> **Answers**
> **a** 9 **b** 6 **c** 1 **d** 5 **e** 7 **f** 10 **g** 8
> **h** 4 **i** 2 **j** 3

2

> **Answers**
> **a** to treat someone with kid gloves
> **b** the current climate **c** to achieve qualifications
> **d** the real world **e** at the end of your tether
> **f** in the long run **g** a rousing speech **h** pocket money
> **i** to do someone a favour **j** to reach a stage

3

> **Answers**
> **a** in the long run **b** do me a favour
> **c** at the end of her tether **d** the current climate
> **e** to treat me with kid gloves **f** the real world
> **g** reached a stage **h** pocket money

Gerunds and infinitives

Grammar folder page 206

1

> **Answers**
> **a** to learn to achieve
> (two examples of the infinitive of purpose)
> to accept
> (infinitive is used after the verb *want*)
> **b** to spray to protect
> (*to protect* is an example of the infinitive of purpose)
> **c** growing sheltering smothering
> (gerund is needed after prepositions)
> **d** to do to get
> (infinitive is used after verbs such as *want* and *tell*)

2

> **Answers**
> **a** gerund **b** gerund **c** infinitive
> **d** infinitive **e** gerund

3

> **Answers**
> Verbs followed by a gerund: mind, feel like, deny, enjoy, risk, suggest, give up
> Verbs followed by an infinitive: promise, refuse, arrange, tend, offer, expect, decide, agree, manage

4

> **Answers**
> **A** forget, regret, go on, remember, try
> **B** start, intend, begin, continue, can't bear
> **C** permit, advise, allow, forbid

5

> **Answers**
> a Jack suggested going to the new Chinese restaurant.
> b Students are not permitted to eat in the classrooms.
> c The police officer forbade anyone to enter the building.
> d Would you mind opening the window?
> e Melinda offered to paint my son's portrait.
> f I hope you didn't forget to buy some apples.
> g I regret wasting so much of my time at school.
> h Despite his injury, he went on playing his violin.
> i Everyone expects him to do well in his exams.
> j Smoking is not allowed on any of that airline's flights.

Speaking 2

1

> **Answers**
> Aim of exams: to find out which pupils can remember what they've been taught
> Types of examinees:
> 1 The petrified
>   a persuade yourself that there is nothing to worry about
>   b make a plan of campaign
> 2 The disorganised
>   a draw up a timetable
>   b find a study partner

At the end of the day, no matter how you look at it, you are at school to learn. And to remember. And it is this last bit that causes all the problems. So they have exams. That way, those in charge can find out which of their pupils remembers $x = y \times 4t$ and which haven't a clue what x is in the first place. Not everyone approaches exams in the same way and not everyone revises in the same way. It does help if you can identify what sort of examinee you are and how to get the best out of yourself.

1 The petrified

These are the people for whom the word 'exam' induces a massive upsurge in heart rate, clammy palms and a desire to run very far away and never come back. Never mind that all through the terms they can get eight out of ten without really trying, sit them in a silent classroom with a clock ticking away the minutes and a pile of spotless white paper before them, and everything they ever knew vanishes from their minds. If you are one of these, here is what to do:

a) About three weeks before the exam, sit yourself down firmly and have a chat with yourself. What is an exam? A test. How many tests do you have every term? Dozens. How do you get on? Fine. Right, so why worry because they have called this one an exam? Would you stop eating burgers if they suddenly called them calorie challenged stomach fillers?

b) Draw up a plan of campaign for the first five minutes of the exam. It is known that 80% of all panicking occurs in the first few moments after the invigilator says 'You may now turn over your papers.' Count slowly to ten, then back to one. Take three deep breaths and tell yourself that even if you could not answer a single question, the sun would still rise tomorrow. Life would go on and you would have another chance. There is always another chance; you never blow life in one go.

2 The disorganised

This is the soul who works flat out for German literature for days and days and then wakes up to discover that German literature isn't till next week and she has two hours to master three terms of physics. This species is also likely to start rereading *Vanity Fair* (the classic novel) and then find a fascinating piece about hair highlights in *Vanity Fair* (the magazine) and waste a whole evening. This is what you do:

a) Draw up a timetable. Set yourself one hour for a specific topic and then schedule yourself a fifteen minute break. That break can be used for anything from making Marmite and cheese sandwiches (marvellous for the brainpower) to washing your hair. But, when it is over, it is back for the second hour.

b) Find a study partner. If you are not the most orderly person, it can be a real bonus to have a friend who is studying the same subjects to keep you on the straight and narrow. Again, allow yourself little treats during the evening and nag each other into completing the task in hand.

2

The main points made by the speaker are that there are two types of examinees: the petrified and the disorganised. The petrified should sit down and try to relax about three weeks before the exam, then draw up a plan of campaign for the first five minutes of the exam. The disorganised should draw up a timetable and find a study partner.

Writing folder 12

Descriptive, narrative and discursive articles pages 182–183

1

> **Suggested answers**
> a
> A You have to describe the difficult conditions that students have to live in and you have to discuss ways of making the best of those conditions. You have to narrate examples from your own friends' experience.

B You have to describe one modern means of communication and you have to discuss how it has changed your life (in both positive and negative ways). There will be a narrative element in the examples that you give from your own experience of this means of communication.

C You have to describe the week's work experience programme that you took part in (this will include an element of narration) and you have to discuss how the programme could be improved.

D You have to describe what facilities are already available and you have to discuss why one particular additional facility would be of benefit to your community.

E You have to describe the types of punishments and rewards used in schools in your country and you have to discuss what you think is good and bad about this system, including suggestions for improvements. There will be some narration in your account of your own experience of punishments and rewards at school.

b
No narrative element is appropriate in D as it is a formal proposal.

Unit 30

pages 184–187

Reading

2

Answers
a 3 b 8 c 1 d 5 e 4 f 7 g 2 h 6

Listening

Interviewer: Why should we employ you, Mr Higgins?

Mr Higgins: You won't find anyone better suited to this job than I am. I've usually made a great success of any jobs that I've taken on. And I badly need this job because my wife is expecting and I've been out of work for six months now.

Interviewer: Why should we employ you, Miss Smith?

Miss Smith: As we've been discussing, I have the experience and qualifications that you ask for in your advertisement for the post. I'm a good team player. I can take the instructions and I have the desire to make a thorough success of this job.

Interviewer: Are you willing to take calculated risks, Mr Higgins?

Mr Higgins: Oh yes, most certainly. Life is a risk. All business involves risk and you can't win anything if you don't take risks.

Interviewer: And are you willing to take calculated risks, Miss Smith?

Miss Smith: I wonder if you could define calculated risks for me? Perhaps you could give me an example of the sort of risk that you have in mind and the stakes that are involved?

Interviewer: Which of the jobs you have held have you liked least, Mr Higgins?

Mr Higgins: All my jobs had their good and bad points, but I've always found that if you want to learn, there's plenty to be picked up along the way. Each experience was valuable. In my first job, I had, of course, to do a lot of very straightforward, routine jobs but I used the spare time and energy I had to learn as much as I could about office procedures, which has I think stood me in very good stead in later jobs.

Interviewer: And which of the jobs you have held have you liked least, Miss Smith?

Miss Smith: I suppose the job I last held was the worst. The people I was working with were very backbiting and unpleasant and management were pretty inefficient. The job was also not nearly challenging enough for me at this stage in my career, which is why I decided it was time to move on.

Interviewer: Now, Mr Higgins, in what areas do you feel that your last boss could have done a better job?

Mr Higgins: Oh, I've always had the highest respect for my last boss. He has taught me so much that I don't think he really could have done a better job. He's really brought me to the point where I'm ready for greater challenges, which is why I'm here now.

Interviewer: Now, Miss Smith, in what areas do you feel that your last boss could have done a better job?

Miss Smith: It's hard to know where to begin. He's lazy. He's inconsistent in his judgements and he is very poor at motivating people and at delegating work. It is hard for me to see how he ever got to a management position being as incompetent as he is.

2

Answers		
Phrase	Used by	Context
badly need	Mr Higgins	I badly need this job
take instructions	Miss Smith	I can take instructions
I wonder if	Miss Smith	I wonder if you could define calculated risks
good and bad points	Mr Higgins	All my jobs had their good and bad points
which is why	Mr Higgins	which is why I'm here now
it's hard to know	Miss Smith	It's hard to know where to begin

Using a range of structures

Grammar folder page 207

2

> **Answers**
> **a** 1 walked/cycled 2 should 3 saves
> **b** 1 used 2 went 3 would 4 been 5 got/had
> **c** 1 had 2 was 3 realised 4 would 5 had 6 was
> **d** 1 how/if/whether 2 had 3 would 4 had 5 Had
> 6 been 7 have 8 was/were 9 have 10 am

3

> **Sample texts**
> **A** I am very much against the proposed new factory. Firstly, it will involve cutting down a lovely wood, which would be a great loss to all of us who live here and enjoy the local countryside in our leisure time. In addition, constructing a factory would make traffic problems considerably worse than they already are. Last but not least, the output from the factory would lead to increased air and water pollution. In other words, the quality of life in this area would deteriorate in a number of different but equally important ways.
> **B** It was an excellent film. I particularly liked the way the main actress presented her character. The plot was also developed in a very effective and rather unusual way. The camerawork was strikingly original and I found the music very haunting too.

Vocabulary

2

> **Answers**
> **A a** 4 **b** 1 **c** 2 **d** 3
> **B a** 3 **b** 4 **c** 2 **d** 1

Speaking 2

1

> **Answers**
> **a** bad advice – it will be hard to hear you.
> **b** bad advice – both should hear you, but you should be talking to your partner rather than the examiner.
> **c** bad advice – you will probably be harder to understand if you talk too quickly. Neither too fast nor too slow is ideal.
> **d** bad advice – just speak clearly.
> **e** bad advice – this is going too far. Of course you must speak clearly and not too fast but it is not natural to say every word distinctly in English. Little words like *of* and *the* are often swallowed. It will sound unnatural if you give too much stress to unimportant words.

> **f** good advice
> **g** bad advice – it is certainly good advice to make eye contact with the examiner but all the time would be inappropriate and would make the examiner feel uncomfortable. In Part 3, for example, you are talking to the other candidate and not to the examiner.
> **h** bad advice – you must talk distinctly. You can't get any marks unless the examiner can hear and understand what you are saying.

Units 26–30 Revision

Vocabulary

> **Answers**
> **a** scenery **b** exposure **c** erosion **d** Predictably
> **e** unexpected **f** regardless

Reading

> **Answers**
> 1 B 2 C 3 A 4 D 5 B 6 A 7 C 8 C

Grammar

> **Answers**
> 1 an 2 work/write 3 to 4 had 5 no 6 for
> 7 how 8 were 9 do/perform 10 so